Holocaust, Genocide, and the Law

Holocaust, Genocide, and the Law

A Quest for Justice in a Post-Holocaust World

MICHAEL BAZYLER

OXFORD
UNIVERSITY PRESS

OXFORD
UNIVERSITY PRESS

Oxford University Press is a department of the University of Oxford. It furthers the University's objective of excellence in research, scholarship, and education by publishing worldwide. Oxford is a registered trade mark of Oxford University Press in the UK and certain other countries.

Published in the United States of America by Oxford University Press
198 Madison Avenue, New York, NY 10016, United States of America.

First Edition published in 2016

Library of Congress Cataloging-in-Publication Data

Names: Bazyler, Michael J., author.
Title: Holocaust, genocide, and the law : a quest for justice in a post-holocaust world / Michael Bazyler.
Description: New York : Oxford University Press, 2016. | Includes bibliographical references and index.
Identifiers: LCCN 2016011937 | ISBN 9780195395693 ((hardback) : alk. paper)
Subjects: LCSH: Genocide (International law) | International criminal law. | Holocaust, Jewish (1939–1945)—Influence. | World War, 1939–1945—Law and legislation.
Classification: LCC KZ7180.B39 2016 | DDC 345/.0251—dc23 LC record available at https://lccn.loc.gov/2016011937

9 8 7 6 5 4 3 2 1

Printed by Edwards Brothers Malloy, United States of America

Note to Readers
This publication is designed to provide accurate and authoritative information in regard to the subject matter covered. It is based upon sources believed to be accurate and reliable and is intended to be current as of the time it was written. It is sold with the understanding that the publisher is not engaged in rendering legal, accounting, or other professional services. If legal advice or other expert assistance is required, the services of a competent professional person should be sought. Also, to confirm that the information has not been affected or changed by recent developments, traditional legal research techniques should be used, including checking primary sources where appropriate.

(Based on the Declaration of Principles jointly adopted by a Committee of the American Bar Association and a Committee of Publishers and Associations.)

To Karen

&

To Nina, Gigi, and Bianca

May they grow up in a world without genocide

CONTENTS

PART THREE The Holocaust as a Catalyst for Modern International Criminal Justice

LIST OF ILLUSTRATIONS

BOOK COVER

CHAPTER 1

CHAPTER 2

CHAPTER 3

CHAPTER 4

CHAPTER 5

CHAPTER 8

CONCLUSION

ACKNOWLEDGMENTS

This book has its origins in 2000, when I began teaching a new law school course at Chapman University titled *Holocaust and the Law* and currently titled *Holocaust, Genocide, and the Law*. Professor Marilyn Harran, Director of the Rodgers Center for Holocaust Education and Stern Chair in Holocaust Education, heard my lament that the Holocaust and its relationship to the law was not taught in law schools and suggested that I debut my course at Chapman as a visiting professor. President James Doti readily agreed. Eight years later, when I joined the Chapman law faculty, President Doti greeted me with the warm words, "Michael, welcome home!"

And what a wonderful home it has been. I am grateful for the support of dear friends and colleagues at Chapman, and especially President Doti, Chancellor (now President) Danieli Struppa, Vice Chancellor Richard Redding, law school deans John Eastman, Scott Howe, and Tom Campbell and associate deans Daniel Bogart, Jayne Kacer, and Donald Kochan.

This book would not have been possible without the assistance of the wonderful staff of our law library, and most especially Research Librarian Sherry Leysen, who with good cheer succeeded in locating and verifying the most obscure of my research and cite-checking requests. Sherry's contribution is throughout this book. Student assistants (many now attorneys) include Alison Bollbach, Veronica Borenstein, Anna Caludac, Elaine Dick, John Evans, Brandon Howard, Nicole Hughes, Daniel Kim, Madeline Liebreich, Grace Nguyen, Heidi Post, Matt Putterman, Kaylee Sauvey, and Wendy Yang.

I am extremely grateful to colleagues in law and history who took the time to read many of the chapters and provide rich input. These include Marilyn Harran, Justice Richard Fybel (with whom I am honored to co-teach *Holocaust, Genocide, and the Law*), Ambassador (and professor) David Scheffer, and professors Israel Charny, Kevin Heller, Gregory Stanton, and William Schabas. Attorneys Joan Daniels and Kristen Nelson provided excellent edits. Professor Christopher

Browning undertook a rich email discourse about the legality of the Holocaust, which greatly helped to shape my thinking of this always provocative issue. The works of Donald Bloxham, Lawrence Douglas, David Fraser, Peter Hayes, Kevin Heller, Michael Marrus, Kristen Rundle, John Roth, William Schabas, and Bettina Stangneth served as driving engines for much of this study.

I am deeply indebted to my Oxford editor Blake Ratcliff for his strong support and always encouraging emails, especially during my challenging phases of this project. Thank you, Blake, for your patience! Chris Collins initially took on the project as editor at Oxford, and editorial assistant Alden Domizio shepherded it to its completion. I also thank Project Manager Balamurugan Rajendran at Newgen Knowledge Works Pvt. Ltd, who oversaw the production of the book and was my main contact throughout the production process.

A special thanks goes to my independent editor Bonny V. Fetterman, a wise guide and dear friend without whom this book would not have been possible.

Critical research was done during my fellowship at Yad Vashem in Jerusalem, as a holder in 2006–2007 of the Baron Friedrich Carl von Oppenheim Chair for the Study of Racism, Antisemitism, and the Holocaust. I especially thank Dan Michman, Tikva Fatal, and Iael and Eliot Nidam-Orvieto for their friendship and support. David Bankier, the late and esteemed head of the Institute for Holocaust Research at Yad Vashem, would always stop whatever he was doing when I popped into his office to discuss the project.

Back in Southern California, inspiration always came from William Elperin, President of the 1939 Society, and our dear Holocaust survivor members. Lunches with Professor Michael Berenbaum always yielded new insights and greatly helped to shape the book. Dr. Robert Feldman, WWII navigator, and Mrs. Joan Feldman made me most welcome at their Rancho Mirage home and provided both inspiration and a wonderful getaway to be able to finish this project. Endre Balogh, photographer extraordinaire, made the cover of the book possible. And I most fortunate to have Mrs. Maria Supikova née Dolezalova on the cover. I hope that her story motivates the young readers of this work.

I wish to remember two superb scholars no longer with us: Stephen Feinstein and David Cesarani. Their much-too-early deaths left a gaping hole in our community and in my life.

The guiding spirit has been Benjamin Ferencz, a hero to all of us in the field of Holocaust and genocide studies. Thank you, Ben, for your friendship and inspiration. This book ultimately is a personal tribute to you.

INTRODUCTION

On July 14, 2008, at a press conference in The Hague, the seat of the International Criminal Court (ICC), Chief Prosecutor Luis Moreno Ocampo announced his decision to file charges of genocide and crimes against humanity against President Omar al-Bashir of Sudan. Al-Bashir thereby became the first head of state to be charged with genocide before an international criminal tribunal. The charges and the warrant for al-Bashir's arrest arose out of the Sudanese government's brutal campaign against its own non-Arab citizens in the Darfur region of Sudan. The ICC chief prosecutor explained why he was seeking to indict al-Bashir for genocide: "These 2.5 million people are in camps. They [al-Bashir's forces] don't need gas chambers because the desert will kill them."[1] Moreno Ocampo did not need to explicitly refer to the Holocaust to evoke its presence. The mere use of "gas chambers" was understood by all as referring to the genocide committed by the Nazis against the Jews.

This book is about why Moreno Ocampo invoked the memory of Nazi Germany's most notorious method of mass murder as a justification for his decision to bring genocide charges against al-Bashir. I aim to demonstrate that the murder of approximately six million Jews during the Second World War by Nazi Germans and their collaborators is not only one of the best known and most horrific events in human history but also the most significant event to have shaped the corpus of international law and the legal systems of many nations since that time. In the field of law, we are living in a post-Holocaust world.

Since the end of the Second World War, a substantial body of law has emerged to address issues related to the Holocaust, genocide, and other mass atrocities. This constellation of issues has been gathered in this book under a category I call "post-Holocaust law." But it is far from a random collection. Rather, as I will show, post-Holocaust law can be viewed as a discrete body of law, developed historically over time and in an organized fashion. For the last fifteen years, I have been teaching this body of law through a law school course I originated, first titled

Holocaust and the Law and currently *Holocaust, Genocide, and the Law*. My aim here, as in my course, is twofold: first, to show how various areas of law have developed as a direct response to the Holocaust; and second, to tell the story of the Holocaust through the prism of law.

This book is about the relationship of the Holocaust to law and law to the Holocaust, the defining catastrophe of the last century that has cast its long shadow over this one. And its influence will continue long after all of us are gone. Just as today we are the cultural descendants of the ancient Greeks and Romans, so too will the tragedy of the Jews and the legalized brutality of the Nazis be studied and probed far into the future. Already, it is a universal symbol of wickedness in our globalized world.

More than a half-century since the end of the Second World War, interest in the Holocaust is greater than ever. Films, novels, and historical studies about the events of the Second World War seem never-ending, with the public in the United States, Europe, and around the world continuing to display keen interest in both newly discovered historical data and fictional renderings of Holocaust events. More news stories about the Holocaust have been published in the last two decades than in the previous fifty years. Holocaust historian Omer Bartov comments on the centrality of the Holocaust in our culture:

> More than fifty years have passed since the final defeat of Nazism, and yet its presence in our minds seems to be stronger than ever. This demands explanation. After all, public interest in events of the past normally diminishes as they recede in time .... But the case of Nazism, and especially of the Holocaust, is different. There are episodes in history whose centrality can only be recognized from a chronological distance. The mass of inexplicable, often horrifying details is endowed with sense and meaning only retrospectively, after it has passed. Gradually such events come to cast a shadow over all that had previously seemed of greater significance, reaching backward and forward, until they finally touch our normal lives, reminding us with ever growing urgency that we are the survivors of cataclysms and catastrophes that we never experienced. The Holocaust is such an event.[2]

Moreover, just when it appears that we have learned all we can about the Holocaust, new information is discovered that sheds new light on the subject.

In the 1990s, historians, lawyers, politicians, and the media began taking renewed interest in the financial crimes that took place during the Nazi era. As a result of class action civil lawsuits filed in the United States, political pressure by the American government and political figures at both the federal and state level, along with new historical studies that emerged as a result of this renewed interest, the extent of the theft of Jewish and non-Jewish assets by the Nazis and their collaborators began for the first time to be fully appreciated sixty years after the events took place.

In the twenty-first century, we are likewise discovering new facts. In 2006, the Red Cross finally agreed to release a treasure trove of documents produced and collected by the Germans during the war detailing their brutalities. The Allies turned them over to the Red Cross after the war to help survivors locate their relatives or to learn the fate of those who perished during the war. The International Tracing Service Holocaust Archive in Bad Arolsen, Germany, the ancient small town in northern Germany where the Red Cross has been storing the materials since the end of the war, contains the largest collection of data detailing the Nazi machinery of persecution. The Archive totals approximately fifty million pages relating to around seventeen million victims. Stored over the last seventy years in six buildings, the archive is now available to researchers and the general public online and in various memorials and museums around the world. The files allow survivors and their descendants as well as researchers to view actual images of transportation lists, Gestapo orders, concentration camp registers, slave labor booklets, and death books – lists of deceased victims. These documents produce new insights about both the Jewish genocide and the murder and persecution of other groups targeted by the Nazis.

An important symbol of the continuing vitality of the Holocaust is the adoption by the UN General Assembly in November 2005 of a resolution designating January 27—the day in 1945 when Auschwitz was liberated by the Soviet army—as "International Day of Commemoration in Memory of the Victims of the Holocaust." At the commemoration ceremony, UN Secretary-General Kofi Annan noted that the Holocaust was the impetus for the establishment of the United Nations, created as a means to help prevent future acts of genocide. This move by the General Assembly has now led to the official recognition by over thirty countries of January 27 as International Holocaust Remembrance Day to remember the genocide of the European Jews.[3]

Memory of the Holocaust is also being maintained by the various Holocaust museums and memorials established throughout the world. Israel established the Yad Vashem Holocaust Research and Commemoration Center in 1953, and in the following decades, many additional memorial sites and museums have been erected worldwide. In 2013, the US Holocaust Memorial Museum marked its twentieth anniversary, and the museum continues to be one of the most visited tourist sites in Washington, D.C. In May 2005, on the sixtieth anniversary of the end of Second World War, the "Memorial to the Murdered Jews of Europe" opened in Berlin, located literally in the shadow of the razed Reich Ministry where Hitler and his cohorts plotted the extermination of European Jews. In 2014, Hungary observed "Hungarian Holocaust Memorial Year—2014" to mark the seventieth anniversary of Germany's invasion of Hungary in March 1944 and the deportation of more than 400,000 Hungarian Jews to Auschwitz in German-occupied Poland, where 80 percent were gassed upon arrival.[4]

The year 2015 brought on a further slew of remembrance and commemoration events: the seventieth anniversary of the liberation of Auschwitz (as noted, on January 27, 1945, by the Soviet Red Army); the seventieth anniversary of the end of the Second World War in Europe when Germany unconditional surrendered (V-E Day, May 7–8, 1945); and the beginning of the greatest criminal trial in modern history, when twenty-two major Nazis were put on trial by the Allies before the International Military Tribunal in the southern German city of Nuremberg in Bavaria (November 20, 1945). On December 9, 2015, UN Secretary-General Ban Ki-moon added another day to our international commemoration calendar: "International Day of Commemoration and Dignity of the Victims of the Crime of Genocide and of the Prevention of this Crime," intended to coincide with the day in 1948 when the General Assembly adopted the UN Convention on the Prevention and Punishment of the Crime of Genocide.

Why is memory of the Holocaust actively kept in public view while other tragedies have faded into history? For those other than the families of victims, the Holocaust has become a near-universal paradigmatic event representing evil. This is reflected in the use of terms like "Hitler," "Nazi," and "fascism" as epithets connoting supreme wickedness. Analogies referring to some current event as being "another Holocaust" abound. The post-Holocaust cry of "Never Again" has entered the vocabulary of humankind. Political scientist John Torpey explains:

> Far from a merely local event of little relevance to those outside the Euro-Atlantic world, the Holocaust has emerged as the principal legacy of the twentieth century with respect to the way our contemporaries think about the past. The perfidy of the Nazi assault on European Jewry has emerged as a kind of "gold standard" against which to judge other cases of injustice and to which advocates seek to assimilate those instances of human cruelty and oppression for which they seek a reckoning.[5]

This is a recent phenomenon. Torpey points out that it is only "over the past two decades or so, [that] the Holocaust [has become] . . . the 'true emblem' of our age."[6] As a result, "the paradigmatic status of the Jewish catastrophe for our time has helped others who have been subjected to state-sponsored mass atrocities to gain attention for those calamities—though hardly all of them, to be sure."[7] In other words, memory of the Holocaust has opened up historical memories of other genocides. It has also become a call to action when shades of "another Holocaust" anywhere in the world are feared or are already taking place.

The Holocaust added a significant word to the world's vocabulary: genocide. This is the crime for which ICC prosecutor Moreno Ocampo sought to have al-Bashir indicted in The Hague. Under international law, it is the gravest crime possible, known today as the "crime of crimes." Genocide, a word of modern origin, was coined in 1944 by Raphael Lemkin, a Polish and Jewish jurist who escaped from Nazi-occupied Poland in 1939 and eventually settled in the United States. Lemkin is also the father of the UN Genocide Convention, the treaty that in 1951 made genocide an international crime. While other mass murders of targeted groups have occurred in history, Lemkin's neologism (from the Greek *geno-* for race or tribe and the Latin *cide* for killing) finally gave the crime its legal name. The term has a precise legal definition as an international crime specifically defined in the Genocide Convention. It is this legal definition that gives it practical significance by creating the legal obligation to bring perpetrators of this particular crime (known today by the French-language originated term genocidairies) and other mass atrocities to justice before national and international tribunals.

Our greater awareness of mass atrocities perpetrated subsequent to the Holocaust now includes the murder of over 1.5 million Cambodians by the Khmer Rouge regime that took over Cambodia in the mid-1970s; the murders of thousands of Bosnian Muslims, Serbs, Croats, and Kosovars in the 1990s in the aftermath of the messy breakup of Yugoslavia; the 1994 genocide in Rwanda when hundreds of thousands of Tutsis and Hutu moderates were murdered by Hutu extremists over a period of one hundred days; and the genocide in the Darfur region of Western Sudan that began in 2003.

Darfur, the first genocide of the twenty-first century, led to an unprecedented awareness campaign in the Western world, with nongovernmental organizations (NGOs) like *Not On Our Watch, World Without Genocide* and *United to End Genocide* specifically devoted to citizen-led activism seeking to persuade the United States and other countries to take action to stop genocide. Critically, many of these NGOs were created by college students, thereby perpetuating anti-genocide activism into the future. In 2005, the UN Security Council referred the situation in Darfur to the International Criminal Court (ICC). Created in 1998, the ICC is the first permanent international criminal tribunal in history, fulfilling the dream of those who created the Nuremberg trials in 1945 that no individual, regardless of status, rank, or position, is immune from criminal prosecution under international law for mass atrocities. This denial of impunity under international law even to heads of state remains the most important gift that Nuremberg has bestowed upon humanity. This legacy was resurrected at the end of the Cold War by the Security Council in the 1990s with the creation of the modern-day progenies of Nuremberg: the International Criminal Tribunal for the former Yugoslavia and the International Criminal Tribunal for Rwanda.

The genocide of the Jews and other crimes by the Nazis continue to drive legal discourse about present-day atrocities, no matter where they occur. In 2009, Bangladesh created a special domestic court to adjudge individuals for crimes committed in 1971, during Bangladesh's secession war from Pakistan (when the region was known as East Pakistan). Although not an international court, Bangladesh named it the "International Crimes Tribunal." In so doing, Bangladesh aimed to establish the court's *bona fides* by connecting it to the first international tribunal in history, the International Military Tribunal established in 1945 at Nuremberg to prosecute the so-called Nazi Major War Criminals. According to the court's website: "The Tribunal is a domestic judicial mechanism set up under national legislation and it is meant to try *internationally recognized crimes and that is why it is known as 'International Crimes Tribunal.'*"[8]

In 2014, the Bangladeshi court issued its most important decision, convicting former pro-Pakistani militia leader Motiur Rahman Nizami of murder, rape, and looting arising from his activities fighting against East Pakistan's secession in the 1970s. It sentenced him to death by hanging. In the course of its 204-page judgment, the tribunal found Nizami criminally responsible for the execution of leading Bangladeshi intellectuals by engaging in "Gestapo-like attacks."[9] And so close to seventy years after the end of the Second World War, a local court in faraway (from Europe) Bangladesh resorted to a Nazi analogy to prove to the world the heinous behavior of the accused. And like Moreno Ocampo, the court characterized the defendant's acts with the "G-crime": Nizami "committ[ed] genocide by killing professionals and intellectuals"—even though (as will be discussed) seeking to wipe out political opponents, even the *intelligentsia* of a group, does not amount to genocide under the Genocide Convention. But for the local court, as with the ICC prosecutor, only the G-crime will do.

As these two examples show, the legal legacy of the Holocaust remains with us. Yet despite widespread interest in the Holocaust and an abundance of courses and books on the subject, there remains one glaring gap: The subject is rarely examined through the prism of the law. This book is written to fill that gap. My intention is not only to describe and analyze the legal aspects of the Holocaust and its aftermath but also to understand the consequences of the Holocaust for the law today and into the future.

Of the topics covered in this book, I make special mention here of the following salient points. First, this book begins with a contention that some may find perplexing: the Holocaust was a legal event and the unfolding catastrophe can be told as legal history. In his 2015 bestseller, *Black Earth*, Yale historian Timothy Snyder maintains that one of the critical factors that enabled the wholesale murder of Jews and other groups was the lawlessness and chaos in the states destroyed by Germany's invading armies.[10] I make a case for the opposite and argue that it was the *legalized* barbarism in Nazi Germany and Nazi-occupied territories between the years 1933 and 1945 that made the massive killings of the Holocaust possible. As I aim to show in Chapter 1, the groundwork for the murder of six million Jews and other persecuted minorities was established almost entirely within the legal framework of German law.

The persecution of the Jews in Germany upon the Nazis taking power in 1933 began with legal decrees excluding Jews from the daily life of society and taking away their rights as German citizens. With Germany's subsequent invasion into most of Europe beginning in 1939, Nazi-issued laws, decrees, and other legal measures in the occupied territories became the primary means by which Jews and other persecuted groups were arrested and then subjugated. Law became one of the leading instruments by which Jews and other victims were stripped of their assets, then their dignity, and eventually their lives. It set the stage for the German people first to accept and then to participate in the increasing scale of persecution that made the creation of human death factories such as Auschwitz possible. At the infamous Wannsee Conference in 1942, where the decision to implement the "Final Solution to the Jewish Question in Europe" was coordinated among the various branches of the German government and the military, seven of the fifteen men sitting around the table were lawyers.

Without law and lawyers, the Holocaust would not have occurred. After a lifetime of working at the intersection of ethics, genocide, and the Holocaust, philosopher and ethicist John Roth in 2015 came to a startling conclusion: "philosophy can expedite genocide."[11] So can law.

Second, it is significant that the first reaction to the Holocaust was a legal one: the act of putting the so-called "Major War Criminals" on trial from November 1945 to October 1946 in Courtroom 600 of the Palace of Justice in the German city of Nuremberg. The trials of the twenty-two top-ranking surviving Nazis before the International Military Tribunal created by the victorious Allies proved to be a model for numerous trials over the next seventy years, including trials before international and national courts of Germans, Austrians and their Eastern European Nazi collaborators.[12] In reviewing these criminal trials, including the other Nuremberg trials (of doctors, jurists, industrialists, and generals of mass murder squads) and national trials held in Germany, Israel, and the United States, I also note the educational and historical importance of these trials—especially in light of the fact that soon there will be no one to prosecute for the crimes of the Holocaust, and no eyewitnesses available to testify at trial.

Third, civil litigation for the financial crimes of the Nazi-era has been a relatively late development in the quest for post-Holocaust justice. Beginning in the 1990s, civil lawsuits in the United States finally confronted the massive robbery of the Jews that took place during the Nazi era. Due to the onset of the Cold War, the Allies largely abandoned this task soon after the war ended. A half-century later, a legal and political movement arose finally bringing a measure of justice by returning stolen Jewish assets to their owners or heirs. As a result of American-centered litigation, political pressure, and new historical studies issued by European governments and private corporations, the extent of the theft of Jewish and non-Jewish assets by the Nazis and their collaborators began to be fully appreciated sixty years after the events took place. Consequently, beginning in 1998, more than $8 billion was paid out over the next decade by European governments and private entities for their wartime and postwar reprehensible behavior. In 2000, German industry and the German government paid $5 billion in compensation to former still-living Jewish and non-Jewish victims used as slaves during the war. German pharmaceutical companies that participated in gruesome medical experiments in SS-run concentration camps likewise participated in the German settlement. European insurance companies that failed after the war to honor insurance policies issued to Jews before the war finally paid out on such policies. Swiss banks, followed by their German, Austrian, French, and even British and American counterparts doing business in Nazi Europe, were accused of confiscating the bank accounts of Jewish depositors. The banks finally began returning moneys to surviving depositors or their heirs sixty years after the war. The Swiss banks class action suit that began the modern Holocaust restitution movement settled in 1998. Administered since then by Brooklyn federal judge Edward Korman, it paid out over $1.28 billion to 457,100 claimants.[13]

In late 2015, after more than a decade of litigation, France agreed to compensate American survivors who were deported in French trains to Nazi death camps in Poland. Under an accord brokered by the Obama administration, $60 million is being paid out to eligible claimants. The accord was overseen by Ambassador Stuart Einzenstat, who has now worked for three administrations (Clinton, Bush, and Obama) on Holocaust restitution issues.

And then there is Nazi looted art. Art looted by the Nazis and discovered to have been in the collections of the most prominent museums in the world, galleries, and even in private hands for the last half-century also began to be returned in the 1990s to rightful owners. The successful saga of Los Angeles resident Maria Altmann and her lawyer Randy Schoenberg to recover five Klimt paintings stolen from Mrs. Altmann's family by the Austrian Nazis—told in the 2015 feature film *Woman in Gold*—is the best known of such cases. But it is just the tip of the iceberg of Nazi looted art yet to be returned to proper owners. As these words are written in 2016, a German government art commission is sorting through a stash of over 1400 paintings coincidentally discovered in 2013 in the Munich apartment of Cornelius Gurlitt, to determine which were stolen from Jewish families. Gurlitt inherited the collection said to be worth up to one billion dollars from his father Hildebrand Gurlitt, an art dealer who traded in works confiscated by the Nazis. When the recluse Gurlitt died at age eighty-one, by his bed lay a suitcase with a Claude Monet landscape inside. The discovery of a Monet in a suitcase left by a dead man in a hospital was only the latest revelation in the strange Gurlitt art saga.

Fourth, the legacy of Nuremberg permeates the current rules of international criminal law. Current prosecutions before both national and international tribunals for the international crimes of war crimes, crimes against humanity, and genocide are only taking place because of what took place seventy years ago in Nuremberg. As aptly stated by Louise Arbour, the former chief prosecutor for the modern Yugoslav and Rwandan war crimes tribunals, "Collectively, we're linked to Nuremberg. We mention its name every single day."[14]

The foundation of the modern-day international human rights legal system was created as a reaction to the prewar international law norm that what a country does to its own people is not a concern of international law. In 1945, the Nuremberg prosecutors had to confront this unyielding principle of state sovereignty when seeking to charge the Nazis on the dock with crimes against humanity stemming from their state-sanctioned persecution of German Jews beginning in 1933. The Nuremberg judges acquitted the Nazi leaders of these charges, because the acts took place in Germany against other German nationals and before Germany went to war in 1939. No more. Today, the various international human rights treaties make the mistreatment by a ruler of his or her nationals a proper subject for international law—regardless of whether these atrocities were committed during a war or in peacetime. The UN Security Council, under its mandate to maintain "international peace and security" in Chapter VII of the UN Charter, regularly monitors, condemns, issues sanctions, and at times even sends troops into countries where the local population is threatened with genocide, crimes against humanity, ethnic cleansing, or any other mass atrocity.

Fifth, legal philosophy ("jurisprudence" is what we call it in the legal academy) has been transformed—alongside the transformations to Judeo-Christian theology and Western secular philosophy—by what took place between 1933 and 1945. It is impossible to be a legal philosopher today without confronting the legal theories created by Nazi jurists—just like it is impossible for postwar Christian ethicists to discuss Christian philosophy without confronting the role of the Church during the Holocaust, or for rabbis to discuss Judaism after the war without confronting such daunting philosophical questions as "Where was God when over one million Jewish children were being slaughtered?"

Sixth, as already noted in the above-mentioned indictment of al-Bashir before the ICC at The Hague or the conviction of Nizami in Bangladesh, the language of the Holocaust is used continuously today to exemplify the worst displays of wickedness. Want to denounce a situation? Compare it to the Holocaust. Want to characterize a person as evil? Liken him or her to a Nazi, "another Hitler," or acting like the Gestapo. Want to call attention to a humanitarian crisis? Call it a genocide. While the misuse of Holocaust terminology is rampant, it is important to remember that the precise use of language is the trademark of good legal analysis and remains the most helpful contribution that a lawyer can bring to a discussion of any subject.

Finally, one example of the ubiquitous presence of Nazism and the Holocaust in our present-day culture is the scholarly debate (and, at times, not so scholarly) about the uniqueness of the Holocaust. As Gavriel Rosenfeld pointed out in 2015:

> Since the 1990s, the idea that the Nazi murder of the Jews differs substantially from other cases of genocide has been intensely discussed among historians, journalists, and other writers. Of late, critics of uniqueness, such as Timothy Snyder, Donald Bloxham, and Dirk Moses, have clashed with defenders of the concept, thereby shedding light on the ongoing struggle to shape the memory of the Nazi past.[15]

The debate is encapsulated in a book entirely devoted to the subject titled *Is the Holocaust Unique?*[16] First published in 1996, it is now in its third edition. The need to update the book on a regular basis is driven by the desire of each new generation of scholars to add their voices to the debate and, unfortunately, additional mass atrocities that continue to beg a comparison to the Holocaust. One of the new essays is by Ben Kiernan of Yale University's Genocide Studies program, who pronounces in the opening sentence of his essay: "[T]he Nazi Holocaust of the Jews was history's most extreme case of genocide."[17]

But why the need by each new set of victims to reach the apex of genocide? Since the Holocaust is the manifestation of supreme evil, other victim groups seek to validate their suffering by arguing that what happened to their people is "as bad as the Holocaust." And if what happened to the Jews also happened to others, then for survivors, descendants of survivors and for some Jews who feel affinity to the Holocaust, this diminishes the tragedy of the Holocaust. The genocide of the Jews in the mid-20th century must remain more horrible than any other genocide, lest it be less thought of.[18] In my view, the impulse to compare national or racial tragedies, when no one's tragedy should be diminished, is not a useful endeavor for post-Holocaust justice.

This book is divided into three parts: *The Legal History of the Holocaust and Genocide; Legal Reckoning with the Crimes of the Holocaust*; and *The Holocaust as a Catalyst for Modern International Criminal Justice*. Part I (Chapters 1 and 2) provides the history of the Holocaust as a legal event and explains how genocide has become known as the "crime of crimes" in both international law and popular discourse. Part II discusses specific post-Holocaust legal topics: the criminal prosecution of Nazi war criminals before international and national courts over the last seventy years (Chapters 3 and 4); Holocaust restitution civil litigation centered in the United States and the use of this litigation as a model for recognition of financial crimes committed during other mass atrocities (Chapter 5); laws in Europe criminalizing the denial of the Holocaust and current efforts to criminalize denial of other genocides (Chapter 6); and the impact of Nazi crimes on post-Holocaust legal philosophy (Chapter 7). Part III examines the Holocaust as a catalyst for post-Holocaust international justice (Chapters 8 and 9), specifically the resurrection of the Nuremberg process as a model for modern-day international criminal prosecutions and how genocide is prosecuted today before both national courts and international tribunals.

It is my hope that addressing all of these issues under the rubric of "post-Holocaust law" will focus attention on the legal means for redressing historical wrongs, obtaining justice for victims, and preventing future genocides, all under the long shadow of the Holocaust. In so doing, we must keep in mind the distressing reality confronting today's students studying the Holocaust that "Never Again" has sadly turned into the reality of "Again and Again." As Israeli Holocaust historian Yehuda Bauer puts it, "[The Holocaust] happened because it could happen ... And because it happened once, it can happen again.... Although no event will ever be repeated exactly, it will, if it is followed by similar events, become the first in a line of analogous happenings."[19] Bauer expresses hope that the "Holocaust can be a precedent, or it can become a warning. My bias is, in a sense, political. I believe we ought to do everything in our power to make sure it is a warning, not a precedent."[20] This book is part of that effort.

PART ONE

The Legal History of the Holocaust and Genocide

1

The Holocaust

A Legal History

This chapter will focus on the system of legalized barbarism that existed in Nazi Germany and the German-occupied territories between the years 1933 and 1945. While histories of the Holocaust abound, no history of the Holocaust has been written from a legal point of view. The discussion below aims to do this by presenting the Holocaust as a legal event. In that regard, it is important to remember that the persecution of the Jews began with the myriad of anti-Jewish laws enacted during the Nationalist Socialist era, from the notorious (the Nuremberg laws of 1935) to the petty (a November 27, 1933, decree forbidding the listing of Jewish holidays on office calendars; a December 1935 decree forbidding German judges from citing legal commentaries by Jewish authors). Such laws were used to gradually transform the status of Jews from citizens to noncitizens to subhumans not even worthy of life.

In Nazi Germany, it was the law itself that first made daily life for Jews difficult if not impossible. Later, it became an instrument by which life itself could be summarily extinguished. By the time the gas vans came to the German-occupied Soviet Union in November 1941 and the human slaughter factories began operating in German-occupied Poland later that winter, the groundwork for the murder of the six million Jews and other persecuted minorities had been laid almost completely within the legal framework of existing German law.[1] Richard L. Rubenstein, a writer on post-Holocaust theology, states with some irony, "The Nazis committed no crime at Auschwitz since no law or political order protected those who were first condemned to statelessness and then to the camps."[2]

A. NAZI GERMANY AS A LAW-BASED STATE

For a long time prior to the rise of the Nazis, Germany had a well-developed and sophisticated legal system. German law, and along with it German philosophy, was well known, respected, and emulated internationally for many years prior to the Nazis coming to power in January 1933. Legal theorists worldwide, including in the United States, looked to German jurisprudence as a source of inspiration for their writings up to the beginning of the Second World War. In pre-Nazi Weimar Germany, lawyers played an important role, judges were independent, and a law-based state with a constitution protecting individual rights existed in a manner not too dissimilar to the United States.

The jurisprudential doctrine favored in the West during the first part of the twentieth century was legal positivism, the theory that legal rules are valid only when duly promulgated, passed, adopted, or otherwise "posited" by a governmental institution having the authority to prescribe rules for a particular community. Written laws (statutes) passed by a legislature is the paradigmatic example of positive law. Morality or natural law (God's law or laws derived from nature or reason) are not proper sources of law in a positivist-based state.

The Nazis, upon coming to power, recognized German society's devotion to written laws. For this reason, they made sure that all of their horrific acts could be based upon some legal decree. For example: In 1938, when Nazi leader Hermann Göring "suggested in the course of a discussion . . . that German travelers could always kick Jewish passengers out of a crowded compartment on a train, the Propaganda Minister Josef Goebbels replied: 'I would not say that. I do not believe in this. There has to be a law.' "[3]

Nathan Stoltzfus and Henry Friedlander provide some reasons why Nazi Germany was a law-based state:

> Nazi legal guidelines had called for laws to be written in clear, easily understandable language that reflected the "national feeling for justice and morality." [. . .] The judicial system played a decisive role in the Nazi regime's efforts to provide the majority with a sense of *Rechtssicherheit,* of stability and legal predictability. Adhering to the formal appearance of the rule of law, the regime anchored the disenfranchisement and dispossession of the German Jews in German law and thereby turned the law into a [legal] means of persecution. The German judicial system was one reason the Holocaust resembled machine-like mass murder rather than a Czarist pogrom.[4]

Margarete Buber-Neumann, a survivor of both the Soviet gulag and a Nazi concentration camp, brilliantly points out in her memoirs how the two camp systems brought out differences in the national cultures of the two nations: there was a "blundering, often stupid brutality" at the Soviet gulag camp Karaganda, she says, and a "refined, law-abiding sadism" at the Nazi concentration camp Ravensbrück.[5]

B. THE NAZIS COME TO POWER THROUGH LAW

Adolf Hitler and his Nazi cohorts used law to seize power and transform the Weimar Republic of Germany, which had come into being in 1919, into the Third Reich dictatorship in 1933. The Weimar Republic, the democratic republic that succeeded the German Empire defeated in the First World War, was a fractious parliamentary democracy. Numerous political parties competed for power, with no party able to receive a majority in the German parliament.[6] One of these was the Nazi Party, formally known as the National Socialist German Workers Party (*Nationalsozialistische Deutsche Arbeiterpartei*, or NSDAP in German). The ideology and party platform of the NSDAP were based in large part on hatred of the Jews, blaming both German Jews and Jews worldwide for Germany's defeat in the First World War and for its postwar economic troubles. Targeting Jews was an integral part of the Nazis' racist vision that saw the German "Aryans" as the master race, the Europeans living to the east of Germany as subservient and inferior, and the Jews as the major threat to German supremacy or even existence.[7]

On the eve of Hitler's ascendancy, the worldwide effects of the Great Depression of 1929 made Weimar Germany even more politically unstable. This economic situation placed an additional strain on German civil society. The Nazi Party exploited these economic woes by blaming the problem on the Jews. Furthermore, at the end of the First World War, Germany was forced to agree to the terms of the Versailles Treaty, under which the new Weimar Republic was obligated to pay significant reparations to the Allies for the war. The Nazis argued that Germany lost the war because a "fifth column" of internal traitors (naming specifically the Jews) had stabbed Germany in the back—this despite the fact that many German Jews had served in the military during the war.

In the elections that took place in July and once again in November 1932, no political party won a majority of seats in the parliament. The NSDAP, with a party platform that promised to reform the moribund democratic system and heavily laden with anti-Jewish propaganda, won the largest number of seats (more than a third). President Paul von Hindenburg, the conservative head of state, personally disliked Hitler, but was convinced by his advisers to give the NSDAP the right to form a minority government through alliance with other conservative politicians. They gambled that once in office, Hitler would moderate his views. Experienced politicians, they believed that they could also control Hitler. As a result, on January 30, 1933, Adolf Hitler became chancellor, or prime minister, of Weimar Germany. This date marks the beginning of the Nazi or National Socialist period in German history.

Hitler and his Nazi cohorts soon consolidated their rule and established a dictatorship through various political and legal machinations. As chancellor, Hitler's main concern was to eliminate all political opposition. On February 27,

1933, less than one month after Hitler took office, the German parliament, the Reichstag, was set aflame under suspicious circumstances. Hitler blamed the Reichstag fire, which many suspected was set by the Nazis, on his Communist opponents, and then used this as an excuse for a further wave of political repression.[8] As a first step, Hitler convinced President von Hindenburg to sign, on the basis of Article 48 of the Weimar Constitution, "the Reichstag Fire Decree" (officially called *Presidential Decree for the Protection of People and State*). Article 48 allowed the president of the republic to rule by "emergency decrees" under certain circumstances and without the prior consent of parliament. The Reichstag Fire Decree was the first step toward the establishment of a single-party dictatorship. The decree was never abolished during Nazi rule. In effect, Hitler ruled for the next twelve years under what amounted to martial law.

New elections for the Reichstag were called for March 5, 1933, and this time the Nazis, together with an allied party, the German National People's Party (DNVP), won a slight majority in the German parliament. (The NSDAP itself won 44 percent of the vote). Following the elections, on March 24, 1933, the Nazis were able to pass in the German parliament the *Law for Removing the Distress of the People and the Reich*. Commonly known as the "Enabling Act," this law gave Hitler the authority to rule by decree for four years. The state reverted to laws now being issued in a classic dictatorial manner—mostly through decrees issued by Hitler or his inner circle.

Arrests of political opponents now became commonplace. Two days before parliament's passage of the Enabling Act, the Nazis established their first major concentration camp on the grounds of an old munitions factory in Dachau, near Munich in southern Germany. Sent to Dachau were political opponents, mainly Communists and Social Democrats, including parliamentarians who were now conveniently absent when the vote on the Enabling Act was taken. (Eighty-one Communist parliamentarians and twenty-six Social Democrats had been arrested by then and so were not present for the vote.) Dachau remained a concentration camp for the entire twelve years of Hitler's reign until liberated by the Americans on April 29, 1945.[9]

On July 14, 1933, one-party rule became a reality when the Nazi-dominated German parliament enacted the "Law Against the New Formation of Parties," enshrining the monopoly of power to the NSDAP. By that time, many of the Nazis' political opponents had been arrested and sent to concentration camps, exiled, or murdered.

While German President von Hindenburg was still nominally functioning as head of state, his failing health removed him as an effective counterweight to Hitler. After von Hindenburg's death on August 2, 1934, Hitler combined the positions of president and chancellor. Hitler was now no longer just the German chancellor but from that day on the "Führer," the supreme leader. All laws, including the constitution, were now subsumed to the will of Hitler under the so-called "Führer principle" (*Führerprinzip*). Essentially, the Führer principle meant that law was replaced by the political decisions of Hitler, who as the representative of the German people (*Volk*) became the supreme lawmaker. In 1942, Reich Justice Curt Rothenberger explained: "The judge is on principle bound by the law. The laws are the orders of the Fuehrer (Adolf Hitler). . . . [W]ith the Fuehrer a man has risen within the German people who awakens the oldest, long forgotten times. Here is a man who in his position represents the ideal of the judge in its perfect sense, and the German people elected him for their judge—first of all, of course, as 'judge' over their fate in general, but also as 'supreme magistrate and judge.' "[10]

Within a year of becoming chancellor, Hitler was able to announce the end of the Weimar Republic and the beginning of the "Third Reich,"[11] the supposed successor to the two earlier glory eras of German history—the medieval Holy Roman Empire, until its dissolution in 1806 by Napoleon's armies, and the German Empire of 1870–1918. The Nazis also called their rule the beginning of "The Thousand Year Reich." The Third Reich lasted for a little over twelve years, until Nazi Germany's defeat in May 1945.

The twelve-year Nazi reign is usually divided into two six-year periods: 1933–1939 and 1939–1945. During the first six years, Hitler consolidated his power in Germany, annexed Austria into the Third Reich through the so-called *Anschluss* (union with Germany) in March 1938, and took over a part of Czechoslovakia (the Sudetenland) also in March 1938, and then the remainder of the Czech portion of the Czechoslovak Republic (Bohemia and Moravia). Slovakia, allowed to be nominally independent, became in reality a satellite state of Nazi Germany. Great Britain and France had consented to the ceding of the Czech territory to Germany through a legal instrument: the four-power (Germany, Italy, France and the United Kingdom) Munich Pact of 1938.[12] The second period, 1939–1945, began with the German military invasion of Poland on September 1, 1939, following the Hitler-Stalin Non-Aggression Pact, which included a secret protocol carving up Poland between Germany and the Soviet Union. With this act of German aggression, Great Britain and France recognized the policy of appeasement to be a failure and declared war on Germany. This marked the beginning of the Second World War.

C. LEGAL MEASURES AGAINST JEWS IN THE REICH

Historians describe Germany's war against the Jews culminating in the Holocaust as a gradual process that unfolded in four stages: "identification and definition" (1933–1935), "expropriation and emigration" (1935–1939), "concentration" or "ghettoization" (1939–1941), and "extermination" or "annihilation" (1941–1945).[13]

Upon coming to power, the Nazis began the process of identifying the Jews of Germany and separating them from public life. In March 1933, a few months after assuming office, the Nazis called for a general boycott of Jewish-owned businesses. It is in this period that Nazi storm troopers (*Sturmabteilung*, or SA) began to mark the window displays of shops owned by Jewish shopkeepers with a Jewish Star of David and the word *Jude* (Jew).

On April 7, 1933, laws barring Jews from government service were enacted. These laws also banned Jews from being professors at public universities, teachers in public classrooms, and doctors at state medical institutions. One of the laws prohibited Jewish students from entering the legal profession. The same month, the Interior Ministry imposed a quota limiting admission of "non-Aryans" to German schools and universities to 1.5 percent. On May 10, 1933, books by Jewish authors and other "degenerate" writers were burned at mass rallies.

It is estimated that in 1933 the non-Aryan population of Germany was about 600,000 or 1 percent. The number of non-Aryans in government service was approximately 5,000, or 0.5 percent of the total government personnel—a very small number. The Nazis' first targets were those 5,000 individuals in government jobs. The first major anti-Jewish law, predating the infamous Nuremberg Laws, which came two years later, was the *Law for the Reestablishment of the Professional Civil Service*, enacted on April 7, 1933. Like much antisemitic legislation, this law carried an innocuous title; however, the law expelled from government service all Jewish civil servants. In a gesture to the wartime hero and aging president of Germany, Paul von Hindenburg, the law initially exempted Jewish veterans of the First World War from expulsion. The exemption did not last long; Jewish veterans were banished from their government jobs soon after Hindenburg's death in August 1934.

Between the civil service law of April 1933 and the Nuremberg Laws of September 1935, both the German federal government and the German states enacted various categories of anti-Jewish legislation, some major and some minor, but all meant to make life extremely difficult for Jews living in Nazi Germany. These included an April 19, 1933, decree entered by the State of Baden, prohibiting the use of the Jewish language (Yiddish) in cattle markets; a May 13, 1933, decree issued by the State of Prussia decreeing that Jews could only change their names to other Jewish names; a November 27, 1933, law issued by the Federal Reich Interior Ministry forbidding the listing of Jewish holidays on office calendars; and a May 5, 1934, decree issued by the Reich Propaganda Ministry forbidding the appearance on stage of Jewish actors. In May 1935, the German army was declared "all-Aryan," meaning free of those whom the Nazis defined as Jews. As Sarah Ann Gordon explains:

> No indignity appeared too trivial to legislate. . . . [Jews] were denied entrance to parks, they could no longer own automobiles, and Jewish

> publications and associations were prohibited. They could not use public telephones or automatic ticket machines, visit the countryside, restaurants, railway or bus station waiting rooms, "Aryan" hairdressers, and sleeping or dining cars on trains. They could not buy newspapers or periodicals, sell their books, buy books in bookstores, receive "smokers' cards," shop during normal shopping hours, or receive a full ration of meats, cereals, and milk. After 1942 they were no longer permitted to keep pets; they were required to turn them in to dog pounds for extermination because they had been "tainted" by " 'Jewish blood.' . . . By 1941 there were no buffers left between Jews and the Nazi state."[14]

From September 11 to 15, 1935, the Nazis held a party congress in the southern German city of Nuremberg, considered by Hitler to be the most German of German cities because of its ancient history. The Nuremberg Laws were drafted on the last two days of the congress and passed by a special session of parliament held at Nuremberg. The Nuremberg "Reich Citizenship Law" of September 15, 1935, deprived German Jews of citizenship, limiting German citizenship to persons of German or "kindred" blood.[15] As a result, those whom the Nazis considered to be non-German were now deprived of the civil rights possessed by citizens of the state. The Nuremberg *Law for the Protection of German Blood and German Honor* forbid marriage and extramarital sexual intercourse between Jews and citizens of German or "kindred" blood. Jews were also forbidden to employ in their households German women younger than forty-five years of age. Individuals arrested for violating the Nuremberg Laws were called *Rassenchander*, or "race polluters."

In examining German legislation enacted during the Third Reich, it is important to note that the Nazis defined Jews by genealogy rather than religion, using the bogus concept of a Jewish "race." In Nazi Germany, a person did not have to practice Judaism in order to be legally considered a Jew; lifelong Christians with Jewish ancestry were Jews, and so forced to wear the yellow star and transported to the "East." Of course, practitioners of Judaism were the primary victims, but the Nazis classified as Jews many persons who did not consider themselves as such.

Since the Nazis classified Jews on the basis of race and not religion, they were now forced to develop an entire set of legal rules to determine who would be classified as a Jew and who would be an Aryan. The practical problem involved Germans who had some Jewish heritage but did not consider themselves to be Jews. These individuals were labeled *Mischlinge*, a German word for half-breeds, mixed ancestry, or mongrels. *Mischlinge* who had three Jewish grandparents were legally considered Jews, and so fell under the category of the anti-Jewish legislation. Non-Jews who had fewer than two Jewish grandparents could sometimes keep themselves out of the Jewish category.[16]

Illustration 1 A sign posted in front of a fence in Germany reading "Jews are not wanted here. Jews are our misfortune," circa 1935. US Holocaust Memorial Museum, photograph 66668.

Since specific definitions were now required, supplementary decrees were drafted by government lawyers. The first supplementary decree to the Reich Citizenship Law, published on November 14, 1935, defined as Jewish (1) all persons who had at least three full Jewish grandparents, (2) those who had two Jewish grandparents and were married to a Jewish spouse, or (3) those who belonged to the Jewish religion at the time of the law's publication or who had converted to Judaism or entered into such commitments at a later date. From November 14 on, therefore, the civil rights of these legally defined Jews were canceled, their voting rights abolished, and Jewish civil servants who had kept their positions owing to their veteran status were now forced into retirement. On December 21, 1935, a second supplemental decree ordered the dismissal of Jewish professors, teachers, physicians, lawyers, and notaries who were state employees and had been granted exemption. What this meant was that one's religion did not matter, nor the religion of one's parents. The critical legal fact for determination of who was to be considered a Jew was the religion of one's grandparents.

A November 26, 1935, supplementary decree to the *Law for the Protection of German Blood* specified the various categories of forbidden marriages, depending on whether one of the parties was classified as a *Mischlinge* of the first degree (two Jewish grandparents) or a *Mischlinge* of the second degree (one Jewish grandparent). The Nuremberg Laws also criminalized certain sexual relations. The original April 1935 decree made it illegal to have sexual relations between Jews and Germans. The 1935 Supplementary Decree forbade sexual relations between Jews and persons of "alien blood." This now required a definition of "alien blood." Twelve days after the issuance of the supplementary decree, a circular from the Reich Ministry of the Interior clarified the ambiguity: alien blood referred to "Gypsies, Negroes, and their bastards."

A major legal hurdle encountered by experts attempting to interpret the Nuremberg Laws was the definition of "intercourse." Litigation on this question even came before the Supreme Court of Germany— and the German high court judges infused its decision with Nazi ideology, making their animus toward Jews obvious. (And this was in the early years of Nazi rule, when opposition to the Nazi version of law was still possible). In its December 1935 decision, the Supreme Court stated: "The term 'sexual intercourse' as meant by the *Law for the Protection of German Blood* . . . is also not limited to coition. It includes all forms of natural and unnatural sexual intercourse—that is, coition, as well as those sexual activities with a person of the opposite sex which are designed, in the manner in which they are performed, to serve in place of coition to satisfy the sex drive of at least one of the partners."[17] The court further explained that bodily contact was not necessary and that even a verbal proposition for sex violated the law. *The Law for the Protection of German Blood* of 1935, broadly interpreted by the highest court in the land, was also strictly enforced, and those caught violating the law received severe punishment.

Other laws making life difficult for Jews followed. Under a decree of August 1938, Jews were compelled to add a middle name to their legal name: "Israel" for Jewish males and "Sarah" for Jewish females and for such a name to appear in all identifying documents.[18] In October of that year, passports of German Jews were marked with the letter "J" for *Jude*.[19] The same month, another decree completed an earlier process by forbidding Jews from practicing law in Germany.

Concurrent with the anti-Jewish legislation, the German racial state also adopted a policy of what today would be called ethnic cleansing: to make Germany—and later the conquered territories annexed into the German Reich—*judenrein* ("free of Jews") through forced emigration. And while Germany did not want its *Juden*, it did want their property. A streamlined bureaucratic process was developed by the Nazis' Jewish specialist Adolf Eichmann whereby in one day a German or Austrian Jewish family could be legally stripped of all its assets in exchange for exit visas allowing them to leave the country within a matter of weeks with little more than the clothes on their backs. In turn, the looted booty, which included clothing, household objects, and other personal possessions that once belonged to Jews, were sold at government-organized public auctions (popularly known as "Jew auctions"), or simply handed out free as emergency relief.[20] It was grand larceny, on a scale unseen in the modern world.

Further legislation during this time was used to pressure Jews to emigrate from Germany. In September 1937, a Nazi decree freed Jews from "protective detention" from such places as Dachau if they emigrated. In October 1937, Heinrich Himmler, head of the *Schutzstaffel* (SS), the elite corps of the Nazi Party, announced that Jews returning to Germany would be sent to concentration camps.

During this period, a series of mob actions against Jews took place in several German cities. Following the violence, there generally appeared a new round of anti-Jewish legislation, further crippling Jewish life in Germany (which after March 1938 included Austria and annexed Czech territories). Seventy months into Nazi rule, the increasing violence reached its apex on the night of the November 9, 1938, in the infamous *Kristallnacht* ("Night of the Broken Glass"), a nationwide coordinated pogrom (mob action) instigated by the Nazi leadership and executed by the police and state agencies, the SA and the SS. The major feature that night was the burning of over a thousand synagogues and the destruction and looting of 7,500 Jewish-owned shops (hence the term "broken glass"). According to official reports, ninety-one Jews were killed during that night and about 30,000 were sent to concentration camps in its aftermath. On November 12, 1938, the German government issued a decree imposing a collective fine of one billion Reich marks on the German Jewish community. Another decree ordered German insurance companies to make payment to the state rather than to the Jewish shop owners who carried insurance for their losses.[21]

A written report of a meeting held on November 12, 1938, under Göring's chairmanship shows the law-based measures taken in the aftermath of *Kristallnacht.*

> *Göring:* Today's meeting is of decisive importance. I have received a letter on the Fuehrer's orders by the Head of Staff of the Fuehrer's Deputy, [Martin] Bormann, with instructions that the Jewish Question is to be summed up and coordinated once and for all and and solved one way or another . . .
>
> . . .
>
> *Fischböck* [speaking for Seyss-Inquart]: We already have a precise plan for this in Austria. . . . In Vienna there are 12,000 Jewish artisans' businesses and 5,000 Jewish retail stores. . . . According to [our] plan, then, 3,000 to 3,500 of the total of 17,000 businesses would remain open, and all the others would be closed. This is calculated on the basis of investigation for each separate branch and in accordance with local requirements. It has been settled with all the competent authorities and could start tomorrow, as soon we get the Law which we requested in September, which would authorize us to withdraw trade licenses generally, without any connection with the Jewish question. It would be quite a short Law.
>
> *Göring*: I will issue the regulation today.
>
> . . .
>
> *Göring*: I must say that this proposal is marvelous.
>
> . . .
>
> *[Walter] Funk*: . . . I have prepared a Regulation for this matter which states that from January 1, 1939 Jews are forbidden to operate retail stores and commission agencies, or to operate independent artisans' businesses. They are also forbidden to hire employees for this purpose, to offer such services, or to advertise them or accept orders. Where any Jewish trade is carried out it will be closed by the police. From January 1, 1939 a Jew can no longer be the manager of a business, in accordance with the Law for the Organization of National Labor, of January 20, 1934.[22]

The initial two stages of the persecution of the Jews described above were critical in preparing the German public at home and the German military in the East for what was to come. Having become acclimated to the widespread persecution of their Jewish neighbors and the eventual elimination of Jews from everyday life through legal means made the subsequent mass deportation and murder of the Jews seem legitimate to the majority of non-Jewish Germans.

D. WAR, OCCUPATION LAW, AND GHETTOIZATION IN OCCUPIED EUROPE

The first public pronouncement threatening all European Jews with annihilation was made by the German head of state on January 30, 1939. On that day, Hitler gave a speech before the German parliament, the Reichstag, and received momentous applause when he spoke the following words:

> If the international Finance-Jewry inside and outside of Europe should succeed in plunging the peoples of the earth once again into a world war, the result will be not the Bolshevization of earth, and thus a Jewish victory, but the annihilation of the Jewish race in Europe.[23]

Nine months later, in September 1939, war did come—but at the instigation of Hitler, with Germany's invasion of Poland. In 1940, Germany continued the war with the invasion of France, Belgium, and the Netherlands. In June 1941, Germany invaded the Soviet Union, putting an end to the Hitler-Stalin Non-Aggression Pact. The numbers of Jews under German Nazi occupation grew with every military success, as Norway, Denmark, France, Belgium, Greece, and southern Europe fell under German control. With the conquest of Poland, the largest Jewish population in Europe totaling three million came under German rule. Invasion of the Soviet Union forced another two million Jews living in the Ukraine, Belorussia, and Russia under the Nazi orbit.

As the territory of the Third Reich expanded, lawyers in the Reich's Ministry of Justice were recruited to work with the German military to formulate the laws that would apply in the territories that became formally or informally part of the Third Reich. The scheme they developed was initially based on existing principles of international law dealing with laws of occupation, applicable to this day. For territories annexed directly into the German state after military occupation (i.e., Austria after the *Anschluss*, the Alsace-Lorraine region of France, and the western portions of Poland annexed into the Reich by a Hitler decree of October 8, 1939), German law would apply, including the anti-Jewish decrees discussed above. For areas under German occupation and direct administration (i.e., the Protectorate of Bohemia and Moravia and the General Government of Poland, the central part of Poland that also was made a German protectorate) occupation laws would apply. The right as occupier to promulgate new rules and orders, and to formulate them in Germany, was technically in conformance with the international laws of occupation. Territories under puppet regimes (i.e., Vichy France, Hungary, Romania, and Slovakia) would be ruled by laws passed by the new regimes, but the freedom of these regimes to pass legislation was circumvented by the pressure of the German authorities as to what laws could or could not be passed.

In the occupied territories, two new sets of laws had to be promulgated: (1) laws dealing with the underground resistance to the German regime, and (2) laws that would apply to the large Jewish population that had now come under German rule as a result of the German military victories in Poland, central Europe, and the western Soviet Union. How the occupied lands would be ruled varied. In the non-annexed portions of Poland (the General Government), a civilian administration was set up headed by Hitler's lawyer Hans Frank. In occupied France and Belgium there was a military government. As for the judicial process in the occupied territories, Hitler's policy was to "leave the courts at home."[24] But even in the western part of Poland that was annexed into the Reich, "the SS and police alone, not the judicial authorities, were to have total control."[25] For non-Jews this meant judgment by a Gestapo court-martial; for Jews, even the summary court-martial was dispensed with "because the Jews were, in any case, no more than fair game for the police. These were measures against which the judicial authorities could not or would not protest, since they 'only' involved Jews."[26]

A critical problem facing the German occupiers was the increasing resistance from the local population. Here again law was used to deal with the problem. On orders from Hitler, Field Marshal Wilhelm Keitel issued on December 7, 1941, the infamous "Night and Fog" Decree (*Nacht-und-Nebel-Erlass*), authorizing extraordinary measures in all occupied territories. Political suspects would simply "disappear" to special detention facilities where, following a summary court proceeding, they would face the death penalty or, if fortunate, imprisonment. The Justice Ministry lawyers who drafted these decrees justified them on the ground of necessity in order to protect German troops against terrorist acts or insurgency.[27]

Another pseudo-legal tool was the use of so-called "atonement measures"—collective punishment for attacks on Germans or German property. These innocent individuals were summarily shot. As Diemut Majer notes: "In these actions, most of which took place in public with forced attendance by the entire Polish population, the hostages were either singled out from lists carefully drawn up by the police (blacklists) or picked at random from the population of the community where the crime was committed ('from the environment of the criminal')."[28]

As for the Jews in the occupied territories, the Nazi planners decided to concentrate them inside Jewish ghettos, euphemistically termed "Jewish residential districts" (*jüdische Wohnbezirke*). These were sealed-off city neighborhoods where the Jews would be forced to live together under conditions of terrible overcrowding and limited rations. Punishment for leaving the Jewish ghetto without a special permit was death. But even here, the veneer of legality was observed. The official reason given for the establishment of ghettos was public health and safety.

Der Gouverneeur des Distrakts Krakau, Krakau 15.IV.9[illegible]
Abteilung Wirtschaft
Unterabt. Treuhandverwaltung.

Zl.21.069/F.

Vollmacht

für

Name: Karl NAGEL

Anschrift Krakau Hotel Bristol

Auf Grund der Verordnung über die Beschlagnahme von privaten Vermögen im Generalgouvernement bestelle ich Sie als Treuhänder für

Mühle und Grossbäckerei ZIARNO

Krakau Zablocie 25

Sie sind zu allen gerichtlichen und aussergerichtlichen Geschäften und Rechtshandlungen ermächtigt, die die Verwaltung obenbezeichneten Vermögens erforderlich macht.-Ihre Ermächtigung ersetz in diesen Rahmen jede gesetzlich erforderliche Vollmacht.-Mit der Zustellung dieser Verfügung verliert der Eigrntümmer des von Ihnen Verwalteten Vermögens das Recht darüber zu verfügen

Nähere Anweisungen: Für die Geschäftführung gilt die erlassene Dienstanweisung.-

Generalgouvernement
Der Gouverneur des Distrikts Krakau
Abt. Wirschaft
Unterabt. Treuhandverwaltung.
Unterschrift.-

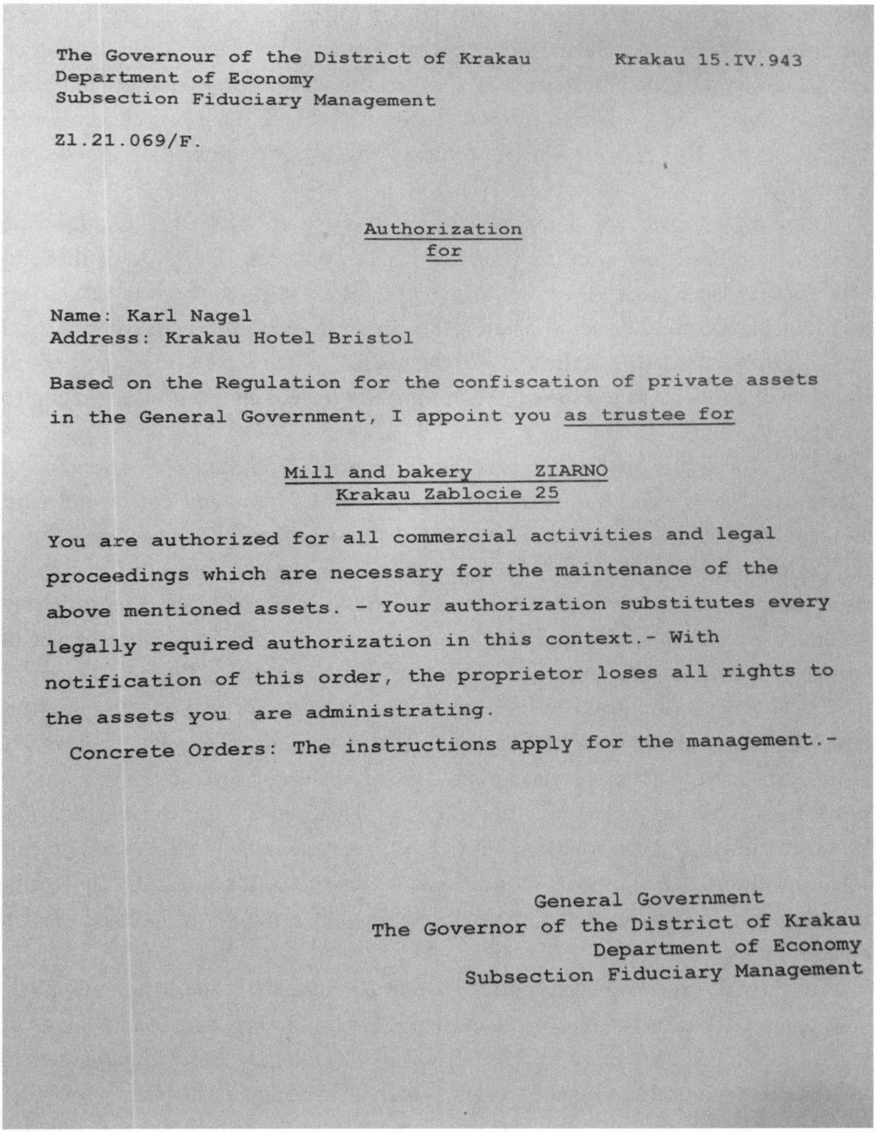

The Governour of the District of Krakau   Krakau 15.IV.943
Department of Economy
Subsection Fiduciary Management

Zl.21.069/F.

Authorization
for

Name: Karl Nagel
Address: Krakau Hotel Bristol

Based on the Regulation for the confiscation of private assets in the General Government, I appoint you as trustee for

Mill and bakery   ZIARNO
Krakau Zablocie 25

You are authorized for all commercial activities and legal proceedings which are necessary for the maintenance of the above mentioned assets. - Your authorization substitutes every legally required authorization in this context.- With notification of this order, the proprietor loses all rights to the assets you are administrating.

Concrete Orders: The instructions apply for the management.-

General Government
The Governor of the District of Krakau
Department of Economy
Subsection Fiduciary Management

Illustration 2 Authorization for seizure of large mill and bakery owned by the Finder family in Cracow. 1940. Courtesy of Miriam Finder Tasini.

Jews had to be segregated because they spread infectious diseases (e.g., typhus), mounted resistance to German occupation, or were involved in plundering or black market activities.[29] Other laws allowed the seizure of Jewish-owned businesses (Illustration 2), Bank accounts, automobiles, and even bicycles could be legally seized. This process was repeated in the other countries conquered by Germany.

Following issuance of decrees ordering Jews to move to the ghettos, the Germans ordered Jewish communities with a population of 10,000 or more to establish Jewish Councils, known as *Judenrat*, as a means through which to implement Nazi orders directed against the Jews. The *Judenrat* acted as the local Jewish government within the walls of the ghetto, responsible for the daily life of the ghetto. These included the establishment of a Jewish ghetto police and ghetto courts.[30]

Raul Hilberg summarizes the precarious situation that ghetto Jews now found themselves in: "Before the war, these Jewish leaders had been concerned with synagogues, religious schools, cemeteries, orphanages, and hospitals. From now on, their activities were going to be supplemented by another quite different function: the transmission of German directives and orders to the Jewish population, and the use of Jewish police to enforce German will; and finally, the deliverance of Jewish property, Jewish labor, and ultimately Jewish lives to the German enemy."[31]

The Jewish victims tried to keep a semblance of ordinary life in the ghettos. Israel Gutman, historian of the Warsaw Ghetto, explains: "The Polish Jews . . . adjust[ed] rapidly to a situation that continuously changed and grew worse. Foodstuffs were smuggled into the ghettos, illegal workshops existed, schools functioned without permission, and public prayers were held although this was forbidden. . . . [D]espite conditions of terror, [underground cells] published secret newspapers and maintained contact among the isolated Jewish communities."[32]

Interestingly, and largely forgotten, is that the first analysis of the tapestry of laws promulgated by the Nazis in conquered Europe was conducted by the great legal scholar Raphael Lemkin. His *Axis Rule in Occupied Europe*, published in 1944, is best remembered as the work in which he introduced the term "genocide" (see Chapter 2), but the book was much more than that. In this study, Lemkin compiled an exhaustive list of laws enacted by the Nazis for the persecution of the conquered populations in seventeen countries. Lemkin was first and foremost a lawyer, and so he applied his fine legal mind to analyzing these German occupation decrees. His goal was to demonstrate Nazi brutality through law. Daniel Marc Segesser and Myriam Gessler describe the motivations for this study:

> Lemkin was convinced that many of his potential readers were inclined to believe that the Axis regimes could not possibly be as cruel and ruthless

> as they had been told so far. It was therefore important to show the readers that the occupation of large parts of Europe had been marked by grave outrages against humanity and international law as well as against human rights, morality and religion and that the occupants had not even refrained from using law to commit their crimes. The publication of a collection of occupation laws was essential, Lemkin believed, for a clear understanding of the Axis regimes. . . . Lemkin wanted to show his reader how the German authorities had organized their occupation of large parts in violation of international law and that . . . they had used a unilaterally utilitarian conception of law—law is what is useful to the German nation—to give the impression of a legal behaviour.[33]

Lemkin's analysis was unique in that no one had studied the German occupation as it was taking place or discussed it in terms of jurisprudence. As Michael Ignatieff explains:

> Here's a lawyer who looks at this horror and tries to understand it as a system of law. His key insight was that occupation, not just in Poland but right across Europe, had inverted the whole tradition of European jurisprudence. So, that you have these incredible insane decrees. Food distribution, for example, in Poland, is entirely racialized. You get food depending on your racial category. Jews get almost no food at all. Other examples: marriage law in occupied Holland was organized on racial grounds. Germans responsible for getting Dutch women pregnant were not punished, as would be the case in any normal code of military justice or honor. They were rewarded because the resulting child would be a Nordic Aryan addition to the master race. Lemkin was the first scholar to notice the insanity of this kind of jurisprudence, to understand its unremitting racial bias, and to see that the extermination of groups that he begins to pick up evidence of is not an accidental or incidental cruelty of occupation, but the very essence of the whole program.[34]

And so, even before the extent of the killings was realized in the West, Lemkin recognized the genocidal purpose from his study of Nazi occupation laws. Strangely, no one continued on the legal road started by Lemkin in analyzing law in the German-occupied territories. Postwar studies of Nazi law abound, but invariably they focus on anti-Jewish laws promulgated during the first six years of Nazi rule.[35] Almost completely missing are analyses of law after the start of the war in 1939. Both historians and law scholars tend to stop at the borders of the German Reich and fail to examine how law operated in the countries under Nazi rule. One work is an exception: Diemut Majer's monumental study, *Non-Germans under the Third Reich: The Nazi Judicial and Administrative System in Germany and Occupied Eastern Europe, with Special Regard to Occupied Poland 1933–1945*, first published in German in 1981 and translated into English in 2003.

In her study, Majer examines the entire legal machinery of Germany during the Third Reich, including the police and SS, and how they all became mobilized in the mission of subjugation and, for the Jews and the Roma (Gypsies), annihilation. The work provides a detailed analysis of the various German laws, decrees, regulations, and other legal pronouncements issued by the German conquerors toward their subjects in Eastern Europe, whom the Nazis considered racially inferior and who were described with a new legal term: *fremdvölkische* (literally aliens or "foreign people").[36] Basic to the concept of Nazi Germany's occupation decrees was the principle of "special law" (*Sonderrecht*), meaning a separate body of rules for the *fremdvölkische* based on the concept of "racial *inequality*" for "non-Germans."[37]

The most extreme application of "special law" took place in occupied Poland, with the German occupiers issuing a myriad of decrees covering the legal treatment of Polish Jews and Christian Poles. Here the concept of law loses all meaning. As Majer explains, "the arbitrary measures of the SS and the police . . . had nothing to do at first with 'criminal prosecution' in the sense meant by the police at the time."[38] Rather, she writes, these were acts of " 'unbridled terror' characterized by innumerable 'blind programs of action,' (such as the mass seizures and deportations), but above all by the arbitrary justice of the SS and the police . . ."[39] All that the " 'courtlike' institutions of the police . . . had in common with the concept of a court was their name . . .," she concludes. "[T]hey were nothing but a mere instrument of a random terror . . ."[40]

Throughout German-occupied Europe all Jews (including children) were legally bound to wear and prominently display on their clothing a yellow Star of David. If found without one, they were subjected to severe punishment. But this was just the tip of the legal iceberg. Another notorious example of a "special law" is the *Law Against Poles and Jews* of December 4, 1941, applied both in the Reich (where tens of thousands of Poles were conscripted for labor in Germany) and in the annexed portions of Poland. In the *Justice Case* in Nuremberg, the American court summarized the law:

> Poles and Jews convicted of specific crimes were subjected to different types of punishment from that imposed upon Germans who had committed the same crimes. Their rights as defendants in court were severely circumscribed. Courts were empowered to impose death sentences on Poles and Jews even where such punishment was not prescribed by law, if the evidence showed "particularly objectionable motives." And, finally, the police were given *carte blanche* to punish all "criminal" acts committed by Jews without any employment of the judicial process.[41]

Even the language of the law changed. Majer's study contains an appended glossary describing "Traditional German Legal Terms" and "National Socialist Legal Terminology." A mere perusal of the glossary starkly demonstrates the corruption of the legal language by the Nazi regime. Terms that seemingly describe innocuous legal procedure are transformed by the Nazi political and judicial authorities into euphemisms for the massive destruction of peoples and the rendering of human beings not as subjects protected by the law but as objects to be used as necessary for the betterment of the German race. Majer explains: "To a great extent the Nazi terms do not correspond to the traditional German legal terminology, nor do they correspond to legal terms in other languages. . . . Most of the Nazi terms were coinages, new creations, or a misuse of older terms."[42]

One last extralegal element needs to be considered alongside the law: massive corruption. As Majer observes: "It was an open secret that corruption and profiteering were the order of the day in the German departments and that in the General Government 'not all principles of the homeland were preserved' . . . "[43] Of course, for Jews and other persecuted groups this was a good thing. Almost every Jewish survivor has a story of being saved, or saving a loved one, through the payment of a bribe.

Despite all these harsh measures, as Timothy Snyder points out, "[T]his was not yet a Holocaust."[44]

E. EXTERMINATION: THE LEGAL HOLOCAUST

The Holocaust, the systematic, state-sponsored plan to murder all Jews, began with the invasion of the Soviet Union in June 1941—code named Operation Barbarossa—and ended with the collapse of the Third Reich itself in 1945. This was the extermination stage, and the one usually thought of when mention is made of the Holocaust. To the Nazis, the Jews became *lebensunwertig*, "life unworthy of life."

Germany's surprise invasion of the Soviet Union in June 1941 was in breach of the German-Soviet Non-Aggression Treaty signed by the two countries in August 1939. The invasion was cataclysmic, with a staggering number of casualties unknown in any previous conflict. Approximately thirty million Soviet civilians and soldiers lost their lives; twenty million of these were civilians. On the German side, estimates of military casualties on the Eastern Front range from 800,000 to 2.7 million, depending on whether German losses are counted before or after the Soviet counterattack in 1942.

At the outset, German military forces achieved rapid victories against the Red Army, capturing a massive amount of Soviet territory, including all of the Ukraine, Belorussia, and the Baltic region. The German military succeeded also in capturing a large portion of Western Russia before it was turned back at the outskirts of Moscow in early December.

Mass killings began to take place as soon as the German troops entered Soviet territory. These were authorized pursuant to two orders issued to the German armed forces: the Barbarossa Jurisdiction Order and the Commissar Order. The Barbarossa Jurisdiction Order, distributed on May 14, 1941, became the German soldier's charter for partisan warfare, essentially giving legal cover for the shooting of anyone suspected of being a partisan. The order, as Valerie Hébert sums up, "suspended courts-martial for civilians suspected of sabotage or guerilla warfare, allowed and encouraged the summary killings of these individuals and collective reprisals against whole communities, and explicitly relieved the army of the obligations to punish German soldiers who had committed crimes against civilians."[45] Since no definition of "commissar" or "partisan" was set out in the two orders, civilian Jews posing no resistance to the fighting military or to the occupation authority became subjects for fair game of mass shootings. The Commissar Order, issued on June 6, 1941, by the German Armed Forces High Command to commanders just two weeks prior to the invasion of the Soviet Union, read: "[T]he originators of the Asiatic-barbaric methods of fighting are the [Soviet] political commissars.... Therefore, if taken while fighting or offering resistance, they must, on principle, be shot immediately."[46] As Hébert points out: "[T]he language of the military directives blurred the lines between civilian and combatant, Jew and partisan, unlawful belligerent and ideological foe."[47] Other orders, more explicit, legally sanctioned mass murder of civilians. For example, the September 1941 Hostage Reprisal Order called for the execution of fifty to one hundred Communists (never defined) for every German life lost to insurrection in the occupied territories.

Part and parcel of Hitler's military campaign was the war against the Jews. Holocaust historian Saul Friedlander explains how virulent antisemitism, apart from any military goals, motivated Hitler's apocalyptic campaign against the Jews:

> Only one group was hounded all over the continent, to the very last individual, to the very last day of German presence: the Jews.... [I]dentifying the Jews as the enemy of humankind [was] preached by the ultimate bearer of all authority: Adolf Hitler. His message may not have been shared by all, but *his* were the guidelines for the policies of total extermination.... [W]e are brought back to a peculiar brand of apocalyptic anti-Semitism, the extraordinary virulence of which remains the only way of explaining both the physical onslaught against *all* Jews living within German reach *and* against any part of human culture created by Jews or showing any trace of the Jewish spirit.... Hitler's goals, mainly his vision of an apocalyptic final struggle against the Jews, were metapolitical. This vision invested the core of his movement with the fervor of a crusading sect.[48]

The process leading to the extermination of the Jews was not linear but took place in fits and starts and developed out of the military circumstances that brought an increasing number of Jews under Nazi control. The killing of millions of Jews by brutal murder or by gassing in human slaughterhouses such as Auschwitz was also reached in stages.

During the invasion of the Soviet Union, four special action murder squads known as the *Einsatzgruppen* followed the regular German army into newly conquered territory. Operating just behind the advancing German troops, these mobile killing squads would round up and murder all the Jews and other "undesirables" such as the Roma (commonly known as Gypsies), perceived Communist political leaders, professionals, and "criminals," often with assistance from the local populace. The German army, known as the *Wehrmacht,* also was heavily involved in the killings. Later on, German police battalions—initially organized to keep order in the occupied territories—joined in the killing process. Of the *Einsatzgruppen* generals who ordered the mass murder of Jews and were put on trial at Nuremberg, the majority were lawyers or legally trained. As Hilary Earl correctly observes: "The collective biography of these men dispels the myth that educational attainment inoculates us against us against genocide. The opposite seems true."[49] Law degrees, especially, seemed to be the gateway ticket to genocide.[50]

The people rounded up were transported either by foot or by truck to a remote location, ordered to dig pits to serve as mass graves, forced to strip naked, and shot at close-range. By such means, the *Einsatzgruppen* squads and their local collaborators managed to murder approximately 1.4 million Jews as well as members of other religious, national, and political groups. They murdered these men, women, and children one by one, bullet by bullet, town by town, and city by city. These massive killings lifted the scale of Nazi atrocities to totally new levels.

One of the most notorious of such massacres took place at Babi Yar, a ravine outside Kiev, the largest city in the Ukraine. Shortly after their capture of Kiev in September 1941, the Germans ordered all Jews of Kiev to appear on a particular morning at a specific location in the city. From there, the Jews were forcibly transported in groups of ten or more to Babi Yar. Over the next two days, a unit of the *Einsatzgruppen,* with the support of a battalion of Waffen-SS soldiers, the military arm of the Nazi Party, and local Ukrainian collaborators, systematically shot dead by machine-gun fire over 33,000 Jews. Operational Situation Report No. 101, sent from the field to Berlin and captured after the war, states that at least 33,771 Jews from Kiev were killed at Babi Yar on September 29 and 30, 1941.

The Jewish population in the Baltic territories was also almost totally exterminated by mass shootings, carried out by the Germans with the assistance of local collaborators. Quoting from Christoph Dieckmann's landmark study on murder

Illustration 3 An SS soldier shooting at a man's head over a mass grave, circa 1941, Vinitsa, Ukraine (USSR). Yad Vashem, photograph 3385/1.

in Lithuania, Timothy Snyder writes: "[T]he 'Lithuanian countryside was transformed in the second half of 1941 into a giant graveyard of the Lithuanian Jews.' By his [Dieckmann's] reckoning, some 150,000 Jews were murdered in Lithuania by November 1941. . . . Deporting Jews had proven to be impossible. What was possible was murdering them where they lived. This was a Holocaust."[51]

The firing squads, however, were having a negative psychological effect on the troops, especially when it came to large-scale murders of defenseless women, children, and babies. In the days soon after the war started, Hitler had signed a law authorizing the so-called T-4 euthanasia program, by which an estimated 70,000 mentally and physically handicapped Germans were gassed to death between 1939 and 1941 as part of Hitler's plan to "purify" the German master race. Gassing now became the favored method of murder, with the gassing done onsite in mobile killing vans in occupied Soviet territory and in stationary death camps in occupied Poland.

By June 1942, approximately fifteen gas vans were put at the disposal of the *Einsatzgruppen* operating in occupied Soviet territory. The victims were packed into the back of closed vans where they were murdered by the use of gas, usually carbon monoxide piped into the closed space of the van through a hose attached to the van's tailpipe. The bodies were then unloaded from the vans, and either buried in mass graves or incinerated in open flames. The Nazis murdered approximately 700,000 persons through this method, with roughly half in occupied Soviet territory and the rest in camps solely devoted to mass murder, which they built in German-occupied Poland.

Mobile van gassings proved an inefficient method for the murder of millions. As with the mass shootings, the executioners were still being traumatized, this time either when the doors of the vans were opened and bodies taken out, or from the screams of the victims during the piping of the gas. The gas vans also frequently suffered mechanical failure and so the murder process did not go smoothly. The stationary human slaughterhouses located in occupied Poland became the means by which the Nazis implemented what they called the "Final Solution to the Jewish Problem in Europe."

The first extermination camp was set up in the Polish village of Chełmno in December 1941. Death camps in other parts of occupied Poland (Bełżec, Treblinka, Sobibor, Majdanek, and Auschwitz-Birkenau) soon followed. The victims were Jews who had earlier been forced into ghettos. The hell of the ghetto now became preferable to the next stage: "resettlement," a euphemism for transport by railroad cattle cars or trucks to these camps. The ghettos were now to be forcibly liquidated, and these *Aktionen* (roundups) were carried out by special units of the German police and the SS. The orders were transmitted through the *Judenrat* heads and enforced by the Jewish ghetto police. One of the most horrid incidents took place in the Łódź ghetto in Poland. On September 2, 1942, the

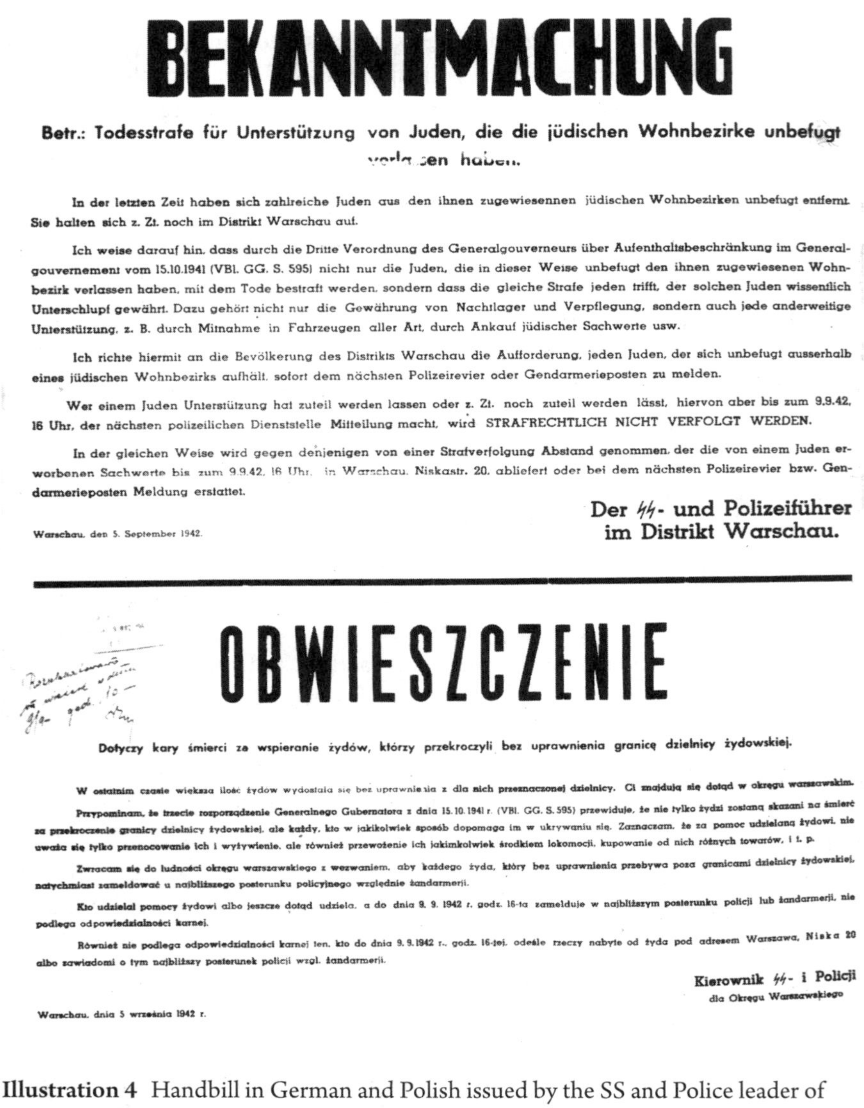

BEKANNTMACHUNG

Betr.: Todesstrafe für Unterstützung von Juden, die die jüdischen Wohnbezirke unbefugt verlassen haben.

In der letzten Zeit haben sich zahlreiche Juden aus den ihnen zugewiesennen jüdischen Wohnbezirken unbefugt entfernt. Sie halten sich z. Zt. noch im Distrikt Warschau auf.

Ich weise darauf hin, dass durch die Dritte Verordnung des Generalgouverneurs über Aufenthaltsbeschränkung im Generalgouvernement vom 15.10.1941 (VBl. GG. S. 595) nicht nur die Juden, die in dieser Weise unbefugt den ihnen zugewiesenen Wohnbezirk verlassen haben, mit dem Tode bestraft werden, sondern dass die gleiche Strafe jeden trifft, der solchen Juden wissentlich Unterschlupf gewährt. Dazu gehört nicht nur die Gewährung von Nachtlager und Verpflegung, sondern auch jede anderweitige Unterstützung, z. B. durch Mitnahme in Fahrzeugen aller Art, durch Ankauf jüdischer Sachwerte usw.

Ich richte hiermit an die Bevölkerung des Distrikts Warschau die Aufforderung, jeden Juden, der sich unbefugt ausserhalb eines jüdischen Wohnbezirks aufhält, sofort dem nächsten Polizeirevier oder Gendarmerieposten zu melden.

Wer einem Juden Unterstützung hat zuteil werden lassen oder z. Zt. noch zuteil werden lässt, hiervon aber bis zum 9.9.42, 16 Uhr, der nächsten polizeilichen Dienststelle Mitteilung macht, wird STRAFRECHTLICH NICHT VERFOLGT WERDEN.

In der gleichen Weise wird gegen denjenigen von einer Strafverfolgung Abstand genommen, der die von einem Juden erworbenen Sachwerte bis zum 9.9.42, 16 Uhr, in Warschau, Niskastr. 20, abliefert oder bei dem nächsten Polizeirevier bzw. Gendarmerieposten Meldung erstattet.

Warschau, den 5. September 1942.

Der SS- und Polizeiführer
im Distrikt Warschau.

OBWIESZCZENIE

Dotyczy kary śmierci za wspieranie żydów, którzy przekroczyli bez uprawnienia granicę dzielnicy żydowskiej.

W ostatnim czasie większa ilość żydów wydostała się bez uprawnienia z dla nich przeznaczonej dzielnicy. Ci znajdują się dotąd w okręgu warszawskim.

Przypominam, że trzecie rozporządzenie Generalnego Gubernatora z dnia 15.10.1941 r. (VBl. GG. S. 595) przewiduje, że nie tylko żydzi zostaną skazani na śmierć za przekroczenie granicy dzielnicy żydowskiej, ale każdy, kto w jakikolwiek sposób dopomaga im w ukrywaniu się. Zaznaczam, że za pomoc udzielaną żydowi, nie uważa się tylko przenocowanie ich i wyżywienie, ale również przewożenie ich jakimkolwiek środkiem lokomocji, kupowanie od nich różnych towarów, i t. p.

Zwracam się do ludności okręgu warszawskiego z wezwaniem, aby każdego żyda, który bez uprawnienia przebywa poza granicami dzielnicy żydowskiej, natychmiast zameldować u najbliższego posterunku policyjnego względnie żandarmerji.

Kto udzielał pomocy żydowi albo jeszcze dotąd udziela, a do dnia 9. 9. 1942 r. godz. 16-ta zamelduje w najbliższym posterunku policji lub żandarmerji, nie podlega odpowiedzialności karnej.

Również nie podlega odpowiedzialności karnej ten, kto do dnia 9. 9. 1942 r., godz. 16-tej, odeśle rzeczy nabyte od żyda pod adresem Warszawa, Niska 20 albo zawiadomi o tym najbliższy posterunek policji wzgl. żandarmerji.

Kierownik SS- i Policji
dla Okręgu Warszawskiego

Warschau, dnia 5 września 1942 r.

Illustration 4 Handbill in German and Polish issued by the SS and Police leader of the Warsaw District announcing the death penalty for those who assist Jews that left the Warsaw Ghetto without authorization, September 5, 1942. USHMM, photograph N08686.

Germans ordered Mordechai Chaim Rumkowski, the head of the *Judenrat*, to prepare 20,000 people for deportation: the sick, the elderly, and the children. On September 4 at 4:00 p.m., Rumkowski delivered his infamous "Give Me Your Children" speech, urging parents to give up their children so that the remaining adults could survive: "[W]e must take upon ourselves the carrying out of this decree. I must carry out this difficult and bloody operation, I must cut off limbs in order to save the body! I must take away children, and if I do not, others too will be taken, God forbid."[52] Adam Czerniaków, the Jewish head of the Warsaw ghetto, took another route when given a similar order in July 1942: he committed suicide by swallowing a cyanide capsule rather than execute the order.

Throughout German-occupied Poland and other parts of occupied Europe, Jews in hiding and also their protectors risked capital punishment under German occupation law if captured. The directive of September 5, 1942 (Illustration 4) threatens death to anyone aiding Jews. The directive was issued in Warsaw during the mass deportations of Jews from the Warsaw ghetto to the Treblinka death camp, 100 kilometers away. Between late July and September 1942, the Germans deported around 265,000 Jews from the Warsaw ghetto to Treblinka, and murdered them upon arrival. From July 1942 through November 1943, a mere sixteen months, the Germans and their Ukrainian auxiliaries managed to murder between 870,000 and 925,000 Jews at Treblinka. The handbill, in German and Polish, reads:

Announcement
Death Penalty for Aid to Jews who have left the Jewish residential areas without permission.

Recently many Jews have left their designated Jewish residential areas. For the time, they are in the Warsaw District.

I remind you that according to the Third Decree of the General Governor's concerning the residential restrictions in the General Government of 10.15.1941 (VBL GG. S. 595) [abbreviation for Verordnungsblatt Generalgouvernement, p. 595] not only Jews who have left their designated residential area will be punished with death, but the same penalty applies to anyone who knowingly provides refuge to such Jews. This includes not only the providing of a night's lodging and food, but also any other aid, such as transporting them in vehicles of any sort, through the purchase of Jewish valuables, etc.

I ask the population of the Warsaw District to immediately report any Jew who resides outside of a Jewish residential area to the nearest police station or gendarmerie post.

Whoever provided or currently provides aid to a Jew will not be prosecuted if it is reported to the nearest police station by 16:00 hrs [4 pm] on 9.9.42.

> Likewise, those who deliver valuables acquired from a Jew to 20 Niska Street or the nearest police or gendarme post by 16:00 hrs. on 9.9.42 will not be prosecuted.
>
> — The SS- and Police Leader for the Warsaw District Warsaw, *September 5, 1942*

By 1943, Jews and other persecuted groups from all over Europe were being systematically rounded up and transported "to the East," where they were either murdered immediately upon arrival in the gas chambers of Auschwitz and the other killing centers or selected for work, from which they were expected to perish through extermination-through-labor (*Vernichtung durch Arbeit* in German).

The Zyklon-B poison gas used in the gas chambers—a common pesticide especially modified for its nefarious purpose—was manufactured, supplied, and delivered by the German company Degesch, controlled by German chemical companies Degussa and I.G. Farben. The crematoria where the dead bodies were burned was constructed by another German company, Tesh & Stabenow, and modified from the standard crematoria used for cremation of the deceased. The Nazi crematoria were specifically designed for mass murder and operated continuously in order to dispose of hundreds of thousands of bodies.

The death and concentration camp system was aimed to murder as many Jews as possible with the minimum number of Germans involved in the process. Death camps like Sobibor, Treblinka, and Bełżec were constructed solely for the purpose of killing. Although Auschwitz, where about a million people were murdered, was the most infamous of the Nazi death camps, it did have factories and other industries where prisoners were worked to death under the German death-though-work program. Overall, between eight million and ten million people—both Jews and non-Jews—were forced to work as slaves during the Nazi era. The slaves worked not only for the SS and the Nazi military machine but also toiled under the most horrific conditions for German private industry. German companies, large and small, utilized this slave labor, and included such notable firms as Mercedes-Benz, Volkswagen, BMW, and Siemens. The I.G. Farben Company, a leading German chemical company broken up after the war because of its intimate involvement with the Nazis, built the Buna factory in nearby Monowitz adjacent to the Auschwitz complex in order to exploit this slave labor.

The policy of extermination of every Jew in Europe originated in Germany proper through a criminal state conspiracy, and implemented through secret orders. On July 31, 1941, Reichsmarschall Hermann Göring issued a secret directive to Reinhard Heydrich, head of the Reich Security Head Office (RSHA):

> I hereby charge you with making all necessary preparations in regard to organizational and financial matters for bringing about a total solution of

> the Jewish question in the German sphere of influence in Europe. Wherever other governmental agencies are involved, these are to cooperate with you. I charge you furthermore to send me, before long, an overall plan concerning the organizational, factual and material measures necessary for the accomplishment of the desired solution of the Jewish question.[53]

Göring's directive to Heydrich was put into state policy six months later at the Wannsee Conference, a seemingly ordinary meeting of high-level bureaucrats that took place on January 20, 1942, at a villa just outside Berlin. At this meeting, convened by Heydrich and assisted by Adolf Eichmann, one of the chief architects of the "Final Solution," the participants were informed of the plan to murder all eleven million Jews of Europe. Heydrich called the meeting of the heads of the main German ministries to coordinate the mechanics of preparing and carrying out the mass murders. The brutality of the Final Solution contrasts with the seeming sophistication of the individuals who acceded to it. Of the fifteen participants at Wannsee, seven had advanced law degrees.

We can surmise that Göring's July 1941 secret directive to Heydrich and the ensuing Wannsee Conference were taken up under the direct order of Hitler, even though a so-called "Führer Order," calling for the extermination of all Jews, has never been found. As Valerie Hébert notes: "Although it is clear that a decision for the wholesale destruction of European Jews was made sometime in the latter half of 1941, no [written] order has been found that can be traced back to Hitler directly."[54]

Reichsmarschall Hermann Göring's secret directive to Reinhard Heydrich in July 1941 put into motion the plans for the Final Solution. But it was Himmler, head of the SS and Heydrich's immediate boss, who "adopted the destruction of European Jewry as his own sacred task."[55] Himmler became the ultimate lawgiver in the occupied Eastern territories, possessing "such wide plenary powers that he was, in effect, in a position to lay down the law in the East."[56] Memoranda from Himmler confirm both the existence of the policy of extermination and that it was conducted in accordance with Hitler's wishes. At the end of the July 1942, Himmler wrote to the head of the SS Central Office: "The occupied Eastern territories will be cleared of Jews. The implementation of this very hard order has been placed on my shoulders by the Fuehrer."[57] Auschwitz commandant Rudolf Höss, testifying in Nuremberg, remembered that in the summer of 1941 he was summoned to Berlin by Himmler:

> He told me something to the effect—I do not remember the exact words—that the Führer had given the order for a final solution of the Jewish question. We, the SS, must carry out that order. If it is not carried out now then the Jews will later on destroy the German people. He had chosen Auschwitz

> on account of its easy access by rail and also because the extensive site offered space for measures ensuring isolation.[58]

From January to May 1944, Himmler gave three speeches to high-ranking army and navy officers in which he declared that Hitler had given him the mission of exterminating the Jews.[59] With regard to Roma and Sinti, the other victim group slated for complete annihilation, historians have discovered a decree issued by Himmler on December 16, 1942, which initiated the deportation of all Roma and Sinti from the German Reich to Auschwitz-Birkenau. The deportations of the Roma and Sinti continued until 1945, and encompassed further deportations from eleven European countries. "By the end of the war, some 500,000 Roma and Sinti perished as a result of starvation, extreme cold, exhaustion . . . medical experiments, maltreatment, and by poison gas."[60]

Unlike the earlier publicly announced laws in the Reich stripping Jews of their civil rights and property, the extermination directives were never published in a law gazette. Secrecy was meant to lull the victims into believing that "resettlement to the East" was something other than transportation by train to their deaths. Jews in Auschwitz, for example, were forced to write letters to their families back in the ghettos extolling the good life they were experiencing upon resettlement. Soon after, many of the letter writers were gassed. Even at the point of death, deception continued. Arrivals at Treblinka encountered a fake train station; it included a wooden clock with painted numerals permanently indicating 6 o'clock, signs reading "ticket window," "cashier," and "station-master," and timetables falsely indicating train connections. At the Bełżec death camp, Kurt Gerstein, head of the Technical Disinfection Service of the Waffen SS, remembers what he observed there in August 1942:

> The next morning, shortly before 7 a.m. someone announced to me: "In ten minutes the first transport will come!" In fact the first train arrived after some minutes, from the direction of Lemberg [today Lviv in the Ukraine]. 45 wagons with 6,700 people of whom 1,450 were already dead on arrival. Behind the barred hatches children as well as men and women looked out, terribly pale and nervous, their eyes full of the fear of death. The train comes in: 200 Ukrainians fling open the doors and whip the people out of the wagons with their leather whips.
>
> A large loudspeaker gives the further orders: "Undress completely, also remove artificial limbs, spectacles etc." Handing over valuables at the counter, without receiving a voucher or a receipt. The shoes carefully bound together . . . because on the almost 25 metre high heap nobody would have been able to find the matching shoes again. Then the women and girls [go] to the barber who, with two, three scissor strokes is cutting off all hair and

> collecting it in potato sacks. . . . Then the procession starts moving. In front a very lovely young girl; so all of them go along the alley, all naked, men, women, children, without artificial limbs. I myself stand together with *Hauptmann* Wirth on top of the ramp between the gas chambers. Mothers with babies at their breast, they come onward, hesitate, enter the death chambers! At the corner a strong SS man stands who, with a voice like a pastor, says to the poor people: "There is not the least chance that something will happen to you! You must only take a deep breath in the chamber, that widens the lungs; this inhalation is necessary because of the illnesses and epidemics." On the question of what would happen to them he answered: "Yes, of course, the men have to work, building houses and roads but the women don't need to work. Only if they wish they can help in housekeeping or in the kitchen."[61]

Gerstein was a German engineer and SS officer brought to Bełżec in 1942 to correct inefficiencies in disinfection operations. Arrested by the French after the war as a high-ranking SS official, he wrote a report in a Paris prison about what he had seen, just before committing suicide.

Even when the tide of the war turned against the Germans—when the Soviets pushed the German military westward after the Battle of Stalingrad in January–February 1943 and the Americans and British troops landed at Normandy in June 1944—the killings continued. Hungarian Jewry, the last large Jewish community standing in Europe, were no longer immune to the German destruction machine after the German invasion of the satellite state of Hungary on March 19, 1944. In the ensuing eight weeks, between May and July 1944, and under the supervision of SS Lieutenant Colonel Adolf Eichmann, who came to Budapest alongside the German troops to oversee the operation, 437,000 Hungarian Jews were sent to their deaths at Auschwitz. The destruction of Hungarian Jewry followed the pattern of the former mass murder of the Jews in Poland, except at a much more rapid pace. The first step was ghettoization. In April 1944, Hungarian authorities ordered the approximately 500,000 Hungarian Jews living outside Budapest to move to large cities, where they were enclosed within selected city blocks. These ghettoes were then cleared out within a matter of weeks. Hungarian Jewish leaders were forced to coordinate the deportations. Approximately 145 train transports for Auschwitz left mostly Budapest in the spring and summer of 1944. Eighty percent were gassed on arrival. Deportations resumed in fall of 1944 on a lesser scale and were supplemented by death marches. In the end, over half a million Hungarian Jews were murdered during that year.

Was the extermination program legal? The most direct answer was given by Konrad Morgen, an SS judge given the mandate by SS chief Heirich Himmler to investigate and prosecute crimes committed by SS personnel in concentration camps. Morgen doggedly prosecuted both corruption and unauthorized killings in eight camps. Yet when Morgen learned of the mass exterminations after a visit to Auschwitz in 1943, he was powerless to do anything about it. As he explained to his American interrogators after the war: "I saw that those killings, by being ordered, were legal in the sense of National Socialist law and therefore I could not take any direct action on this sector."[62]

F. AFTERMATH

On May 7, 1945, after the capture of Berlin by the Soviet Red Army, Germany agreed to an unconditional surrender. A week earlier, Hitler committed suicide in his underground bunker. Europe now lay in ruins and its population decimated. Political scientist R. J. Rummel, in his now-classic *Death By Government*, estimates that "[t]he Nazis murdered from about 15,000,000 to over 31,600,000 people, most likely closer to 21 million men, women, handicapped, aged, sick, prisoners of war, forced laborers, camp inmates, critics, homosexuals, Jews, Slavs, Serbs, Czechs, Italians, Poles, Frenchmen, Ukrainians and so on."[63]

The figure usually cited for the number of Jews murdered by the Nazis and their supporters is six million. This round number is an approximation, which appeared immediately after the war at the Nuremberg trials (the Nuremberg indictment used the figure of 5.7 million and described it as a conservative estimate), and was later verified through several calculations. According to German Holocaust historian Wolfgang Benz, writing in *The Holocaust Encyclopedia*, "The best estimate of the death toll of European Jews in the Holocaust, on the basis of the latest research, is that at least 6 million persons were murdered by gas or shootings or died of starvation and physical abuse."[64]

Estimates for other persecuted groups are: 90,000–200,000 Roma and Sinti; 200,000–300,000 people with disabilities; 5,000–10,000 gay men; and approximately 2,500 Jehovah's Witnesses. Other large-scale groups of victims of the Nazi killing machine include over three million Soviet POWs and approximately 1–1.5 million political dissidents.

In the summer of 1945, Europe lay in ruins. Hundreds of cities were reduced to rubble. Eight million people were displaced. The continent was on the brink of famine. President Harry S. Truman, while touring Germany in July 1945 on the eve of the Potsdam Conference, observed the "long, never-ending procession of old men, women, and children wandering aimlessly along the autobahn and the country roads carrying, pushing or pulling what was left of their belongings."[65] The same scene was repeated throughout Europe. The death toll and destruction caused by the Nazis and their collaborators during their twelve-year reign was unprecedented in human history.

2

Naming the Crime

Genocide

A. THE HISTORICAL BACKGROUND OF THE TERM "GENOCIDE"

1. Lemkin's Word

Because the word "genocide" is so readily known and both used and overused, those first confronting its etymology are surprised to learn that it is of relatively recent origin. Though human history is full with cases of one nation, tribe, or group of people being completely wiped out by another nation, tribe, or group, the word "genocide" itself did not even exist before the Second World War and arose directly out of the Holocaust.[1] Its inventor, Raphael Lemkin, was a Jewish legal scholar who fled Poland shortly after the German invasion. It is the legal background of the word's originator and the purpose for the invention of the term—to make this behavior an international crime recognized by the community of nations as illegal through a multilateral treaty—that puts the term "genocide" solidly within a legal framework.

Raphael Lemkin was born in Bezwodene, Poland (then part of Western Russia), in 1900 and died in the United States in 1959. Originally a linguistics student, he switched his university studies to law after developing a keen interest in cases of historical massacres. According to Lemkin's autobiography, he was influenced at an early age by Polish writer Henryk Sienkewicz's Nobel Prize-winning novel *Quo Vadis*, which described the massacres of early Christians during the reign of the Roman Emperor Nero.[2] Lemkin was both absorbed with and aghast at the inhumanity of these acts and began studying other acts of man's inhumanity toward his fellow human beings. As a young university student, Lemkin was distressed to learn that in the twentieth century the Turkish perpetrators of what later became known as the Armenian genocide were never punished for their acts. Lemkin turned to the study of law because he thought that this profession would best qualify him for "the task of making the destruction of groups of human beings punishable."[3] When told by one of his university professors that international law does not concern itself with acts committed by rulers within their own territory because these rulers are protected by the notion of state sovereignty, Lemkin objected: "Sovereignty cannot be conceived as the right to kill millions of innocent people."[4] Lemkin's response was to propose an international crime for which individuals committing such acts against a group of people, whom he labeled "a collectivity," could be punished irrespective of national boundaries. In effect, Lemkin was proposing the now-recognized rule of universal jurisdiction by which individuals committing certain heinous crimes are considered *hostis humani generis* (outlaws of all mankind) and can be prosecuted by any national court regardless of where the crime was committed.[5]

After graduating from law school at the University of Lvov in 1926, Lemkin taught criminal law and worked as a criminal prosecutor in Warsaw. Lemkin still dabbled in international law in his off-hours. At a League of Nations–sponsored international law conference held in Madrid in 1933, the thirty-three-year-old lawyer first introduced his international law crime, which he then called the crime of "barbarity"—a forerunner of his later term, "genocide." As stated in his conference paper: "Whosoever, out of hatred towards a racial, religious or social collectivity, or with a view to the extermination thereof, undertakes a punishable action against the life, bodily integrity, liberty, dignity or economic existence of a person belonging to such collectivity, is liable for the crime of barbarity. . . . The above crime will be prosecuted and punished irrespective of the place where the crime was committed and of the nationality of the offender, according to the law of the country where the offender was apprehended."[6]

The proposal went nowhere. While the winds of war were already blowing in Europe with Hitler's rise to power earlier that year, the law delegates in Madrid and at subsequent legal conferences where Lemkin continued to present his proposal ignored his pleas. Lemkin, of course, exhibited prescience. Despite efforts by Great Britain and France to placate Hitler by acceding to his demands for more territory, war could not be avoided. After the German invasion of Poland in 1939, Lemkin was drafted into the Polish army and was wounded in battle. Following Poland's rapid defeat, he escaped to Sweden and from there eventually made his way to the United States. Left behind in Poland were his parents, whom he never saw again. More than fifty members of his family would perish in the Holocaust. No longer just a student of mass murder and group violence, he now experienced it personally.

Lemkin taught at Duke University before joining President Franklin D. Roosevelt's War Department. In 1944, he published his now-classic book, *Axis Rule in Occupied Europe*, where he described the brutalities inflicted by Nazi Germany upon the occupied nations of Europe. Winston Churchill, in a speech referring to Nazi atrocities broadcast in August 1941 over the BBC, had remarked,

"We are in the presence of a crime without a name." In *Axis Rule,* Lemkin gave that crime a name: "genocide."[7]

"By 'genocide,'" he wrote in 1944, "we mean the destruction of a nation or of an ethnic group. This new word . . . is made from the ancient Greek word *genos* (race, tribe) and the Latin *cide* (killing) . . ."[8] Genocide is "a coordinated plan of different actions aiming at the destruction of essential foundations of the life of national groups, with the aim of annihilating the groups themselves."[9] *Axis Rule* was well received, including a front-page review in the *New York Times Book Review*.[10] And the word struck a chord. As William Schabas notes, "Within months [of publication of *Axis Rule in Occupied Europe* in November 1944], it was being used widely to refer to Nazi atrocities."[11]

2. Genocide at the Nuremberg Trials

On October 18, 1945, "genocide" entered the English, French, Russian, and German languages when the word appeared, without attribution to its inventor, in the criminal indictment issued against the top Nazi war criminals.[12] In charging the Nazi leaders with Count Three—war crimes—the Nuremberg indictment explained that in the course of committing such crimes, the Nazis "*conducted deliberate and systematic genocide, viz.*, the extermination of racial and national groups, against civilian populations of certain occupied territories, in order to destroy particular races and classes of people, and national, racial or religious groups, particularly Jews, Poles and Gypsies."[13] Justice Robert Jackson, the chief American prosecutor and lead organizer of the London Conference, also made use of Lemkin's neologism in a planning memorandum distributed to the British, Soviet, and French delegates in June 1945.[14] Lemkin then sought out various members of the prosecution team and lobbied to have the term utilized during the trial. And he succeeded. Although genocide was never expressly identified as a crime at the Nuremberg trials, it appeared numerous times as a descriptive term for the atrocities that took place during the Nazi era, both before the International Military Tribunal at Nuremberg (IMT) and during the Subsequent Nuremberg Proceedings, the twelve later trials of other top Nazis at Nuremberg before American judges (see Chapter 3). As Hilary Earl notes, "[e]ven if none of the 207 war criminals [tried by the Allies between 1945 and 1949] were indicted specifically for 'genocide,' the word peppers the record of the thirteen Nuremberg trials. . . ."[15]

3. Father of the Genocide Convention

Getting genocide on the books of international law—codifying it as an international law crime—became Lemkin's obsession for the remainder of his life. The central address to do so was the United Nations, established in June 1945 as a successor to the League of Nations. Lemkin's first success in making genocide an international crime took place on December 11, 1946. On that day, the UN General Assembly at its first session unanimously passed Resolution 96 (I), titled "The Crime of Genocide." The resolution did three things. First, it defined genocide in broad terms as "a denial of the right of existence of entire human groups, as homicide is the denial of the right to live of individual human beings . . ."[16] Second, it noted that because genocide "shocks the conscience of mankind, results in great losses to humanity . . . and is contrary to moral law and to the spirit and aims of the United Nations," its "punishment . . . is a matter of international concern." Finally, and most importantly, it recognized genocide as a "crime under international law."[17]

Since a General Assembly resolution has no binding effect, G.A. Res. 96 (I) requested the United Nations' Economic and Social Council to prepare a draft of an anti-genocide treaty. Lemkin's efforts were being rewarded, but it took five more years for his original dream to come to fruition. On December 9, 1948, the first step was reached when the UN General Assembly issued the final text of a treaty, the "Convention on the Prevention and Punishment of the Crime of Genocide" (also called the "Genocide Convention"), which the member states were invited

Illustration 5 Ratification of Genocide Convention, Lake Success, NY, by representatives of Korea, Haiti, Iran, France, and Costa Rica and UN officials. Oct. 14, 1950. Raphael Lemkin (back row, right, standing). Courtesy of the United Nations, photograph 66374.

to join as state parties. By the terms of the treaty, at least twenty states needed to join for the Convention to come into force. This occurred on January 12, 1951.

Lemkin's singular efforts to criminalize genocide took their toll on his health. Falling gravely ill in 1948 following passage of the Genocide Convention, Lemkin's diagnosis of his own illness was "Genociditis, exhaustion from work on the Genocide Convention."[18] He lived for eight more years.[19] On August 28, 1959, Lemkin died of a heart attack in a New York City at age fifty-nine, "friendless, penniless, and alone, leaving behind a bare rented room, some clothes, and a chaos of unsorted papers."[20] Seven people attended his funeral. Buried at New York's Jewish Mount Hebron Cemetery in Queens, New York, his tombstone simply reads: "Father of the Genocide Convention."

While Lemkin's legacy has long been known and recognized by Holocaust historians and genocide scholars, his name remains obscure to the general public and even to the legal profession. Lemkin's word, however, has now achieved recognition beyond his dreams. Genocide has now become synonymous with extreme evil and, as noted by William Schabas in his legal treatise on genocide, the "crime of crimes."[21] A Google search today yields over twenty-six million entries for the term.[22]

Nevertheless, Lemkin's naming "the crime of crimes" and his instrumental role in outlawing it under international law could only go so far. As Omer Bartov explains, "Lemkin was an extraordinary man . . . and he did show that if you are committed and as obsessed—and he indeed was a lonely, obsessed, compulsive person—you may, under the right circumstances . . . be able to make a huge difference . . . [But] doing that alone did nothing as such; it was a beginning, not an end."[23] Naming the crime and preventing it are two different matters.

B. THE GENOCIDE CONVENTION

The postwar impetus for the Genocide Convention can be traced back to one event: the reading on October 1, 1946, of the judgment by the judges of the IMT. Lemkin would later describe that day as "the blackest day" of his life.[24] Lemkin encountered two major disappointments upon reading the IMT judgment. First, his prized word "genocide" did not appear in the judgment. Second, the Nazi arch-criminals were found guilty only for crimes that took place after the start of the Second World War on September 1, 1939. This is so, despite that fact that they had been in power since 1933, and for six years had engaged in state-sanctioned persecution of the Jews, including murder, expulsion, and massive theft. Yet according to the Nuremberg judgment, the defendants on the dock committed no crime on the books for all these acts prior to the outbreak of war, at least no crime under international law.

The three principal crimes charged at Nuremberg were crimes against peace (or waging an aggressive war), war crimes, and crimes against humanity (CAH). The only charge that could possibly cover prewar conduct was CAH, but this crime had a major limitation under the Nuremberg Charter: it required that the acts of inhumanity against any civilian population—such as murder, extermination, enslavement, and deportation—must have been committed "before or during the war."[25] This is the "war nexus" or "armed conflict nexus" element of CAH, meaning that under the Nuremberg principles the accused Germans could not be charged with CAH unless the crime was committed in the context of, or a prelude to, an armed conflict. Here is the paragraph that made October 1, 1946, the blackest day of Lemkin's life:

> With regard to crimes against humanity, there is no doubt whatever that political opponents were murdered in Germany before the war, and that many of them were kept in concentration camps in circumstances of great horror and cruelty. The policy of terror was certainly carried out on a vast scale, and in many cases was organised and systematic. The policy of persecution, repression and murder of civilians in Germany before the war of 1939, who were likely to be hostile to the Government, was most ruthlessly carried out. The persecution of Jews during the same period is established beyond all doubt. *To constitute crimes against humanity, the acts relied on before the outbreak of war must have been in execution of, or in connection with, any crime within the jurisdiction of the Tribunal. The Tribunal is of the opinion that revolting and horrible as many of these crimes were, it has not been satisfactorily proved that they were done in execution of, or in connection with, any such crime. The Tribunal therefore cannot make a general declaration that the acts before 1939 were crimes against humanity within the meaning of the Charter* but from the beginning of the war in 1939 war crimes were committed on a vast scale, which were also crimes against humanity; and insofar as the inhumane acts charged in the Indictment, and committed after the beginning of the war, did not constitute war crimes, they were all committed in execution of, or in connection with, the aggressive war, and therefore constituted crimes against humanity.[26]

The German persecution of Jews prior to the outbreak of the war was therefore not considered a crime that could be prosecuted by the IMT at Nuremberg. For the rest of his life, Lemkin channeled his professional and personal tragedies into an all-out effort to make genocide—whether committed in times of peace or war—an international crime. More than two years later, he achieved his first success when on December 9, 1948, the final language of the Genocide Convention was formally voted on and approved at the Third Session of the UN General Assembly in Paris.

1. Legislative History

The premier international body that came out of the war was the United Nations, the legal successor to the League of Nations.[27] It was during the various UN sessions that the Convention's terms were worked out. The Convention's agreed-upon language was inevitably a matter of compromise. The final definition of the crime of genocide differs from Lemkin's original definition of genocide, with certain acts (i.e., cultural genocide) and certain groups (i.e., political groups) excluded under the treaty because the UN delegates could not agree on their inclusion.

Under international law procedure, agreement to a treaty's terms does not yet make the treaty legally binding. Rather, upon its adoption, the proposed treaty is then open for ratification or accession. Generally, a minimum number of ratifications or accessions is required for a treaty to come in force. Under the terms of the Genocide Convention, ratification or accession by at least twenty states was necessary. It took another three years for this to occur. On January 12, 1951, the Genocide Convention gained legal force after Egypt became the twentieth state to ratify the treaty.

Then came another hurdle: getting the United States to become a party, since it was not one of the twenty states. Unfortunately, Lemkin did not live to see that day. On December 11, 1948, just two days after the United Nations opened the Genocide Convention for signature, President Harry Truman signed the treaty. However, for the next four decades, the Senate could not muster the required two-thirds majority to ratify the Convention.[28] A stubborn minority of senators continued to oppose making the United States a party to the Convention. They feared that the legal and quasi-legal racial discrimination practiced in the American South against African-American citizens could be construed as a form of genocide. If the United States became a party to the treaty, the argument went, America's participation would be used as a legal bludgeon against it.[29] And the fear was not without foundation. In December 1951, the Civil Rights Congress, an early civil rights organization, presented a paper to the United Nations at a meeting in Paris titled *We Charge Genocide: The Crime of Government Against the Negro People*, accusing the US government of practicing genocide under the terms of the Genocide Convention.[30] In reaction, Lemkin published an opposition editorial in the *New York Times* arguing that "by no stretch of the imagination can one discover in the United States an intent or plan to exterminate the Negro population. . . . By confusing genocide with discrimination[,] injustice is done not only to existing international law but also the good name of some democratic societies which might be unjustly slandered for genocide."[31] Lemkin's aim was to counter an argument being made against Senate ratification, now made real by this petition, as part of his efforts to have the United States join the Convention. Lemkin did not succeed. At his death in 1959, the United States was not a party.

The end of Jim Crow laws in the South and other civil rights–era achievements certainly made the arguments that the United States was practicing genocide less potent. These were now replaced by another obstacle to Senate ratification: skepticism that the United States should be a party to human rights treaties in general. This anti-interventionist agenda by a substantial minority of the Senate kept it from ratifying the treaty. It was not until 1986, during the Reagan administration, that proponents succeeded in gaining Senate ratification.

The hero of the ratification movement was Wisconsin Democratic Senator William Proxmire. Beginning in 1967, Proxmire would make daily speeches on the floor of the Senate urging approval of the Genocide Convention. On February 11, 1986, after nineteen years and 3,211 speeches, the full Senate finally took a vote and ratified the treaty that had been signed by President Truman forty years earlier. The full Congress then passed a law making it a federal crime to commit genocide.[32] No one has yet been prosecuted in the United States under this law.

2. Definition of Genocide

The term "genocide" has a legally defined meaning, set out in Article II of the Genocide Convention:

> In the present Convention, genocide means any of the following acts committed with intent to destroy, in whole or in part, a national, ethnical, racial or religious group, as such:
> a. Killing members of the group;
> b. Causing serious bodily or mental harm to members of the group;
> c. Deliberately inflicting on the group conditions of life calculated to bring about its physical destruction in whole or in part;
> d. Imposing measures intended to prevent births within the group;
> e. Forcibly transferring children of the group to another group.[33]

The Genocide Convention does not create a court for the prosecution of genocide; rather it leaves prosecution to any tribunal competent to prosecute perpetrators. Since no international court existed to prosecute individuals for genocide for the first forty-five years of the Convention's existence, the Article II definition remained unused for close to a half-century. This changed remarkably since the mid-1990s, when individuals involved in atrocities in the former Yugoslavia and Rwanda began to be indicted for genocide by the UN-created ad hoc tribunals. These first-ever genocide trials before an international criminal tribunal led to the first practical examination of what the words in Article II actually mean. As a result, we now have a remarkable body of court decisions issued by the ad hoc tribunals giving practical meaning to the words first penned in 1948 (see Chapter 8).

The first impression from reading the definition of genocide in Article II is its imprecision and ambiguity. For this reason, the judges of the international ad hoc tribunals who utilize the Article II definition to determine guilt or innocence of accused perpetrators have been struggling for the last two decades to make the definition workable. Despite these problems, the Article II definition is the one that lawyers, jurists, and legal scholars must live with and interpret, since it is the only authoritative definition of the crime of genocide under international law.

There have been significant controversies in the field of genocide studies in recent years over how to describe the boundaries of genocide—"where mass murder stops and the ultimate human crime starts. Yet the term is far more than a tool of historical or moral analysis. Its use brings momentous political and legal consequences and is therefore bound to be highly contested."[34] For historians and other social scientists, a perpetual testing and redefining of categories comes naturally. Judges, on the other hand, have to be precise because their opinions have specific effects to the defendants on the dock. All alternative formulations are not legally binding.[35] In terms of law, the only relevant definition of genocide for purposes of criminal prosecution is the one found in the Genocide Convention. This is the definition used to determine whether the defendant is a genocidaire.

Every crime contains two elements: the prohibited act (the *actus reus* of the crime) and the state of mind (*mens rea*) that the accused must possess at the time when the prohibited act was committed. The same is true of the Genocide Convention, which makes genocide a crime under international law. For an individual to have committed the crime of genocide, the prosecution (whether before an international court or a domestic court) must prove that both elements were present at the time of its commission. What makes genocide an international crime of a special order (the "crime of crimes") is its *mens rea*: the genocidaire must intend to destroy in whole, or (as interpreted today) in substantial part, an enumerated group ("national, ethnical, racial or religious group") given special protection by the Genocide Convention.[36] This particular "group intent"—the specific intent to destroy an enumerated victim group—distinguishes genocide from any other crime under international law. We now turn to these elements.

3. *Actus Reus* of Genocide—The Prohibited Acts

The *actus reus* element is found in subsections (a) through (e) of Article II, enumerating the limited number of ways a genocide can be committed. Ironically, even the precise and specific acts that constitute genocide have been criticized as being too broad or too narrow.

Must There Be Actual Physical Destruction?

Genocide is first and foremost the crime of group destruction. The UN General Assembly's Declaration on Genocide, passed unanimously in 1946 as the precursor to the Genocide Convention, expressed this understanding when it described genocide as "a denial of the right of existence of entire groups, as homicide is the denial of the right to live of individual human beings."[37] Article II, however, does not limit the *actus reus* element of genocide solely to acts that result in complete physical extermination or extinction of a group, or even to instances of mass murder. Rather, it makes other acts that fall short of mass murder as also legally constituting genocide. Thus, in addition to subsection (a)—"killings members of the group"—genocide can also include: (b) "Causing serious bodily or mental harm to members of the group"; (c) "Deliberately inflicting on the group conditions of life calculated to bring about its physical destruction . . . in whole or in part"; (d) "Imposing measures intended to prevent births within the group"; and (e) "forcibly transferring children of the group to another group."

To date, all successful prosecutions for genocide before the ad hoc tribunals have been of individuals charged with killing members of a protected group.[38] The only act short of killing found to constitute genocide is rape, recognized in the *Akayesu* decision of the International Criminal Tribunal for Rwanda (ICTR). In *Akayesu*, the ICTR Trial Chamber placed rape within paragraph (b) as constituting acts "[c]ausing serious bodily or mental harm to members of the group."[39] Even in that instance, the genocidaire was charged with the killing of other members of the group along with the charge of rape.

Recognizing the seriousness of the crime, it is unlikely that an international prosecutor would ever charge anyone with committing genocide without there being deaths, especially massive deaths. The only possible exception would be the instances where the perpetrators aim to destroy the protected group by preventing births within the group or forcibly transferring children from the group. Because these are acts that aim to destroy the group by biological means, they are also likely to be prosecuted as genocide. As of this writing, however, no one has been prosecuted for these enumerated acts of genocide.

British political scientist Martin Shaw argues for expanding the *actus reus* of genocide by including other modes of behavior. As he explains:

> Lemkin was surely right that to understand genocide, we should see killing and physical harm as elements of the broader process of social destruction. The Nazis did not aim simply to kill subject peoples, even the Jews: they aimed to destroy their ways of life and social institutions. Lemkin was correct to stress the integrated, multi-dimensional nature of the attack, and not to fall into the trap (as later writers have) of separating physical violence from social destruction.[40]

Shaw expresses the frustration of many outside the legal field who find the legal formulation of what acts can constitute genocide as being too narrow. While nonlawyers like Shaw may offer extralegal definitions of genocide, for legal purposes the range of acts that constitute genocide remains confined to instances when mass murder or group destruction by other means, as set out in Article II (a) through (e), had taken place. As Lemkin explained when nonlawyers suggested that racial discrimination in 1950s America amounts to genocide: "Genocide implies destruction, death, annihilation, while discrimination is a regrettable denial of certain opportunities of life. To be unequal is not the same as to be dead."[41]

Must the Destruction Be Systematic?

On August 10, 1999, a lone gunman attacked the children and staff of a Jewish daycare center in Los Angeles. Buford O. Furrow, Jr., a thirty-seven-year-old member of the neo-Nazi group Aryan Nations, sprayed at least seventy rounds with a high-powered assault rifle into the lobby of the center. Furrow wounded five individuals: three young children, a teenager, and an adult. After the shooting spree, Furrow hijacked a car and fled. About an hour later, he gunned down Joseph Ileto, a Filipino postman delivering mail. After turning himself in, Furrow confessed to scouting several prominent Jewish institutions in the Los Angeles area before stumbling upon the Jewish community center. In 2001, as part of a plea bargain, Furrow pleaded guilty to sixteen felony counts, including the murder of Mr. Ileto, in exchange for the prosecution not seeking the death penalty. He was sentenced to life without parole. Furrow, who expressed no remorse over the killing of Mr. Ileto or the wounding of the individuals at the daycare center, said he targeted the daycare center because of his hatred of Jews. He also told authorities that if Mr. Ileto had been white, he would not have killed him. According to the police, Furrow intended for his acts to be a "wake-up call to America to kill Jews."[42]

Could Furrow have been charged with genocide even though he murdered only one individual and wounded several others? A credible argument can be made that Furrow's state of mind at the time of his acts meets the *mens rea* of genocide. If Furrow intended, as he set out on his racially motivated killing spree, to kill as many Jews as possible, his murder of even one Jew meets the requirement of *intending* to destroy a substantial part of a protected group. On the other hand, if Furrow set out to kill one particular Jewish person because of his hatred of Jews, then the killing is racially or religiously motivated murder but not genocide.

It appears that under the text of the Genocide Convention, Furrow's acts meet the *actus reus* elements of genocide. Article II (a) speaks of "killing members of the group" without specifying the number of members of the protected group that must be killed for the killings to constitute genocide. Assuming that Furrow had the sufficient intent for the crime of genocide, Furrow committed one count of genocide and five counts of attempted genocide under the Genocide Convention.

Commentators interpreting the Genocide Convention appear to agree with this result. John Heidenrich explains: "[I]f an ordinary gang of thugs kill a person simply because that person belongs to a particular nationality, ethnicity, race, or religion, that one murder is, legally speaking, an act of genocide."[43] Many genocide scholars disagree with this interpretation. These critics note that a person charged with the death of a single individual—even if the individual's intent was to destroy a substantial or even an entire protected group—should be tried for a homicide, that is, murder, and not genocide. To do otherwise, diminishes the severity of the crime of genocide. During the drafting process of the Convention before the United Nations, delegates from the representative nations specifically considered this quantitative issue. The United States, in particular, was troubled by a result where genocide could be found in instances where the number of victims is small.[44] The British agreed, noting that the murder of one individual constitutes homicide and not genocide.[45]

The proponents of the view requiring actual substantial destruction also point to the "Preamble of the Rome Statute," which created the modern International Criminal Court (ICC) to try perpetrators of genocide and other serious international crimes. The Rome Statute appears to exclude random murders targeted at members of a protected group from its jurisdiction by limiting genocide and other international crimes covered by the statute to "unimaginable atrocities that deeply shock the conscience of humanity," "such grave crimes [that] threaten the peace, security and well-being of the world" and "the most serious crimes of concern to the international community as a whole."[46]

Must Genocide Involve State Action?

For many genocide scholars the killings must not only be large but also involve state action. Sociologist Irving Louis Horowitz explains that genocide "is not simply a sporadic or random event"; it must be systematic "and conducted with the approval of, if not, direct intervention by, the state apparatus."[47] The insertion of the "substantiality" and "state action" requirements to the *actus reus* element of the crime is, of course, contrary to the very words of the Genocide Convention. The Yugoslav ad hoc tribunal specifically held that "state action" was not necessary.[48] With the rise of such nonstate groups as ISIS that practice genocide, the argument for requiring "state action" makes even less sense. If one or more leaders of ISIS were to put on the dock for destroying a substantial part of the Yazidis religious group in Iraq, they surely should be prosecuted for genocide despite the fact that ISIS, regardless of its self-anointed description of a state, is not a nation state.

Why Are Only Certain Groups Protected by the Genocide Convention?

Lemkin had a broad definition of the groups that can be victims of the international law crime he called "genocide." The Genocide Convention, in Article II, is more narrow, protecting from genocide only "national, ethnical, racial or religious" groups. Two significant questions arise from this categorization: (1) Since the Convention does not provide a definition for these four protected groups, how are they to be defined? and (2) Why does the Convention limit its protection to these four groups? (The latter question is usually set out as a criticism of the Convention for failing to include "political groups" within its protection.)

While the drafters might have believed that the descriptions "national, ethnical, racial or religious" are so obvious that they do not require any definition, the reality is quite different. As John Quigley observes: "By limiting genocide to acts intended to affect only certain types of groups, the drafters of the Genocide Convention created more complexity than they realized. The very existence of a group may be disputed. Even if the group is found to exist, an accused may deny that fact, thereby casting doubt on whether he had an intent to destroy it. Or an accused may act against a person thinking they belong to a group that in fact does not exist."[49]

For close to five decades, these definitional issues did not need to be confronted because no one was prosecuted for genocide under the treaty. The problem arose when the words of the law had to be applied to specific facts, after the UN Security Council created in the 1990s the ad hoc tribunals and in its mandate gave these tribunals the authority to criminally prosecute individuals for genocide. Now these words had to be applied to specific situations and against specific criminal defendants.[50]

Failure to precisely define the four protected groups in the Genocide Convention led to problems in the very first set of international prosecutions for genocide in the 1990s before the International Criminal Tribune for the former Yugoslavia (ICTY) and the ICTR. In the prosecution before the ICTR of Jean-Paul Akayesu, the first person convicted of genocide by an international tribunal (see Chapter 9), the defendant argued that he could not be prosecuted for genocide since the Tutsi victims of the Rwandan genocide do not constitute "a national, ethnic, racial or religious group" separate from the Hutu perpetrators. The ICTR Trial Chamber rejected his argument, finding that the Tutsi were indeed a distinct ethnic group targeted by the Hutu ethnic group. As the Trial Chamber explained:

> The Chamber notes that the Tutsi population does not have its own language or a distinct culture from the rest of the Rwandan population. However, the Chamber finds that there are a number of objective indicators of the group as a group with a distinct identity. Every Rwandan citizen

> was required before 1994 to carry an identity card which included an entry for ethnic group . . . being Hutu, Tutsi or Twa. The Rwandan Constitution and laws in force in 1994 also identified Rwandans by reference to their ethnic group. . . . The Rwandan witnesses who testified before the Chamber identified themselves by ethnic group, and generally knew the ethnic group to which their friends and neighbours belonged. Moreover, the Tutsi were conceived of as an ethnic group by those who targeted them for killing.[51]

The last point is critical. It is of no consequence if the targeted individuals do not constitute or even conceive of themselves as members of the protected group. What counts is the perception of the *perpetrators*. When the Nazis targeted Jews in their belief that Jews constituted a separate race, a scientific finding that Jews do not constitute a separate race does not mean that the Holocaust was not a genocide. Under the Nazi racial theories, Christians with at least three Jewish grandparents were also considered part of the "Jewish race," and so the murder of such Christians based on this belief likewise constitutes a genocide.

The ICTY also recognizes that the relevant analysis is, as Quigley puts it in his genocide legal treatise, a matter of "a group in the eye of the [perpetrator] beholder."[52] In the *Jelisić* case, the Trial Chamber explained: "[I]t is more appropriate to evaluate the status of a national, ethnical or racial group from the point of view of those persons who wish to single that group out from the rest of the community. . . . It is the stigmatization of a group as a distinct national, ethnical or racial unit by the community which allows it to be determined whether a targeted population constitutes a national, ethnical or racial group in the eyes of the alleged perpetrators."[53] Since the essence of the crime of genocide is based upon the mental state of the perpetrator, it is perfectly acceptable to base the crime on the subjective belief of the perpetrator. The law still defines the crime—rather than the offender—but bases it on the offender's state of mind at the time of the commission of the crime.[54]

As for the issue of the exclusion of political groups from the protection of the Genocide Convention, the drafters expressly considered this question and ultimately decided to exclude political groups from the categories of protected groups. The purported rationale given was that the other groups listed—national, racial, ethnic, and religious—have a quality of permanency, while political allegiances can be easily changed. A Communist today can become a capitalist tomorrow. Lemkin himself raised this rationale. As Schabas explains, "Raphael Lemkin said political groups lacked the permanency and specific characteristics of the other groups, insisting that the Convention should not risk failure by introducing ideas on which the world was deeply divided."[55] Polish jurist Manfred Lachs, who also participated in the drafting of the Convention, added, "Those who needed protection most were those who could not alter their status."[56]

Of course, the characterization of national, racial, ethnic, and religious groups as being immutable is not entirely correct. Individuals can, and do, change their nationalities and religions. Even ethnicity and race are not permanent, with persons of mixed race or ethnicity deciding with which group to self-identify. The real reason for excluding the term "political" from the group descriptions was more practical: fear by representatives of some member states that inclusion of the term would open up these states to prosecution for political crimes under the Genocide Convention. Schabas concludes: "It is clear that political groups were excluded from the definition for 'political' reasons rather than reasons of principle."[57]

Some have argued for a long time that the exclusion of political groups from the legal definition is the most defective feature of the Genocide Convention and have campaigned to amend the Genocide Convention by adding political groups as a protected group.[58] This campaign appears to have little chance of success considering that the original definition in the Genocide Convention has remained unchanged for the last half-century and was incorporated without amendment into the definitions of the crime of genocide in the statutes for the ad hoc international tribunals for the former Yugoslavia and Rwanda and the Rome Statute establishing the ICC.

Another possibility is to enact a domestic criminal statute that does not merely incorporate the international legal definition of genocide, but expands the definition to include political groups within the protected class of victims. Some states in criminalizing genocide in their domestic penal codes have specifically added "political groups" within the list groups protected by the crime of genocide.[59] Canada, in its domestic legislation, takes a whole other approach by completely avoiding any list of groups but instead criminalizing the intent to destroy, in whole or in part, any "identifiable group of persons, as such, that, at the time and in the place of commission, constitutes genocide according to customary international law or conventional international law or by virtue of its being criminal according to general principles of law recognized by the community of nations. . . ."[60]

Should "Cultural Genocide" Be Considered Genocide?

One issue that arose in the course of the drafting of the Genocide Convention during debates both before the General Assembly of the United Nations and its Economic and Social Council was whether the Convention should also include the crime of "cultural genocide." The term "cultural genocide" refers to "acts aimed at the destruction of a group by elimination of its cultural attributes, as opposed to the actual physical destruction of the group."[61]

Those suggesting that intentional destruction of a group's culture should be part of the crime of genocide present an attractive argument.[62] Eliminating or destroying the cultural features of a group—such as suppression of its language or religion—is in fact an insidious way to destroy the group, as its cultural features are what makes the group distinctive. Proponents of this view argue that this is in effect equivalent to physically destroying the group. The term today is often associated with acts directed toward indigenous peoples or other ethnic minorities within a country or region with the aim of eradicating the particular and long-standing way of life of such a minority.[63] Examples include the suppression of Tibetan culture and religion by the People's Republic of China in its efforts to assimilate the Tibetan people into China; the suppression of the Kurdish culture in Turkey, which, until recently, included a ban on the use of Kurdish language in schools, media, and other public fora; the forced assimilation of the Aboriginal indigenous people into the dominant European culture of Australia that took place during the first two centuries since colonization (and similar acts which took place against the Maoris in New Zealand); and the suppression of the culture of Native Americans in the New World.

Initial drafts of the Genocide Convention did include reference to cultural groups as one of the protected groups under the Convention. In the end, however, the proponents' arguments were rejected by the General Assembly during its final vote, and so destruction of a group's culture is not included in the acts criminalized by the Convention. There is one exception. While cultural genocide was left out of the final version of the Genocide Convention, "a shadow of the idea reappeared in the final version, which lists the forcible transfer of children from one group to the other as a punishable act."[64]

The primary reason why the UN delegates rejected the inclusion of "cultural genocide" as a crime under the Convention was the belief that the destruction of cultural attributes of a group does not rise to the level of physical destruction, which is the main aim of the Convention. The debate, however, continues, with some scholars and even jurists vigorously arguing that the Genocide Convention definition should be amended to include within the legal definition of genocide both the destruction and attempted destruction of a group's culture.[65] No court has yet to proclaim an instance of cultural genocide.

4. *Mens Rea* of Genocide: "With Intent to Destroy, in Whole or in Part"

In the *mens rea* analysis, it is important to recognize the differences between the *political* uses of the word "genocide" to describe various forms of collective violence directed at ethnic and religious minorities, and the more demanding *legal* definition of genocide that requires compelling and unambiguous evidence of a specific "intent to destroy."

The *Dolus Specialis* (Special Intent) of Genocide

Proving genocidal intent is both the most important and the most difficult task in prosecuting an individual for the crime of genocide.[66] As Article II of the Genocide Convention notes, the commission of acts specified in subsections (a) through (e) alone does not make out the crime of genocide. It must be shown that, at the time the perpetrator committed any of the (a) through (e) acts, the perpetrator also held a certain state of mind, or *mens rea*. That requisite state of mind is found in the following language: "acts committed with *intent to destroy, in whole or in part, a national, ethnical, racial or religious group.*"

Using American criminal law parlance, genocide is then a "specific intent" crime, meaning that the defendant must have harbored the specific intent set out in the Genocide Convention to commit the acts. The specific intent requirement is two-fold. First, because genocide can only be committed intentionally, committing one or more of the (a) through (e) acts negligently or recklessly does not signify the crime of genocide. Or put another way, there is no such thing as reckless genocide or negligent genocide.[67] Second, the crime of genocide requires not only a general intent to commit the acts specified in (a) through (e) but also a second intent, called the specific intent or special intent (*dolus specialis* in Latin) in criminal law phraseology. For genocide, the perpetrator must have intended to commit acts (a) through (e) with a second intent: "*the intent to destroy*," in whole or in part, the enumerated victim group.[68] The ICTY, in one of its decisions, explained: "It is in fact the *mens rea* which gives genocide its speciality and distinguishes it from an ordinary crime and other crimes against international humanitarian law. The special intent which characterizes genocide supposes that the alleged perpetrator of the crime selects his victims because they are part of a group which he is seeking to destroy."[69]

Quigley, in his legal treatise analyzing the Genocide Convention, expresses the two intents necessary for the crime of genocide a bit differently; nevertheless, he reaches the same result:

> Genocide is distinguished from other serious offenses by the element of intent. For genocide, victimization of human beings is a necessary, but not the sole element. Acts directed against human beings must be committed with an intent to destroy a group to which the immediate victims belong. No matter how culpable the actor [is] towards these immediate victims, this additional element is required. The act against the immediate victims must reflect a culpable state of mind in regard to the group. Thus, genocide encompasses a dual mental element: one directed against the immediate victims, and a second against the group.[70]

The prosecution must prove both of these intents by a criminal standard, usually expressed in the United States as "beyond a reasonable doubt." It is an element difficult to prove, as criminal proceedings before the ICTY and the ICTR have shown. In those courts, a number of defendants indicted for genocide have been found not guilty of the crime—even though the court conceded that a genocide in fact took place—because the prosecution could not prove beyond a reasonable doubt that the defendant harbored these legally required intents at the time of the killings. As explained by Quigley, "In most prosecutions to date, it has been clear that the accused caused harm to specific victims in ways falling within the subparagraphs [(a) though (e)] of Article II of the Genocide Convention. What the accused has typically denied is having acted with intent to destroy the group of which the victims were members. The several acquittals that have been entered on genocide charges have resulted from the court's conclusion that the prosecution had not proved the intent to destroy."[71]

A helpful way of looking at this is to distinguish between "intent" and "outcome." Even if the outcome is the mass murder of thousands of individuals or more, it does not mean that the accused on the dock possessed the necessary intent for genocide, that is, to destroy the protected group in whole or in part. We examine this subject further in Chapter 8.

The Meaning of "in Part"

In *Axis Rule*, Lemkin explained that genocide means "the destruction of a nation or an ethnic group."[72] While not expressly stated, the implication is that the entire victim group must be eradicated, or, at the least, the defendant must have intended to destroy the entire group even if the final result was not the group's extinction. Using the Holocaust as our paradigmatic standard, we can surely conclude that Hitler and his cohorts committed genocide of the Jews even if the Nazis failed in their purported ultimate goal of killing every Jew on the face of the earth or, for that matter, all of the Jews of Europe.[73] For this reason some have argued that unless the perpetrator's goal is to kill all of a given people, the individual did not commit genocide regardless of the number of people actually killed. Just as homicide is the extinction of the life of an individual, genocide is the extinction of the life of an entire group.

This argument, however, is contrary to the actual words of the Genocide Convention. Article II states that the necessary intent possessed by the perpetrator at the time of commission of any of the acts enumerated in subparagraphs (a) through (e) is not only the intent to destroy the group "in whole" but also "in part." Quigley explains how the term "in part" was inserted into the genocidal intent element of the offense: "As the drafting proceeded, some participants worried that persons accused of genocide might argue that they did not intend to destroy the entire group, but only a portion of it. So the drafters added the phrase 'in whole or in part.' "[74] At the same time, Quigley points out: "The phrase 'in part' has eluded precise application. By one reading, it imports a minimum numerical requirement" to the *mens rea* element of genocide.[75] The United States, in ratifying the Genocide Convention in the late 1980s, filed with the UN an Understanding as part of its ratification, noting that it interprets "in part" to mean "in substantial part." While the United States' Understanding did not further define the term "substantial," when genocide was made a federal crime by the US Congress in the aftermath of the Convention's ratification, the federal penal statute criminalizing genocide under American law added the explanation that "substantial part" means destruction of "such numerical significance that the destruction or loss of that part would cause the destruction of the group as a viable entity within the nation of which such group is a part."[76]

The ad hoc tribunals have come to the same understanding about the need to show substantiality. The ICTR, for example, has held that the *mens rea* element "requires the intention to destroy a considerable number of individuals who are part of the group."[77] The ICTY likewise explained in the *Krstić* Trial Chamber decision that "an intent to destroy only part of the group must nevertheless concern a substantial part thereof, either numerically or qualitatively."[78] These decisions show that the Understanding filed by the United States earlier, interpreting "in part" as being "in substantial part," has now become accepted international law.

If intent to physically destroy a part of a protected group is sufficient to meet the *mens rea* element, this leads to two other questions: (1) how many members of a protected group must the perpetrator intend to destroy for the "intent to destroy . . . in part" requirement be met, and (2) what proportion of a protected group must actually be destroyed for the destruction to qualify as a partial destruction? Since the Genocide Convention does not provide an answer, international tribunals trying individuals for genocide have to fill in the meaning to both these questions.

In the previous section, we dealt with the second question concerning the substantiality of the crime. However, the focus here is not on the result, but on the mental state of the defendant: how large a part of a protected group must the actor intend to destroy to possess the requisite *mens rea* of genocide? There is no single answer. As Schabas points out in his detailed discussion of the issue, for some scholars the perpetrator must intend to destroy a substantial or significant part of the protected group. For others, "[g]enocide can occur with the specific intent to destroy a small number of a relevant group."[79] Intent to destroy a statistically small number of a protected group can meet the genocidal intent if the individuals targeted comprise the leaders of a protected group. As the *Krstić* Appeals Chamber noted, "In addition to the numeric size of the targeted portion, its prominence within the group can be a useful consideration. If a specific part of the group is emblematic of the overall group, or is essential to its survival, that may support a finding that the part qualifies as substantial within the meaning of Article 4."[80] Ultimately, a hard-and-fast rule—whether expressed numerically or by percentage—cannot be given. Rather, the usual legal answer applies here: what qualifies as "intent to destroy . . . in part" and also meets the substantiality requirement will depend on the facts of the particular case.

5. Genocide-Related Crimes: Conspiracy, Incitement, Attempt, and Complicity

The Genocide Convention in Article III criminalizes other acts that fall short of genocide but that are still punishable under the Convention as genocide-related crimes. These four crimes are: (1) conspiracy to commit genocide; (2) inciting others to commit genocide; (3) attempted genocide; and (4) complicity in genocide. Most domestic genocide statutes also criminalize such acts, consistent with the scheme in their penal codes that likewise outlaw acts that fall short of the actual crime.[81] All criminal statutes, for example, punish in some form or another not only those who kill another human being without cause (for example, not in self-defense), that is, murder, but also those who are complicit in the murder, enter into a conspiracy to murder another human being, attempt to kill but are unsuccessful in their efforts, or incite another person by words or deeds to actually commit the killing. For some of these related crimes, a person receives the same punishment as the actual perpetrator, while for others the punishment may be less. The same rule goes for genocide-related crimes.

Conspiracy to Commit Genocide

Conspiracy as an international crime was first recognized at the Nuremberg proceedings of the senior Nazi leaders, where the defendants were charged with three substantive crimes—crimes against peace, war crimes, and crimes against humanity—*and* conspiracy. Conspiracy was also charged at the later Nuremberg zonal trials.[82]

The Genocide Convention continues this recognition of conspiracy as a separate international crime by noting in Article III that a person can be found guilty of "conspiracy to commit genocide." Both the ICTY and ICTR statutes recognize the separate crime of "conspiracy to commit genocide."[83] The first person to be convicted of conspiracy to commit genocide was Jean Kambanda, a former prime minister of Rwanda. Conspiracy was one of the slew of charges to which Kambanda pled guilty before the ICTR in 1998 and received a life sentence. Since that time, other defendants before both the ICTY and ICTR have been charged with conspiracy to commit genocide, with some being convicted of the charge (see Chapter 9).

To date, no one has been charged, and thereby convicted, solely of conspiracy to commit genocide. Prosecutors at both ad hoc tribunals have included the conspiracy charge as part of their indictments for genocide and genocide-related crimes solely in instances when they believe that a genocide actually took place and was committed by a group of individuals. Additionally, no one has yet been found guilty of conspiracy to commit genocide but acquitted of genocide itself. Therefore, the existence of conspiracy to commit genocide as an inchoate crime remains only a theoretical possibility.[84]

Last, since genocide is practically always a group crime—unlike murder, for example, where there can be just one guilty party—conspiracy to commit genocide can always be charged alongside the main crime of genocide. As a result, a court can increase the sentence of a convicted genocidaire by issuing separate sentences for each crime. The practice of the ad hoc tribunals, however, has been to conflate the separate convictions into one across-the-board sentence.

Incitement to Commit Genocide

The Genocide Convention also would punish those who incite others to commit genocide. Criminalizing incitement is always a risky proposition since it criminalizes pure speech and so may be used to stifle freedom of expression. During the drafting of the Convention, the US delegation was specifically concerned with that danger.[85] At the same time, taking their cue from the fiery speeches of the Nazi leaders against the Jews, the drafters recognized that genocide often begins with public speeches by those in power urging others to take action against a victim group.[86]

The balance is struck with the added requirements to the actual crime. The incitement must be "direct and public," meaning that the speech must expressly urge the listeners to take immediate action against members of a protected group. It must also be done in a public forum (including transmission via television, radio, or some technological means; incitement to genocide via email, text, Facebook, or other electronic messaging today would surely qualify) in order for "incitement to genocide" to take place.[87] Here a distinction exists with the crime of complicity to commit genocide. Privately urging someone to commit genocide, in other words, private incitement, can make an individual guilty of complicity to genocide, but only if an actual genocide took place. Since incitement to genocide, however, is a preparatory or inchoate crime, technically a person can be convicted for incitement to genocide even if actual genocide never took place (akin to the crime of attempted genocide—see discussion below). To date, however, no one has ever been charged with the inchoate aspect of the crime.

The most prominent convictions for incitement to genocide came in a set of cases before the ICTR of individuals involved in radio broadcasts urging Hutus to kill Tutsis, and even giving specific locations where the victims could be located (see Chapter 9). Finally, it should be kept in mind that almost all individuals charged with incitement to genocide can also be charged with complicity in genocide (see discussion below) since complicity in genocide by aiding and abetting someone to commit genocide also includes the act of incitement.[88] In practical terms, therefore, charging someone with incitement to genocide in addition to the charge of genocide seems superfluous.

Attempted Genocide

For almost all crimes found on the books of domestic legal systems, if an individual attempts to commit the enumerated crime, but fails to do so, he or she can be found guilty of the separate crime of "attempt to commit crime X" or "attempted X." For example, an individual who intends to kill someone, shoots at the intended victim but misses, does not go free. Society considers that individual both culpable enough and sufficiently dangerous that the individual is guilty of "attempted murder," a separate crime on the books that often carries a lesser penalty of imprisonment.

The Genocide Convention likewise recognizes the "crime of attempt to commit genocide" or, more simply put, "attempted genocide" (akin to "attempted murder," "attempted robbery," etc.). The Yugoslav and Rwanda ad hoc tribunals, by incorporating the crimes listed in the Genocide Convention, likewise criminalize attempts to commit genocide. However, while the crime is on the books, to date no one has ever been prosecuted for attempted genocide either before the ad hoc tribunals or in any domestic court.[89]

Complicity in Genocide

Complicity to commit genocide is recognized as a separate crime under Article III of the Genocide Convention, and likewise adopted by the statutes establishing the ICTY and the ICTR. The basis for recognizing criminal liability for complicity comes from domestic legal systems. As Schabas points out, "Probably all criminal law systems punish accomplices, that is, those who aid, abet, counsel and procure or otherwise participate in criminal offenses, even if they are not the principal offenders."[90] In the United Kingdom, the United States, and other British-derived legal systems, complicity is not a separate crime, but a means to find an accomplice to a crime guilty for acts committed by the principal when the accomplice shares the same *mens rea* as the principal. For example, if A and B plan to kill C, and A shoots C and kills him, B is also guilty of murder even though B did not pull the trigger because B's *mens rea* was the same as that of A, the actual perpetrator of the crime. B, in that instance, is said to have aided and abetted A in the crime and is charged the same as a principal in the crime.[91] As explained by the judges at one of the later US trials at Nuremberg, "The person who persuades another to commit murder, the person who furnishes the lethal weapon for the purpose of its commission, and the person who pulls the trigger are all principals or accessories to the crime."[92] Under Anglo-American law, the person is not charged with a separate crime of aiding or abetting, or complicity, but rather is charged along with the actual perpetrator of the crime itself and is subject to the same punishment.

The Genocide Convention crime of complicity treats the analysis differently. An accomplice to genocide can be found guilty of a separate crime of complicity even though the accomplice's *mens rea* was less than that of the perpetrator. For example, the ICTY Appeals Chamber in *Prosecutor v. Krstić* reversed the Trial Chamber's conviction of a Bosnian Serb general of genocide, but found him guilty of "complicity to commit genocide." The Appeals Chamber treated the complicity conviction as less heinous than the overturned genocide conviction by reducing the defendant's sentence from forty-six years to thirty-five years imprisonment.

This result makes it appear that the crime of "complicity to genocide" is somehow a lesser or secondary offense to the crime of "genocide," but as Schabas points out, "when applied to genocide, there is nothing 'secondary' about it. The 'accomplice' is often the real villain, and the 'principal offender' a small cog in the machine. Hitler did not, apparently, physically murder or brutalize anybody; technically, some might describe him as 'only' an accomplice to the crime of genocide."[93] Another way of explaining this is that in genocide the general principles of criminal liability can sometimes be turned on their head. For genocide, the individuals who actually perpetrate the killings or the other *actus rea* of the crime are only accomplices, while the *real* perpetrators are the leaders who plan and order the carrying out of these acts for the purpose of committing genocide.

What is the *mens rea* for the crime of complicity to commit genocide? The *Krstić* Appeals Chamber explained that the "conviction for aiding and abetting genocide [is proper] upon proof that the defendant knew about the principal perpetrator's genocidal intent. . . ."[94] Krstić participated in the 1995 mass murder of 8,000 Bosnian Muslims in Srebrenica, the largest wartime mass murder on European soil since the Second World War. Even though the prosecution had not proven that Krstić had the intent to destroy the Bosnian Muslims as a group when he participated in the Srebrenica mass killings, the Appeals Chamber found that he "had knowledge of the genocidal intent of [his superiors]" to destroy the Bosnian Muslims when they ordered Krstić and others to carry out the killings.[95] Krstić was therefore found guilty of complicity to genocide because "he assist[ed] the commission of the crime [of genocide] knowing the intent [of others] behind the crime."[96]

Of course, mere knowledge as sufficient *mens rea* is not enough. Krstić also had the necessary *actus reus* of the crime of genocide by participating in the killings at Srebrenica. Quigley points out that the minimum *mens rea* of knowledge for the crime of complicity to genocide must be tempered by some common sense limitations, otherwise an ordinary foot soldier would be liable for complicity to genocide by the mere awareness that his superiors' purpose in ordering the killings was to destroy the enumerated group.[97] Last, related to complicity to genocide, the ICTY created another form of group complicity called Joint Criminal Enterprise (JCE) (see Chapter 8).

6. Proving Genocide

How does the prosecution prove a case for genocide? As with any criminal prosecution, the easiest way to do so is through a direct confession of the defendant, who admits both to carrying out any one of the genocidal acts set out in Article II (a) through (e) and to the harboring of specific intent to commit those acts. For example, the defendant confesses that he intended to destroy a specific national, ethnic, racial, or religious group and thereafter either killed members of that protected group or directed others to do so.

Another means is through the testimony of witnesses who can affirm that the defendant made statements corroborating genocidal intent and admitted to the commission of the genocidal acts. Commission of the acts (a) through (e) can also be proven by eyewitness testimony in those instances when the defendant denies participation or involvement. The defendant's denials are likely to be rejected by the trier of fact when a percipient witness credibly testifies that he or she was present at the scene and *saw* the defendant commit any of the acts set out in subsections (a) through (e) *and* heard the defendant express the intention to destroy the group.

The participation of defendants in the destruction of a protected group and their reasons for doing so can also be confirmed through documents, such as written orders, letters, or other written communications. As will be shown in Chapter 3, the Nuremberg prosecutions of the Nazis provide an excellent demonstration of how documents can be utilized to convict defendants of international crimes by showing both the defendants' participation in the acts and the intentions behind the defendants' acts. The trial of Adolf Eichmann in Israel likewise shows the important use of documents to find a defendant guilty. In the trial of Saddam Hussein, Saddam's signature on written orders to kill innocent civilians at Dujail proved critical to a verdict of guilty for crimes against humanity.

In reality, however, most defendants on trial for genocide or other serious international crimes do not confess or make such incriminating statements. They are more likely to plead ignorance and lack of involvement. Documents may also be nonexistent because defendants, realizing the criminality of their behavior, may not put their orders in writing or may destroy any incriminating documents. In such cases, genocide must be proven by circumstantial evidence. The previous discussion noted the difficulty of proving the specific intent of genocide. For this reason, demonstrating that "the accused did it" (the *actus reus*) is often easier than proving "why the accused did it" (the *mens rea*).

Prominent British barrister Geoffrey Robertson, citing jurisprudence from the ad hoc tribunals for the former Yugoslavia and Rwanda, has summarized well the many ways that genocidal intent can be proven short of a confession or a "smoking gun" document:

- [T]he intent can be inferred from words, or deeds, or by a pattern of purposeful action.
- The intent can also be inferred from the general context in which other culpable acts were committed systematically by the same perpetrator group or by others.
- Other facts, such as the scale of atrocities committed, their general nature in a region or a country, or the fact of deliberately and systematically targeting victims on account of their membership of a particular group, while excluding the members of other groups, can also enable the inference of genocidal intent to be drawn.[98]

One example will suffice to demonstrate how genocidal intent can be proven through circumstantial evidence. The defendant is on trial for genocide for intending to physically destroy an enumerated group by engaging in acts criminalized in subsection (c): "deliberately inflicting on the group conditions of life calculated to bring about its physical destruction in whole or in part." How to prove that defendant harbored the specific intent to commit acts enumerated in subsection (c)? In 1947, while the Convention was being drafted, UN Secretary-General Trygve Lie, in a commentary about this subsection and with the Holocaust as a recent backdrop, explained as follows:

> Obviously, if members of a group of human beings are placed in concentration camps where the annual death rate is thirty per cent to forty per cent, the intention to commit genocide is unquestionable. There may be borderline cases where a relatively high death rate might be ascribed to lack of attention, negligence or inhumanity, which, though highly reprehensible, would not constitute [circumstantial] evidence of intention to commit genocide.[99]

The current plight of the Rohingya Muslim ethnic minority in Buddhist-majority Burma (also known as Myanmar) may be one of those borderline cases under category (c). The Rohingya face severe legal and actual discrimination, including being legally barred from practicing certain professions. They are also forced to live in specific areas that are cut off from the rest of the population by barbed wire and barricades. As a result, they are denied vital services and access to food sources. Thousands have fled on boats to escape persecution, but have been turned back. If massive deaths follow, this may be sufficient proof that certain Burmese government officials are "deliberately inflicting on the group conditions of life calculated to bring about its physical destruction in whole or in part" and therefore harbor the necessary *mens rea* for genocide.[100]

Last, because domestic penal statutes require proof of a criminal act and concurrent intent beyond a reasonable doubt, international penal tribunals, composed of judges selected from domestic legal systems, likewise require such level of proof to find the defendant guilty of genocide. As Quigley explains, "International law has not independently developed . . . [culpability] concepts, but draws on domestic law, where such matters have been analyzed by courts in great detail. The presumption is that when treaty drafters formulate a penal offense, they operate from concepts found in domestic penal law."[101] This evidentiary standard has been expressly codified in the Rome Statute of the International Criminal Court. Article 66(3) of the Rome Statute states that "to convict the accused, the Court must be convinced of the guilt of the accused beyond a reasonable doubt."[102] The Rules of Procedure and Evidence of the Yugoslav and Rwanda ad hoc tribunals likewise adopted the same evidentiary standard, stating that "[a] finding of guilt may be reached only when the majority of the Trial Chamber is satisfied that guilt has been proved beyond a reasonable doubt."[103]

The criminal standard of "proof beyond a reasonable doubt" imposes a much higher burden of proof on the prosecution than the standard of evidentiary proof required in civil cases, formulated in common law jurisdictions as "proof by a preponderance of the evidence." This high standard of proof for all criminal cases, coupled with the special difficulties of proving specific intent in criminal prosecutions for genocide, makes the task of convicting a defendant for genocide particularly difficult.

7. Punishment

The Genocide Convention makes it clear that anyone who commits one of the enumerated acts listed in Article II, regardless of whether they act in a public or private capacity, shall be criminally punished.[104] Genocide, therefore, is an international crime carrying individual criminal responsibility.

The Convention provides that persons charged with genocide shall be tried by the state in which they committed the act or by an (unnamed) international criminal tribunal with jurisdiction over the matter as decided upon by the Contracting Parties.[105] That tribunal today is the ICC. However, prosecution is preferred by domestic tribunals under the complementarity principle of the ICC.[106] This means that the ICC can only step in when national judicial systems fail to prosecute. This can be demonstrated by the fact that the state is either unwilling or unable to bring perpetrators of genocide and other mass atrocities to justice—or when the Security Council votes to refer the matter to the ICC (as was done with Darfur). A more detailed discussion of punishment is set out in Chapter 9, discussing specific genocide prosecutions before international and domestic courts.

C. USE AND MISUSE OF GENOCIDE TERMINOLOGY

1. Using and Misusing the G-Word: Why Words Matter

Because of its unique status in the hierarchy of crimes, genocide has achieved the status of not just being an international crime but as a symbol of suffering of the most extreme; and one that almost every victim group seeks to appropriate for itself. John Torpey correctly points out that "[t]he enshrinement of the term 'genocide' as the 'crime of crimes' thus makes it almost a *sine qua non* in the pursuit of greater attention for the wrongs that have befallen a particular group."[107]

The emotive power of Lemkin's word, as put by Michael Ignatieff, has led to "banalis[ing] [genocide] into a validation of every kind of victimhood."[108] Or as Alain Destexhe puts it: "Thus the word genocide fell victim to a sort of verbal inflation. . . . It has been applied freely and indiscriminately to groups as diverse as the blacks of South Africa, Palestinians and women, as well as in reference to animals, abortion, famines and widespread malnutrition, and many other situations. The term genocide has progressively lost its initial meaning and is becoming dangerously commonplace."[109] Schabas in his *Unimaginable Atrocities,* labels this phenomenon "The Genocide Mystique," devoting an entire chapter to the subject.[110]

Jurists and other legal scholars who designate a massacre as a crime against humanity (and what can be more terrible than a crime against the whole of humanity?) or a war crime are denigrated because they failed to characterize the event as a genocide. Schabas explains: "The word 'genocide' itself has a strange, mysterious effect. For victims, it presents itself as a badge of honour, the only adequate way to describe their suffering or that of their ancestors. Those who question whether the word is appropriate in given circumstances are sometimes dismissed as 'deniers.' "[111] And more: it is not enough that the victim group itself views the atrocity committed against it as genocide; the whole world must recognize that the atrocity rose to the level of being a genocide. As explained by German politician Markus Meckel, when urging his government in 2015 to finally recognize the terrible events that took place in the eastern Anatolia as a genocide, "Anyone who does not use this term is basically giving the suffering and the catastrophe a lesser meaning."[112]

The judicious use of the term "genocide" is important, not just for the simple reason that misuse of terminology amounts to telling lies about the events taking place but also for practical purposes. As Ignatieff points out: "All these rhetorical issues are of some importance because calling every abuse or crime a genocide makes it steadily more difficult to rouse people to action when a genuine genocide is taking place."[113] If the term genocide is to retain its impact as "the crime of crimes," it must be used within a certain framework. The only recognized available framework is that found in the Genocide Convention.

What conclusions can we draw about the status of Lemkin's neologism in the twenty-first century? As David Bosco has incisively pointed out, "The word genocide may be too powerful for its own good. It conjures up images of a relentless and irrational evil that must be confronted massively. It is almost paralyzing. We are used to fighting crime; genocide seems to require a crusade."[114] Akhavan similarly refers to the "dreaded *g* word"[115]—dreaded not only because it denotes atrocities of the worst kind but because its appearance in political and legal discourse more often obfuscates rather than clarifies.

In the prevention of atrocities arena, seeking to label an event as a genocide often needlessly shifts the focus from what needs to be done to halt the ongoing atrocities to theoretical arguments about whether the genocide label fits. And we now know that even if all agree that a genocide is ongoing, it does not mean individual states or the international community will take action. In 1994, the Clinton administration feared characterizing the Rwandan atrocities with the G-word lest it will be required to take military action to stop the mass murders. This led to the now notorious incident of State Department spokeswoman Christine Shelby refusing to utter the word "genocide" in a televised press conference in 1994 as the Rwandan genocide was unfolding. The most she would admit was that "acts of genocide" were taking place, but noted that this did not amount to "genocide." Shelby refused to answer a reporter's insistent question of how many "acts of genocide" amount to genocide. In his celebrated volume about the Rwandan genocide, Philip Gourevitch called this incident the "semantic squirm."[116]

In contrast, during the Bush presidency Secretary of State Colin Powell had no compunction in 2004 to label the massacres in Darfur as genocide.[117] Yet, the recognition by the United States that a genocide was ongoing in Sudan led to little action to stop the genocide. At most, President George W. Bush allowed the Security Council to refer the Darfur situation to the ICC by instructing the American ambassador not to cast a veto.

The repeated pinning of the genocide label on Darfur by the United States was not done to rally the international community to stop the genocide in Sudan; rather it became merely another instance of demonizing a regime it did not like by using the worst possible epithet against it. And so Akhavan asks: "Is it better to not call a genocide 'genocide' and do nothing, or is it better to call a genocide 'genocide' and still do nothing?"[118] With regard to Darfur, he points out that "much controversy arose concerning the use of the *g* word itself, but not concerning the everyday horrors confronted by the victims in Sudan."[119]

David Scheffer, the first holder of the US Ambassador-at-Large for War Crimes Issues (and currently Northwestern University law professor) concludes that the term "genocide" carries too much baggage and weighs down the decision-makers (whether at the United Nations or in individual governments) from responding to events which occur in his so-termed "atrocity zone." As Scheffer diplomatically explains, "The prospect of the term genocide arising in policy making too often imposes an intimidating brake on effective responses."[120] For purely practical reasons, Scheffer prefers the more generic and less-loaded term "atrocity" (or its cognate "atrocity crimes").[121] Since the invoking of the G-word clouds rather than clarifies reality and thereby acts as an obstacle to genocide prevention, Scheffer's suggestion that the use of the G-word in the world of genocide prevention is best avoided appears to be sound.

2. When Is It Proper to Characterize a Historical Event as a Genocide?

Is it proper to use the genocide label to describe events that took place before the enactment of the Genocide Convention? For some, the answer is "no." One can argue that to pin the label genocide upon an event that occurred prior to the existence of the Genocide Convention amounts to unfairly accusing alleged perpetrators of committing a crime that was not "on the books" when the event took place. The analogy, of course, breaks down when we apply it to the Holocaust, since the mass murder of the Jews during the Nazi era also took place before the enactment of the Genocide Convention. Yet, as discussed above, Lemkin specifically coined the term "genocide" to describe the events of the Nazi era. This is one reason why many describe the Holocaust as the paradigmatic genocide. Genocide scholars likewise use the Holocaust as the standard by which to measure other genocides. And victim groups aim to convince others that the atrocities suffered by their kin should likewise be called a genocide because of similarities to the Holocaust.

The debate surrounding the proper use of the "genocide" label for historical purposes manifests itself today most prominently around one event: the massacres of the Armenians during the First World War and shortly thereafter. In all, between 1 million and 1.5 million Armenians died between 1915 and 1920 as a result of the forcible expulsion by Turkish authorities of the entire Armenian population from eastern Anatolia into the deserts of Mesopotamia, a region now in modern-day Iraq, Kuwait, and Syria. The expulsion was carried out through forced marches, where the expelled Armenian civilians died for lack of food, water, or shelter. Many were also murdered by local Kurdish and Turkish populations that the Armenians encountered during the forced marches. Village-by-village mass killings led to additional deaths.

Was this genocide? There is no dispute that the Armenian minority in Ottoman Turkey was a distinct ethnic and religious group, and so would be a protected group under the Genocide Convention. There is also little doubt that three *actus rea* of genocide were committed. With regard to subsection (a) "killing members of the group," there is no dispute that a substantial number of Armenians, whether in the tens or hundreds of thousands or a million or more were killed. With regard to subsection (b) "causing serious bodily or mental harm to members of the group," there is also no dispute that the same number of Armenians incurred serious bodily and mental harm. With regard to subsection (c) "deliberately inflicting on the group conditions of life calculated to bring about its physical destruction in whole or in part," the forced deportation of the Armenians ("conditions of life") inflicted conditions that brought about the physical destruction of a substantial part of the Armenian people. In 1915, approximately 2.5 million Armenians were living in the Ottoman Empire. By 1923, only about 200,000 Armenians remained. In all, two-thirds of the Armenian population living in Ottoman Turkey in 1915 was gone by 1923, either deported or massacred by the Ottoman government.[122]

Did the Ottoman leaders also possess the necessary *mens rea* "intent to destroy, in whole or in [substantial] part" the Ottoman Armenians by committing acts (a), (b), and (c)? Geoffrey Robertson deftly summarizes the circumstantial evidence of genocidal intent on the part of the Ottoman Turkish rulers who initiated the expulsions and killings:

> [The Ottoman rulers] were well aware, throughout the time when the deportations were underway, that they had turned into death marches. The Armenians were dying in their tens of thousands, and those who put them in these conditions did nothing to extract them or bring the conditions to an end by, for example, protecting the deportees or punishing those who attacked them. There is ample evidence that the CUP [Committee of Union and Progress, the Young Turks who wrestled rule from the Ottoman sultan] leadership knew of these massacres. The US ambassador, Henry Morgenthau, says he complained several times to Interior Minister Talaat Pasha about his government's "extermination" policy, and quotes Talaat as replying: "*We have already disposed of three quarters of the Armenians; there are none left in Bitlis, Van and Erzenum. The hatred between the Turks and the Armenians is now so intense that we have got to finish with them. If we don't, they will plan their revenge.*" In a modern war crimes trial, the ambassador's testimony would be relied on as evidence of an admission by Talaat to the knowledge (*mens rea*) sufficient for guilt of genocide, under the command responsibility principle.[123]

To buttress their claim, the Armenians and their supporters point to the links between the Holocaust and the Armenian genocide. The Armenians and their supporters also marshal two additional pieces of evidence: (1) the reported utterance by Hitler in August 1939 to his generals in explaining that they would all enjoy impunity from prosecution for the naked attack on Poland, since "[w]ho remembers now the extermination of the Armenians?"[124] and (2) Raphael Lemkin apparently not only had the contemporaneous murder of the Jews in mind but also the earlier murder of the Armenians when coining the term "genocide."[125]

Turkey steadfastly refuses to recognize the massacres of the Armenians as a genocide. At the most, the official position of the Republic of Turkey is to label the events as the "so-called Armenian genocide," but this is a disrespectful use of the word and hardly its recognition. According to Turkey, the forced dislocation was "a war-related dislocation and security measure" that led to unfortunate deaths.[126] Under the Turkish narrative, aspirations of Armenian nationalists for independence in the waning days of the Ottoman Empire made the Armenian minority a security risk. Because the Armenians took arms against the Ottoman government, they were relocated due to their political aims, and not their ethnicity or religion. But according to British historian Donald Bloxham, "nowhere else during the First World War was the separatist nationalism of the few answered with the total destruction of the wider ethnic community from which the nationalists hailed."[127] Turkey also claims that not all Armenians were targeted for deportation, with much of the Armenian population in Istanbul untouched by the events, that the usually cited figure of 1.5 million deaths is an exaggeration, and that a comparable number of Turks also perished during the same period.

In 2014, on the ninety-ninth anniversary of the Armenian genocide, some movement toward recognition was made when Turkish President Recep Tayyip Erdoğan offered condolences to the victims and their descendants and spoke of the "inhuman consequences" of the Armenians' expulsion. However, he did not speak of genocide. Nevertheless, this was the first time that any Turkish head of state, or for that matter any high-ranking Turkish government official, acknowledged the suffering of the Armenians on one of the most sacred days for the Armenian people. In 2015, on the centenary of the massacres, Turkish Prime Minister Ahmet Davutoglu issued an even stronger statement of condolence: "We once again respectfully remember Ottoman Armenians who lost their lives during the deportation of 1915 and share the pain of their children and grandchildren."[128]

To counter Turkish denial, the Armenian community and their supporters have mounted an extremely successful worldwide campaign to have as many governmental bodies as possible—national legislatures, state and provincial legislatures, and city councils—*officially* recognize the Armenian genocide.[129] Each year on April 24, marking the day in 1915 when Armenian intellectuals were arrested in Istanbul and the mass-scale massacres which soon followed, every American president since President Ronald Reagan has made a speech marking the occasion of the Armenian genocide, though only President Reagan used the actual G-word.[130] President Barack Obama pledged during his election campaign that he would recognize the genocide, but he has never used the term publicly for fear of offending America's close ally Turkey.[131]

The high point of recognition came in April 2015, on the centenary of the Armenian genocide, with commemorations around the world and daily media stories about the events of 1915. That month, Pope Francis, during a mass, labeled the events as genocide. Austrian and German parliaments followed suit, passing resolutions commemorating the centenary and specifically using the G-word. The European Union did the same.

Ironically, Turkey's steadfast denials and its various high-profile public protests have been counterproductive by making the Armenian genocide even more well known. Next to the Holocaust, the Armenian genocide today is the most well-known genocide in human history—and the only mass atrocity to which the word "genocide" is invariably attached. Hitler's statement of "Who remembers now the extermination of the Armenians?" is certainly false today. In 2009, American journalist and lawyer Michael Bobelian published a book on the recognition campaign, labeling the Armenian genocide in the subtitle as "a forgotten genocide."[132] Even if that description had some credence in 2009, it surely is no longer true after the 2015 centenary remembrances around the world.

There are intrinsic problems, however, with efforts to have political bodies—whether parliaments of individual nations, or international bodies like the European Union and the UN General Assembly—reach back into history and declare an event to have been a "genocide." First, politicians and diplomats are not neutral judges who base their decisions upon an analytical application of the facts to the law.[133] They are also not legitimate historians whose task is to research and explain past events based on archival data they discover and analyze through extensive research. Rather, their decisions are based on political expediency and maintenance of good diplomatic relations with other governments. Armenia, for example, will not recognize the Ukrainian *Holomodor* as a genocide for fear of antagonizing its good neighbor Russia, with whom it seeks to maintain friendly relations and receives protection against its less-friendly neighbors. Russia's position is that the famine of the 1930s was not a genocide but yet another in a series of brutal events committed by Stalin against all of the peoples making up the former Soviet Union.[134] Likewise, Israel will not call the massacres of the Armenians a genocide since this would offend Turkey, the only Muslim-majority state with whom the Jewish state maintains political and military ties.[135] To underscore the political nature of this decision, when Israel-Turkey relations began to deteriorate after Israel's military operation in 2010 against a Turkish ship carrying activists seeking to break Israel's blockade of Gaza, one of the first reactions in the Israeli parliament was to call for the official recognition of the Armenian genocide. A similar call—a law to criminalize the denial of the Armenian genocide—went out in the Russian parliament in 2015 when Turkey shot down a Russian military jet involved in the Syrian conflict.[136]

My point here is not to reject the genocide label for the mass murders and deportations of the Armenians beginning in 1915—the genocide label fits—but rather to point out that the political arena is not the best place to debate history. There are too many other competing agendas going on. It is also important to recognize when the debate becomes too centered on the word itself rather than the issue at hand—obtaining for the Armenians a long-overdue acknowledgment and apology from Turkey for the sufferings of their ancestors. As Thomas DeWaal observes: "For most Armenians, it seems that no other label could possibly describe the suffering of their people. For the Turkish government, almost any other word would be acceptable."[137] In regard to the Armenian genocide, the use of the G-word stands in the way of any possibilities for reconciliation, even if the genocide designation for a historical atrocity is proper.

PART TWO

Legal Reckoning with the Crimes of the Holocaust

3

Prosecution of Nazi War Criminals at Nuremberg

Nuremberg is not just a city in Bavaria. It also refers to the greatest criminal trial in modern history.[1] The word "Nuremberg" today is uttered in courtrooms of The Hague in the Netherlands, Arusha in Tanzania, Dhakka in Bangladesh, Phnom Penh in Cambodia, and even in the military courtrooms of that tiny sliver of American-leased property in Cuba called Guantánamo. Seventy years after the International Military Tribunal (IMT) trial first began on November 20, 1945, Nuremberg has become the lodestar for how perpetrators of genocide and other mass atrocities should be dealt with in every corner of the globe.

A. INTERNATIONAL MILITARY TRIBUNAL AT NUREMBERG

After the defeat of the German army in the battle of Stalingrad in February 1943, followed by the D-Day invasion of the Western Allies on the beaches of Normandy in June 1944, it became apparent that Germany was going to lose the war. What to do then with the German leaders? The Führer, Adolf Hitler, was arch-criminal No. 1 and it was not unreasonable to believe that he would be captured to face the fate determined by his captors. All agreed that he and the other German leaders who brought so much death and destruction—the six years of war that resulted in fifty-five million dead and left Europe in rubble—should be punished. But *how* was a question that the Allies had never unanimously answered.

1. The Rocky Road to Nuremberg

On January 13, 1942, representatives of the nine European countries then occupied by Germany issued the St. James Proclamation from their exile seats in London.[2] In it, they announced that at the end of the war those responsible for war crimes would be punished. Twenty-one months later, as the tide of the war had turned, Stalin, Churchill, and Roosevelt issued on October 30, 1943 a joint Moscow Declaration "Statement of Atrocities" promising that "the major criminals . . . will be punished by a joint decision of the Governments of the Allies."[3]

Despite these legalist statements, it was not at all clear that the courtrooms of Europe would be where the Nazi war criminals would have to answer for their crimes. Roosevelt's Secretary of State Cordell Hull stated in October 1943: "If I had my way, I would take Hitler and Mussolini and Tojo and their accomplices and bring them before a drumhead court martial, and at sunrise the following morning there would occur an historic incident."[4] There were excellent reasons for rejecting the judicial route. First was the lack of any precedent for the creation of an international criminal tribunal. Napoleon Bonaparte was not put on trial after his defeat at Waterloo in 1815 but instead sent into exile. Second was the bad experience in the aftermath of the First World War when the Allies sought to try the German Kaiser Wilhelm II, but who subsequently escaped and obtained refuge in the Netherlands. The Allies did force the postwar German Weimar Republic to prosecute some lower-ranking Germans for war crimes in the infamous Leipzig trials. These trials, however, proved to be a disaster, as the German judges meted out very lenient sentences and the few convicted were either freed early or allowed to escape from prison. And so there was a clear consensus on the part of the Allies not to repeat Leipzig and allow the Germans to try their own.

At the three-day Tehran summit in late 1943, Josef Stalin made the sensible suggestion during dinner to summarily execute Nazi General Staff officers, but used the not-so-sensible number of 50,000. Churchill was appalled and stormed out, until he was cajoled by Roosevelt to return.[5] It would be wrong, however, to regard Churchill as being the defender of the rule of law. Churchill also favored a soldierly solution: a drumbeat court-martial followed by summary execution of the leading Nazis, although the number Churchill had in mind was much smaller than Stalin's.

By the time of the Yalta Conference in February 1945, there was still no agreement as to what to do with the captured German leaders. Roosevelt was now opposing summary execution of captured German leaders. He and his advisers countered that such a policy would lead to charges equating the Allies with the Nazis. Instead, the Americans now pressed for postwar trials of Germans involved in wartime atrocities and criminality.

On the American side, the most ardent proponent of an American-style criminal judicial process was Roosevelt's Secretary of War Henry Stimson. Stimson set out his rationale in a letter to the president on September 5, 1944: "It is primarily by the thorough apprehension, investigation, and trial of all the Nazi leaders and instruments of the Nazi system of terrorism, such as the Gestapo, with punishment delivered as promptly, swiftly, and severely as possible, that we can demonstrate the abhorrence which the world has for such a system and bring home to the German people our determination to extirpate it and all its fruits forever."[6] Stimson's opponent on this issue was Roosevelt's Secretary of Treasury Henry Morgenthau. The Morgenthau Plan, under which Germany would be stripped of its industrial capacity so that it no longer could wage war, also called for the summary execution of the German leaders. Roosevelt was initially receptive to Morgenthau's ideas, but he eventually turned to favor Stimson's view. Stimson saw Morgenthau's Jewish background and thirst for revenge for the mass murder of his brethren as coloring his judgment.

On the British side, one of the major proponents of holding a criminal trial was the brilliant legal scholar Hersch Lauterpacht, an Eastern European–born Jew schooled in interwar Poland and Vienna who immigrated to Britain before the start of the war. By the time of the war, Lauterpacht held the prestigious chair as the Whewell Professor of Law at Cambridge University. Writing in 1942, he argued that for international law of war to have any meaning, it must be enforced when violated: "For the cause of international law demands not only the punishment of persons guilty of war crimes. It requires that such punishment shall take place in accordance with international law. . . . [In] so far as the punishment of war crimes is intended to take place within the framework of a legal process, it will enhance both its effectiveness and the respect for international law if such limitations as the law of nations imposes are rigidly adhered to."[7]

Across the ocean, the Jewish Harvard law professor Sheldon Glueck, also rarely mentioned by Nuremberg biographers, was arguing the same. In a 1943 *Harvard Law Review* article, Glueck called for the establishment of an international criminal tribunal to prosecute Germans.[8] In the Soviet Union, another Jewish scholar, Professor Aron Trainin of Moscow University, set out the legal underpinning for putting the leading Nazis on trial for violating international law. Trainin's 1944 text, *Hitlerite Responsibility Under Criminal Law*,[9] was translated into English and widely read and studied by those who came to create the tribunal at Nuremberg.

In April 1945, the French came out in favor of a trial. The British, however, were still adamantly opposed. As late as April 12, 1945, less than a month before the war ended, the British War Cabinet formally communicated to the Americans that Britain would not accept a trial for Hitler and his cohorts, since "the question of their fate is a political, not a judicial, question."[10]

The next month, with victory in Europe, the British finally came around. Stalin likewise favored holding a trial, although Stalin's vision of what the trial should look like differed significantly from the American view.[11] As summarized by the *New York Times*, "The Soviet Union, which had lost millions of its people during the war, wanted the Nazis executed with as little folderol as possible."[12]

The Americans had a different idea. As explained by Justice Robert Jackson in a speech before the annual conference of the American Society of International

Law: "You must put no man on trial under the forms of judicial proceeding, if you are not willing to see him freed if not proven guilty. If you are determined to execute a man in any case, there is no occasion for a trial; the world yields no respect to courts that are merely organized to convict."[13] It was this speech that led to Jackson being tapped as chief prosecutor of the IMT. An important goal for the Americans was to make prosecution of the top Nazis a history lesson for the German people.[14]

A general agreement was ultimately reached among the foreign ministers of the Four Allied nations at a UN conference in San Francisco in May 1945 that a trial by an international military tribunal of the top Nazis would take place. The American view had prevailed. Those behind Nuremberg, largely Americans, had a vision that the first trial would be only the beginning of a lengthy process that would mete out justice to both first-ranking and second-ranking perpetrators of the Nazi regime.

The London Conference: Creating the IMT

On May 2, 1945, President Harry Truman offered Robert Jackson, a longtime Roosevelt confidant and former attorney general whom Roosevelt had appointed to the US Supreme Court, the position of chief prosecutor in the contemplated tribunal. Jackson, age fifty-three, accepted. The Supreme Court would soon adjourn for the summer, and Jackson believed that he would be back in time for the regular start time of the fall session, the first Monday in October. Of course this did not happen. Jackson became the first and only Justice to ever take a leave of absence from the Supreme Court.

With Jackson in charge, the war's victors met in London beginning June 26, 1945, to create the tribunal out of whole cloth. They called their court the International Military Tribunal (IMT). The IMT would try the so-called "Major War Criminals" on charges that the tribunal would issue and under procedure that it itself established. The prosecutors would be lawyers from each of the four leading Allied powers (the United States, the United Kingdom, the USSR, and France). The judicial panel deciding guilt or innocence would be composed of eight judges, one primary and one alternate, from each of these Allied powers.

On August 8, 1945, the delegates from the four nations issued an IMT Charter. The Charter imbued the court with jurisdiction to try individuals charged with three specific international law crimes:

- *Crimes Against Peace*: namely, planning, preparation, initiation, or waging of a war of aggression, or of a war in violation of international treaties, agreements, or assurances;
- *War Crimes*: namely, violations of the laws or customs of war. Such violations shall include, but not be limited to, murder, ill-treatment

or deportation to slave labor or for any other purpose of civilian population of or in occupied territory, murder or ill-treatment of prisoners of war or persons on the seas, killing of hostages, plunder of public or private property, wanton destruction of cities, towns, or villages, or devastation not justified by military necessity;

- *Crimes Against Humanity*: namely, murder, extermination, enslavement, deportation, and other inhumane acts committed against any civilian population, before or during the war, or persecutions on political, racial, or religious grounds in execution of or in connection with any crime within the jurisdiction of the tribunal, whether or not in violation of domestic law of the country where perpetrated.

In addition, the defendants were going to be charged with a fourth crime, common though not unique to Anglo-American law: conspiracy. The idea for charging the Nazis also with conspiracy came from a young Jewish lawyer on Stimson's staff, Murray Bernays. According to Bernays, the Nazi group of chieftains were akin to an organized crime syndicate. "The crimes and atrocities were not single or unconnected," wrote Bernays, "but were the inevitable outcome of the basic criminal conspiracy . . . based on the Nazi doctrine of racism and totalitarianism. . ."[15] This charge would appear in the Nuremberg Charter as "common plan or conspiracy to commit any of the foregoing crimes."[16]

2. The Trial

The prosecution teams divided among themselves the task of proving each crime. The Americans took on the task of proving conspiracy, which became Count 1. The Americans by far had the largest staff on hand, numbering over six hundred. Jackson's lead deputy was Thomas Dodd, who later became a US Senator from Connecticut. His other lead deputy was Telford Taylor, who succeeded Jackson as chief prosecutor for the subsequent Nuremberg trials. William Jackson, Justice Jackson's son, who graduated from Harvard Law School in 1944 and later became a prominent New York attorney, served as personal assistant to his father. Also sitting at the prosecutor's table as assistant trial counsel was the young navy captain Whitney Harris, another lead prosecutor, who later wrote a bestselling book on the IMT trial entitled *Tyranny on Trial*[17] and until his death at age ninety-seven in 2010 was a leading spokesperson for the legacy of Nuremberg.

The job of the British prosecutors was to prove Count 2, crimes against peace. Heading the British team was Hartley Shawcross, attorney general for the United Kingdom and a barrister with much courtroom experience. Shawcross' second-in-command was David Maxwell Fyfe, also a prominent barrister, who ended up doing most of the work as lead of the British prosecution team and was arguably the most effective prosecutor at Nuremberg.

Evidence of war crimes and crimes against humanity, Counts 3 and 4, were handled by the Soviets and the French; the Soviets for the Eastern Front and the French for the Western Front. The original chief French prosecutor was Francois de Menthon, the former attorney general of France, who resigned in January 1946 to take up active politics and was replaced by Auguste Champetier de Ribes, a close colleague of Charles de Gaulle. Andrei Vishinsky, the chief prosecutor of the notorious Stalinist trials of the 1930s, assumed responsibility for the Soviet team at Nuremberg. The actual Soviet prosecution in the courtroom was led by Ukrainian jurist Roman A. Rudenko.

We know from the transcripts of the London Conference that the four powers almost failed in their efforts to establish the IMT. Kirsten Sellars describes some of the tensions: "The American delegate threatened to walk out over the question of the court's location, the French delegate objected to plans to bring charges of crimes against peace, the British fretted over the risk of German countercharges, and the Soviets refused to countenance a definition of aggression. . . . Until the final day, none of them could be sure that a tribunal would be established at all. . . .[18]

The Defendants

As far as we know, the defendants at Nuremberg never killed anyone by their own hands. The twenty-one defendants on the dock were all representatives of the Nazi regime captured after the war and now charged as international criminals. The lead defendant and dominant personality was Reichsmarschall Hermann Göring. From the outset, the fifty-two-year-old Göring aimed to run the show. Answering the indictment in court, he wanted to make a statement after pleading not guilty. Sir Geoffrey Lawrence, the presiding judge, curtly cut him off. Later, Göring began passing notes to various defense attorneys, recommending trial strategy; he again was stopped by Judge Lawrence. Joining Göring on the dock were: Foreign Minister Joachim von Ribbentrop; Hans Frank, Hitler's personal lawyer appointed by Hitler as governor-general of occupied Poland; Rudolf Hess, Hitler's former deputy; Ernst Kaltenbrunner, chief of SS Security; Alfred Jodl, chief of operations of the Wehrmacht, the regular German army; Wilhelm Keitel, Chief of the High Command of the Wehrmacht; Karl Dönitz, head of the navy and Hitler's chosen successor as chancellor; Erich Raeder, former head of the navy; Fritz Sauckel, head of the slave labor program; Alfred Rosenberg, Reich Minister for the Eastern Occupied Area; Albert Speer, Minister of Armaments and War Production; Wilhelm Frick, Minister of the Interior; Julius Streicher, founder of the infamous antisemitic daily *Der Stürmer*; Arthur Seyss-Inquart, Minister of the Interior and Governor of Austria; Konstantin von Neurath,

Minister of Foreign Affairs and later Reich Protector of Bohemia and Moravia; Baldur von Schirach, head of the Hitler Youth; Walther Funk, former Minister of Economics and head of the Reichsbank; Hans Fritzche, head of the Radio Division of the Propaganda Ministry; Hjalmar Schacht, also former Minister of Economics; and Franz von Papen, former chancellor and ambassador to Austria.

Martin Bormann, Deputy Führer and Hitler's secretary, was tried in abstentia. Years later it was discovered that he had died in 1945. The industrialist Gustav Krupp von Bohlen und Halpach was dropped as a defendant when the judges learned post-indictment that he was senile and so unable to stand trial. Robert Ley, head of the German Labor Front, committed suicide in jail before the trial started.

Hitler shot himself in the bunker before being captured by the Red Army. SS chief Heinrich Himmler, who was also in charge of the death camps in the East, fled to the British zone. Upon capture, he ingested a cyanide capsule while being examined by a British doctor. Chief Nazi propagandist Josef Göbbels also committed suicide.

Last, the IMT Charter indicted six former Nazi organizations: the leadership corps of the Nazi Party; the SS, along with the Security Service (SD) as an integral part; the Gestapo; the storm troopers (SA); the General Staff and High Command of the German armed forces (the Wehrmacht); and the Reich cabinet. This was done pursuant to Article 9 of the Charter, by which the IMT could declare a defendant a member of a "criminal" group or organization. Article 10 then permitted the competent national authority of any signatory to bring individuals to trial before national, military, or occupation courts for the crime of membership in a criminal organization. In such a subsequent trial, Article 10 provided that the criminal nature of the group or organization need not be proven de novo.

The Defense Attorneys

The Charter vested the choice of defense attorneys on the accused. German attorneys, about two dozen with some being former Nazi Party members, were chosen to represent the defendants. As a common defense tactic, they and their clients also sought to shift blame onto the missing defendants from the dock: Hitler, Himmler, Göbbels, and Bormann. Prosecutor Thomas Dodd observed, "It would be relieving to hear one of them admit some blame for something. They blame everything on the dead or the missing."[19]

The Judges

The problem here was selectivity, because only judges from the four Allied powers would judge the defendants. The American judge was Francis Biddle, former attorney general under Roosevelt. The British judge was Sir Geoffrey Lawrence, the sixty-year-old former Lord Chief Justice of England. Lawrence presided over the proceedings as the chief judge of the IMT. Jackson believed that the selection of a British judge as president of the court would lessen the perception that the Americans were playing too large a role in the trials. Judge Lawrence acted superbly during the trial, preserving the dignity of the proceeding by reigning in parties and counsel when courtroom decorum was interrupted. Making sure that the defendants received their day in court, Judge Lawrence "bent over backward to let the defense handle the witnesses . . . in any way it chose."[20] Much of the positive legacy of Nuremberg is owed to his fine performance as the presiding jurist. The French judge was Henri Donnedieu de Vabres, a former international criminal law professor who also spoke fluent German. The Soviet judge was Iona Nikitchenko, who presided over some of the Stalinist show trials. Nikitchenko did not inspire confidence that he would dispassionately listen to the evidence when he stated in London before the trial even began: "We are dealing here with the chief war criminals who have already been convicted and whose conviction has been already announced by both the Moscow and Crimea [Yalta] declarations."[21]

Each of the four countries also appointed an alternate judge, who made up part of the full bench. The alternates did not have an official vote in any decision, but played an active role in deliberations.

Illustration 6 Chief US prosecutor Justice Robert Jackson delivers the prosecution's opening statement at the International Military Tribunal war crimes trial at Nuremberg, Nov. 21, 1945. US Holocaust Memorial Museum, photograph 03547.

The Trial Begins

The Soviets wanted to hold the trial in the four-power-occupied Berlin, but the location finally chosen was the German city of Nuremberg (Nürnberg or Nuernberg in German) in Bavaria, located in the American zone of occupation. This ancient city in southern Germany had been the cradle of Nazism. It was the location of the massive Nazi Party rallies between 1933 and 1938, and it was during the 1935 Nazi Party Congress that the infamous anti-Jewish Nuremberg Laws were introduced into the German legal code.

Like many other German cities, Nuremberg had been heavily destroyed by Allied bombing, but it still had a large standing courthouse, the Palace of Justice, and an adjoining jail.

A formal indictment was issued on October 6, 1945, in Berlin, where the Soviets insisted on holding the opening session. Jackson flew into Nuremberg for the first time a few weeks before the trial was due to start. Earlier, Jackson's team had architects and construction experts flown in from America to transform Courtroom 600, the chamber where the trial was to be held, to fit the needs of the trial. Windows were cut into the walls to enable camera teams to film the proceedings. IBM installed special equipment, never used before, for simultaneous translation between English, Russian, French, and German. The courtroom was enlarged to accommodate the audience.[22]

Shortly before 10 a.m. on November 20, 1945, the elevator from the cellar brought out the defendants, in groups of three, from the jail below into Courtroom 600. Each of the defendants pleaded "Not Guilty" to the indictments charged. The next day, Robert H. Jackson, the chief prosecutor for the United States, made his opening statement:

> The privilege of opening the first trial in history for crimes against the peace of the world imposes a grave responsibility. . . . The wrongs which we seek to condemn and punish have been so calculated, so malignant and so devastating that civilization can not tolerate their being ignored, because it can not survive their being repeated. . . .

As he closed his opening address, fifty-six transcript pages later, Jackson addressed the judges directly:

> The real complaining party at your bar is Civilization. . . . Civilization asks whether law is so laggard as to be utterly helpless to deal with crimes of this magnitude by criminals of this order of importance. It does not expect that you can make war impossible. It does expect that your juridical action will put the forces of International Law . . . on the side of peace."[23]

Journalist William Shirer of CBS News noted at the time: "My spine throbbed as Jackson used the power of language to build up his masterly case against the Nazi barbarism. We have heard today one of the great trial addresses of history."[24]

The Prosecution Case

For the next 217 days, excluding a two-week Christmas recess, the trial continued. In all, 240 witnesses were called to the stand and 2,630 documents also entered into evidence. At the London conference, the delegates debated whether to use the Anglo-American adversarial system of the common law, or the European inquisitorial system of civil law. It was finally decided that the adversarial system would be used at Nuremberg, but the traditional rules of evidence found in Anglo-American criminal trials were relaxed.[25] Since the trial was not before a jury of laypeople, there was less of a chance of prejudice before the professional bench. Moreover, Jackson noted the "impossibility of covering a decade of time, a continent of space, a million acts, by ordinary rules of proof, and at the same time finishing this case within the lives of living men."[26] The prosecution case was divided into two stages. In the first stage, the prosecutors sought to establish the criminality of various components of the Nazi regime. In the second stage, the prosecution focused on establishing the guilt of individual defendants.

The Americans went first and concluded their presentation of the evidence by the end of the year. The British, French, and Soviet prosecutors then laid out their respective cases. The prosecutors rested their case in March. To a large extent, the prosecution's case was a trial by documents, generated by the Germans themselves, that fell into Allied hands. These included original military, diplomatic, and government files of the Nazi regime. Signed by many of the defendants, they were highly incriminating.[27] The strategy to rely heavily on captured documents over eyewitness testimony was made by Jackson, since the former was more reliable than the latter, and with less surprise. Eyewitnesses could be impeached or discredited on cross-examination. Moreover, the crimes were so staggering that eyewitness testimony might be viewed as exaggerated. As Jackson noted: "We must establish incredible events by credible evidence."[28]

Reliance on documents, however, contributed to the monotony of the proceedings. Each document, or portion thereof, that became part of the evidence had to be read in its entirety during court proceedings and translated simultaneously into four languages. Many trial days consisted of nothing more than lengthy readings by prosecutors. Novelist Rebecca West, reporting on the trial for *The New Yorker*, characterized it as "a citadel of boredom."[29]

Nine days into the trial, the American prosecution broke up the monotony by screening a documentary film as part of their case. The film, *Nazi Concentration and Prison Camps*, was made especially for the trial. The images of endless heaps of dead bodies and scenes of misery upon the liberation of the camps had a profound impact on the courtroom spectators. Göring's reaction: "And then they showed that awful film and it just spoiled everything."[30] Lawrence Douglas calls the screening of the film one of "the Nuremberg trial's most spectacular moments" and adds that "[t]his use of film in a juridicial setting was unprecedented."[31]

Jackson, in his opening address, explained to the court: "We will show you these concentration camps in motion pictures, just as the Allied armies found them when they arrived. . . . Our proof will be disgusting and you will say I have robbed you of your sleep. . . ."[32] Confronting head-on an accusation that Allied charges of German atrocities might be exaggerated (as was done, it turned out, during the First World War), Jackson added: "I am one who received during this war most atrocity tales with suspicion and skepticism. But the proof here will be so overwhelming that I venture to predict not one word I have spoken will be denied."[33] It was the brilliant decision of Justice Jackson and his staff to present scenes from the actual locations where the Nazis had committed their crimes. If the judges themselves could not visit the crime scenes during the course of the trial, the prosecutors would bring these scenes before the court. To this day, this footage remains as our most vivid memory of the Holocaust, now widely available on YouTube.[34]

Live Witnesses

The IMT trial also featured testimonies of hundreds of live witnesses. Thirty-three witnesses testified for the prosecution. One of the most effective was Marie Claude Vaillant-Couturier, a thirty-three-year-old non-Jewish woman arrested by the Germans in France and sent to Auschwitz as a political prisoner. Put on the stand by French prosecutors, Mme. Vaillant-Couturier provided powerful eyewitness testimony about what she saw at Auschwitz in 1942. She described how an orchestra played happy tunes as Jewish prisoners were separated upon arrival: those destined for slave labor and those that would be immediately gassed. She told of a night when she was "awakened by horrible cries. The next day we learned that the Nazis had run out of gas and the children had been hurled into the furnaces alive."[35]

On January 3, 1946, prosecutors called SS officer Dieter Wisliceny to the stand. Wisliceny, an Eichmann associate, described how he had helped to organize the deportation of Jews to extermination camps.

PROSECUTOR SMITH BROOKHART: "What became of the [Hungarian] Jews to whom you already referred, the approximately 450,000?"

WISLICENY: "They were all brought to Auschwitz and brought to the final solution."

BROOKHART: "Do you mean they were killed?"

WISLICENY: "Yes, with exception of perhaps 25 to 30 percent who were used for labor purposes."[36]

That same day, the prosecutors also put on the stand SS General Otto Ohlendorf, commander of an *Einsatzgruppe* unit who testified how his men killed 90,000 people, mostly Jews, in the aftermath of Germany's invasion of the Soviet Union.

On April 16, Rudolf Höss, commandant of Auschwitz, testified, put on the stand by defense counsel for Ernst Kaltenbrunner.[37] This decision badly misfired. Instead of helping Kaltenbrunner, Höss, speaking directly and matter-of-factly, implicated not only Gestapo chief Kaltenbrunner but a number of the other defendants in their role of extermination of Jews and other victims.

The Defense Case

Eighty witnesses testified for the defense, including nineteen of the twenty-one defendants.[38] For the most part, the defendants were unrepentant, including Göring. Their usual line of defense was that they did not know of the atrocities committed or, if they knew, the acts were done on orders of Hitler, Himmler, or Göbbels, and not theirs.

Justice Jackson, in his closing address, neatly summarized the defendants' line of defense:

- Of Göring, "A number-two man, who knew nothing of the excesses of the Gestapo which he created, and never suspected the Jewish extermination program, although he was the signer of over a score of decrees which instituted the persecution of that race."
- Of Hess, "A number-three man, who was merely an innocent middleman transmitting Hitler's orders without ever reading them, like a postman or delivery boy."
- Of Ribbentrop, "A foreign minister who knew little of foreign affairs and nothing of foreign policy."
- Of Keitel, "A field marshal who issued to the armed forces but had no idea of the results they would have in practice."
- Of Frank, "A governor general of Poland who reigned but did not rule."
- Of Frick, "A minister of interior who knew not even what went on in the interior of his own office, much less the interior of his own department, and nothing at all about the interior of Germany."

Beginning on March 13, 1946, Göring spent three days explaining his innocence. Judge Lawrence gave Göring and his defense counsel wide leeway in presenting their evidence. On March 18, Jackson began his cross-examination of Göring. Much has been written about the supposedly ineffective cross-examination conducted by Jackson, at least on the first day of the cross-examination.[39] One of the judges later wrote that "Göring quickly saw the elements of the situation, and as his confidence grew, his mastery became more apparent. Jackson looks beaten and dead tired."[40]

On the second and third days, Jackson recovered, as he pinned down Göring for his role in anti-Jewish measures.

JACKSON: "Then you published on 12 November a decree, also under the Four Year Plan, imposing a fine of a billion marks for atonement on all Jews?"

GÖRING: "I have already explained that all these decrees at that time were signed by me and I assume responsibility for them."

JACKSON: "Well, I am asking you if you did not sign that particular decree? I am going to ask you some further questions about it later."

GÖRING: "That is correct."[41]

Illustration 7 Defendant Hermann Göring testifies in his defense at the International Military Tribunal in Nuremberg, US Holocaust Memorial Museum, photograph 80239.

All agree that British prosecutor David Maxwell Fyfe's cross-examination of Göring shined. "[T]here was no question that the tenor of the cross-examination changed when Fyfe took the lectern."[42] Maxwell Fyfe was able to pin down Göring for issuing various decrees contradicting established rule of warfare, such as execution of Royal Air Force flyers who escaped from a POW camp and the shooting of Soviet POWs. He also sought for Göring to take responsibility for the extermination of the Jews. Göring denied even knowing of the policy.

> MAXWELL FYFE: Will you please answer my question: Do you still say neither Hitler nor you knew of the policy to exterminate the Jews?
>
> GÖRING: As far as Hitler is concerned, I have said that I do not think so. As far as I am concerned, I have said I did not know, even approximately, to what extent these things were taking place.
>
> MAXWELL FYFE: You did not know to what degree, but you knew there was a policy that aimed at the extermination of the Jews?
>
> GÖRING: No, a policy of emigration, not liquidation of the Jews. I knew only that there had been isolated cases of such perpetrations.[43]

Over the next four months, most of the other defendants took the stand. Some claimed they had merely been following orders, even though the IMT Charter specifically precluded that defense. Most, as noted, sought to pin the blame on Hitler and the other Nazi leaders. The defense concluded its case on July 25, 1946. The next day, the prosecutors began to deliver their closing arguments, with Jackson going first. These were followed by closing arguments from the defense. On August 31, 1946, the defendants made their final statements. On September 2, after 216 days of court hearings over a period of eleven months, the judges retired for deliberations.

The Verdicts

On September 30, the judges began to announce their verdicts. Over the next two days, they took turns reading aloud the court's judgment. When finished on October 1, 1946, the court disbanded. Twelve of the defendants were sentenced to death. Three received life imprisonment. Four received long prison terms. Three defendants—Franz von Papen, Hjalmar Schacht, and Hans Fritzche—were acquitted. Found guilty as criminal organizations were Nazi Party leadership corps, the Gestapo, the SS (with the exception of the SS mounted regimes), and the SD. Acquitted as criminal organizations were the Reich cabinet, the Wehrmacht General Staff, and the Wehrmacht High Command.[44]

With regard to Count 1, conspiracy, the tribunal found only a conspiracy to wage aggressive war. Conspiracy did not attach to the other crimes charged. And conspiracy only applied to those German leaders who participated in the formulation or refinement of a concrete plan to wage a war of aggression. Mere knowledge of these plans or even actual involvement in the economic preparation for wars of aggression did not result in criminal guilt under the common plan or conspiracy.

For crimes against peace, the judgment recognized that aggressive war was "the supreme international crime" for which even a head of state could be brought to account. The charge, ruled the court, was not ex post facto. Leaders who purposefully attacked neighboring counties without cause must have known that their deeds were illegal. It would be unjust to allow these policymakers to escape justice merely because no one had been charged with that crime in the past.

With regard to war crimes, the judgment rejected the argument that rules of war had become obsolete, citing as precedent under The Hague Convention of 1907. Germany's policy of fighting a "total war" was impermissible, and leaders who set the policy for total war were war criminals.

With regard to crimes against humanity (such as extermination and enslavement of civilian populations on political, racial, or religious grounds), the judges interpreted that crime strictly, requiring a wartime nexus for conviction. As noted earlier, the defendants could be guilty of crimes against humanity only for actions that were committed after the start of the Second World War on September 1, 1939, but not during the first six years of Nazi rule, from 1933 to 1939.

Post-Conviction

On October 16, 1946, the defendants sentenced to death were executed by hanging in the early hours in the prison gymnasium. It was a private affair, with only a handful of official witnesses. Göring avoided his scheduled execution by ingesting a cyanide capsule that was somehow slipped into his prison cell. Bormann was never found. The executioners scattered the ashes by disposing them in the Isar River in Munich so that no trace would remain of these individuals.

3. Major Criticisms of the IMT

When the IMT convened in Nuremberg, the reaction from the legal academy and the politicians was mixed. For some, the special horror of the Second World War required an exceptional legal remedy, lest international law showed itself unworthy to the task. For many others, however, the IMT was a court set out to do "victor's justice," with faulty law, faulty procedure, and an unbalanced match between the prosecution and the defense. Charges of retroactivity and selectivity were the criticisms most often heard.

Ex Post Facto, or The Principle Against Retroactivity (*Nullum Crimen Sine Lege*)

The most severe criticism hanging over the tribunal was that it convicted the German defendants in violation of the principle against retroactivity set out in the Latin maxim *Nullum crimen sine lege* ("no crime without a law"). In other words, the crimes set out in the Charter were not criminal at the time that the Germans committed their acts. Of the four crimes charged, crimes against peace was the one most susceptible to the retroactivity charge, and so proved the most contentious. The American notion of charging the German leaders of the crime of waging an aggressive war was vigorously challenged as early as 1944 by the British and the French. At the London conference, Jackson sought to assuage his Western counterparts: "We propose to punish acts which have been regarded as criminal since the time of Cain and have been so written in every civilized code."[45]

The legal basis relied on by the Americans for charging the Nazi leaders for the crime of starting an aggressive war was the Kellogg-Briand Pact of 1928. Under the pact, fifteen nations, including Germany, agreed that recourse to war as a means of resolving conflicts between nations was now illegal. However, while the 1928 Kellogg-Briand Pact could be cited as making war illegal, nothing in the pact made individual statesmen criminally responsible for having led their countries to war. As one contemporary noted at the time: "There is no convention or treaty which places obligations explicitly upon an individual not to aid in waging an aggressive war."[46] It was a gap in positive law, and one that the prosecutors and the legal theorists behind them sought to fill by relying on principles of customary international law. To critics, however, this was nothing more than politics masquerading as law.[47]

Crimes against humanity also was new and viewed as ex post facto. The draftsmen of the charge could point to no treaty that criminalized "crimes against humanity." As to war crimes, the ex post facto argument was not legitimate. Foot soldiers and officers had been convicted of violating rules of war mistreating noncombatants and captured combatants since the nineteenth century. And recent German law confirmed this rule. In the 1921 *Llandovery Castle* case,[48] still being taught in law schools around the world, two German submarine officers were found guilty of war crimes by a German court in Leipzig for ordering in 1918 the sinking of a Canadian hospital ship and then shooting at the survivors on lifeboats to cover up their crime. The German judges rejected their defense that the officers were following orders of the submarine captain, since they were bound not to follow the patently illegal order. However, the notion that heads of state and other high-ranking political and military leaders—as opposed to foot soldiers or their military commanders on the battlefield—can be criminally accountable for war crimes was a subversive idea.

VICTOR'S JUSTICE, OR "THE VANQUISHED ARE AT THE MERCY OF THE VICTOR"

As Göring wrote on the indictment handed to him: "The victor will always be the judge and the vanquished the accused." The counterargument is that victor's justice was impossible to avoid. According to Lauterpacht, writing in 1944 to urge the Allies to put the Germans on trial: "In the existing state of international law it is probably unavoidable that the right of punishing war criminals should be unilaterally assumed by the victor."[49]

The charge of victor's justice could have been avoided if the judges came from neutral countries or were even anti-Nazi German jurists. But this was not done. And sitting among the judges was a Soviet judge, coming from a country that itself committed aggressive war against Poland in 1939 and Finland in 1940.

THE "SO YOU TOO" DEFENSE (*TU QUOQUE*)

It is no defense to murder to say that other people have also murdered. And the Allies made sure to protect themselves against the "so you too" argument (expressed in Latin as *tu quoque*) by writing into the Charter that this defense would be prohibited at trial.[50]

The prosecuting powers themselves, however, were coming into court with unclean hands, especially the Soviets. But if any state was entitled to retribution, it was the Soviet Union. In the brutal history of humanity, no other tragedy compares to the scale of death and destruction brought by Germany in the years between 1941 and 1945 to the territories of present-day Russia, Belarus, and the Ukraine. During the forty-seven months of what is known in the region as the Great Patriotic War, approximately thirty million Soviet civilians and soldiers lost their lives. Twenty million of these were civilians. Moreover, a large measure for the defeat of Nazi Germany can be credited to the Red Army and its successful march all the way to Berlin.

4. The Holocaust at Nuremberg

AT TRIAL

The IMT trial, as mentioned earlier, was not about the Holocaust. The primary focus was on the defendants' crime of waging an aggressive war. Nevertheless, the persecution of Jews was a running theme of the proceedings, from the trial indictment to the closing statements and judgment.[51] During the trial, the prosecutors presented considerable evidence about the mass murder of the Jews. Many captured German documents discussed anti-Jewish measures. The most compelling evidence came from the Soviet team. The official policy of the Soviet Union was "Do not divide the dead."[52] In the Soviet narrative, all of its nationalities had suffered equally under Hitler. Nevertheless, as part of their evidence of the Nazis' "crimes against humanity," the Soviet prosecution submitted data of the extermination of hundreds of thousands of Jews. The Soviets also put on the stand two witnesses, both Jewish, who provided eyewitness accounts of the extermination of Jews in Poland and Lithuania. Samuel Reizman, one of the organizers of the revolt in the Treblinka death camp, testified that Treblinka had thirteen gas chambers in which Jews were executed. Most persons sent there, he said, were murdered within ten minutes of their arrival.[53] Abraham Sutzkever, the great Russian/Yiddish poet who came to live in Israel after the war, was sent to the Vilna ghetto after the Nazis entered Vilna in 1941. He testified how tens of thousands of Jews were murdered shortly after, including his infant son.[54] The Soviets also put on the stand Severina Smaglevskaya, a non-Jewish Polish prisoner at Auschwitz. Smaglevskaya testified how Jewish "women carrying children in their arms or in carriages, or those who had larger children, were sent into the crematory together with their children. . . . [W]hen the greatest number of Jews were exterminated in the gas chambers, an order was issued that the children were to be thrown into the crematory ovens or the crematory ditches without previous asphyxiation with gas."[55]

The French likewise presented evidence of mass murder of the Jews. As noted earlier, Mme. Vaillant-Couturier, a non-Jewish political prisoner at Auschwitz, testified about extermination measures she observed there.

M. DUBOST: What do you know about the convoy of Jews which arrived from Romainville about the same time as yourself?

VAILLANT-COUTURIER: When we left Romainville the Jewesses who were there at the same time as ourselves were left behind. They were sent to Drancy and subsequently arrived at Auschwitz, where we found them again 3 weeks later, 3 weeks after our arrival. Of the original 1,200 only 125 actually came to the camp; the others were immediately sent to the gas chambers. Of these 125 not one was left alive at the end of 1 month. The transports operated as follows: when we first arrived, whenever a convoy of Jews came a selection was made. First the old men and women, then the mothers and the children were put into trucks together with the sick or those whose constitution appeared delicate. They took in only the young women and girls as well as the young who were sent to the men's camp. Generally speaking, of a convoy of about 1,000 to 1,500, seldom more than 250 . . . reached. The rest were immediately sent to the gas chamber. At this selection also, they picked out women in good health between the ages of 20 and 30 years, who were sent to the experimental block; and young girls and slightly older women, or those who had not been selected for that purpose, were sent to the camp, where like ourselves, they were tattoed and shaved. There was also, in the spring of 1944, a special block for twins. It was during the time when large convoys of Hungarian Jews—about 700,000—arrived. Dr. Mengele, who was carrying out the experiments, kept back from each convoy twin children and twins in general, regardless of their age, so long as both were present. So we had both babies and adults on the floor at that block. Apart from blood tests and measuring I do not know what was done to them.

M. DUBOST: Were you an eye witness of the selections on the arrivals of the convoys?

VAILLANT-COUTURIER: Yes, because when we worked at the sewing block in the spring of 1944, the block where we lived directly faced the stopping place of the trains. The system had been improved. Instead of making the selection at the place where [the trains] arrived, a side line now took the train practically right up to the gas chamber . . . right opposite our block, though, of course, separated from us by two rows of barbed wire . . . we saw the unsealing of the cars and the soldiers letting men, women, and children out of them. We then witnessed heart-rending scenes; old couples forced to part . . . mothers made to abandon their young daughters, since the latter were sent to the camp, whereas mothers and children were sent to the gas chambers. All these people were unaware of the fate awaiting them. They were merely upset at being separated, but they did not know that they were going to their death. To render their welcome more pleasant at this time—in June-July 1944—an orchestra composed of internees, all young and pretty girls in little white blouses and navy blue skirts . . . who played during the selection, at the arrival of the trains, gay tunes such as the "Merry Widow," the "Barcarolle" from the "Tales of Hoffmann," and so forth. They were then informed that this was a labor camp and since they were never brought into the camp they saw only the small platform surrounded by flowering plants. Naturally, they could not realize what was in store for them. Those selected for the gas chamber, that is, the old people, mothers, and children, were escorted to a red-brick building.

M. DUBOST: These were not given an indentification number?

VAILLANT-COUTURIER: No.

DUBOST: They were not tattooed?

VAILLANT-COUTURIER: No. They were not even counted.

DUBOST: You were tattooed?

VAILLANT-COUTURIER: Yes, look. (The witness shows her arm). . . .[56]

Closing Statements

In their summations, both the French and British prosecutors spoke about the mass murder of the Jews. Chief British Prosecutor Hartley Shawcross focused on the special role of the Jews in the Nazi program:

> There is one group to which the method of annihilation was applied on a scale so immense that it is my duty to refer separately to the evidence. I mean the extermination of the Jews. If there were no other crime against these men [the defendants], this one alone, in which all of them were implicated, would suffice. History holds no parallel to these horrors.[57]

Shawcross also provided one of the most effective examples of bringing the Holocaust into the IMT courtroom by reading from an affidavit of a German engineer Hermann Graebe, manager of a German building firm in Nazi-occupied Ukraine. In his affidavit, Graebe described witnessing one instance of the mass murder of Jews.

> On October 5, 1942, when I visited the building office at Dubno, my foreman told me that in the vicinity of the site Jews from Dubno had been shot in three large pits, each about 30 meters long and 3 meters deep. About 1,500 persons had been killed daily. All the 5,000 Jews who had still been living in Dubno before the pogrom were to be liquidated. As the shooting had taken place in his presence, he was still much upset. Thereupon, I drove to the site accompanied by my foreman and saw near it great mounds of earth, about 30 meters long and 2 meters high. Several trucks stood in front of the mounds. Armed Ukrainian militia drove the people off the trucks under the supervision of an SS man. The militiamen acted as guards on the trucks and drove them to and from the pit. All these people had the regulation yellow patches on the front and back of their clothes, and thus could be recognized as Jews. My foreman and I went directly to the pits. Nobody bothered us. Now I heard rifle shots in quick succession from behind one of the earth mounds. The people who had got off the trucks—men, women, and children of all ages—had to undress upon the orders of an SS man, who carried a riding or dog whip. They had to put down their clothes in fixed places, sorted according to shoes, top clothing, and underclothing. I saw a heap of shoes of about 800 to 1,000 pairs, great piles of underlinen and clothing. Without screaming or weeping, these people undressed, stood around in family groups, kissed each other, said farewells, and waited for a sign from another SS man, who stood near the pit, also with a whip in his hand. During the fifteen minutes that I stood near I heard no complaint or plea for mercy. I watched a family of about

> eight persons, a man and a woman both about fifty with their children of about one, eight and ten, and two grown-up daughters of about twenty to twenty-nine. An old woman with snow-white hair was holding the one-year-old child in her arms and singing to it and tickling it. The child was cooing with delight. The couple were looking on with tears in their eyes. The father was holding the hand of a boy about ten years old and speaking to him softly; the boy was fighting his tears. The father pointed to the sky, stroked his head, and seemed to explain something to him. At that moment the SS man at the pit shouted something to his comrade. The latter counted off about twenty persons and instructed them to go behind the earth mound. Among them was the family, which I have mentioned. I well remember a girl, slim and with black hair, who, as she passed close to me pointed to herself and said "Twenty-three [years old]." I walked around the mound and found myself confronted by a tremendous grave. People were closely wedged together and lying on top of each other so that only their heads were visible. Nearly all had blood running over their shoulders from their heads. Some of the people shot were still moving. Some were lifting their arms and turning their heads to show that they were still alive. The pit was already two-thirds full. I estimated that it already contained about 1,000 people.[58]

Judgment

The Holocaust also appeared in the judgment in a section titled "Persecution of the Jews."

> The persecution of the Jews at the hands of the Nazi Government has been proved in the greatest detail before the Tribunal. It is a record of consistent and systematic inhumanity on the greatest scale. . . . In the summer of 1941, plans were made for the "final solution" of the Jewish question in Europe. This "final solution" meant the extermination of the Jews, which early in 1939 Hitler had threatened would be one of the consequences of an outbreak of war, and a special section in the Gestapo under Adolf Eichmann, as head of section B4, of the Gestapo, was formed to carry out the policy . . . Adolf Eichmann, who had been put in charge of this program by Hitler, has estimated that the policy pursued resulted in the killing of 6,000,000 Jews, of which 4,000,000 were killed in the extermination institutions.[59]

Because of the documents uncovered and eyewitness testimony at the trial, one of the most important nonlegal legacies of the IMT trial (and of the subsequent Nuremberg Military Tribunal trials) was the preservation for posterity of the critical evidence of the Holocaust. While the historiography of the Holocaust that came out of the trials was imperfect, it was invaluable. Already in 1946, this legacy was recognized. As Charles Wyzanski Jr. wrote: "[I]f it had not been for the trial and the diligent efforts of the staff of able lawyers and investigators, acting promptly and in response to the necessities of legal technique, the important documents in which the defendants convicted themselves might never have been uncovered. . . . [This has] given historians much of the data which the world will require for proper evaluation of the causes and events of World War II."[60]

And so the first great book on the history of the Holocaust, Raul Hilberg's *The Destruction of the European Jews*, was made possible only because its historian author was able to mine the documents unearthed by the prosecution team to conduct their case at Nuremberg, which he found in 1951 in Alexandria, Virginia, where they filled 28,000 linear feet of shelf space in a federal records center. As Hilberg later recollected, "What I found inside was absolutely extraordinary. . . . It took but one glance at all these documents to realize that their contents could not be read by one individual in a lifetime."[61] Since Hilberg, countless scholars have followed his legal paper trail to research and write histories of that era.

B. THE LATER NUREMBERG TRIALS

Following the conclusion of the IMT trial in 1946, the Palace of Justice for the next three years became the scene of twelve more trials of Germans from the Nazi elite. When the four-party delegations first met in London in the summer of 1945, there was discussion about having a subsequent international military tribunal for the top Nazis not prosecuted before the IMT. The souring of relations between the Soviets and their Western allies soon made it obvious that there would be no subsequent IMT proceedings. Since the plan of an IMT2 was dead, it now became the responsibility the Allied military prosecutors in each of the various occupation zones to conduct their own trials, applying the law that came out of the London Charter and the IMT judgment.

Though the IMT was disbanded, the American Office for Chief of Counsel for War Crimes (OCC) stayed put. Change of personnel followed. Taking over from Jackson was one of his deputies, Telford Taylor, given the rank of brigadier general. Taylor's task was to assemble a fresh team of prosecutors to try the second tier Nazis not tried before the IMT. These individuals were either already in American military custody or living in the American zone of occupied Germany. The Americans were most keen to prosecute German industrialists, none of whom faced trial before the IMT. Gustav Krupp was dismissed after indictment because of his senility, and the IMT judges refused the prosecution's request to have him replaced by his son Alfried Krupp, the real brain of the Krupp empire during the war. And so Alfried Krupp, Frederich Flick and their associates, along with the bosses of the I.G. Farben chemical concern, each had their own trial as part of the three industrialist trials conducted by the OCC.

Most trials took place in the same Courtroom 600 where the IMT trial was conducted. Formally these were military proceedings, since the trials proceeded under the auspices of the US Army. And so the courts of this "Other Nuremberg" or Subsequent Nuremberg Proceedings are referred to as the Nuremberg Military Tribunals (NMTs).[62] The NMT panels were composed primarily of state judges, some from the state supreme courts, and other American legal actors who volunteered to come to occupied Germany to mete out justice to the indicted Nazis.

1. The Twelve NMT Trials

On December 20, 1945, a month after the IMT trial started, the quadripartite Control Council that governed Allied-occupied Germany enacted an occupation law, Control Council Law No. 10 (CCL10), authorizing each of the four powers to carry on with such prosecution in its own zone of occupation as it might see fit. On January 4, 1946, at the IMT trial and a few weeks after enactment of CCL10, Colonel Telford Taylor presented the prosecution case against the German High Command. His eloquence led to his appointment as lead prosecutor in the later Nuremberg trials, with Taylor eventually spending more time at Nuremberg prosecuting Nazis than any other Allied lawyer.

On October 1, 1946, the IMT issued its verdicts and disbanded. A week later Jackson resigned and returned to the Supreme Court. With his resignation, Jackson presented a final report to President Truman. In his report, Jackson saw the need for additional trials: "A very large number of Germans . . . remain unpunished. There are many industrialists, militarists, politicians, diplomats, and police officials whose guilt does not differ from those who have been convicted except that their parts were at lower levels and have been less conspicuous."[63]

Taking its authority from CCL10 and following Jackson's suggestion to Truman, the OCC from 1947 to 1949 staged twelve trials against 177 defendants. Similar trials were simultaneously being conducted in the French, British, and Soviet zones of occupation.[64] Ultimately, however, prosecution of Nazi war criminals in the years following the war became largely an American endeavor. The Americans had conducted the greatest number of trials in their zone of occupation and held in custody the largest population of convicted war criminals, three times as many as the British and the French.[65]

The indictments in the twelve NMT trials followed a common pattern. Count 1, akin to the IMT trial, charged conspiracy, except here it was conspiracy to commit war crimes and crimes against humanity and not crimes against peace.

However, no defendant was convicted of Count 1.[66] Count 2 charged war crimes, and Count 3 charged crime against humanity. Count 4 charged membership in a criminal organization, if the defendant belonged to a Nazi organization declared criminal by the IMT. In a few cases, some defendants were charged with crimes against peace.

Despite accusations of bias by those who wanted to shut down the American war crimes program in occupied Germany, the American prosecutors and judges committed an exemplary job of providing due process to the defendants before the NMT. Heller concludes that, "with very few exceptions, the tribunals did everything they could do to provide the defendants with fair trials."[67] He does point out that (1) the prosecutors "enjoyed significant material and logistical advantages over the defense," and (2) the "prosecutors relied heavily on incriminating statements made by the defendants without the benefit of counsel."[68]

The same criticisms made of the IMT trial—both at the time and thereafter—reappear with the NMT. The trials were nothing more than victor's justice, the ex post facto prohibition [*nullum crimen sine lege* ("no crime without a law")] was breached, and the Allies were guilty of some of the same crimes, the *tu quoque* ("you too"/"so-did-you") defense. The NMT judges had an easier time dealing with the first two, since those were already rejected by the IMT, and so they had precedent to follow. Interestingly, even though the *tu quoque* defense was prohibited, some of the tribunals allowed this defense to come in.

On October 25, 1946, less than four weeks after the IMT judgments were issued, the US military brought indictments in *Case No. 1*, against twenty-three Nazi physicians and scientists in what is known as the Doctors' Trial and formally named *United States v. Karl Brandt, et al.* Defendants included Karl Brandt, personal physician to Adolf Hitler; Siegfried Handloser, chief medical officer in the German armed forces; and Paul Rostock, dean of the medical faculty at the University of Berlin whom Brandt made chief of a new department for medical science and research toward the end of the war. The trial marked the first appearance of a female defendant at Nuremberg: Herta Oberheuser, a doctor at the Ravensbrück concentration camp who performed medical experiments on prisoners, inflicting wounds on her subjects in order to simulate wounds of German combat soldiers in the field.

The defendants were charged with war crimes and crimes against humanity based on their responsibility for murders and other atrocities committed on prisoners, including gruesome medical experiments. Verdicts were announced on August 19, 1947, with sixteen defendants found guilty and seven acquitted. Seven defendants were sentenced to death, five sentenced to life imprisonment, with sentences for the others ranging from twenty to ten years. Brandt was hanged.[69] Handloser was sentenced to life imprisonment, later reduced to twenty years. He was released seven years later, as part of the Cold War release program

Illustration 8 Defendant Herta Oberheuser standing at the defendants' bench, Nuremberg Medical Trial, Trial #1, 1946, Yad Vashem, photograph 3397/59, courtesy of Dr. Robert Levi.

initiated by the Western allies. Oberheuser was sentenced to twenty years' imprisonment, later reduced to ten years, and then released in 1952. She returned to practice medicine, but then lost her medical license in 1956 after a former Ravensbrück inmate recognized her. Rostock was the highest-ranking defendant to be acquitted; the court could not find sufficient proof of his complicity in the medical experiments.

Case No. 2, brought a month later began, was unusual since it involved only one defendant, German Air Force Field Marshal Erhard Milch. Milch was accused of war crimes and crimes against humanity for mistreatment of civilians of occupied territories, including the use of slave labor and medical experiments. As in the Doctors' Trial, Milch was also charged with mistreatment of German nationals, characterized as crimes against humanity. The American judges acquitted Milch of crimes against humanity involving the medical experiments, but found him guilty of war crimes and crimes against humanity with regard to the use of slave labor by the Luftwaffe, the German air force, during the war. Milch was sentenced to life imprisonment, but was released in 1954. He died in 1972.

On January 4, 1947, while the Milch trial was still ongoing, the United States brought *Case No. 3*, known as the Justice Trial and formally titled as the *United States v. Josef Altstoetter, et al.* The fifteen defendants were German jurists holding leading legal positions under the Nazi regime who played a role in transforming German criminal law into an instrument of terror, in the manner described in Chapter 1.

The defendants included judges, officials in the Ministry of Justice, and high-ranking court administrators. The indictment charged the defendants as participating in "a nationwide government-organized system of cruelty and injustice . . . perpetrated in the name of the law. . . ."[70] In an oft-quoted phrase from the indictment, during the Nazi era "[t]he dagger of the assassin was concealed beneath the robe of the jurist."[71]

The German jurists were charged with war crimes and crimes against humanity. The war crimes count focused on the so-called Night and Fog Decree (*Nacht-und-Nebel-Erlass*) issued for the occupied territories and authorizing the arrest, furtive transport, and secret trial by special courts of the Reich Justice Ministry. Roughly one-half of those who were seized were executed.[72] Some of the defendants were involved in the drafting or implementation of the decree. Other defendants were involved in enacting and carrying out various other special decrees targeting persecuted groups, the most drastic (as discussed in Chapter 1) being the Law Against Poles and Jews of December 4, 1941. Crimes against humanity dealt with similar acts of judicial murder, but committed within the Reich against German Jews and political opponents. According to the indictment, the German legal institutions created for this "reign of terror" and the legal proceedings that followed lacked "even a semblance of fair trial or justice."[73]

Case No. 3 was completely novel. Never before, not even before the IMT, had prosecutors sought to argue that misuse of the law and legal institutions can rise to the level of being a war crime or a crime against humanity. In essence, the three American judges were asked to hold that legal actors *like them* doing their job as judges and other legal officials *according to the law* of their nation were international criminals. The case was crafted and led by Charles M. LaFollette, a former Republican congressman from Indiana who was offered the position of an NMT judge but decided in 1946 to join the prosecution team.[74] Taylor made LaFollette his chief deputy. Taylor recognized the novelty of the charges by noting in his Final Report that "to jurists [*Case No. 3* is] perhaps the most interesting of all the Nuremberg trials."[75] The prosecution team included as assistant counsel Sadie B. Arbuthnot, the first female to take the podium at Nuremberg.

Eleven months later, the American judges issued their verdicts: eleven defendants were found guilty and four were acquitted. Four defendants (Franz

Illustration 9 Nuremberg Trials prosecutor Sadie B. Arbuthnot stands at podium in Nuremberg courtroom, 1947, the Nuremberg Justice Trial, Trial #3, 1947, courtesy of Historical & Special Collections, Harvard Law School Library, photo 1998.1.60.

Schlegelberger, Herbert Klemm, Rudolf Oeschey, and Oswald Rothaug) were sentenced to life, with the others receiving sentences between five to ten years. None of the defendants served out their full sentence. As example, Schlegelberger, the principal defendant, was released in 1951 and received a full state pension until his death at age ninety-four.

In Chapter 1, we examined the corruption of German law under the Nazis. Here, we briefly focus on the acts of the four defendants adjudged most seriously by the tribunal to see what made them international criminals in the eyes of the law and why, as the court ruled, "we see no merit in the suggestion that Nazi judges are entitled to the benefit of the Anglo-American doctrine of judicial immunity."[76]

Oswald Rothaug was Presiding Judge of the Special Court at Nuremberg from 1937 to 1943 (he was later transferred to Berlin to serve as Senior Prosecutor in the People's Court), and now was sitting as a criminal defendant in the same courthouse where he judged others. Rothaug presided over the notorious Leo Katzenberger case, the sixty-eight-year old head of the Nuremberg Jewish community whom Rothaug sentenced to death for "racial pollution" based on Katzenberger's friendship with his younger female neighbor. His pronouncements from the bench and his judicial opinions were openly antisemitic and also prejudiced against Polish defendants. In one case, he spoke of the "Polish subhuman race."[77] Rothaug began the Katzenberger trial with the infamous Nazi proclamation "The Jews are our misfortune."[78]

Rudolf Oeschey was a fellow judge of Rothaug at Nuremberg and succeeded Rothaug as Presiding Judge of the Special Court. He sentenced to death, among others, a Polish widow named Sofie Kaminska, under the Law Against Poles and Jews for scuffling with a German policeman. In the tribunal's opinion, "this is . . . a case of such a perversion of judicial process as to shock the conscience of mankind."[79] Oeschey likewise expressed openly his prejudices against Jews and Poles.

Franz Schlegelberger, described by Taylor as "[t]he principal defendant in the Nuremberg dock" in *Case No. 3*,[80] was a more complex figure because he was not a Nazi fanatic, and so was representative of the legion of German jurists who joined the Nazi cause. Schlegelberger was already an accomplished jurist when the Nazis came to power. He had served as a judge and was a respected scholar when he became the deputy chief of the Reich Justice Ministry. At one point, he even served as Acting Minister of Justice. Schlegelberger was one of the principal drafters of the Law Against Poles and Jews and assisted its implementation in the occupied Eastern Territories. The prosecution presented numerous instances of Schlegelberger creating, implementing, and enforcing Nazi policy under the guise of law. Schlegelberger dismissed judges who imposed what he considered to be too lenient sentences. He also intervened in cases when Hitler disagreed with a court decision. In one case involving a German Jew named Markus Luftglass, the court sentenced the seventy-four-year-old defendant to thirty months' imprisonment for the crime of hoarding eggs. Hitler, upon reading a news story of the verdict, informed Schlegelberger that he wanted the defendant to be sentenced to death. Schlegelberger's missive of October 29, 1941, explains what took place next: "On receiving the Führer's command passed on to me by the Minister of State and Head of the Chancellery I handed over the Jew, Markus Luftglass, who was sentenced by the Special Court at Kattowitz to 2-1/2 years' imprisonment, to the Secret State Police for execution."[81]

In his defense, Schlegelberger argued that he harbored no personal animus toward Jews. He testified that his personal physician was half-Jewish and that his best friend was a Jewish judge whom he earlier saved from execution. He claimed that even though he viewed Hitler as an enemy of the rule of law, he continued to work for the Hitler regime so that he could moderate Nazi excesses. If he resigned, Schlegelberger argued, a Nazi zealot would take his place and pervert the law even more. Schlegelberger retired in 1942 at age sixty-six. His successor Otto Thierack was indeed more cruel, essentially turning over the administration of justice to the SS and the police.

In the end, the American judges found that Schlegelberger "loathed the evil" for which he was responsible but yet traded his intellect and ability for a "mess of political pottage and for the vain hope of personal security."[82] The court pointed out that upon retirement, Hitler awarded Schlegelberger 100,000 reichsmarks and permission to purchase a farm as reward for "good and faithful service."[83] The court found Schlegelberger to be a tragic figure who nevertheless deserved severe punishment for committing acts that amounted to war crimes and crimes against humanity.

Concurrently with the Justice Trial, the NMT prosecutors started another trial in the Palace of Justice, *Case No. 4* and formally known as *United States v. Oswald Pohl et al.* This was the first of three cases brought against high-ranking SS officials involved in the operation of a vast empire throughout occupied Europe: concentration and labor camps, mines, and factories all run by the SS. SS boss Heinrich Himmler committed suicide by swallowing a cyanide capsule shortly after being captured by the British, and so the lead defendants were his underlings. Lead defendant Oswald Pohl was the chief of the economic and administrative department of the SS. According to the prosecution, approximately ten million persons were imprisoned in the camps. Specific charges against Pohl and sixteen others included imprisonment of civilians of foreign countries and prisoners of war; exploitation of these individuals as forced laborers; medical experiments conducted on prisoners; and plundering of their property. The case closed nine months later and verdicts issued on November 3, 1947. Three defendants were acquitted. All the defendants were acquitted of crimes against peace, but convicted (save one) of both war crimes and crimes against humanity. Three defendants were sentenced to death, but only Pohl was hanged. None of the other convicted defendants (including four sentenced to life imprisonment) served their full terms, all released by 1951.

On February 8, 1947, *Case No. 5*, and formally known as *United States v. Friedrich Flick et al.* (Flick Trial) began, the first of three industrialist trials. Five other officials of the Flick concern were also indicted. Specific counts included slave labor and spoliation and "Aryanization" of property in occupied countries. The defendants argued that they had no choice but to work with the Nazis or, as summarized by Taylor, "their ostensible agreement with Nazi racial ideas were self-protective measures described by Flick as 'howling with the wolves.'"[84] In less poetic terms, Flick explained: "After the [Nazi] seizure of power, every industrialist in the long run had to get into some sort of relationship with the new holders of power."[85] And, incredulously, he maintained that the Jewish-owned companies he acquired under the Nazis were legitimate business deals.[86]

Flick was found guilty of economic plunder and given a seven-year prison sentence. Three of his co-defendants were acquitted and two were given prison terms ranging from six years to two and a half years. Taylor describes the judgment as "exceedingly (if not excessively) moderate and conciliatory"[87]—code words for lenient. As for misuse of legal doctrine, the judges accepted the defendants' defense of "necessity"—a narrow defense in criminal law, recognized only in the most extreme circumstances when a defendant commits a crime only because he or she would be killed or suffer serious bodily harm for failure to comply. No evidence was offered that these defendants would suffer such a fate if they refused to plunder or employ slave labor at the Flick plants. And the punishment meted upon them by the court soon became irrelevant. Just three years later, Flick was released and his company returned to him. In 1972, at the time of his death, he was one of the world's wealthiest individuals.

On May 3, 1947, *Case No. 6*, the second industrialist trial and commonly known as the Farben Trial began.[88] Twenty-four officials of the I.G. Farben industrial concern, dissolved by the Allies through Control Council Law No. 9, were indicted, with one dismissed before verdict. In terms of lack of scruples, there has never been a corporate giant like Farben. Working closely with the Nazi leadership, the company coordinated the takeover of entire factories in Poland, France, Norway, and the Soviet Union on the heels of Germany's invasions of these countries. Its volume of plunder was enormous. Farben also supplied the Zyklon-B poison gas for the mass murder in concentration and death camps. It built its Buna Werke factory next to Auschwitz, striking a business deal with the SS to supply it with Auschwitz prisoners to work as slaves in the factory. Over 80,000 prisoners worked as slaves for Buna Werke, with a life expectancy of three to four months—and less if they worked in the nearby Farben mines. At the direction of the Farben bosses, the slave workers were driven mercilessly to increase production. Those unable to work were sent to Birkenau, the camp adjoining Auschwitz, to be gassed.

Taylor explained that "[i]n the prosecution's mind, the evidence against the Farben defendants was the strongest of all the industrialist trials."[89] The judges thought otherwise. Ten defendants were acquitted, the largest percentage of any of the twelve trials. Others were convicted either for plunder or use of slave labor, or both, as war crimes or crimes against humanity, both with quite lenient prison terms. Most were soon released and many became captains of banking and industry in postwar West Germany.[90]

On May 10, 1947, indictments were filed in *Case No. 7*, also known as the *Hostages Case*. The defendants were twelve German army generals involved in Germany's conquest and occupation of Greece, Albania, and Yugoslavia. Defendants were charged with various war crimes, especially reprisals against civilian populations for partisan activity and execution of POWs. This was the first trial of the generals of the regular army, the Wehrmacht; the High Command (Trial No. 12) being the second. Two generals were sentenced to life imprisonment, with the other convicted defendants receiving sentences between fifteen and twenty years. Two defendants were acquitted. All convicted were released within three years by the American occupation authorities.

The judgment contained some strange notions of international law. All three countries had a high rate of resistance to the occupation, with irregular militias—called partisans—attacking German soldiers. The German army's response was to inflict collective punishment, that is, one hundred random civilians shot for every German soldier killed. The court decided that such responses do not violate international law. With regard to partisans, the court held that upon capture they were not entitled to status and protection of lawful belligerents. As for hostages, the court explained that while "the idea that an innocent person may be killed for the criminal act of another is abhorrent to every natural law . . . it is not our province to write international law as we would have it—we must apply it as we find it. An examination of the available evidence on the subject convinces us that hostages may be taken in order to guarantee the peaceful conduct of the populations of occupied territories and, when certain conditions exist and the necessarily preliminaries have been taken, they may be, as a last resort, shot."[91] This strange pronouncement, however, was irrelevant since the court held that these conditions and preliminaries were not met by the German army. In harsh language it condemned the acts of the Wehrmacht:

> Mass shootings of the innocent populations, deportations for slave labor and the indiscriminate destruction of public and private property, not only in Yugoslavia and Greece but in many other countries as well, lend credit to the assertion that terrorism and intimidation was the accepted solution to any and all opposition to the German will. . . . The guilt of the German occupation forces is not only proven beyond a reasonable doubt but it casts a pall of shame upon a once highly respected nation and its people.[92]

The last sentence is critical, since it flies in the face of the myth held by most Germans that the Wehrmacht had "clean hands" during the war. The attraction of this myth is not surprising, considering that 20 million Germans served in the army. To accept the Nuremberg judges' findings in this case and in the *High Command Case* (see below), "would have implicated vast portions of German society in Nazi crime."[93]

Case No. 8, United States v. Ulrich Greifelt, et al. and commonly known as the *RuSHA (Rasse- und Siedlungshauptamt) Case*, was the second SS case before the NMT, and involved fourteen (including thirteen members of the SS) defendants associated primarily with the SS Main Race and Resettlement Office and the SS Main Office for Repatriation of Racial Germans. These offices, under the supervision of SS chief Himmler, were the backbone of the Nazi racial program. The trial featured the other female defendant at Nuremberg, Inge Viermetz, accused of abducting Polish children with Aryan features who were brought to the Reich for "Germanization" under the so-called *Lebensborn* program. Defendants were accused of crimes against humanity by taking part in "a systematic program of genocide, aimed at the destruction of foreign nations and ethnic groups, in part by murderous extermination, and in part by elimination and suppression of national characteristics."[94] While the court found that "thousands upon thousands" of foreign children were kidnapped, the prosecution did not prove that the *Lebensborn* Society officials were involved in the kidnappings. Viermetz was the only defendant acquitted of all charges. Three others were released for time already served. The others received sentences ranging from life imprisonment to ten years. None served their full sentences, with those not dying in prison released by 1955.

Case No. 9, United States of America v. Otto Ohlendorf, et al. is commonly known as the *Einsatzgruppen Case.*[95] On July 30, 1947, indictments were issued and verdicts announced on April 10, 1948. As discussed in Chapter 1, the *Einsatzgruppen* were special military units of the SS attached to the regular Germany army whose specific task was to round up and execute Jews and Soviet commissars in captured Soviet territory beginning in mid-1941. The killing method was by bullet, with mobile gas vans later used to make the killings more efficient and less traumatic

Illustration 10 Fifteen-year-old Maria Dolezalova testifies as a prosecution witness at the Nuremberg RuSHA Trial, Trial #8, Oct. 30, 1947. Because of her "Aryan" features, Maria was spared from death and forced to live with a German family after the Germans on June 9, 1942 destroyed the town of Lidice, Czechoslovakia and murdered most of its inhabitants as group reprisal for the assasination of SS leader Reinhard Heydrich. Children suitable for "Germanizing" were placed with SS families in the Reich and raised as Germans. US Holocaust Memorial Museum, photograph 07341, courtesy of Hedwig Wachenheimer Epstein.

for the *Einsatz* personnel, who had to murder women and children eye-to-eye at close proximity. Approximately one million Jews and others were "liquidated" in this manner.[96] The twenty-four defendants were either commanders or subordinate officers of these units. Chief Prosecutor Benjamin Ferencz (and today at age ninety-six the last living Nuremberg prosecutor) began his opening speech:

> May it please your Honors: It is with sorrow and with hope that we here disclose the deliberate slaughter of more than a million innocent and defenseless men, women, and children. This was the tragic fulfillment of a program of intolerance and arrogance. Vengeance is not our goal, nor do we seek merely a just retribution. We ask this Court to affirm by international penal action man's right to live in peace and dignity regardless of his race or creed. The case we present is a plea of humanity to law. . . . The defendants were commanders and officers of special SS groups knows as Einsatzgruppen—established for the specific purpose of massacring human beings because they were Jews, or because they were for some other reason regarded as inferior peoples. . . . We shall show that these deeds of men in uniform were the methodical execution of long-range plans to destroy ethnic, national, political, and religious groups which stood condemned in the Nazi mind. Genocide, the extermination of whole categories of human beings, was a foremost instrument of the Nazi doctrine.[97]

Ferencz presented his case solely through documents—field reports sent to Berlin detailing the numbers killed and locations—and rested after two days. The defense next took 136 days to present their defense.[98] Their chief argument was that they were simply following orders and believed that all Jews had to be killed for reasons of military necessity. Asked to explain why it was necessary to murder Jewish babies, infants, and children, SS General Otto Ohlendorf, the chief defendant who first admitted at the IMT trial that his *Einsatzgruppe* D killed some 90,000 Jews, explained: "[T]he children were people who would grow up and surely being the children of parents who had been killed, they would constitute a danger no smaller than that of the parents."[99]

All defendants were convicted, with fourteen of the twenty defendants who reached verdict condemned to death. The remainder received sentences ranging from life to time served. The Cold War impacted greatly the fate of these defendants. Only four death sentences were carried out, with the remainder of the defendants set free by mid-1958.

On August 17, 1947, *Case No. 10*, the third and last of the industrialist cases, began with the filing of an indictment against Alfried Krupp, head of Krupp Industries, and ten of his associates in the *Krupp Case*. Defendants were charged with crimes against peace and exploitation of slave labor, with tens of thousands of slaves working for the Krupp concern during the war. All were found guilty and given prison terms ranging from twelve years to two years and ten months. Krupp was given a sentence of twelve years and his family enterprise was taken away from him.

The postscript to the Krupp trial provides another egregious example of the postwar rejection of the achievements of the NMT. Krupp was released after just four years in prison, and his properties were restored to him. In 1957, *Time* magazine featured Krupp on its cover, lauding his contribution to restoring the economy of West Germany. His wartime deeds were barely mentioned. By that time, Krupp had become the richest man in Europe.

On November 1, 1947, the indictment in *Case No. 11*, known also as the *Ministries Case*, was filed. Prosecuted were members of the German diplomatic corps and others involved in international affairs during the Nazi era. Since the defendant diplomats and others participated in formulating or executing Germany's invasions of many of its neighbors and beyond, a large focus of the *Ministries Case* was the contours of the crime of waging an aggressive war, as enunciated by the IMT. The tribunal followed IMT precedent that waging an aggressive war amounts to "crimes against peace." The indictment also included war crimes and crimes against humanity committed against Jews and Slavic populations through "a systematic program of genocide" of these peoples. For crimes against peace, the court held that complete blame cannot be placed on Hitler, since it would not have been possible to wage aggressive wars without the devotion and skill of the men around him. Five defendants were convicted of crimes against peace, the *only* defendants in the twelve trials to have been so convicted. Two defendants were acquitted. Others received prison terms ranging from twenty-five years to time served. The court's judgment was issued on April 14, 1949, the last of the NMT judgments. The next month, the Federal Republic of Germany was created out of the three Western occupation zones.

On November 28, 1947, indictments in *Case No. 12*, the so-called *High Command Case*, were filed.[100] The defendants, Hitler's Wehrmacht generals, were charged with crimes against peace by participating in invasions of neighboring European states. As in the *Ministries Case*, this tribunal found that the generals could be found guilty if they were in a position to shape or influence the planning, initiation, or continuance of the war. Crimes against peace during the Second World War were not a "one-man crime" of just the Commander in Chief of the German Forces. Generals who planned aggression with Hitler could be guilty under international law; field commanders could not. As the court explained:

> Thus, it is a defendant's power to shape or influence State policy rather than rank or status which determines a defendant's criminality under the charge of Crimes Against Peace. International law condemns those who, due to their actual power to shape and influence the policy of their nation, prepare

> for, or lead their country into or in an aggressive war. But we do not find that, at the present stage of development, international law declares as criminals those below that level who, in the execution of this war policy, act as the instruments of the policy makers. Anybody who is on the policy level and participates in the war policy is liable to punishment. But those under them cannot be punished for the crimes of others.[101]

The court rejected the superior orders defense made by the German generals since "[t]he practical effect [of this defense is] to say that all the guilt charged in the indictment was the guilt of Hitler alone. . . . [T]o recognize such a contention would be to recognize an absurdity."[102] Defendants were also charged with war crimes and crimes against humanity for implementing orders that they knew were patently illegal, since they called for the execution of POWs and civilians.

Verdicts were issued on October 27, 1948. Eleven of the thirteen generals present to hear the verdicts (one committed suicide while in custody) were found guilty; two were fully acquitted. To the prosecution's surprise, none of the generals on the dock were convicted of crimes against peace, only of war crimes and crimes against humanity, since none met the court's leadership requirements. Two received life sentences, which they did not serve, while others received prison terms ranging from twenty-five years to time served, with the former also released early. As this last Nuremberg trial was ongoing, the Soviets began the blockade of Berlin. Germany was now our friend and ally. What happened next reflected this new reality.

2. "Noel, Noel, What the Hell"

Taylor's original plan for the NMT was to hold at least thirty-six trials.[103] He later maintained that with sufficient time and resources, he could have convicted between 2,000 and 20,000 defendants.[104] As it was, the American prosecutors were lucky to be able to bring to judgment the 177 Germans put on trial. But the world was a different place in 1949 than it was in 1946, when the trials started. In March 1946, Winston Churchill gave his Iron Curtain speech in Fulton, Missouri. Once again, as with his prewar warnings about Hitler, Churchill was right. Soviet dictator Josef Stalin never fulfilled his pledges made to the United States and Britain at the 1945 Yalta Conference to facilitate free elections in Eastern European states liberated by Soviet troops, instead turning them into satellite states tethered to the Kremlin. By 1949, the Eastern European states of Poland, Czechoslovakia, Hungary, and others freed by the Red Army had been transformed into people's republics. The Western Allies feared that other European states would follow. Western Germany was now the first line of defense against the spread of

Communism. Congressional delegations visiting Germany were putting pressure on the NMT prosecutors to close up shop and move on. The Germans were now our friends and the Russians our enemy.

The Cold War began seeping into the NMT courtrooms. As Taylor was to report to the secretary of the army upon conclusion of his assignment: "On the whole, it was apparent to anyone connected with the entire series of trials under Law No. 10 that sentences became progressively lighter as time went on."[105] The presiding judge of the *High Command Case* (the last of the NMT proceedings that began in December 1947 and ended in October 1948) candidly wrote to his son as the trial was ongoing "that his hatred of the Soviets and fear of a Soviet invasion of Nuremberg were so profound that the defendants' crimes no longer seemed 'so bad' to him."[106]

As the verdicts were issued for each of the trials, American politicians stateside and elites in Germany began a campaign to free those convicted by the American occupation courts, including the NMT. The government of Chancellor Konrad Adenauer, not long after the establishment of the Federal Republic in May 1949, publicly announced its objectives of seeking to "pardon . . . offenses . . . arising from the bygone period of distress and transition."[107] In the German parliament, "speakers from every German political party except the Communists attacked the theory of the trials—or the continued imprisonment of convicts—or both" and called for a single, sweeping amnesty.[108] German clergy and veterans groups likewise played a large role in the process; it soon became of the favorite subjects of the German press. The amnesty campaign raised four arguments: (1) the trials lacked legality since no war crimes were committed; (2) the trials applied ex post facto laws; (3) the trials were victor's justice; and (4) the defendants were only following orders.

General Lucius Clay, the head of the American occupation zone, held firm, but his successor, John McCloy, who now became known as the US High Commissioner for Germany, buckled. Soon after arriving in Germany in September 1949, McCloy began pardoning or severely reducing the sentences of those serving prison sentences at War Crimes Prison Nr. 1, the Landsberg Prison outside of Munich. In his own words, the death sentences of "only the worst of the worst" would be confirmed.[109] The last hanging at Landsberg took place in 1951.[110] By May 1952, only thirty-five men out of an original 142 convicted by the NMT courts remained at Landsberg.[111]

In May 1958, thirteen years to the month after the war ended, the Americans' Nazi prosecution program formally ended with the closure of War Crimes Prison Nr. 1.[112] The last of the NMT defendants walked out of Landsberg a free man. The German politicians and clerics who joined the daily protesters outside of Landsberg to free the "beacons of the German *Volk* in their struggle for justice and the reconciliation of nations" had won. [113] And Krupp and Flick were not only freed, but their empires were returned to them. Others also went on to prominence in the new Federal Republic of Germany. American complicity with the Germans in the scrubbing of history went even so far that "the Americans hesitated even to use the words 'war crimes' and 'war criminals' in later public discussions. . . . When they sought to inform the public at all, they spoke frequently in terms of common crimes ever more remotely connected with the war and Nazism."[114] The British felt the same. On April 12, 1948, the Overseas Reconstruction Committee of the British cabinet agreed that "no further trials of war criminals should be started after 31 August, 1948."[115]

Benjamin Ferencz, chief prosecutor in the *Einsatzgruppen* NMT trial, in a letter to his former boss Telford Taylor in December 1951, expressed his frustration.

> I notice in this morning's paper that a group of our Landsberg friends have been given their freedom as a Christmas present. These include . . . three Einsatzgruppen boys, Schubert, Jost and Nosske. Schubert confessed to personally supervising the execution of about 800 Jews in a humane manner to avoid the moral strain on the execution squad. You may recall that the deadline for cleaning up Simferopol was Christmas 1941 and that Schubert managed to kill all the Jews by then. So for Christmas ten years later he goes Scot free. Who says there is no Santa Klaus? Nosske was the one whom the other defendants called the biggest bloodhound of the day after the sentences were imposed and [he] only received twenty years. Now Nosske is free to join former Gen. Jost whose command ordered a fourth gas van when the three in operation executing women and children were insufficient to do the job properly. Noel, Noel, what the hell.[116]

A bitter Taylor penned an article for *The Nation* in 1951 titled "The Nazis Go Free."[117] And so, "[t]he history of the [NMT] trials, in short, is the (early) history of the Cold War," [118] with justice being the first casualty. Reading about the eventual fate of the convicted NMT defendants invokes only feelings of outrage. According to Valerie Hébert, "the [Nuremberg] trials' goals of justice and education were a failure."[119] Soon, the NMT proceedings became ancient history, the forgotten stepchildren of the IMT.

3. Legacy of the NMT

Photos of Göring and his fellow defendants on the dock in Courtroom 600 have become iconic in the post-Holocaust era. Documentaries and YouTube videos about the IMT trial abound. Not so for any of the NMT trials. The sole exception (with regard to films) is the Hollywood classic *Judgment at Nuremberg*, a fictional account of the Justice Trial made in 1961. But even that film is often confused with the IMT trial. This is a shame, because the NMT trials are as worthy of post-Holocaust memory as the IMT.

First, as Kevin Heller points out, "[t]he tribunals generated a massive documentary record of Nazi criminality, one that dwarfs the IMT." He explains:

> [T]he transcripts of the twelve trials run 132,855 legal-size pages and include the testimony of more than 1,300 witnesses and the contents of more than 30,000 separate documents. The twelve judgments, in turn,—which total 3,828 pages—reflect the factual density of the trials, describing at great length everything from Hitler's transformation of the German courts into "a nationally organized system of injustice and persecution" (Justice) to the role that German industrialists played in financing Hitler's rise to power and equipping the Nazi war machine (Flick, Farben, Krupp) to how the Reich planned its various invasions and wars of aggression (Ministries).[120]

Robert Kempner, one of Taylor's deputies, described the trials as "the greatest history seminar ever held."[121] As Heller notes, "th[e] vast historical record [produced by the NMT trials] will be of use to lawyers and historians for decades to come."[122]

Unlike at the IMT, the Holocaust was front and center in all of the twelve NMT trials. Because the Holocaust was not a major focus of the IMT, it was during the American zonal trials that the world learned in detail how these murders took place and the important segments of German society that participated in them. Moreover, the American prosecutors made a conscious decision to try to place the extermination of the Jews within the framework of the law, labeling it a genocide, though the crime was not yet officially on the books. In the end, the evidentiary and documentary record meant that "only the most committed apologist could maintain that the Holocaust—and the Nazis' other crimes—beyond number—were 'fable, not fact.' "[123]

Second, the NMT trials also became the first set of tribunals to apply the jurisprudence created by the IMT and thereby solidifying it as legal precedent. The "Nuremberg crimes" set out in the Charter were now applied to another set of German defendants. The NMT tribunals, in the words of Kevin Heller, "took the raw materials provided to them—the London Charter, the IMT judgment, Law No. 10—and honed them into a coherent system of criminal law, one in which crimes were divided into elements, modes of participation were precisely identified, and defenses made available but cabined within reasonable limits."[124] This, in turn, set the precedent for the Nuremberg jurisprudence that today forms the corpus of international criminal law (see Chapter 8).

The most important principle confirmed by the NMT was of individual criminal responsibility under international law. As the judgment in the *High Command*

Case put it: "[I]t would be an utter disregard of reality and . . . legal shadow-boxing" to rule that a state is responsible for atrocities while those who "devise and execute" these polices are immune from legal culpability.[125] And as the *Einsatzgruppen Case* judgment noted, the NMT defendants were "in court not as members of a defeated nation but because they are charged with crime. They are being tried because they are accused of having offended against society itself, and society, as represented by international law, has summoned them for explanation."[126]

Of course, the NMT tribunals had an easier time to deal with this issue, since they could rely on the IMT precedent. Once the IMT judgment announced that the so-called arch-criminals like Göring and seventeen of his co-defendants were criminally responsible for war crimes and crimes against humanity, it was logical for the NMT judges to hold the same for the second-tier Nazis before them.

The NMT judges also harkened back to Justice Jackson's poisoned chalice reference, realizing that they were creating a precedent that applies to all international criminals going forward. As the judgment in the *Ministries Case* explained:

> We must not forget that guilt is a personal matter; that men are to be judged not by theoretical, but by practical standards; that we are here to define a standard of conduct of responsibility, not only for Germans as the vanquished in war, not only with regard to past and present events, but those which in the future can be reasonably and properly applied to men and officials of every state and nation, those of the victors as well as those of the vanquished. Any other approach would make a mockery of international law and would result in wrongs quite as serious and fatal as those which were sought to be remedied.[127]

Crimes against peace—the "supreme crime" before the IMT—did not fare as well before the NMT, and is one reason why it has yet (if ever) to become part of modern international criminal law jurisprudence.[128] Many of those charged with crimes against peace were acquitted of that charge before the NMT. Responsibility for crimes against peace was limited only to those who set policy and so knowingly participated in the preparation, planning, initiation, or waging of an aggressive war. In contrast, criminal responsibility for war crimes and crimes against humanity was not limited to high-echelon officials.

Third, the NMT trials also created their own significant jurisprudence. For example, the Medical and Justice Trials, by rejecting defendants' claims that they had acted in accordance with existing German laws, established the norm that the accused cannot validly assert immunity from prosecution because he or she acted in accordance with the law of the state where the international crime took place. This is in contrast to the IMT judgment, where, as Heller points out, "there is remarkably little criminal law. . . . nothing on evidence and procedure; almost nothing on modes of participation, defenses, or sentencing. Even the discussion of the crimes themselves is relatively cursory and unsystematic. The NMTs, by contrast, addressed all of those areas in detail."[129]

Fourth, the American judges in these later trials conscientiously considered the evidence and dismissed charges and acquitted defendants for whom the prosecution could not show guilt beyond a reasonable doubt. This helped to confirm the international norm that accused international criminals, no matter how serious the atrocities they are accused of, must receive a fair trial. Without the later NMT trials at Nuremberg, the IMT trial would be viewed less favorably today and would have a lesser impact on international criminal law. As David Glazier has pointed out: "[T]he twelve U.S. Nuremberg trials judged seven times as many defendants as the International Military Tribunal (IMT) and addressed a broader spectrum of international criminal law issues. . . ."[130]

Finally, there is the unfortunate negative legacy of the NMT: the trials being the first instances of Nazi perpetrators literally getting away with mass murder. The 177 defendants actually prosecuted by Taylor and his team represented only a small percentage of prosecutable "Major War Criminals." More egregious, even most of those put on trial escaped the punishment imposed on them. Of the twenty-eight death penalties issued by the American judges at the NMT trials, twenty-one were converted to prison terms; sixty-nine of the seventy-four prison sentences handed in for revision were reduced; and thirty-two detainees were released immediately. As noted earlier, the last NMT defendant was set free by the Americans in 1958. Among those were the industrialists, granted clemency by McCloy in January 1951, setting the message that at most they were "white collar criminals." Convicted insider traders today serve longer sentences than those served by Flick, Krupp, and the I.G. Farben executives.

4

National Prosecutions of Nazi War Criminals

In 1948, the UN War Crimes Commission published its so-called Central Registry of War Criminals and Security Suspects (CROWCASS). The CROWCASS list contained over 60,000 names.[1] Only a minuscule number were ever prosecuted. This chapter discusses some of the notable prosecutions, focusing on three countries: Germany, Israel, and the United States.

A. PROSECUTIONS IN GERMANY

The successful postwar movement in West Germany in the late 1940s and 1950s to free Germans found guilty by the Allied occupation tribunals meant that the new Bonn Republic was not going to seriously prosecute Nazis in their midst. Eight million Germans were members of the Nazi Party at the end of the war, and they and their families wanted to move on. Forgetting the immediate past was a worldwide phenomenon, not just in Germany, but it was in Germany that the motto went "Let the past lie." If the past was to be remembered, it would be the past of Germans as also victims of the war.[2] It would not have been surprising if no Nazi trials took place in the Bonn Republic. Nevertheless, there remained a committed few who were not ready to sweep the crimes of the Nazi era under the rug. These included some politicians, journalists, legal actors, and survivors. Included also in this group were German Jews who returned home after the war. Among them was a Jewish lawyer named Fritz Bauer, who played a leading role in the Frankfurt Auschwitz trial discussed in this chapter.[3] Bauer lived out the war years in neutral Sweden and returned to Germany in 1949, the same year that the Federal Republic of Germany was formed by the Western allies. A decade later Bauer became chief prosecutor in State of Hesse (where Frankfurt is located) and remained in this position until his death in 1968. A Jewish Nazi-hunter living in postwar Germany was not a well-liked man. Bauer once commented: "When I leave my office, I enter enemy territory."[4] Through efforts of Bauer and others, more than 6,000 Nazis stood trial in West Germany. Another 100,000 were investigated but never tried.[5]

For proponents of prosecution, the first problem was the upcoming statute of limitations. Under the German Penal Code, all forms of criminal homicide are subject to a statute of limitations. The German parliament (Bundestag) agreed to extend the limitations period for murder for Nazi crimes, but not for manslaughter, which expired in 1959. From that year on, Nazi killers could only be prosecuted for *murder* or the lesser crime of *accomplice to murder*. In 1968, the Bundestag made accomplice to murder more difficult to prosecute through a change in the criminal code. From then on, an accomplice to a crime could receive the same sentence as the actual perpetrator only if both shared the same *mens rea*. Otherwise, the accomplice to murder had to receive a lesser sentence, with fifteen years being the maximum sentence.[6]

Another obstacle was that West German jurists refused to accept the Nuremberg precedent on the ground that these international and occupation tribunals convicted on the basis of ex post facto laws. This demonization of Nuremberg and everything that it represented reached its apex in 1951 when the Federal Ministry of Justice and the newly created Federal Supreme Court purged "Allied Control Council Law 10" from German law books, with the first president of the Supreme Court labeling it a "foreign cell" in German jurisprudence.[7] And so, without the Nuremberg trials as a precedent, the resurrected courts of the Federal Republic turned to German penal law for bringing Nazi war criminals to justice. As a result, in all German prosecutions for Nazi crimes over the last seventy years, no German was charged with committing war crimes or crimes against humanity. Rather, these individuals were tried as common criminals, charged with murder and the derivative crimes of complicity to murder and manslaughter, and the latter soon became unavailable because of the statute of limitations. The problem was that the way a common criminal would be tried under German law for a murder of one human being simply did not fit the mass atrocities perpetrated by Germans.

Compounding the problem of prosecuting for Nazi crimes was that the Allied denazification campaign instituted by the Allies was a total failure. The few who lost their positions soon regained them. In 1949, West Germany passed an amnesty law that reintegrated 30,000 civil servants and professional soldiers back into society. A second amnesty law enacted two years later (the infamous "131 law") provided for a general amnesty for all Nazi-era state officials who had been sacked in 1945, giving them the right to a state job in the new Bonn republic. And this amnesty decree covered judges and other legal actors from the Nazi period. Consequently, the postwar West German judiciary and almost the entire legal establishment became rife with former Nazis. Approximately 80 percent of judges and prosecutors during the Nazi era returned to their old jobs.[8]

The combination of judging Nazi mass murderers as common criminals and prosecution before judges and by prosecutors who just a few years earlier themselves were enforcing Nazi law, led to an obvious result: only the most guilty would be prosecuted and, when put on trial, these would either be acquitted or receive very lenient sentences. While there was a spate of prosecutions and convictions from 1945 to 1949 under the watchful eyes of the occupation authorities, these soon died down with the creation of the Federal Republic. From 1950 to 1957, prosecutions significantly dropped.

A major transition took place in 1958, after the Ulm *Einsatzgruppen* trial (which we will examine in this chapter), and in its wake, the creation of a dedicated government unit to investigate cases of possible Nazi criminality. The ZS—short for the Central Office of the Land Judicial Authorities for the Investigation of National Socialist Crimes of Violence (*Zentrale Stelle der Landesjustizverwaltungen zur Aufklärungen national-sozialistischer Gewaltverbrechen*), abbreviated as the Central Office (*Zentrale Stelle*)—was created by state prosecutors in Ludwigsburg and began operations on December 1, with the Ulm trial's chief prosecutor Erwin Schüle as its head. It was given a limited mandate. Schüle and his team were not tasked to conduct actual prosecutions. Instead, the ZS's job was to investigate suspected cases of Nazi criminality and then turn over the dossier for cases it felt were prosecutable to local prosecutors. The ZS also could not investigate crimes committed in Germany, including German concentration camps like Dachau. Its jurisdiction was limited to crimes committed on foreign territory by Germans and others now living in the Federal Republic. The principal focus was crimes in the East, principally in concentration camps in occupied Poland and other mass killing sites in the Baltics and the Soviet Union.

From 1958 to 1993, the ZS launched more than 120,000 investigations, of which 4,853 led to actual prosecutions.[9] Its mission, however, was not an easy one. The public was reluctant to provide information. Suspects, when investigated, often covered for each other or refused to cooperate. ZS investigators were mockingly referred to as *Nestbeschmutzer*, literally those who soil their own nests. Moreover, the murders were so thorough that few or no survivors who could provide eyewitness testimony remained. Finding non-Jewish bystanders who witnessed the killings was also difficult since these, for the most part, were now living behind the Iron Curtain. By the time the Cold War ended, many of these witnesses were no longer alive, or considered less credible due to the long passage of time between the crimes and prosecutions. In total, including the early round of prosecutions immediately after the war, 6,498 individuals were convicted of Nazi crimes. Of these only 169 received life sentences.[10]

The accepted myth that the real evildoers were the Nazi leaders—Hitler, Himmler, and Goebbels—or the "three-men crime" theory,[11] neatly translated into distinctions that existing German penal law made between a perpetrator

(*Täter*) under German Penal Code § 211[12] and an accomplice (*Gehilfe*) under §§ 26 and 27. If the three Nazi leaders were perpetrators, then everyone else was an accomplice. Those who killed intentionally but without the *mens rea* elements of murder could initially be found guilty of manslaughter under Penal Code § 212, but this option became unavailable after 1960 since it carried a fifteen-year statute of limitations. An effort that year to extend the limitations period beyond 1960 failed in the Bundestag. This failure is all the more egregious since international law in the post-Holocaust era does not recognize a limitations period for war crimes and related atrocities.[13] And so those brought to trial after 1960 for the genocide committed in the conquered territories of the East were in most instances adjudged to be accomplices to these gruesome crimes, with the real culprits ensconced in Berlin at the time, since they killed on the orders of their superiors.

The maximum sentence of life imprisonment (the death penalty being abolished in 1949) was reserved for the so-called "excess perpetrators"—the few sadists who killed for personal pleasure and thus fit within the *mens rea* requirement of § 211 that the killer must have harbored "blood lust" at the time of the killing. The trial process thus became, in the words of Jörg Friedrich, "a search for the mens rea in skulls of the agents of the mass extermination, a search for private excesses in the routine activities [of mass murder]."[14] A finding of excesses (*Exzesstat*) thus became the *sine qua non* for a conviction of murder.

Another category of murderers included those who had internalized the racial hatred of the Nazi leaders and so killed for that reason, but even when the prosecution could prove that the defendant was an unrepentant Nazi, the court was still most likely to issue a verdict of accomplice liability or (guilt for manslaughter before 1959) rather than murder. Killings—even mass killings—committed according to the orders issued was not murder. In the end, between 50 and 85 percent of defendants found guilty by German courts for committing Nazi crimes were adjudged to be accomplices to murder.[15]

In this section, we focus on two significant prosecutions during the old Federal Republic: the so-called Ulm *Einsatzgruppen* trial in 1958 and the Frankfurt Auschwitz trial in 1963. Each of these trials brought to light a different aspect of the Holocaust. The German SS defendants in Ulm were responsible for one of the thousands of the open-air mass killings of Jews that took place on the heels of Germany's June 1941 invasion of the Soviet Union. These murders were done face to face and bullet by bullet, with over one million Jews murdered in all. The SS defendants in the Frankfurt Auschwitz trial a decade later were killers of a different sort: overseers of the largest human slaughterhouse in human history. Their killings were depersonalized, done on a mass scale through chambers filled with human beings killed *en masse* with the Zyklon-B poison gas. The total number killed in Auschwitz was also around one million.

1. The Ulm *Einsatzgruppen* Trial

In 1958, the ten defendants who stood trial in Ulm were still robust men, and so unlike today could not avoid prosecution on grounds of ill health.[16] The heart of the case came down to the claim that these ten defendants had all taken on active leadership roles in the murder squad known as *Einsatzkommando (EK) Tilsit.* EK Tilsit's sole task was to execute Jews, Communists, and other resisters across a twenty-five-mile stretch of the Lithuanian border with Germany. The unit was so named because it was formed from members of the Security Service (SD) and the Gestapo in the German border town of Tilsit (today located in Russia and called Sovetsk) in East Prussia across the Lithuanian border. EK Tilsit first began its murder operations after entering Soviet-occupied Lithuania on June 21, 1941, as part of Operation Barbarossa. The killings were done in three Lithuanian border towns with large Jewish populations.[17] The murder of 5,000 people, mostly Jews, was part of the larger killings of Jews carried out by *Einsatzkommando* 3, of which EK Tilsit was a unit. The total number murdered from July to November 1941 by *Einsatzkommando* 3 was 137,346, according to the meticulous tally kept by its head, Karl Jäger.[18] *Einsatzkommando* 3 was in turn a unit of *Einsatzgruppen* A, attached to Army Group North during the invasion of the Soviet Union. *Einsatzgruppen* A operated in the former Baltic states of Lithuania, Latvia, and Estonia.

The first killings took place in Garsden, within days after the German invasion. A year earlier, Garsden became part of the Soviet Union with the takeover of the Baltic states by the Soviet Union in 1940. The town was on the border of the German Reich, with the German city of Memel just seventeen kilometers away, annexed by Germany in March 1939. Of the population of 3,000, one-half was composed of Jews, making Garsden one of the typical poor *shtetl* towns dotting Eastern Europe. The German takeover of Memel, part of Lithuania, led the Jews of Memel to flee across the border, increasing Garsden's Jewish population in the years before the German invasion. In a routine that duplicated itself a thousand-fold throughout now German-occupied Eastern Europe, the male Jews of Garsden were made to dig their own mass grave, and then shot in groups of ten at the foot of the grave by members of the SD and the Gestapo. In all, 201 Jewish men were murdered by the pit on June 24, and their bodies covered in dirt. A few months later, the Jewish women and children, who had been kept in a barn, were killed in a similar manner. By the end of the year, Garsden and the surrounding towns were declared *judenrein* (cleansed of Jews).

After the war, the surviving members of EK Tilsit returned to West Germany, starting new lives and reintegrating themselves into postwar German society. Their prosecution in 1958 happened because of sheer coincidence, due to the hubris of one individual. By the mid-1950s denazification proceedings had ceased. German local prosecutors had no incentive to prosecute individuals who committed crimes in the conquered territories and outside their immediate jurisdiction. The Allies also began freeing the senior Nazis that they convicted. Many incriminated individuals therefore began to come out of hiding, no longer fearing prosecution. Among them was Bernhard Fischer-Schweder, who had shed his alias to sue in April 1955 for the restoration of his civil service status after being fired from his job. Fischer-Schweder's unsuccessful suit in the Ulm labor court first caught the attention of the press, and then the local prosecutor's office, especially since the media revealed that he was a former SS *Oberführer* (brigadier general). Offended by his perceived mistreatment by the German court and what he considered to be false accusations by the press, Fischer-Schweder wrote a critical letter to the editor.[19] As to why he registered in Ulm under an alias and provided false information about his wartime status, he replied "I had no reason to bring up things that I was not asked about."[20]

Fischer-Schweder's public protests led the state prosecutor of Baden-Wuerttemberg, the German state where Ulm was located, to quietly investigate him. The investigation never proceeded very far. In 1956, a new prosecutor, Erwin Schüle (who later would become the first head of the ZS), took over. Schüle expanded the investigation. Rather than just bringing charges against Fischer-Schweder, Schüle began searching for the whereabouts and fates of the other former members of EK Tilsit. His research revealed that none were prosecuted, or even investigated, for their role in the Holocaust in Lithuania. Schüle made it his goal to put the massacres on the Lithuanian-German border in the context of the entire genocide of the Jews in Lithuania, where 90 percent of the Jewish population (one of the highest in Europe) had been murdered by the end of the war.

While it may seem surprising today, local Germans knew little about the open-air killings committed in the East at the outset of the war, when over one million Jews were murdered on occupied Soviet territory. The returned soldiers did not talk about what they did in the East; only whispers abounded.[21] Schüle's team began by seeking out survivor organizations in Germany and abroad. They also reached out to individual survivors and witnesses, sought materials in archives at Yad Vashem Holocaust Research and Commemoration Center in Israel, as well as the expertise of historians to build their case. These included records of the major *Einsatzgruppen* trial at Nuremberg. The investigators also discovered the existence of five operational reports from the field setting out the activities of EK Tilsit. One report, *Ereignismeldung* #14, dated July 6, 1941, stated:

> From Tilsit three large cleansing actions [*Grosssäuberungsaktionen*] were carried out, and the following were shot:
> - in Garsden 201 people

> - in Krottingen 214 people
> - in Polangen 111 people
>
> In Garsden, the Jewish population supported the Russian border guards in the defense against the German attack. In Krottingen, during the night of the occupation one officer and two billeting officers were surreptitiously shot by the population. In Polangen, on the day after the occupation one officer was furtively shot by the population. In all three large operations, Jews were predominantly liquidated. To be found among them, however, were also Bolshevik functionaries and snipers, who had been handed over as such to the Sicherheitspolizei in part by the Wehrmacht.[22]

In all, the field reports showed that EK Tilsit had carried out eleven mass executions in barely two weeks after the invasion. Despite their best efforts, Schüle's team could not locate any survivors to testify, attesting to the efficiency of the killings. As a result, only one Jewish witness testified at trial: Josef Warscher, a Buchenwald camp survivor who headed the Munich-based *Israelitische Kultusvereinigung*. As put by Warsher during his testimony, "Jews were so thoroughly destroyed in these areas that hardly any survivors remain."[23]

The Defendants

Schüle initially charged Fischer-Schweder with murder, along with two other individuals: Hans-Joachim Böhme and Werner Hersmann. The indictment described them "as murderers, having carried out the premeditated mass murder of people out of base motives and with cruel intentions."[24] Fischer-Schweder served as chief of police of nearby Memel and was identified by numerous witnesses as one of the commanding officers on the scene in at least three of the massacres. He was charged with the murders of 711 individuals. Böhme and Hersmann served as commanders of EK Tilsit. Both were charged with 5,108 counts of murder through the cleansing operations that they carried out. The investigators learned that one other commander, Erich Frohwann, committed suicide a month after the war ended. Three other members of EK Tilsit also committed suicide once they found out that they were being investigated.

Hans-Joachim Böhme, thirty-three years old at the time of the shootings and a member of the Nazi Party since 1933, entered the SS in 1938. Educated and trained as a lawyer, Böhme attained the rank of *SS-Standartenführer*, the highest rank below general. After the war, Böhme started a new life in the small town of Reinstorf near the northern city of Lüneburg. Though he registered under his own name, Böhme hid his particulars by registering under a false passport he obtained during his days in the Gestapo. He claimed that he was a German refugee fleeing from Eastern Germany.

Werner Hersmann, thirty-eight years old in 1941, was the most senior officer below Böhme in the EK Tilsit unit still alive. Hersmann joined the party in 1930 and the SS a year later. By his own account, he remained a committed Nazi even after the war. In 1950, Hersmann was put on trial for the murder of five Germans who publicly turned against Nazism a month before the war ended. Hersmann led the SS squad that executed these five resisters. Found guilty, he was sentenced to eight years' imprisonment. In 1954, Hersmann was paroled. Rather than move into the shadows, Hersmann took an active role as a Nazi apologist, joining those who worked for the release of convicted Nazis. A major figure in this far-right movement was Rudolf Aschenauer, a young attorney based in Munich, who represented Otto Ohlendorf, the chief defendant at the *Einsatzgruppen* trial in Nuremberg. Aschenauer thereafter carved out a legal career representing former Nazis, and took on Hersmann as his client. Aschenauer *de facto* became the lead defense counsel in the Ulm trial, with the other defense counsel often taking cues from his actions.[25] The other seven defendants were initially charged as accessories, accused of "aiding and abetting [*Beihilfe*] deliberately through word and deed in the mass executions carried out by the above mentioned perpetrators at the same time and location."[26] The indictment read that they were being charged with "hundreds of counts of aiding and abetting in murder."[27]

Schüle later asked for a murder conviction for Pranas Lukys, the only non-German defendant, based on evidence produced at trial. Lukys served as a Lithuanian police chief who had assisted the Germans in numerous executions. Fleeing the Red Army, he resettled in Germany after the war, first under a false name and then under his real name.

Five of the defendants charged as accomplices (Werner Kreuzmann, Gerhard Carsten, Franz Behrendt, Harm Harms, and Edwin Sakuth) had been longtime police officers.[28] One, Werner Schmidt-Hammer, had never joined the Nazi Party, and his defense counsel made wide use of this fact to distinguish his client from the fellow co-defendants. Schmidt-Hammer, however, led the shooting squad on the day of the first shooting at Garsden. After the war, he became an optometrist.

Edwin Sakuth worked at the SD office in Memel, a branch of Hersmann's Tilsit office, and coordinated the early shootings with Fischer-Schweder and Frohwann. Carsten headed a border police post operated under Harms and had participated in several mass executions.[29] Behrendt likewise worked under Harms. As director of the border police units, Harms was instrumental in the use of the border police to round up the Jews in the Lithuanian border towns. When arrested, he was working as a shoemaker. Upon interrogation, Harms implicated many of his co-defendants and so proved to be a pivotal witness. Werner Kreuzmann was Böhme's deputy. Sakuth worked at the SD Memel office and coordinated with Fischer-Schweder and Frohwann on the early killings.

The ten men, all officers, were tried for the execution of 5,502 civilians. Notably, none of the actual shooters was put on trial. Schüle explained that "[i]n our view, members of police battalions who took part in executions, so long as they did not commit excesses, should not be investigated as suspects because typically in war these police officers were deployed in close formation by their officer and so a public refusal to carry out orders was impossible."[30] As Schüle was to show at trial, however, refusal to obey an order to shoot innocent civilians in practice carried no penalty. No case has been found of a German soldier punished for such refusal. The real reason for the impunity was that German society was not yet ready to prosecute the ordinary field soldier, even if he was a member of the SS. Hence, the shooter who "did not commit excesses" when repeatedly firing upon innocent women and children at point-blank range at these open-air massacres could be questioned by Schüle and his team, but only as a material witness and not a suspect.

The Trial

The trial began on April 28, 1958, and ended four months later. Presiding was the fifty-three-year-old jurist Edmund Wetzel. Judge Wetzel had never been a Nazi Party member, and so had clean credentials to preside over the trial. Joining him were two other judges, who would determine the verdict in conjunction with six jurors. A majority of two-thirds, or six, was needed to procure a verdict.

For four months, various former German soldiers testified about the involvement of the defendants in the massacres in Lithuania seventeen years earlier.[31] Other witnesses provided background information about the genocide of the Jews in Lithuania, the role of *Einsatzgruppen* A, the command structure of the German occupiers, and the part played by local Lithuanians in rounding up and killing the Jews. Since documents clearly showed defendants to be EK Tilsit members and the number of Jews killed by the unit, their main defense was that they were following orders.

For the initial three defendants charged with murder, the prosecution focused on demonstrating their state of mind at the time of the killings, specifically that they took initiative, displayed hatred of Jews, and went beyond just fulfilling what was Nazi policy at the time. For Fischer-Schweder, witnesses related that at the killing field in Garsden, Fischer-Schweder took out his pistol and shot those Jewish men still alive. During another shooting, Fischer-Schwede had put together an "improvised court" (*Schnellgericht*) to decide which Lithuanians would live or die. He also selected a boy to be killed alongside his father. According to the prosecution, these actions demonstrated that Fischer-Schweder was acting of his own volition and so displayed the base motives necessary to make the case for murder under German law.

As noted, Böhme and Hersmann were co-commanders of EK Tilsit. Böhme portrayed himself as a reluctant Nazi. His incredulous testimony prompted one of the judges to comment: "Come on and prod your heart into action.

Answer for what happened like a man!"[32] Hersmann, on the other hand, was unrepentant and readily admitted to the killings and his role in them. He admitted that he acted on his own volition and believed in the need to murder Jews as enemies of the Reich. As to his *mens rea,* a co-defendant related in his written statement how Hersmann supposedly singled out a Jewish doctor to be shot against the objections of soldiers whom the doctor was treating.[33] One press article opined that Hersmann "is perhaps the only one of the accused who believed truly and deeply in fascist ideology," and the only one "ready to account for the crimes."[34]

The prosecution challenged the necessity of following orders on the pain of death or other severe punishment through a written report submitted by a German historian, Hans-Günther Seraphim, one of the few postwar German academics who studied the Nazi era. In Ulm, he testified: "In more than a decade of research . . . the expert witness has not found a single case that would permit the conclusion that the refusal by an SS officer to execute an extermination order would have led to consequences damaging to his life and limb."[35]

Besides the defense of following orders, the other major defense argument was that all Jews were proponents of "Judeo-Bolshevism" and so naturally would join the terrorist partisans who posed a danger to the German occupation authorities. As Böhme testified: "[T]he destruction of Jews had nothing to do with racial hatred."[36] Of course, the argument falls apart with the murder of children. Böhme's reply was that the children had to be killed "so that they would not make difficulties later for our grandchildren."[37] When asked whether all 5,000 victims, including the murdered Jewish women and children, were "dangerous enemies" of the state, Böhme replied, "It is very difficult to know."[38]

For percipient witness testimony by a non-German, the prosecution brought from Soviet Lithuania Ona Rudaitis, a sixty-seven-year-old retired nurse. Rudaitis testified how coming home from visiting a patient, she ran into a killing operation. Women and children being forced to strip before being led out in groups to a mass grave, where they were immediately shot. She estimated to have seen the murder of two hundred to three hundred Jews.[39] Naturally, she could not identify any of the defendants in the courtroom.

Another star witness was Wilhelm Gerke, a former member of EK Tilsit. Unlike other former members of EK Tilsit, Gerke readily admitted to his role in the killings. He opened his testimony by stating: "I don't want to dodge questions. I don't want to save myself, nor do I want to save any of the others. . . . I want to answer all the questions truthfully."[40] He then tearfully spent a full day on the stand admitting that he himself took part in the execution of at least 813 Jewish women and children. Upon concluding his testimony, Gerke fainted.[41] According to Tobin, Gerke "recalled with specificity that Kreuzmann had been present at the first murder in Garsden, a charge Kreuzmann had been denying throughout the trial. . . . [S]obbing, he told the court how he and Harms had carried out Böhme's orders to murder Jewish women and children in Heydekrug."[42] He also related that after one massacre, Böhme ordered him to "chase" more Jews out of their homes for slaughter because "the numbers killed were too small."[43] He also testified how after one massacre the extermination squad held a banquet at a nearby Lithuanian inn, paying for food and cognac with the money stolen from the victims.[44] What made Gerke's testimony credible was that he was under arrest at the time, after being extradited from Sweden. At a later trial in 1963, Gerke himself was found guilty and sentenced to five years' imprisonment.

Closing Statements

Closing statements by German prosecutors in German courts trying other Germans for Nazi crimes are remarkable. Each reflects the message of the day about Germany's attitude toward coming to terms with its Nazi past. Today, a German prosecutor would readily admit to the active culpability of the German populace from that time. But Germany's *Vergangenheitsbewältigung* [coming to terms with the past] in 1958 manifested itself much differently than after unification and into the twenty-first century. At that time, the guilt of the Germans was seen, at the most, as the failure to protest. It was the guilt of a bystander ("I should have done something"), and not of a perpetrator ("I admit my crimes"). In closing, Schüle reflected that sentiment: "We all have a guilty conscience when we think back to the evil of those times . . . we were all too cowardly [to protest]."[45]

On August 11, ten days later, the defense attorneys began their closing statements. Rudolf Aschenauer, Hersmann's attorney, went first. He did not minimize what had occurred. This was a trial "that concerns the most terrible and unbelievable acts of the history of the Nazi regime against people whose only mistake was being Jewish."[46] But according to Aschenauer, his client and the other defendants had been duped by Hitler and his henchmen to believe in the antisemitism spewed by the Nazi leaders. His client Hersmann had no choice but to follow orders given by his superiors, relying on the well-known German phrase *Befehl ist Befehl* ("An order is an order"). Counsel for the other defendants likewise stuck to the "following orders" defense, the very defense rejected at Nuremberg, but which had no precedential value or even credibility in this proceeding.

The Verdicts

After a week of deliberations, the court announced its verdicts. All ten defendants were found guilty, however, not as principals, but as accessories. Even those in supervisory roles were found only to be supporting the acts of killing. Using the terminology of German criminal law, they were all perpetrators, but not "excess" perpetrators. Sentences ranged from three to fifteen years in prison, relatively light. A clue to the result can be found in the beginning pages of the court's decision: "The court has determined that it was Hitler who gave the verbal orders [for the Final Solution] and that Himmler and Heydrich plotted and carried these out."[47] And so, in the eyes of the court, *none* of the main perpetrators on the scene of these massacres exhibited blood lust, committed excesses, or killed because they internalized the Nazi racial hatred of Jews. They killed even women and children *only* because they were ordered to.

Fischer-Schweder, the original defendant, was found guilty of being an accessory to murder in 526 cases and was sentenced to ten years in prison. Böhme, arguably the most reprehensible defendant, was found guilty of being an accessory to murder in 3,907 cases and was sentenced to fifteen years in prison. Hersmann, his fellow chief of the Tilsit unit, was convicted on 1,656 counts of accessory to murder and sentenced also to fifteen years' imprisonment. Lukys, the only non-German defendant and who made a terrible impression on the court by showing a lack of remorse, was found guilty of being an accessory to murder in 315 cases and was sentenced to seven years in prison.

As to the other defendants, they were also all accessories and not perpetrators and received sentences ranging from seven to three years. The three-year sentence was handed out to the only non–Nazi Party member of the group, Werner Schmidt-Hammer, who was convicted on 526 counts of accessory to murder. Three of the convicted defendants were even allowed to go home after the trial.

Considering sentences passed out by modern international tribunals for atrocities committed in the former Yugoslavia and Rwanda, which themselves tend to lean on the side of leniency (see Chapters 8 and 9), these sentences border on being obscene. And yet the mere fact that all defendants were convicted was viewed by the German prosecutors as a successful result, considering the circumstances of the time. In the preceding seven years, from 1950 to 1957, 38 percent of Nazi prosecutions in West Germany—and these were strongest cases from the thousands selected to go to trial by the prosecutors and a neutral investigating magistrate—ended in acquittals.

Legacy of the Trial

The trial received an immense amount of media attention in the West Germany. Caroline Sharples writes that "[a]lthough the first day of the trial received relatively little coverage, the rest of the proceedings were reported faithfully in the national press, with most publications granting the case at least one substantial paragraph."[48] The trial thereby awakened Germany's awareness to the horrors committed by Germans in the East during the war. As a result, "justice ministers in West Germany . . . completely reversed the existing investigation procedure."[49] Rather than relying on random coincidences, such as how the Ulm case came to be, the state justice ministers decided to start systematically investigating Nazi crimes through the creation of the ZS. While the ZS's authority was circumscribed—it could not itself prosecute but only investigate and only had authority for crimes in concentration camps and other mass killing sites in the East—its creation began a new era for how the German legal system and all of Western Germany would deal with the mass of criminals in their midst. As Sharples aptly states, "It was the Ulm trial, above all, that succeeded in stirring up popular emotions in the Federal Republic."[50]

The Fall of Erwin Schüle

As noted above, the driving personality of the Ulm trial was Erwin Schüle, its chief prosecutor. Without Schüle's appointment in 1956 to investigate the one defendant in the "Fischer-Schweder Case," the trial of the leaders of the EK Tilsit squad would not have taken place.

Rewarded for his success in Ulm by being appointed as the first head of the ZS, Schüle brought his comprehensive approach to this first solely dedicated Nazi crimes unit created since Nuremberg. By all accounts, he did a superb job, launching over 2,000 investigations during his tenure as head of the ZS until 1965. It is therefore a sad postscript that Schüle's career ended on a sour note, akin to the downfall of Kurt Waldheim, the UN Secretary-General exposed a decade later for being a Nazi. East Germany, as part of its campaign to publicize the existence of Nazis in the West German government, revealed that Schüle had been a Nazi Party member, and not just a rank-and-file member but a member of the SA, the so-called Nazi storm troopers. Schüle at first denied the charge, but then explained that he joined the party in 1937 to escape persecution for his anti-Nazi beliefs.[51] The revelation was a major embarrassment for both Schüle and the ZS. Though he stayed on the job after a German probe could not verify his role, he resigned in 1966.[52] Schüle's tragic fall shows how deep the Nazi connection was in Germany, with its chief Nazi hunter exposed as a former Nazi himself.

2. The Frankfurt Auschwitz Trial

Twenty personnel of Auschwitz stood trial in Frankfurt between 1963 and 1965.[53] Like the Ulm trial, this trial in Frankfurt also came about through sheer coincidence. In 1958, an inmate in a German prison named Adolf Rogner sent a letter to Hermann Langbein detailing the whereabouts of Wilhelm Boger, a notorious figure from the Auschwitz camp. Langbein had been a non-Jewish political prisoner in Auschwitz. After the war, he helped create the International Auschwitz Committee, a German organization whose mission was to publicize the horrors of Auschwitz and aid survivors of the camp. Langbein passed on the information to German judicial authorities, but this tip was not taken seriously since Rogner was a convicted criminal. Coincidentally, at around the same time, a trove of Auschwitz documents was discovered in the hands of a survivor who saved the charred remains from a police court building in the former German city of Breslau (today Wroclaw in Poland). The survivor gave these documents to a German journalist who passed them on to Hesse's chief prosecutor, Fritz Bauer. The documents contained execution orders signed by Auschwitz commandant Rudolf Höss. They included the names of those killed, names of personnel involved, and the supposed reasons for the executions. With these documents and a remit from his superiors, Bauer was given the responsibility in 1959 to ferret out and prosecute the individuals who formed the entire crime complex at Auschwitz.

Unfortunately, the upper echelon of Nazi leaders responsible for the mass murders at Auschwitz could not be prosecuted.[54] Rudolf Höss, the most notorious Auschwitz commander, was captured after the war and turned over to the Poles after he testified at the IMT. Tried before a special Polish war crimes court, Höss was found guilty and hanged in 1947 on the grounds of Auschwitz. Adolf Eichmann, responsible in 1944 for sending over 400,000 Hungarian Jews by train to Auschwitz, was captured in Argentina by the Israelis in 1961 and then tried in Jerusalem. Eichmann's well-publicized trial and conviction spurred the German legal establishment to likewise try other Nazis in their midst. One of the most senior was Richard Baer, the last camp commandant of Auschwitz. Bauer arrested Baer, but Baer died while in custody six months before the trial began. And so the twenty defendants eventually at the dock in Frankfurt represented the second-tier perpetrators from Auschwitz.

The Defendants

The lead defendants were Robert Mulka and Karl Höcker, two former deputies to the camp commandant. As second-in-command at Auschwitz, they were in charge of the day-to-day administration of the camp. Indicted also were high-ranking Gestapo personnel at Auschwitz: Wilhelm Boger (who was identified by Rogner in prison) and Oswald Kaduk. Boger was responsible for the camp's security and notorious for torturing prisoners by using the so-called Boger swing, a bar over which inmates were draped, exposing their buttocks and genital area to severe and painful beatings. Kaduk likewise was notorious for torturing prisoners.

The defendants also included physicians and staff members from the camp's hospital, persons involved the selection process on the arrival ramp at Auschwitz-Birkenau and some camp guards. It even included a prisoner, Emil Bednarek, an ethnic German born in Poland. Arrested by the Gestapo in 1940, Bednarek was sent to Auschwitz, where he became a block elder, known in concentration camp slang as a *kapo*. Known for his cruelty, Bednarek was charged with the deaths and maltreatment of fellow prisoners.

The Trial

After an extensive investigation that lasted five years, the trial began on December 20, 1963. After 183 court sessions, it ended on August 20, 1965, with twenty defendants facing the court's verdict. Though Bauer spearheaded the prosecution, he left it to his non-Jewish prosecutors to actually argue the case in court. The defendants among them had nineteen defense attorneys. As in the Ulm trial, this trial featured one noteworthy defense counsel, Hans Laternser, who had previously represented defendants at Nuremberg and other Nazi trials in postwar West Germany.

Over the next twenty months, a massive amount of documentary evidence was introduced and over two hundred witnesses testified. Unlike at Ulm, the investigators were able to locate both Jewish and non-Jewish witnesses who survived Auschwitz and willing to come to Germany to give testimony. Documentary evidence included Zyklon-B request forms with Mulka's signature on them, and authorizations for the sick to be taken to the gas chambers. The Zyklon-B request forms stated that the purpose of the gas was to be for the "resettlement of Jews." Witnesses testified seeing Mulka at the arrival ramp, overseeing the selection process of arriving prisoners to determine which would be sent off to work and which would be gassed. To everyone's surprise, Mulka denied knowledge of any killings at Auschwitz.

Wilhelm Boger, the Auschwitz security chief, claimed that his interrogations were always on the orders of his superiors. He also claimed that he never seriously hurt anyone. Multiple witnesses testified otherwise. One former prisoner testified to seeing Boger kill fifty to sixty people, two at a time, at the Auschwitz execution site. Another prisoner testified seeing Boger shoot ten people. A third former prisoner testified to seeing Boger murder Gypsy children by taking them by their legs and slamming their heads against a wall.

Victor Capesius, known as "The Druggist of Auschwitz," was a pharmacist by training. His tasks included making selections at the train ramp of which arriving prisoners were going to be gassed and which would be allowed to work. He worked alongside the infamous Dr. Joseph Mengele. Capesius was also in charge of the chemicals used at the camp, including Zyklon-B. Though he denied involvement, several former prisoners testified witnessing him at these tasks. After the war, he was arrested by British and American occupation authorities, but released each time. At the time of his arrest in 1959, Capesius was living a normal life, owning both a pharmacy and a beauty parlor.

Witnesses testified about the cruelties of Oscar Kaduk, the SS interrogator responsible for punishing "misconduct," including escape attempts. Kaduk would force inmates to lie on the ground on their backs, where he would then place a board over their throats that he would stand on until the inmate choked to death. One witness testified to seeing Kaduk force women to beg for their lives before shooting them in the feet first and then other parts of their bodies until he finally killed them. Another witness also testified that he had seen Kaduk drive about a dozen children into the gas chamber at gunpoint.

Dov Paisikovic, a *Sonderkommando* (Jewish inmate selected to dispose of the dead), testified about the massive pits used to burn bodies and how other *Sonderkommandos* threw themselves into the fiery pits to end their ordeal. Witness Rudolph Vrba—one of the few escapees from Auschwitz—testified about the extensive theft at Auschwitz and the methodical manner in which Jews were robbed of their clothes and belongings. When Auschwitz was liberated, almost 393,000 men's suits and 863,000 women's dresses were found along with massive amounts of gold teeth that had been extracted from the murdered victims. These did not include the many shipments of stolen goods previously sent back to Germany. A former SS judge, Konrad Morgen, testified that he was sent to Auschwitz to investigate the theft of gold and valuables by Auschwitz personnel. While there, he was shown how the gas chambers operated.

Another witness, Dr. Ella Lingens, was a physician and professor living in Vienna when the Nazis came to power in 1938. Along with her physician husband Kurt Lingens[55] she helped Viennese Jews, including her students, hide from the Gestapo. Arrested in 1942, she was sent to Auschwitz, where she worked as a physician. There, she managed to save some Jews from the gas chambers. At trial, she described the horrendous conditions in the women's camp. Over 10,000 women died in the space of a few months. Inmates not selected for gassing received seven to eight hundred calories of food per day. Typhus was rampant at the camp. The combination of a near starvation regimen, disease, inadequate clothing, and taxing work led to the deaths of many.

The Verdicts

The court was a mixed bench, composed of three judges (with two alternates) and six jurors (and their three alternates). A guilty verdict required a majority of five out of the nine. Unlike at the Ulm trial, the jurors included four women. Similar to the situation in the Ulm trial, all of the judges were part of the judiciary during the Third Reich. Hans Hofmeyer, the presiding judge, repeatedly announced that the trial was not about the mass murder process at Auschwitz, but about specific acts that the defendants committed and their liability under German law. As a result, a single killing committed with *Exzessat* was seen as much worse than being complicit in thousands of murders but done on the orders of others.

As discussed earlier, West Germany declined to apply international law to the prosecution of Nazi defendants. Consequently, simply murdering a mass of defenseless civilians did not make the person a murderer. If the acts were carried out according to orders, the actual executioner could be recognized under German law as an accomplice to the murders. Only by exhibiting cruelty during the mass murder process—the blood lust element of murder—or alternatively possessing provable racial hatred toward the victims could satisfy the *mens rea* element of murder under German penal law.

Given this unfortunate combination of Germans again trying their own and the strict application of German penal law to Nazi crimes, it was no surprise that many of the verdicts were not commensurate to the gravity of the crimes. Nevertheless, the verdicts in Frankfurt in 1965 were harsher than those that came out of Ulm seven years earlier, where no one was found guilty of murder. Of the twenty defendants at this trial, seven were found guilty of murder and sentenced to life imprisonment on the basis of *Exzesstat*. These included defendants Boger, Kaduk, and the *kapo* Bednarek. Mulka and Capesius were also found guilty of murder by killing with *Exzesstat*, but received prison terms of fourteen years and nine years, respectively. This was despite uncontroverted evidence of both defendants committing multiple murders.

Ten defendants were found guilty of being accessories to murder and given sentences anywhere from three to nine years. Among these was Karl Höcker, the second-in-command, who received a seven-year sentence. The court ruled that Höcker was guilty of aiding and abetting the murder of 1,000 prisoners on four separate occasions. In his favor, the court found that that he had been a model citizen after the war and had voluntarily asked for denazification in 1952. Three defendants were acquitted.

Few of the defendants served their full sentence. Boger died in prison twelve years later. Capesius lived for eleven more years after his release. The others found guilty were all released early for medical reasons. Mulka was released after three years and died a year later. Kaduk was moved to a nursing home in 1988 after serving twenty-three years of his life sentence and lived for another nine years, dying in 1997. Bednarek, the former *kapo* sentenced to life imprisonment, was released in 1975. Höcker, the camp adjutant to commandant Baer and sentenced to seven years (but with a reduction for time served), was released on parole in 1970. He returned to his former job as chief cashier at a bank and died in 2000 at age eighty-eight. In 2007, Höcker's photo album from his days at Auschwitz surfaced, containing photos of SS personnel at leisure, around the same time that they participated or assisted in the murder of over 400,000 Hungarian Jews (Illustration 11).

Legacy of the Trial

The Auschwitz trial received even more publicity than the trial at Ulm. The trial and its attendant publicity played an important role in keeping the memory of the horrors of Auschwitz alive for the German public. As Fritz Bauer noted: "One of the most important tasks of this trial is not only to present the horrendous facts . . . [T]he point of this trial [is] to say: 'You should have said no.' "[56]

Illustration 11 Nazi officers and female auxiliaries (*Helferin*) run down a wooden bridge in Solahuette, a resort for German personnel at Auschwitz, July 1944. Photo is one of 116 photos collected by SS officer Karl Höcker (center), stationed at Auschwitz. US Holocaust Memorial Museum, photograph 34586.

For trials in West Germany after the creation of the ZS in 1958, we can summarize that most of those charged were convicted. Some were sentenced to life imprisonment, but most received prison terms that seemed incredibly lenient in light of what they had participated in.[57] Despite the shockingly low rate of prosecutions and then convictions, we can point to one positive legacy. The domestic trials and their reporting by the German media became the vehicle by which the people of the Federal Republic of Germany learned exactly what their fellow Germans had perpetrated in the East. German historians at that time did not write about the recent Nazi past. German cinema and later television, unlike today, were completely ignoring the subject. Germany's confrontation with its past, *Vergangenheitsbewältigung*, was for the most part a judicial phenomenon.

B. THE TRIAL OF ADOLF EICHMANN IN ISRAEL

If any trial can stand alongside the IMT trial in Nuremberg in 1945–1946 as one of the greatest criminal trials in modern history, it is the trial of Nazi SS Lieutenant Colonel (*Obersturmbannführer*) Adolf Eichmann in Jerusalem in 1961–1962. Black-and-white photographs of the fifty-five-year-old Eichmann trapped in the glass booth of the Jerusalem courtroom remain one of the iconic images of justice in our post-Holocaust world. According to British historian David Cesarani, Eichmann has become "a metonym for the entire history of the Nazi persecution and mass murder of the Jews"[58]

It is impossible today to discuss Eichmann without discussing another person who interjected herself into the Eichmann drama: philosopher Hannah Arendt, who coined the phrase "the banality of evil" to describe Eichmann. A German Jewish émigré to the United States, Arendt had been a student of the German philosopher and later Hitler devotee Martin Heidegger before emigrating from Nazi Germany to Paris in 1933 and then fleeing to America in 1941. When Eichmann was captured by the Israeli agents in May 1960, *The New Yorker* hired Arendt to report on the upcoming trial. Arendt flew to Israel but visited the courtroom for only a few sessions. She dropped in and then she left.[59] She also did not interview any of the prosecutors or defense attorneys, the Israeli interrogators in Bureau 06 who spent months with Eichmann, or any of Eichmann's associates either from his Nazi days in Europe or his compatriots in Argentina.

Little is remembered about what Arendt wrote about the Eichmann trial itself. But her *impression* of Eichmann on the stand that she shared with the world, first in her five *New Yorker* articles and subsequently collected in her 1963 book *Eichmann in Jerusalem*,[60] represents one of the major pieces of thought about the nature of evil in our post-Holocaust world.[61] To Arendt, the utter incongruity "between the unspeakable horror of the deeds and the undeniable ludicrousness of the man who perpetrated them" whom she encountered in the Jerusalem courtroom could only be explained by understanding him as an exemplar of the "banality of evil."[62] In the now-famous elucidation of this statement, she explained: "The trouble with Eichmann was precisely that so many were like him, and that the many were neither perverted nor sadistic, that they were, and still are, terribly and terrifyingly normal."[63]

I do not intend to examine whether evil is or can be banal or evildoers normal. But I simply note that Arendt was utterly wrong about Eichmann. To save his skin, Eichmann on the stand was playing the part of a sometimes befuddled and sometimes dutiful bureaucrat who simply was following orders and who never had any hatred of the Jews. And Arendt fell for it. The real Eichmann is exemplified in the statement that he made repeatedly to his compatriots in Budapest in 1944 and then years later in Argentina (that Arendt even quotes in her book): "I will jump into my grave laughing, because the fact I have the death of five million Jews on my conscience gives me extraordinary satisfaction."[64] In Argentina, speaking to Dutch journalist and former Nazi collaborator Willelm Sassen, he explained: "[I]f we had killed 10.3 million, I would be satisfied, and would say, good, we have destroyed an enemy."[65]

In reality, as noted by Holocaust historian Christopher Browning, "Eichmann exemplified willful evil, a man who consciously strove to maximize the harm he did to others."[66] Deborah Lipstadt puts it most succinctly: "He was no clerk."[67] And Bettina Stangneth, in her brilliant *Eichmann Before Jerusalem*, concludes that Eichmann was in fact, a consummate actor who "reinvented himself at every stage of his life, for each new audience and every new alarm.[68] He becomes "subordinate, superior officer, perpetrator, fugitive, exile, and defendant. . . . Eichmann-in-Jerusalem was little more than a mask."[69]

1. Eichmann Before Jerusalem—The Nazi Era

Eichmann's relatively low rank in the Nazi hierarchy belies his deeds. As far as we know (except for one unverified instance mentioned at trial where Eichmann supposedly beat to death a Jewish boy in Hungary in 1944), Eichmann never killed anyone by his own hand. And there is no record of him ever meeting with Hitler. Yet, this so-called Jewish specialist in the SS was responsible for organizing the roundup and deportation of about two million Jews of Central, Southern, and Western Europe to their deaths in Auschwitz-Birkenau and other camps in German-occupied Poland. This grotesque accomplishment came about as a result of two factors: his zeal and his efficiency. The tale of how this seemingly unremarkable Nazi became a mass murderer of unparalleled proportions has been told many times, but never so well as in Bettina Stangneth's *Eichmann Before Jerusalem*, published in German in 2011 and in English in 2014. Stangneth's study is notable for its level of detail. Among other sources, she relied on the complete set of transcripts from the twenty-nine hours of taped interviews that Eichmann gave in 1957 in Argentina to the Dutch Nazi Willem Sassen. In doing so, she produced the best rejoinder to Arendt—not about the nature of evil, but about Eichmann the man.

Eichmann was born in Germany in 1906; his family moved to Austria eight years later. At age nineteen, and a high school dropout, Eichmann began working as a salesman. In 1932, he joined the Austrian Nazi Party and later that year its elite SS unit. Fired from his job, he moved to Berlin after Hitler came to power. In 1934, he was promoted to the rank of SS-*Scharführer* (sergeant) when he joined the Reich Security Main Office. In 1936, he married Vera Liebel. Eichmann's reputation as the leading genocidaire of the Jews came as a result of a career decision: he was going to become the Nazi specialist on the Jews—and he let everyone around him know this. He hired a Hebrew teacher and even visited Palestine in 1937. He claimed also to speak Yiddish (itself a derivative of German).

As the Jewish specialist within the SS, Eichmann took on the responsibility of carrying out the first anti-Jewish goal of the Nazis: to forcibly expel all Jews from the territory of the Reich, first consisting of Germany and then also Austria, and finally the conquered territories in the East that were annexed into the Reich. The concomitant goal of expulsion was to deprive German Jews of their assets. Eichmann eagerly set up the bureaucratic machinery by which Jews would legally be deprived of their property in exchange for an exit visa that gave them the right to leave the Reich.

Eichmann's organizational skills became known to his superiors when he arrived in Austria in March 1938, the same month that the Anschluss took place, and created the Central Office of Jewish Emigration in Vienna. With ruthless efficiency, the Central Office expelled nearly 100,000 Austrian Jews and confiscated their assets. Franz Meyer, a Berlin Jew who visited Vienna, described Eichmann's operation for the court in Jerusalem. It was like "a flour mill connected to some bakery. You put in at the one end a Jew who still has capital and has, let us say, a factory or a shop or an account in a bank, and he passes through the entire building from counter to counter, from office to office—he comes out at the other end, he has no money, he has no rights, only a passport in which is written: You must leave this country within two weeks: if you fail to do so, you will go to a concentration camp."[70]

In September 1939, the same month when Germany attacked Poland, SS chief Heinrich Himmler established the Reich Security Main Office (RSHA), under the command of Reinhart Heydrich. In December 1939, Heydrich created Section IV D 4 ("Emigration and Evacuation") within the RSHA for the central handling of the expulsion of all Jews still in the Reich, primarily to the ghettos in the Eastern territories. In March 1941, a reorganization of the RHSA took place and Eichmann was appointed head of the slightly renumbered Section IV B 4, titled "Jewish Affairs" (*Judenreferat*). By October, 1941, all emigration from the Reich was forbidden. From his position as an RHSA director, Eichmann organized the deportation of over 1.5 million Jews to their deaths. Eichmann's main challenge was logistics: how to round up and transport so many people, and his additional title of "Transportation Administrator" for the "Final Solution" was to make sure that the trains to the death camps ran on time.

As discussed in Chapter 1, the official marker for the change of policy from deportation and ghettoization of Jews to their extermination was the Wannsee Conference that took place on January 20, 1942, outside of Berlin. Organized by Heydrich, the RHSA head announced to fifteen key officials in the government and party the secret plan for the extermination of all European Jewry under the name "Final Solution of the Jewish Question." Jews would no longer be deported to ghettos. Rather, the ghettoes would be closed and the Jews exterminated in the killing centers in occupied Poland. Heydrich told the participants that he had been tasked by Hitler and Himmler to implement the Final Solution. Eichmann was Heydrich's aide at the conference. By this time, he had reached the rank of Lieutenant Colonel, the highest rank he was to achieve in the SS.

Two months after the Wannsee Conference, the new policy was put into effect when the SS began operation of death camps in Bełżec and Sobibor in German-occupied Poland. In July 1942, the Treblinka death camp in occupied Poland opened. Tens of thousands of Jews were sent to these camps from Jewish ghettos in Poland to be immediately exterminated. That same year, Eichmann began deporting Jews from Slovakia and Holland for extermination. On July 10, 1942, following the roundup of French Jews, Eichmann received a cable asking what should be done with 4,000 children held at the Drancy holding camp outside Paris. Eichmann responded that as soon as more trains are dispatched from occupied Poland to France, the "transports of children would be able to roll."[71] The next month, Eichmann ordered the deportation of Jews in Belgium. The destination for all these Jews was now Auschwitz.

On November 17, 1942, Eichmann sent a letter to the Reich Foreign Ministry requesting that the government of now Nazi-allied Bulgaria be approached so that deportation of Bulgarian Jewry could begin "as part of the process of the general solution of the European Jewish problem."[72] In January 1943, Eichmann sent his deputy Dieter Wisliceny to Greece to begin deportation to Auschwitz of the Jews of Greece. Eichmann now sought to have another German ally, Romania, deport its Jews. Eichmann's last notorious deed took place following the entry of German troops into Hungary in March 1944. Shortly thereafter, Eichmann arrived in Budapest to begin deportation to Auschwitz of the last significant Jewish community in Europe. Over the next few months, more than 400,000 Hungarian Jews were sent primarily to Auschwitz to their deaths.

It was Eichmann's job to make sure that no Jew within Germany, German-occupied territory, and even states allied with Germany could escape this edict—and Eichmann rejected every request thereafter to allow any Jew to leave. As his deputy Dieter Wisliceny testified at Nuremberg, this included the period at the end of the war when Himmler himself sought to come into the good graces of the Western allies by ordering the exterminations to stop and releasing some Jews. According to Wisliceny, Eichmann countermanded Himmler's order.[73]

Eichmann's role in the Holocaust was well summarized by Chief Prosecutor Gideon Hausner, in his opening statement: "There was only one man who had ever been almost entirely concerned with the Jews, whose business had been almost entirely with the Jews, whose business had been their destruction."[74]

Eichmann's Escape and Capture

From today's perspective it seems astounding that Eichmann was not captured until 1960. Leading Nazis chose one of two options following Germany's surrender in May 1945: suicide or escape. Eichmann chose the latter by putting on the uniform of a common German soldier. He was detained twice by the US Army but each time managed to flee. He then lived in Germany under a false identity for four years, away from his family. In May 1949, the American Jewish monthly *Commentary* reported on Eichmann: "No one knows whether he is now alive or dead."[75] There were even rumors that he was hiding in Palestine, pretending to be a Holocaust survivor.[76]

In 1950, through an escape route created by officials at the Vatican, Eichmann arrived in Italy and secured a Red Cross refugee passport and an Argentine visa under the name "Ricardo Klement." As Klement, Eichmann arrived in Argentina on July 14, 1950. He took on various jobs: a rabbit farmer, a surveyor, and eventually a position at the Mercedes-Benz plant in Buenos Aires. By the end of 1952, he felt safe enough to have his wife Vera and their three sons join him in Buenos Aires, where a fourth son was born. Vera Eichmann lived under her own name, and so did her sons.[77]

For the next decade, Eichmann freely hobnobbed with the other Nazis who fled to South America after the war. In 1957, the neo-Nazi Willem Sassen taped dozens of hours of private conversations with Eichmann. During these interviews, Eichmann confirmed on tape that he had desired to exterminate all Jews and was sorry that he was not successful in his mission. He pointedly stated that "there are still a whole lot of Jews enjoying life today who ought to have been gassed."[78]

In her research, Stangneth discovered that the West German intelligence service had located Eichmann in Argentina as early as 1952. The CIA did so four years later. Stangneth also revealed that Eichmann even penned a letter to Chancellor Konrad Adenauer, never sent, intended to justify the National Socialist state and its aims.[79] All this was unknown to the Israelis, who sporadically were searching for Eichmann. Nazi hunter Simon Wiesenthal showed more zeal, but his fifteen-year search for the infamous Eichmann from his office in Vienna was unsuccessful, though he confirmed that Eichmann was still alive.[80] In 1960, the Israelis were tipped off of Eichmann's whereabouts by Fritz Bauer, the German Jewish attorney general of the German state of Hesse. The tip to Bauer came from an unlikely source—a blind half-Jewish German emigré lawyer in Buenos Aires named Lothar Hermann whose daughter coincidentally befriended one of Eichmann's sons. The Israeli secret service conducted the capture operation without a hitch. After observing the Eichmann family in Buenos Aires for months and confirming Eichmann's identify, Israeli agents on May 11, 1960, snatched Eichmann near his home as he was getting off the bus after work. Disguising him in an El Al Airline's steward's uniform, the Israeli team sneaked a drugged Eichmann through Argentine customs onto the Israeli plane and flew him to Israel for trial.

2. Eichmann in Jerusalem—The Trial

Why prosecute? In 1965, the Mossad assassinated Herbert Cukors in Paraguay, who had been in charge of the extermination of the Jews of Latvia. They easily could have done the same with Eichmann. However, Israeli Prime Minister David Ben-Gurion specifically instructed that Eichmann should be captured and brought alive if possible to stand trial in Israel before Israeli judges.

Ben-Gurion's announcement of Israel's intention to put Eichmann on trial caused much criticism at that time. No less a personality than former NMT Chief Prosecutor Telford Taylor opined in the pages of the *New York Times* that Israel should turn over Eichmann to an international tribunal. The problem was that no such international tribunal existed, and the UN Security Council was not about to create one in the midst of the Cold War.[81] Turning over Eichmann to the Germans for trial, as some had urged at the time, was also a nonstarter. If the Israelis were seen as being inherently biased against Eichmann, the Germans were exactly the opposite. Besides, Germany was not even asking for Eichmann. Returning Eichmann to Argentina for trial would be even more ludicrous since Argentina sheltered him for years.

Trials of leading Nazis by their victim nations was already an established precedent. After testifying before the IMT, Auschwitz commandant Rudolf Höss was turned over to the Poles for trial before their self-styled Nuremberg tribunal. The same was done with Amon Göth, the notorious commandant of the Placzow concentration camp with whom Oskar Schindler negotiated to save Jews. Dieter Wisliceny, one of Eichmman's chief aides, was turned over to the Czechoslovakians for trial after he testified at Nuremberg. Wisliceny was tried and hanged in Bratislava in 1948, the same fate that befell Höss and Göth in Poland after their trials.

The two major differences with these former national prosecutions was that Israel did not exist at the time of Eichmann's crimes and the crimes were not committed on Israeli soil. Nevertheless, as officially the state of the Jewish people established in 1948, Israel had the same right to try Eichmann as Poland had in trying Höss and Göth and Czechoslovakia had in trying Wisliceny. In doing so, Israel had to make sure that the trial was as fair as possible. In that, they succeed admirably. Eichmann got his day in court. The due process rights Eichmann received in Israel surpassed those given by Poland, Czechoslovakia, and other European states that held Nazi trials of Germans after the war.

The Strange Law Used to Prosecute Eichmann

The indictment charged Eichmann with fifteen counts of committing "crimes against the Jewish people." This domestic criminal statute was enacted by the Israeli parliament (Knesset) in 1950, ten years before Eichmann's capture and the same year that he fled Europe for Argentina. Still on the books, it is formally called the Nazi and Nazi Collaborators Law (NNCL).[82]

The crimes against the Jewish people set out in the NNCL encompassed all manner of persecution of millions of European Jews during the Nazi era, from arrest and imprisonment in concentration camps and ghettos, to theft of property, and deportation and extermination. Charging Eichmann with this crime was superfluous, since all these acts amounted also to war crimes or crimes against humanity, for which there was strong precedent under international law emanating from Nuremberg and which national courts are competent to prosecute. But the charge fit perfectly within the narrative that Israel sought to bring out in the trial: Eichmann, as the self-avowed Jewish specialist of the Nazis, was one of the main implementers of the Holocaust. The generic charges of crimes against humanity and war crimes did not bring out as well this narrative. In Nuremberg, the accused were tried, among other crimes, of committing "crimes against humanity." In Israel, Eichmann was tried for committing "crimes against the Jewish people."

What is this strange crime of *hostis Judaeorum* and how did it come about? The postwar enactment in Israel of the NNCL springs from the insidious method used by the Nazis of recruiting Jewish and non-Jewish prisoners in the concentration camps to maintain order and oversee the fulfillment of work quotas. Such prisoner functionaries were known as *kapos*—a slang term originated by the inmates themselves. Jews were appointed *kapos* in camps where the prisoner population was predominantly Jewish, and they were only in charge of other Jews. Taking on the role of *kapo* could mean the hope of survival for oneself or a family member because of the special privileges the *kapo* received from the German SS authorities running the concentration and labor camps.

A common refrain heard from Jewish survivors of the camps is the cruelty of the Jewish *kapos*. A frequent charge is that the Jewish *kapos* behaved "worse than the Germans"—and this statement reflects in large part the bitterness and shame felt by the authors of such statements toward their Jewish brethren. It also reflects the reality of camp life under a system where much of "the dirty work" would be done by prisoners.

The NNCL was specifically enacted to prosecute such "Nazi collaborators"—the former Jewish *kapos* among the Holocaust survivors who arrived in Israel after the war.[83] After its passage a decade prior to Eichmann's capture, the NNCL began to be used to prosecute Holocaust survivors in Israel. We do not know the exact number of *kapo* trials that took place in Israel. The records of these trials remain sealed and will only be opened seventy years after each of the trials has taken place. According to Israeli scholars, about thirty to forty prosecutions took place between 1951 and 1964,[84] but these are rough estimates. Israeli journalist Tom Segev quotes Supreme Court Justice Moshe Silberg, who felt that punishing *kapos* was detracting from the horror perpetrated by the Nazis: "It is hard for us, the judges of Israel, to free ourselves of the feeling that, in punishing a worm of this sort, we are diminishing, even if by only a trace, the abysmal guilt of the Nazis themselves."[85] With the capture of Eichmann, the NNCL could now be applied to an actual Nazi.

Trial Preparation

During the IMT and NMT trials, the prosecutors were working under extreme conditions among the ruins of Germany, daily encountering difficulties in collecting, collating, and translating the mass of incriminating documents and otherwise putting together their case. Not so, with the Eichmann trial. Here meticulousness ruled the day. The Israeli police set up a special unit, Bureau 06, to assemble relevant documents, interview witnesses, and interrogate Eichmann. The interrogations began in May 1960, shortly after Eichmann's arrival in Israel, and continued until early 1961. Ultimately, 16,000 documents were assembled, many of them bearing Eichmann's signature. The witness list had 108 survivors, historians and other scholars, and non-Jews who came to Israel to testify as prosecution witnesses about their interactions with Eichmann during the Nazi era. Only a few of the witnesses had ever met Eichmann, the SS Jewish Affairs specialist; rather, they were put on the list to testify about each stage of the Holocaust, from deportation and expropriation in Germany and Austria, to extermination by bullets and poison gas in occupied Poland and the Soviet Union.

Chief prosecutor was Gideon Hausner, Israel's attorney general. Assisting him were Yakov Bar-Or and Gabriel Bach, who later became a justice on the Israeli Supreme Court. Much criticism has been directed over the years toward Hausner. It began with Arendt who in *Eichmann in Jerusalem* described Hausner as "very unsympathetic, boring, constantly making mistakes."[86] His brilliant opening statement, in her view, was "cheap rhetoric and bad history."[87] Stephan Landsman diminishes his stature by calling him "a commercial lawyer with no criminal trial experience."[88] And of course there is the critique that Hausner was Ben-Gurion's lackey, dutifully following his boss's orders that the trial be turned into a history lesson.[89] The criticisms are unfair. Hausner performed brilliantly, as did his deputy prosecutors Bach and Ben-Or. Hausner's opening address, which began with the phrase "Standing with me are six million accusers . . ." is considered an iconic moment in Israel's history.

For his defense counsel Eichmann selected Dr. Robert Servatius, a German attorney who had earlier defended Nazis at Nuremberg. Israel paid for the representation and flew Servatius and assistant counsel Dieter Wachtenbruch to Israel. Journalists from around the world came to Israel to report on the trial. Among them was thirty-year-old Holocaust survivor (and future Nobel Peace Prize laureate) Elie Wiesel, then living in Paris, who covered the trial for the New York–based Jewish newspaper *The Forward*.

The Trial Begins

Criminal Case 40/61, *State of Israel v. Otto Adolf Eichmann*, began on April 11, 1961. The panel of judges who considered the Eichmann case were Moshe Landau (presiding), Benjamin Halevy, and Yitzhak Raveh. All three had been born in Germany and came to British Palestine before the war. There would be no chance of mistranslation, since they could hear Eichmann and communicate with him during the trial directly in German. Before the prosecution even

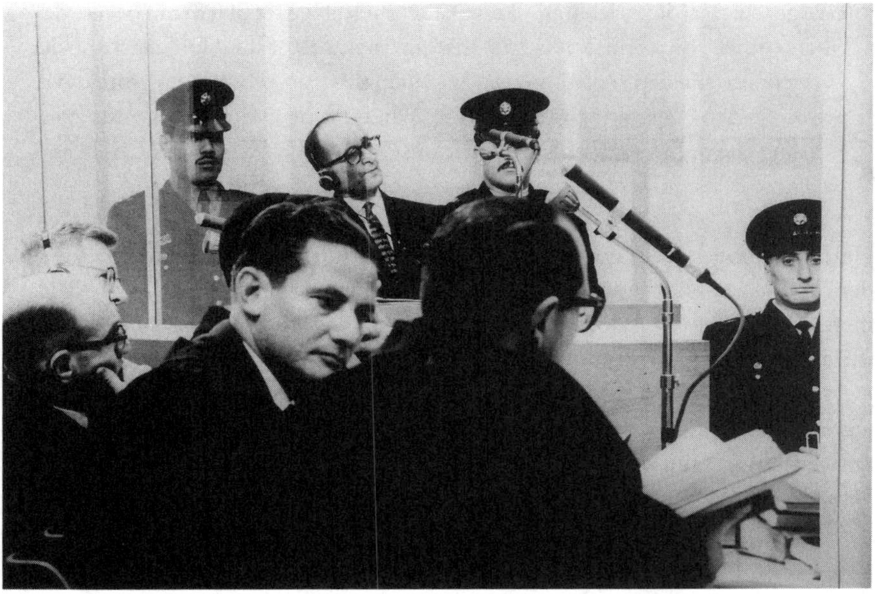

Illustration 12 Adolf Eichmann listens to the proceedings through a glass booth during his trial in Jerusalem, 1961. Chief defense counsel Robert Servatius (far left), chief prosecutor Israeli Attorney-General Gideon Hausner (left), assistant prosecutor Gabriel Bach (middle, facing camera, later a justice on the Israeli Supreme Court), and Adolf Eichmann (back), US Holocaust Memorial Museum, photograph 24373, courtesy of Eli M. Rosenbaum.

brought on their first witness, Servatius made a motion to dismiss the case. He could have made a number of grounds for the dismissal: (1) the trial was illegal because Eichmann was kidnapped from Argentina; (2) the court did not have jurisdiction to try Eichmann because the crimes were not committed on the territory of Israel and took place before the state's establishment; and (3) the law under which Eichmann was being prosecuted was promulgated in 1950, after Eichmann committed his acts, and so this was an ex post facto prosecution. Servatius raised these arguments during the trial, but he chose primarily to base his initial motion on another ground: Eichmann could not get a fair trial before Israeli judges since they were Jews and Eichmann was on trial for "crimes against the Jewish people." The next day, the judges announced their ruling: the motion was denied. As presiding judge Moshe Landau explained:

> [W]hile on the bench, a judge does not cease to be flesh and blood, possessed with human emotions. However, he is required by law to subdue these emotions and impulses, for otherwise a judge will never be fit to consider a criminal

> charge which arouses feelings of revulsion, such as a case of treason or murder or any other grave crime. It is true that the memory of the Holocaust shocks every Jew to the depth of his being, but when this case is brought before us we are obliged to overcome these emotions while sitting in judgment. After considering the arguments of learned Counsel for the Defense, this Court and each one of its judges regards itself as competent to try this case.[90]

Here, the judges were going to put aside their emotions and listen to the evidence. They applied to Eichmann the basic premise of criminal law: "[E]very man is deemed to be innocent and that his case must be tried only on the basis of the evidence brought before the Court."[91]

With the motion denied, Eichmann now had to enter a plea. For each of the fifteen counts, when asked "Are you guilty or not guilty?" Eichmann gave the same answer: "In the sense of the indictment, no." It was not original, with many the Nuremberg defendants mouthing the same phrase.

Hausner then gave his opening argument. His stirring opening words are remembered by every Israeli who listened to the speech, which was broadcast on the radio throughout Israel:

> When I stand before you here, Judges of Israel, to lead the Prosecution of Adolf Eichmann, I am not standing alone. With me are six million accusers. But they cannot rise to their feet and point an accusing finger towards him who sits in the dock and cry: "I accuse." For their ashes are piled up on the hills of Auschwitz and the fields of Treblinka, and are strewn in the forests of Poland. Their graves are scattered throughout the length and breadth of Europe. Their blood cries out, but their voice is not heard. Therefore, I will be their spokesman and in their name I will unfold the awesome indictment.[92]

The Prosecution Case

The prosecution presented its case in chronological order. First came witness testimony about the forced deportation of the Jews from Germany and Austria and the theft of their property before the start of the Second World War. Since Eichmann was the SS deportation specialist for the Jews, it was not hard to prove Eichmann's personal responsibility for these acts. Second came testimony about life in the ghettos in the East after the invasion of Poland in 1939 and the mass shootings of Jews after the invasion of the Soviet Union in 1941. The problem here was that of relevancy: Eichmann had nothing to do with these activities. Third, came testimony of deportation of Jews to extermination camps in Poland as part of the "Final Solution." Eichmann's new role as the SS transportation specialist for the Jews tied him to these acts. In this part of the trial, the prosecution presented testimony about the deportation of over 400,000 Hungarian Jews to their deaths in summer 1944. Since Eichmann was in Budapest in charge of these deportations, tying Eichmann to these acts also was unproblematic. Finally, the prosecution turned to day-to-day operation of the killing centers in German-occupied Poland. Here again there was a relevancy problem since Eichmann was not involved in these operations. The only relevancy was indirect: Eichmann knew the fate that awaited the Jews that he was transporting to the East. From each Holocaust survivor on the stand Hausner elicited as many details as possible before being cut off by Presiding Judge Landau. Exasperated by what appeared to be testimony having nothing to do with Eichmann, Landau openly chastised Hausner, who nevertheless stood his ground.

Hausner's most surprising strategy (wholly irrelevant to Eichmann's guilt) was to ask many of the survivors the same question: Why they did not resist or revolt? His reason for asking was to answer a question on the minds of many Israeli Jews. At the May 1, 1961, session, the forty-year-old Moshe Beisky testified. A "Schindler List" survivor, Beisky was a magistrate at the time; he later became a justice on the Israeli Supreme Court. In his testimony, Beisky related an incident when 15,000 prisoners were forced to watch the hanging of a young boy at the Płaszów camp for the offense of whistling a Russian tune. Hausner interjected: "Fifteen thousand people stood there and opposite them hundreds of guards. Why didn't you attack then, why didn't you revolt?" Beisky's response, according to Hausner in his memoir, "was delivered in a hushed, sometimes inaudible voice, but it was [the] most convincing piece of human truth I have ever heard on the subject. In his response, Dr. Beisky raised the trial to a new moral height."[93]

> First of all, I can no longer—and I acknowledge this—after eighteen years I cannot describe this sensation of fear. This feeling of fear, today when I stand before Your Honors, does not exist any longer and I do not suppose it is possible to define it for anyone. . . . Nearby us there was a Polish camp. There were 1,000 Poles. . . . One hundred metres beyond the camp they had a place to go to—their homes. I don't recall one instance of escape on the part of the Poles. But where could any of the Jews go? [. . .] We were wearing clothes which . . . were dyed yellow with yellow stripes. And that moment, let us suppose that the 15,000 people within the camp even succeeded without armed strength . . . to go beyond the boundaries of the camp—where would they go? What could they do? [. . .] It is not physically possible to present the conditions of those days in the courtroom, and I do not believe, Heaven forbid, that people will not understand this, but I myself cannot explain and I experienced this on my own person . . .[94]

The "sheep-to-the-slaughter" syndrome was also put to rest by Abba Kovner, one of Israel's leading poets who was a partisan during the war and led the Vilna ghetto uprising. As a man of arms, Kovner epitomized the brave Israeli Jew. Turning to the judges, he declared: "The surprising thing, in my opinion, is that a fighting force existed at all, that there was armed reaction, that there was a revolt. This is what was not rational."[95]

On June 18, 1961, Session 100 was held. Eichmann was asked if the extermination of the Jews was legal, even under Reich law. This line of questioning sought to probe Eichmann's defense that he was "following orders." Here is the exchange:

HAUSNER: Do you perhaps know on the basis of which law—was there some German law which empowered or authorized the Senior Commanders of the Security Police and the Security Service or the police to impose death sentences?

EICHMANN: I do not know that; I only know that where there was a State Secretary for Security, that these matters were dealt with by this authority on its own for its area of jurisdiction, without any involvement of the Head Office for Reich Security.

HAUSNER: Was there any law which empowered the Commander or the Commandant of an extermination camp to exterminate people?

EICHMANN: There was certainly no law . . . I do not know about anything else, because I really had nothing to do with that. I only know that people relied on the saying "The Führer's words have the power of law," that was the saying at that time. I myself neither gave orders for these matters nor had anything to do with them.

HAUSNER: Was there any law which allowed Globocnik to exterminate hundreds of thousands, and a quarter of a million Jews from the General Government [of German-occupied Poland]? Here you did have something to do with this, because here you dictated or wrote him the ex post facto, or after-the-event, authorizations for these activities.

EICHMANN: I did obtain orders for this, that is correct, and I have also admitted that, but as for the other aspects, at that time they were not supposed to be of any concern to me, since I had nothing to do with them; that was dealt with by the higher authorities.

HAUSNER: Was there any law which empowered you to carry out the deportations from the Reich and the occupied territories?

EICHMANN: I do not know . . . I was not an independent holder of an office; I obtained my orders from my immediate superiors, I had to comply with these orders.

HAUSNER: And you did not care in any way to know whether they were legal, or whether the orders were illegal, legal or illegal even from the point of view of Reich law—that was of no concern to you?

EICHMANN: If I received the order from my Department Chief, the Head of the Reich Criminal Police and Lieutenant General, then it was on his responsibility, and he would have looked after things appropriately with regard to his superior. It was not up to me to concern myself with this, as a Section Head who obtained the orders from my immediate superior.

HAUSNER: That means that it was of no concern to you whether it was legal or illegal—that did not concern you in any way?

EICHMANN: This question did not arise, as I obtained the orders, the unambiguous and clear-cut instructions of my superior.

HAUSNER: That is precisely why I am asking you whether you were interested to know whether these orders were legal or illegal, "yes" or "no"? Did you ever ask, where are the powers, where is the legal framework on the basis of which we are acting? Did you ever ask this question? Did you concern yourself with that?

EICHMANN: I am not a lawyer. I had to obey, I had only learned the life of a soldier.[96]

The Defense Strategy

With regard to his role as the Jewish emigration specialist, Eichmann's defense was that his goal was the same as the Zionists: to have the Jews leave Europe and come to the historic land of Israel. It was only British intransigence in limiting emigration to Mandate Palestine that thwarted his goal of sending more Jews there. The "Eichmann-as-Zionist" argument broke down, however, when one of the judges pointed out that the Jews of Germany and Austria were not leaving their homes voluntarily.

Forced emigration of Jews, however, was Eichmann's lesser crime. His primary guilt rested from the forced deportation of Jews to the killing centers in the East. Here, Eichmann sought to portray himself at all stages as a dutiful soldier. Others above him made policy, and he was bound to follow it. He made no independent decisions. He was, in his most often repeated defense, "merely a little cog in the machinery that carried out the directives and orders of the German Reich. I am neither a murderer nor a mass murderer."[97]

Where that line of defense completely failed was the deportation of Hungarian Jews to Auschwitz after German troops entered Hungary in March 1944. Eichmann arrived in Budapest in 1944 to coordinate this deportation and knew the fate that would befall them. As noted, in the ensuing ten months, more than 400,000 Hungarian Jews were sent to their deaths, with 90 percent immediately gassed upon arrival at Auschwitz. The Germans knew that the war was already lost. Yet Eichmann in Budapest was fighting his own war: to murder as many Jews as possible, even in defiance of the orders of his superiors. He took every initiative to maintain, or increase, the rate of deportations. This included requisitioning trains that otherwise would have been used for military transport.

There was one document that served as "the smoking gun"—a note that Eichmann sent to the Reich Foreign Ministry just two months before Germany's surrender, when all knew that the war was lost, seeking to stop the emigration of 1,000 Jewish children from Romania to Palestine.

> *Berlin, 3 March, 1945*
> *Secret*
> *To: Foreign Ministry, Attention: Counsellor Herr von Hahn, Berlin Rauchstrasse*
> *Re: Transfer of Jews from the Balkans to Palestine*
> *Documentation: None*
> *According to reliable information which must be kept secret negotiations which might prove successful are being conducted between Jewish leaders in Rumania—through their offices in Constantinople—and Turkey, for the grant of transit visit for one thousand Jewish children and one hundred Jewish adults who will accompany the former on their trip via Bulgaria and Turkey to Palestine.*
>
> *We request every effort to prevent this emigration.*
>
> *By Order*
> *Eichmann*

The document expressly contradicts Eichmann's argument that he was merely a transportation coordinator. His intervention to stop the emigration of the Romanian children had nothing to do with his transportation duties. And so the document proves that Eichmann did not just follow orders but took initiative. The 1,000 Romanian children were prevented from emigrating so they could be killed.[98]

The Verdict and Appeal

On December 13, 1961, the judges returned to announce their verdict. Eichmann was found guilty and sentenced to death. Paragraph 221 of the judgment goes to the heart of the court's guilty verdict:

> [T]he Accused well knew that the order for the physical extermination of the Jews was manifestly illegal, and that by carrying out this order he was committing criminal acts on an enormous scale. To arrive at this finding, we do not have to rely on the Accused, because according to Section 19(b) [dealing with superior orders] the question as to whether an order is manifestly illegal is a question of law, left to be decided by the court according to objective criteria. In any case, we shall also quote his evidence in the matter,

which he gave after much evasion, and as though it needed a great inner effort on his part to realize such a simple truth:

> "Your Honour, President of the Court, since you call upon me to tell and give a clear answer, I must declare that I see in this murder, in the extermination of Jews, one of the gravest crimes in the history of mankind."

And in answer to Judge Halevi:

> ". . . I already realized at that time that this solution by the use of force was something unlawful, something terrible, but to my regret, I was obliged to deal with it in matters of transportation, because of my oath of loyalty from which I was not released." (Session 95, Vol. IV, pp. 35–36)

Not only the order for physical extermination was manifestly illegal, but also all the other orders for the persecution of Jews because of their being Jews, even though they were styled in the formal language of legislation and subsidiary legislation, because these were only a cloak for arbitrary discrimination, contrary to the basic principles of law and justice. . . . This was not a single crime, but a whole series of crimes committed over the years. The Accused had more than enough time to consider his actions and to desist from them. But he did not stop; as time went on, he even increased his activity. [99]

In their judgment, the trial judges commented on Eichmann's credibility on the stand:

> The Accused's evidence in this case was not truthful evidence, in spite of his repeated declarations that he was reconciled to his fate, knowing the gravity of the activities to which he had confessed of his own will, and now his only desire was to reveal the truth, to correct the wrong impression which had been created in the course of time in regard to his activities in the eyes of his people and of the whole world. In various sections of this Judgment, we have pointed out where the Accused was found to be lying in his evidence. We now add that his entire testimony was nothing but one consistent attempt to deny the truth and to conceal his real share of responsibility, or at least to reduce it to a minimum. His attempt was not unskilful, due to those qualities which he had shown at the time of his actions—an alert mind; the ability to adapt himself to any difficult situation; cunning and a glib tongue. But he did not have the courage to confess to the truth, not about how things actually happened, nor about his inner convictions to the acts he committed. We saw him again and again winding his way under the impact of the

> cross-examination, retreating from complete to partial denial, and only when left no alternative, to admission; but of course always taking refuge in the plea that in all matters, great or small, he was acting on explicit orders.[100]

On May 29, 1962, Israel's Supreme Court, sitting as a Court of Criminal Appeal, rejected Eichmann's appeal and upheld the district court's judgment on all counts. After the president of Israel Yitzhak Ben-Zvi rejected his plea of clemency, Eichmann was executed by hanging in Ramla Prison during the night between May 31 and June 1, 1962. His ashes were scattered in the international waters of the Mediterranean so that he would have no final resting place.

3. Legacies of the Trial

Legal scholars have traditionally minimized the importance of the Eichmann trial to international criminal law.[101] According to Leora Bilsky: "[T]his failure by international law scholars to recognize the contribution made by the Eichmann trial to international law stems from its misconception as a Jewish trial arising from, among other things, the sui generis category of crimes against the Jewish people, which formed the legal basis of this trial."[102] Bilsky blames Arendt, who fostered the view of the trial being more political than legal.[103] This negative view is wrong, since the trial provides important precedent in international criminal law.

First, the trial recognized the principle of universal jurisdiction: certain crimes are so abhorrent that the perpetrator can be tried before the courts of any country that has personal jurisdiction over the perpetrator.[104] While the rule was recognized as far back as the nineteenth century—pirates and slave traders were considered universal outlaws—the Eichmann trial brought this concept to the modern atrocity crimes. As noted earlier, Israel tried Eichmann not only because his deeds were committed against the Jews but because they were so horrid. Israel also universalized the trial by prosecuting Eichmann as well for war crimes and crimes against humanity against other victim groups. Thus, the indictment also charged the defendant with persecution of Poles, Slovenes, the Roma (commonly known as Gypsies), and the murder of some eighty children from the Czech village of Lidice, as part of the destruction of Lidice and murder of all its inhabitants in reprisal for the assassination in Prague of Reinhard Heydrich in 1942.[105]

Chile dictator Augusto Pinochet's arrest in Britain in the 1998 has been hailed as the modern recognition of universal jurisdiction as applied to atrocity crimes. In fact, the concept was already enshrined in the Eichmann trial three decades earlier. There was much universalism in the Eichmann trial, though the instrumentality applying universal justice was a domestic court. Because Eichmann was a *hostis humani generis*—an outlaw of all mankind—the trial court rejected

Eichmann's argument that he could be tried only by the state where his acts were committed. This territorial limitation for prosecuting genocide is found in the text of the Genocide Convention. Article 6 states that "[p]ersons charged with genocide . . . shall be tried by a competent tribunal of the State where the act was committed, or by such international penal tribunal as may have jurisdiction. . . ." Read literally, it limits the prosecution of genocidaires by domestic courts only of the country where the genocide was committed. The Israeli District Court rejected this literal interpretation. As it explained: "[T]here is nothing . . . to lead us to deduce any rule against the principle of universality of jurisdiction with respect to the crime in question. It is clear that the reference in Article 6 to territorial jurisdiction, apart from the jurisdiction of the non-existent international tribunal, is not exhaustive."[106] The court's holding is now the consensus rule under international law. No country today limits its prosecutions of genocidaires only to instances where the genocide occurred in its own territory. (See Chapter 9.)

Second, Eichmann was the first person convicted of genocide by any court. The judgment of the Israeli trial court held: "We, therefore, convict the Accused, pursuant to the first count of the indictment, of a crime against the Jewish people, an offense under Section 1(a)(1) of [NNCL], in that during the period from August 1941 to May 1945 . . . he, together with others, caused the deaths of millions of Jews, with the purpose of implementing a plan which was known as the 'Final Solution of the Jewish Question,' with an intent to exterminate the Jewish People." This conviction under Israel's NNCL's domestic crime of "crimes against the Jewish people," as discussed earlier, was nothing more than a reformulation of the crime of genocide as set out in the Genocide Convention, but applied only to one religious/ethnic group: the Jews. In the words of William Schabas: "Whereas the [Genocide] Convention contemplates genocide that is perpetrated against a 'national, ethnical, racial or religious group', the Israeli legislation replaced these words with the expression 'the Jewish people.' "[107]

Eichmann's conviction for genocide in 1961 stands in isolation. No one was convicted of genocide at Nuremberg because the crime was "not on the books" at the time. After Eichmann's conviction, it was not until the 1990s that both domestic courts and international tribunals began prosecuting individuals for genocide (see Chapter 9).

Third, the Eichmann trial continued the concept that evildoers no matter how horrible will be put on trial and that the trial can be a fair one. Israel could have easily assassinated Eichmann. Instead, he was brought to Israel for trial as a continuation of the policy enunciated at Nuremberg. The trial was a model of fairness, providing the defendant with every opportunity to prove his innocence and ranking equally in that regard with the IMT and NMT trials.[108] Moreover, just as not every defendant found guilty at Nuremberg was convicted of every count, so too here the court held: "We acquit the Accused of a crime against the Jewish People, by reason of the acts attributed to him . . . during the period until August 1941." Those acts of persecution of the Jews through forced emigration, deportation, and ghettoization did not amount, according to the court, to genocide of the Jews. Instead the court found these acts to be crimes against humanity under the category of "persecution" of a group. This genocide acquittal was also the first time that any judicial tribunal sought to determine the relationship between genocide and crimes against humanity, an issue not dealt with at Nuremberg and not raised again until the 1990s with the creation of the ad hoc Yugoslavia and Rwanda tribunals. The acquittal also set legal precedent: physical extermination of a protected group is genocide; displacement of the same group and robbery is not. In the prosecution of Bosnian Serb leader Rodovan Karadzić, the Yugoslav tribunal in 2012 specifically relied on this acquittal of Eichmann for the Jewish genocide for acts prior to 1941 as the reason for dismissing the prosecution's charge that Karadzić can be guilty of genocide for persecution of Bosnian Muslims and Bosnian Croats. As the ICTY explained: "Eichmann was convicted of genocide only for those acts which were directed at destroying the group and not displacing it."[109]

Much credit for the fairness of the trial belongs to the three Israeli judges, who worked mightily to cull evidence that demonstrated Eichmann's personal responsibility in the persecution and extermination of, primarily, the Jews of Europe and, secondarily, other victim groups. The promise that the judges made at the outset of the trial to presume innocence and listen to the evidence was fulfilled. And this was an activist court. Rather than just passively listen, Presiding Judge Moshe Landau and his two colleagues often intervened (in German) to ask follow-up questions and sought clarification from Eichmann himself. The same can be said about Eichmann's appeal of his conviction to the Supreme Court of Israel. The Israeli Supreme Court on appeal specifically rejected Eichmann's defense, which it summarized as follows: "The line of defence pursued by the Appellant was that he did nothing relating to the persecution of the Jews except upon orders of his superiors, and that he personally was not competent to determine their fate."[110] Evidence of Eichmann's guilt was overwhelming, both from the trove of captured Nazi documents introduced at trial and testimony of witnesses Höss and Wisliceny at Nuremberg.

One common criticism of the trial is that Ben-Gurion and Hauser sought to turn the trial into a history lesson, putting on the stand witness after witness to testify about atrocities that had no connection to Eichmann. This exasperated the judges, who repeatedly kept questioning Hausner about the relevancy of this testimony. Arendt is especially critical, explaining: "I held and hold the opinion that this trial had to take place in the interests of justice and nothing else."[111] Stephan Landsman elucidates this point: "This Holocaust-wide victim focus . . . produced a flawed template for addressing mass atrocity by shifting the central focus of the trial from establishing the criminal wrongdoing of an accused individual to the twin objectives of creating a historical record of the entirety of the Nazis' genocidal program and using the proceedings for the public airing of a vast array of victims' witness narratives, whether connected to the guilt of the accused or not. . . . The case ceased to focus on Eichmann."[112] In the end, I believe both goals were met. Ben-Gurion got his history lesson, for the Israeli public and the world, and the judges were presented with overwhelming evidence of Eichmann's personal responsibility for many—though not all—of the crimes of the Holocaust presented through the testimony of the Jewish survivors.

The extensive use of survivor witnesses in Jerusalem led to what Landsman calls the invention of the "witness-driven atrocity trial."[113] This shift to in-court narration of the victims' stories created a new template for the prosecution of international atrocity crimes. The use of survivor testimony has become the trial method *de rigueur* for trials before the modern international criminal tribunals.

Last, in discussing the trial's legal legacy, it must be remembered that Hausner and his deputies were not seeking to break new legal ground. Rather, they wanted to situate Eichmann's prosecution as much as possible within existing precedent—from international law, Anglo-American law, and even continental law. That is why "crimes against the Jewish people" is modeled on the text of the Genocide Convention. All Israeli law did is replace the general protected groups of racial or ethnic group of Article 2 of the Convention with the specific term "Jewish people." Throughout the trial, Hausner and his aides often quoted from and relied on preexisting precedent from the IMT at Nuremberg. They also cited frequently existing case law from court decisions in the United States and Britain and legal scholarship from these two countries. The whole point was *not* to create a legacy—but which they did nevertheless, as discussed above.

In 2011–2012, on the occasion of the fiftieth anniversary of the Eichmann trial and appeal, conferences were held in North America, Europe, and Israel examining the trial and its legacy. Today, many international legal scholars recognize the impact of the trial on modern international criminal law. William Schabas, one of the deans of genocide jurisprudence, affirms: "[T]he Eichmann judgments [of the Israeli District Court and Supreme Court] represent pioneering analyses of difficult legal issues whose findings have, by and large, been sustained by the case law that has emerged in the modern renaissance of international criminal law."[114]

C. HUNTING FOR NAZIS IN AMERICA

Eichmann's escape to Argentina after the war showed that South America was a favored destination for Nazis. The so-called "rat line" for escaping Nazis that some German Catholic priests established in the Vatican led directly to Catholic South America.[115]

But not all Nazis hid in Germany or escaped to South America. North America was also a favored destination. Immediately following the war, American intelligence officials plucked more than 1,600 German scientists and relocated them to the United States lest they be captured by the Russians. Other Nazis were used as spies by the CIA during the Cold War. Newly declassified documents and a best-selling book by *New York Times* reporter Eric Lichtbau revealed in 2014 that at least 1,000 former Nazis and collaborators spied for the Americans, with some being protected by US intelligence agencies until the 1990s.[116]

But the largest segment of Nazi war criminals coming to America used the same route as the tens of thousands of refugees from war-torn Europe, gaining entry through America's postwar relaxed immigration laws. The opening of American borders for such refugees allowed Nazis and Nazi collaborators to slip through with the victims. Most ended up in the United States, with some also in Canada. Other favored destinations were Britain and Australia.[117]

In the Cold War era, FBI Director J. Edgar Hoover had no interest in tracking down supposed Nazis in America. Only one person was denaturalized and deported between 1945 and 1978. On March 14, 1973, Hermine Braunsteiner Ryan became the first Nazi war criminal to be extradited from the United States. A former female guard at the Ravensbrück concentration camp who later moved on to the Majdanek camp, she was extradited by the United States to Germany to stand trial. After the war, Hermine Braunsteiner married Russell Ryan, a US Air Force mechanic stationed in Germany. She came to the United States in 1959 and became a US citizen in 1963, living the life of a suburban housewife in Queens. Braunsteiner Ryan was tracked down by Simon Wiesenthal, who was told about her by female survivors living in Israel. She was called by prisoners the "Stomping Mare" for her brutality. But her sole extradition shows the lack of interest of immigration authorities in tracking down Nazis and their collaborators in America.

The turning point came in 1979, with establishment of the Office of Special Investigations (OSI) in the Criminal Division of the US Department of Justice which aggressively began pursuing aging Nazis. The OSI prosecuted over one hundred individuals, most being East European collaborators who slipped into the United States after the war as "refugees." The great majority were discovered not through some tip, but through OSI's use of Nazi documents from archives around the world and matching names with US immigration records. A federal judge once marveled at the ability of OSI "to discover the acts of a single individual across the temporal expanse of fifty years and a distance of an ocean and half a continent."[118] The Simon Wiesenthal Center, in its annual report card of how well countries have prosecuted Nazis, has always awarded the United States an "A" grade.

Australia, Canada, and the United Kingdom chose to go after their suddenly discovered Nazis Nuremberg-style, that is by passing laws that would prosecute such individuals for war crimes and crimes against humanity in their domestic criminal courts.[119] Fearing that criminal prosecution of Nazi cases was likely barred by the ex post facto clause of the US Constitution, the US Congress took a different route. Under the so-called 1978 Holtzman Amendment to the Immigration and Nationality Act (named for New York Congresswoman Elizabeth Holtzman, who introduced the law), the Department of Justice was given a three-part mandate: (1) identify individuals living in the United States who obtained US citizenship by concealing their involvement in Nazi persecution; (2) initiate civil proceedings to revoke their citizenship through denaturalization proceedings in federal court; and (3) deport such persons. American immigration law became the vehicle to go after such Nazis because all individuals seeking to emigrate from Europe to the United States needed to certify on their applications that they did not participate in the persecution of individuals on the basis of race, religion, national origin, or political opinion during the Nazi era. Proof that a naturalized American citizen lied on his and her application in effect allowed the United States to roll back the clock and strip that individual of American citizenship.[120] Under 8 U.S.C. § 1451(a), a certificate of naturalization may be canceled if it was "illegally procured or . . . procured by concealment of a material fact or by willful misrepresentation." Critically, there is no statute of limitations on civil immigration and naturalization fraud claims. Once citizenship was revoked, the United States would then initiate removal proceedings, by which the now denaturalized ex-Nazi would be sent to another country that would take him or her. Despite initial predictions that its work would last no more than a decade, OSI was active for over twenty-five years. With the opening of the Soviet archives in the 1990s, its workload actually increased. The treasure trove of Nazi documents seized by the Soviets brought to light other Nazi persecutors who emigrated to the United States after the war. The majority of persons against whom OSI initiated proceedings were guards at concentration camps and forced-labor camps. Some were former members of some auxiliary local police unit set up by the Germans in the occupied Eastern territories.

American citizenship is a precious commodity, and so immigration authorities cannot just cancel citizenship that they determine was "illegally procured" or "procured by concealment of a material fact or by willful misrepresentation." Rather, due process guarantees of the US Constitution require the federal government to initiate civil denaturalization proceedings in order to obtain an order from a judge revoking citizenship. If successful, OSI must then file a separate removal action to remove the defendant from the country. Even though both proceedings are not criminal, a quasi-criminal burden of proof is imposed on the government to prove its case by "clear, unequivocal and convincing evidence that does not leave the issue in doubt," a standard substantially identical to the "beyond a reasonable doubt" standard of criminal prosecutions. Even after successful denaturalization and deportation proceedings, the defendant remains in the United States until another country is found willing to take the deportable individual. This makes denaturalization and deportation proceedings a long and drawn-out process. Initially heard by a federal immigration judge, the proceedings are subject to appeal all the way to the US Supreme Court.

One case actually reached the Supreme Court, *Fedorenko v. United States*,[121] where the Supreme Court upheld the constitutionality of the Holtzman Amendment. Fedor Fedorenko was a Ukrainian who became a guard in the Treblinka death camp in Nazi-occupied Poland. There was no selection process in Treblinka. Every man, woman, and child arriving there would be immediately sent to be murdered. After OSI successfully denaturalized him, Fedorenko moved back to Soviet Ukraine, where he was put on trial, found guilty, and executed. Other former Nazis chose more hospitable places. Arthur Rudolph, one of the Nazi scientists brought to America, helped develop the Saturn 5 rocket that launched a crew of American astronauts on the first manned flight to the moon in 1969. Rudolph voluntarily gave up his US citizenship and moved back to Germany in 1984 after OSI accused him of working thousands of slave laborers to death while director of the German factory that produced the V-2 rocket during the war. San Francisco resident Elfriede Rinkel, an eighty-six-year-old widow who had worked as a female guard in Ravensbrück and later married a Jewish man, also did not challenge her denaturalization and in 2006 quietly left the country to live out her remaining years in Germany.[122]

The longest set of proceedings undertaken by OSI was against John Demjanjuk, a Ukrainian serving in the Red Army who was captured by the Germans in 1941. Demjanjuk went on to serve as an SS guard in Sobibor, one of the five extermination camps that the Germans built in occupied Poland. In 1952, Demjanjuk emigrated to the United States from Germany, claiming that he had spent most of the war as a prisoner. He lived in Cleveland, where he worked for many years at a Ford auto plant and raised a family. The legal saga to denaturalize and deport Demjanjuk and then try him for his Nazi past began in 1977 in a US immigration court. It lasted over thirty years and took place in courtrooms on three continents. OSI first accused Demjanjuk of being "Ivan the Terrible," a notorious sadistic guard at Treblinka, even though a Nazi ID card provided by the Soviet authorities indicated that Demjanjuk had been based at Sobibor. Witnesses appeared, however, claiming that Demjanjuk was the terrible Ivan of Treblinka. With his citizenship revoked in 1981, Demjanjuk agreed to be removed to Israel to stand trial for being Ivan the Terrible. He thereby became only the second and last non-Israeli besides Eichmann to be tried under the NNCL. Based on the Nazi guard photo ID in his name and witness testimony from Treblinka survivors, he was found guilty in 1988 by the Israeli District Court. Like Eichmann, Demjanjuk was sentenced to death. By the time the case came on appeal to the Supreme Court of Israel, it fell apart. As discussed above, the opening of Soviet archives after the fall of the Soviet Union led to the discovery of other Nazi persecutors living in the United States. For Demjanjuk, the result was exactly the opposite. Newly discovered Nazi documents in Soviet archives pointed to another Ukrainian guard named Ivan—Ivan Marchenko—as being Ivan the Terrible.

Israel could have put Demjanjuk on trial for a second time, not for being the terrible Ivan of Treblinka but for being the not-so-terrible Ivan of Sobibor (the actual death camp where Demjanjuk served)—but took the legalistic route. Since Demjanjuk was extradited to Israel only on the charge of being Ivan the Terrible, the proper procedure after reversal of Demjanjuk's conviction was to roll back the extradition. After spending seven years in an Israeli jail, Demjanjuk returned to the United States, where his citizenship was restored in 1998. OSI then initiated a second round of deportation and removal proceedings for still lying on his entry papers by failing to reveal that he was a guard at Sobibor. In 2009, he was deported a second time, this time to Germany, which was ready to try him. In 2011, Demjanjuk was found guilty for his role as guard at the Sobibor death camp. In the words of Lawrence Douglas, Demjanjuk was the right "wrong man."[123] Demjanjuk was given a five-year sentence, but allowed to stay at German nursing home while his case was being appealed. In 2012, he died at age ninety-one while awaiting the fate of his appeal.

With the pool of potential defendants quickly dwindling, the US Department of Justice in 2010 effectively closed down OSI, merging it with another agency. The merged unit, the Human Rights and Special Prosecution Section (HRSP), investigates and prosecutes modern-day genocidaires who might have made their way into the United States. The mandate of HRSP is listed as "seek[ing] to prosecute human rights violators under the federal criminal statutes proscribing torture, war crimes, genocide, and recruitment of child soldiers . . . [and] human rights violators under U.S. civil immigration and naturalization laws in order to revoke U.S. citizenship or other legal status."[124]

D. RETROSPECTIVE

In 1980, the ZS chief prosecutor announced that his Nazi-hunting office would be closing in a few years. He was incorrect. In the twenty-first century, we are still in the throes of the last batch of persecutions of Nazi war criminals, octogenarians and nonagenarians who are judged to be in sufficiently good health by the courts to be prosecuted for crimes they committed over sixty years or so earlier.

In 2010, as noted above, ninety-year-old John Demjanjuk was extradited from the United States and put on trial in Germany after his American citizenship was revoked for lying on his refugee application in the 1950s. At his 2011 trial in Munich, Demjanjuk was found guilty as an accessory to the murder of

27,900 Jews deported to the Sobibor death camp from Holland during his time there. Though a few Sobibor survivors testified at the trial, none could identify Demjanjuk. His assignment as a guard at this death camp, proved through Nazi documents, was sufficient for the court to adjudge him as an accessory to almost 30,000 murders. According to the court decision: "The guards knew exactly what would happen to the people arriving at the camp, from everyday abuse to gruesome murders. . . . [Duties rotated around the camp] so that every single guard would be involved in all parts of the process."[125] Demjanjuk was given a five-year sentence. In March 2012, he died with his appeal pending. His death also brought to an end prosecutorial efforts to charge him with the deaths of an additional 4,400 Jews during the time that Demjanjuk served later as a guard at the Flossenbürg concentration camp in Bavaria.

The Munich court's acceptance of the prosecution's legal theory that Demjanjuk was an accomplice to 27,900 murders without proof of what he actually did at Sobibor opened up a whole new avenue of prosecutions. Taking the Demjanjuk precedent one step further, a prosecutor in the northern German city of Lüneburg in 2014 charged former SS Officer Oscar Gröning of 300,000 counts of accessory to murder for the approximate number of Hungarian Jews brought to Auschwitz on the orders of Adolf Eichmann, who were gassed during a fifty-seven-day period in 1944 in Auschwitz. Unlike Sobibor, Auschwitz was not only a death camp, and so not every SS member participated in the killing process. The ninety-three-year-old Gröning volunteered for the SS when he was twenty years old. At age twenty-two, he was stationed in Auschwitz. An apprentice banker before the war, Gröning became leader of a squad that collected and sorted valuables taken from Jews arriving by cattle car at the Auschwitz ramp. These belongings were then shipped back to the Reich and distributed or sold. As an SS officer, Gröning directed prisoners to collect the suitcases and clear away the bodies of those who had died on the trains. For this, he was dubbed by the media as the "Bookkeeper of Auschwitz."[126] At this trial, Gröning admitted moral guilt but claimed never to have participated in the selection process or any acts of killing, and the prosecution could prove none. He testified to observing mass gassings and burning of the corpses, but claimed that he himself had no involvement in these actions. After a three-month trial, Gröning was convicted as an accessory to murder and sentenced to four years' imprisonment. The prosecutors successfully argued that simply by sorting banknotes taken from the trainloads of arriving Jews about to be exterminated made him an accomplice to the mass murders because he was part of the machinery of death at Auschwitz. Unlike the Ukrainian Demjanjuk, Gröning was a German and an SS member. He was also stationed at Nazi Germany's most infamous concentration camp, and so his trial and conviction had important symbolic value for Germany—and especially becasue Gröning turned out to be one of the last Germans convicted as a Nazi war criminal.[127]

What made this prosecution different was that, to use modern parlance, Gröning outed himself a decade earlier when in 2005 he began giving interviews to the press recounting his experiences as an SS soldier at Auschwitz. He also appeared in a BBC documentary on the history of the camp. Gröning did so to counter claims of Holocaust deniers that there were no gas chambers at Auschwitz. In an interview with the German magazine *Spiegel*, he also recounted:

> A new shipment had arrived. I had been assigned to ramp duty, and it was my job to guard the luggage. The Jews had already been taken away. The ground in front of me was littered with junk, left-over belongings. Suddenly I heard a baby crying. The child was lying on the ramp, wrapped in rags. A mother had left it behind, perhaps because she knew that women with infants were sent to the gas chambers immediately. I saw another SS soldier grab the baby by the legs [and kill it].[128]

Gröning appears also to have been the only SS officer on trial to have admitted moral responsibility for his actions. "This moral guilt I confess, with remorse and humility before the victims. . . . I beg for forgiveness," he told the court at the start of the trial, in front of several Auschwitz survivors who appeared as co-plaintiffs. As for criminal responsibility, he told the judges: "You must decide on the legal guilt."[129]

Eleven months after Gröning's conviction, a five-judge court in the small northern German town of Detmold found another former Auschwitz guard, Reinhold Hanning, guilty as an accessory to at least 170,000 murders during his time as an SS guard at the camp from January 1943 to mid-1944. The June 2016 verdict came after a four-month trial for the 94-year-old Hanning, a retired dairy farmer. As with Gröning, the prosecution offered no proof at trial that the former twenty-four-year-old SS squad leader actually participated in any killings while stationed at Auschwitz, though he was there when hundreds of thousands of Hungarian Jews were murdered. Presiding judge Anke Grudda in her courtroom address to the defendant explained: "For two and a half years, you watched as people were murdered in gas chambers. . . . You had an important function. With your guard duties, you ensured a seamless performance of the killing machine."[130] Hanning was sentenced to five years' imprisonment; because of his advanced age he is unlikely to serve any prison time.

What are we to make then of the efforts to prosecute Nazi war criminals and collaborators over the last seventy years? Now that this legal enterprise is coming to an end, a legal reckoning is most apt. It is easy to be critical and conclude that the law has not served well the actual victims of Nazi crimes. Efraim Zuroff, the top Nazi hunter at the Simon Wiesenthal Center, estimates that individuals who can be labeled "Nazi war criminals" numbered at least in the hundreds of thousands.[131] Of these, very, very few were put on trial. Whatever justice was dispensed at Nuremberg and thereafter is overshadowed by the massive impunity afforded to hundreds of thousands of German, Austrian, and other perpetrators who were never called to account for their deeds. Historian Donald McKale in his 2012 study, *Nazis After Hitler: How Perpetrators of the Holocaust Cheated Justice and Truth,*[132] paints a most bleak picture of the project and its legacy.

> [T]he majority of Nazi perpetrators of the Holocaust survived without Hitler into the postwar era, a few briefly and most for many years. . . . Neither the perpetrators nor the world experienced an extensive, badly needed reckoning for what, between 1939 and 1945, nearly physically wiped out an entire people of Europe. Tragically, the post-Holocaust world had little sympathy for the victims and thus little will to punish the perpetrators.[133]

McKale is, of course, correct that of the hundreds of thousands of individuals that participated in the persecution of innocent civilians during the Second World War only a minuscule number ever had to answer for their acts.[134] But what makes the post-Holocaust period different from the aftermath of other earlier genocides is precisely the commitment over the last seventy years to bring perpetrators to justice. What Nuremberg and its progenies have done, in the words of legal scholar Mark Drumbl, is to create the "judicialization of World War II atrocities in Europe."[135] The fact that *some* prosecutors around the world had the will to bring Nazi perpetrators to justice, rather than allowing them to live out their lives peacefully, today serves as a model for preventing perpetrators of modern-day genocides and other mass atrocities from escaping prosecution.

5

Civil Litigaton for the Financial Crimes of the Holocaust

It is a truism that no amount of financial remuneration can compensate victims of a genocide for the lives lost, never mind the monetary damages suffered. Yet part and parcel of every genocide is theft. Monetizing losses from a mass atrocity and then seeking compensation from the wrongdoers, both the actual perpetrators and their accomplices, invariably leads to heated discourse in proportion to the painful emotions that arise from the tragedy. Historian Michael Marrus begins his book on Holocaust restitution *Some Measure of Justice* with the words "Spit at it"—uttered by literary critic Leon Wieseltier to his mother about what to do with Germany's offer to make restitution payments to Holocaust survivors.[1] Elie Wiesel, in his preface to Stuart Eizenstat's book *Imperfect Justice* speaks of feeling "reluctant to define the greatest tragedy in Jewish history in terms of money."[2] To put it simply, money and genocide don't go well together. Yet restitution may be the only form of justice available to survivors.

A. STEALING FROM THE JEWS

Economic dispossession of the Jews was a critical part of Nazi Party policy. One of the first actions taken by Hitler's storm troopers was to paint *Jude* (Jew) on the storefronts of Jewish shops as part of the state-sanctioned call on April 1, 1933, for an economic boycott of all Jewish businesses. Law, as discussed in Chapter 1, became an important tool of Nazi thievery, depriving Jews not only of their civil rights but also their possessions. Regulations mandated that Jews detail all their property on government-issued forms. Registration was the first step in the process of both legal and extralegal confiscations. Jews in the Reich fortunate enough to obtain an exit visa had to leave most of the property behind as the price of departure. Part of Adolf Eichmann's evil genius upon arrival in Austria in 1938 was to create a one-stop thievery shop, the Central Office for Jewish Emigration, where Jews within the course of one day would legally turn over their assets to the state in exchange for an exit visa (see Chapter 4).

"Fire sales" of Jewish property became common in the Reich as Jews desperately sought to sell their assets at distressed prices. "Jew auctions" also became a normal part of the German economy, where properties of the departed Jews would be sold off at bargain basement prices. According to Holocaust historian Peter Hayes, "By the summer of 1939, the Third Reich had reduced German Jews to penury and pocketed at least 3 billion of the 7.1 billion reichsmarks in property that they had registered the previous year."[3]

Upon takeover of foreign territories, the properties of the Jews there were likewise confiscated and sent back home as part of the social safety net instituted by the Nazis to keep the civilian populace content. Birkenau contained large warehouses, nicknamed by the inmates "Canada" (for a place of seeming abundance), where goods taken away from arriving prisoners were sorted and then stored. The same trains that would bring Jews to their deaths were then used to ship the plunder back to Germany. The cut hair was used to make ship rope and mattresses, among other products. Prying gold teeth from the mouths of the Jews just gassed by specially designated prisoner "barbers" was part of an efficient method that all possessions of the Jews would be put to good use. The gold was melted down and deposited in an SS bank account.

Extralegal theft was a common phenomenon, with Jews being able to save their life or the life of a loved one by bribing Nazi guards or someone from the local populace. Both *hiding Jews* in exchange for cash or valuables and *hunting for Jews* in exchange for a monetary reward from the German authorities became brisk businesses in German-occupied Europe. Authorities in Berlin became concerned that the amount of extracted gold and other valuable items sent back to Germany from Auschwitz did not total the amount they had anticipated, and so they sent Konrad Morgen, an SS judge with training in investigations, to Poland to conduct an audit.[4] Morgen later was sent to investigate alleged corruption taking place in the Płaszów concentration camp, run by the notorious commandant Amon Göth. In October 1944, the SS arrested Göth for corruption. Göth was accused of violating SS regulations by not turning over to SS authorities the wealth that had been forcibly taken from Jewish prisoners as well as from ghetto residents. Before then, however, Oscar Schindler was able to save the Jews on his list by appealing to Göth's rapaciousness.

The conundrum created by the perversity of German SS law that legally allowed for genocide but punished unsanctioned mistreatment of Jewish prisoners and private theft is aptly noted by Holocaust historian Saul Friedlander: "[SS head Heinrich] Himmler was of course confronted with an ongoing and intractable issue: How to stem wanton murder in an organization set up for mass murder; how to stem widespread corruption in an organization set up for huge-scale looting."[5]

But even the supposedly morally upright Himmler was not immune from thievery. In a letter written in 1942, Himmler counseled: "We have a moral right, an obligation to our people, to take the people who want to kill us, and kill them. But we have no right to enrich ourselves with a single fur, a watch, a single mark, a cigarette, or anything else."[6] In his next letter home, however, he mentions a gold bracelet that he was sending along and a fur coat that would be forthcoming. Both, presumably, were booty stolen from Jewish inmates of his SS concentration camps.

B. RETURNING WHAT WAS STOLEN

Upon Germany's defeat, the goal of returning what was stolen was a high item on the Allies' agenda, though the primary focus was to return state wealth embezzled from the formerly occupied countries.[7] American-based Jewish organizations such as the World Jewish Congress sought to make sure that the robbery of the Jews was not forgotten and presented plans to the Western occupation authorities, especially the Americans, detailing how much was stolen from the Jews and proposals on how it should be returned. The end result, however, was that "the monetary value of compensation payments [to Jewish survivors and heirs] rarely equaled the worth of what individuals lost."[8] The same can be said for restitution to non-Jewish victims.

During the last seventy years, there have been three key periods in Holocaust restitution. The first period was the immediate postwar era, when the Allies sought to recover and return assets stolen by the Nazis throughout Europe (and Jewish property was part of the returned booty). The second period began with the return of German sovereignty in 1949 and featured the agreement by West Germany in 1952 to make payments to the new state of Israel for the next decade and to individual Holocaust survivors during their lifetime. The payments to the still-living survivors continues today, but will end in the next decade when the last of the still-living survivors of the Holocaust will die out. The third period began in the 1990s, more than a half-century after the end of the Second World War, when the subject of the Jewish losses arose again, but this time wholly unexpectedly and with its locus surprisingly in the United States. This section focuses on the three periods.

1. Restitution by the Allies in Occupied Germany

The first materialization of the policy to reimburse victims of Nazi theft were wartime measures intended to harm Nazi Germany's economy. One such measure was the 1944 Operation Safehaven, aimed to block Germany from transferring assets to neutral countries.

Following Germany's unconditional surrender in May 1945, the Allies established the quadripartite Allied Control Council, the legislative body under which occupied Germany would be ruled. The Control Council soon began enacting a series of laws to turn back the massive theft within Germany that took place during the last twelve years. Forcing the Nazis to forfeit their property was an important part of the Allies' strategy in their control of postwar Germany, as vital as putting the wrongdoers on trial. For this purpose, the Allies granted themselves broad discretionary powers to determine what property could be seized.

US Military Government Law No. 52 (the Blocking Control Law), enacted weeks after German surrender, served as the foundation of "Property Control." Law No. 52 made all property in Germany subject to seizure and management by the military government. All transactions involving cultural materials of value or importance and property owned or controlled by religious, educational, cultural, and scientific institutions were prohibited. It also "blocked all property owned or controlled directly or indirectly in whole or in part by the Reich or any political subdivision or agency thereof, the Nazi Party and affiliated organizations, all persons who were high in the political and economic life of Germany, and persons residing outside of Germany." Notably, the "block" applied to any property that had been acquired under duress and allowed the military government the right to seize it. US Military Government Law No. 59, the first of the property restitution laws, was enacted on November 10, 1947. It called for the restoration of identifiable property that had been seized on racial, political, or religious grounds. It also established the principle that a "successor organization" would have the right to claim the assets of those who had perished and to use the proceeds for the relief and rehabilitation of survivors. In August 1947, four German states in the American zone promulgated laws to provide financial indemnification to victims of Nazi persecution. In May 1948, the US Military Government in Germany authorized the Jewish Restitution Successor Organization to recover unclaimed Jewish property and the property of dissolved Jewish communities and associations in the American zone.

In the newly liberated countries, local authorities issued decrees nullifying all transfers made pursuant to German regulations or by German occupation courts. Poland is representative. The June 6, 1945, "Decree on the Binding Force of Judicial Decisions Made During the German Occupation in the Territory of the Republic of Poland" provided that all court judgments delivered during the German occupation were invalid and had no legal effect. The provisions of the 1945 decree were further developed by Polish Supreme Court. The court held that German notarial deeds executed during the occupation, used to "legally" transfer property to the German occupiers, had no legal effect. The 1945 decree also invalidated contracts for property purchased from German administrators or occupier-appointed trustees. Former owners, however, still had to initiate administrative or court proceedings to invalidate the contract. The law had minimal effects on the prewar Polish Jewish population because most had either perished during the war or left the country.

In the end, the efforts to seize stolen wealth and return it to its proper owners was only partially successful. As discussed in Chapter 3, even assets seized from wealthy industrialists convicted at Nuremberg by the American NMT tribunals were soon returned to them upon their release from prison. Furthermore, the Nazis incurred only minor financial penalties for their crimes, which directly impacted the victims' compensation. With the creation of the Federal Republic in 1949, restitution ceased. In East Germany, whatever the Soviets did not seize as war booty and take back home (including entire factories) was nationalized with the creation of the German Democratic Republic and became property of the new German Communist state.

German Jews could reclaim their property after the war in the Western sectors of occupied Germany. One lawyer working on restitution for German Jews and other Nazi victims was Benjamin Ferencz, former chief prosecutor of the NMT *Einsatzgruppen* trial (see Chapter 3). Ferencz stayed in Germany and took on the job as the first director of the United Restitution Organization (URO), a legal aid society based in Frankfurt formed by German Jewish lawyers who fled to Britain during the war. Its task was the restitution of both real estate and movable properties such as bank accounts, securities, jewelry, and furniture stolen from German Jews now living outside of Germany. Ferencz also held the position of director general of the Jewish Restitution Successor Organization (JRS O), the first so-called successor organization set up by the American military administration in 1948 with its office in Nuremberg. The JRSO was designated as the legal successor of heirless property of murdered Jews and defunct Jewish communal groups located in the American zone. The proceeds from the sale of such properties was used to assist Jewish survivors worldwide. Ferencz's other task was to obtain compensation from German companies that employed Jewish slave labor during the war. Eventually, Ferencz and his colleagues were able to reach slave labor agreements with six German companies that used Jews as slaves during the war whereby each of the companies created a compensation fund for its former slaves.[9]

Restitution efforts were also made in the other Eastern European states, but these soon ended as the Soviet-liberated countries fell behind the Iron Curtain. Surviving Jews, in effect, became "double victims": first of the Nazi regime that stole their assets and then of the new Communist regimes that instead of returning what was stolen, nationalized the properties. Restoration of Jewish communal property in Poland and other East European states began taking place only after the fall of Communism.[10]

2. German Reparations to Israel and Survivors

On September 10, 1952, West Germany entered into the Luxembourg Accords, agreeing to pay $845 million in reparations. The first agreement was a bilateral treaty with Israel, the so-called Luxembourg Agreement.[11] The second agreement was with a specially created pass-through entity, the Conference on Jewish Material Claims Against Germany ("Claims Conference") based in New York, by which West Germany would make payment to a limited class of survivors living in the West, to be distributed by the Claims Conference. To this day, Germany recognizes the nongovernmental Claims Conference as the sole representative of world Jewry to deal with Germany for Holocaust-era restitution claims.

The agreements were reached after six months of negotiations with Israeli diplomats and Jewish representatives primarily from the World Jewish Congress (and especially its president Nahum Goldmann). Israel's original demand was $1.5 billion, the supposed cost to be incurred by the new country in absorbing Holocaust survivors who arrived in Israel after the war. The $1.5 billion demand was based on 500,000 survivors coming to Israel, with $3,000 cost for each survivor.

The bilateral treaty between the Federal Republic and Israel came into force in March 1953 and led to the eventual transfer of DM $3 billion in goods and services to Israel.[12] The transfer took place over fourteen years, between April 1, 1953, and March 31, 1966.[13] During this period, Israel received from West Germany a multitude of goods that included such items as ships, cars, factory and medical equipment, technology, and agricultural products. The goods imported into Israel under the agreement constituted between 12 and 14 percent of Israel's annual imports over the next decade—an enormous help to the economy of the new nation.[14]

The agreement between the German Federal Republic and the Claims Conference consisted of two protocols: (1) a promise to enact German laws that would compensate Jewish victims of Nazi persecution for indemnification and restitution claims arising from Nazi persecution and (2) DM $450 million transferred to the Claims Conference for individual payments to Jewish survivors living outside of Israel.[15]

These agreements were, and still are, revolutionary. As Nehemiah Robinson, Jewish activist and principal legal adviser to the Claims Conference at the time, explained: "[I]n no previous case in history had a State paid indemnification directly to individuals, most of them not even its own citizens."[16] David Ben-Gurion, Israel's first prime minister, who gave the green light to negotiate directly with the Jewish people's former enemy, explained: "For the first time in the history of the Jewish people, oppressed and plundered for hundreds of years . . . the oppressor and plunderer has had to hand back some of the spoil and pay collective compensation for part of the material losses."[17] Elazar Barkan calls the Israeli-German agreement "the moment at which the modern notion of restitution for historical injustices was born."[18]

On the German side, the architect of Germany's compensation program was Konrad Adenauer, West Germany's first prime minister. Adenauer's reasons for pushing for compensation were multifaceted. West Germany sought to become a *bona fide* member of the new anti-Soviet Western alliance, and Adenauer, who himself had no Nazi connections, badly wanted to draw a line through the Nazi past. Paying compensation was an effective way to do so. Adenauer also had a problem: many of his technocrat public officials had been former Nazis. The leading ex-Nazi was Hans Globke, Adenauer's chief of staff. In 1936, as an official in the Reich Interior Ministry, the jurist Globke co-authored the definitive commentary on the Nuremberg race laws. Globke also penned the laws that gave all property belonging to concentration camp victims to the German government.[19] And so Adenauer came up with a solution to the problem of so many compromised elites returning to power. As Jeffrey Herf points out: "Given Adenauer's view of the depth of Nazism's roots in the German past and its residues in the postwar era, he shifted the focus regarding the Holocaust away from war crimes trials and toward the somewhat less contentious matter of restitution payments to Jewish survivors and to the State of Israel."[20]

On September 27, 1951, Adenauer made a historic speech before a special session of the German parliament announcing that Germany was ready to negotiate:

> The federal government, and with it the vast great majority of the German people are conscious of the immeasurable suffering that was brought to bear upon the Jews in Germany and in the occupied territories during the period of National Socialism.... [U]nspeakable crimes were perpetrated in the name of the German people which impose upon them the obligation to make moral and material amends, both as regards the individual damage which Jews have suffered and as regards Jewish property for which there are no longer individual claimants.[21]

Adenauer's Christian Democrats and their conservative coalition allies were steadfastly opposed to reparations, so he did not even have support of his own party. Adenauer instead had to seek support from his political opponents, the Social Democrats, who under their leader Kurt Schumacher had closely lost the first postwar German election.[22] When it came time to vote in parliament on whether to negotiate with Israel, the Social Democrats unanimously voted in favor, with a majority of Adenauer's fellow Christian Democrats voting in opposition. As for the other Germany, the official view of the German Democratic

Republic was that it had no moral responsibility to make payments because all the Nazis had been purged from its territory and were now living in the Federal Republic of Germany.

For Israel, entering into an agreement with the state that represented the tormentors of the Jews was one of the most painful decisions it had to make. A common mindset among worldwide Jewry after the war was to shun all things German, whether visiting the country or purchasing German products (German cars being the most visible item). One cannot overestimate the amount of loathing that Jews worldwide and survivors in particular felt toward Germany after the war.[23] When word leaked out that David Ben-Gurion's government was negotiating with West Germany, massive demonstrations took place against accepting such "blood money." These were the first major street demonstrations to take place in Israel since its formation in 1948. In the end, pragmatism won out. Israel badly needed German aid, and so the Israeli Knesset (parliament) by a vote of 61–50 agreed for Israel to negotiate directly with Germany.

Since much of the payments came in the form of goods, German products flooded the Israeli economy. For many years, Israel was the only country outside of Germany where the most common model for a taxi was Mercedes-Benz. For the next twelve years, 15 percent of Israel's economic growth and 45,000 jobs, according to the Bank of Israel, "could be attributed to investments made with reparations monies."[24] Israel also had (and still has) the largest population of Holocaust survivors. The individual payments helped survivors who often came to Israel with nothing more than clothes on their backs to reestablish their lives. Ultimately, more than 250,000 Israelis received some form of compensation from Germany, with the lump sum payments to survivors equaling, on the average, a year's income.[25] For individual survivors, the choice of whether to file an application for compensation also posed a moral dilemma, with a small but significant number of survivors refusing to accept monetary payments from Germany.[26]

In all, since the payments began in 1952, Germany has paid over $70 billion in Holocaust restitution.[27] Over 600,000 Jews surviving the Holocaust received some kind of payment from Germany. A number of survivors in Israel and around the world continue to receive monthly compensation checks from Germany. Others, depending on the level of suffering during the war, received a one-time payment. As example, Jews who escaped to the East into the Soviet hinterland (including this author's parents), received a one-time payment of €2,556.

Finally, a small but important point on terminology. Germany calls its program of Holocaust reparations *Wiedergutmachung,* translated as "to make whole." The Jewish side rejects the term, since making whole in the aftermath of the Holocaust is impossible. I use the term "restitution" to cover both payments/transfer of goods to Israel and individual payments to survivors. In Hebrew, the general term used is *shilumin* ("reparations")—from Jewish legal tradition that denotes punitive payments—as opposed to *pitsuim* ("compensation") since compensation for the Jewish lives lost and monetary losses is impossible.[28]

3. Holocaust Restitution in the 1990s—A Measure of Justice Fifty Years Later

The modern-era Holocaust restitution campaign had very strange beginnings. It started with three class action lawsuits filed in New York federal court in 1996 against Swiss banks for failure to return bank accounts and other deposits by Jews in neutral Switzerland during the Hitler era. The private banks and the Swiss National Bank were also accused of trading with Nazi Germany in looted assets, including gold stolen by the Nazis. The campaign proceeded with further class action litigation, this time against European insurance companies for failure to honor Holocaust-era insurance policies. Holocaust survivors then began filing class action suits against German companies for profiting from the slave labor of Nazi victims, the same unresolved issue that Nuremberg prosecutor Benjamin Ferencz was handling through the 1950s. French and Austrian banks were also sued for persecuting their Jewish customers. Finally, there was Nazi looted art. Museums, galleries, and private collectors, first those located in the United States and then in Europe, began to be sued in American courts by survivors or heirs seeking the return of, or compensation for, art looted by the Nazis from Jewish families that came into the hands of these persons and entities after the war.

Why the United States?

In my 2003 book *Holocaust Justice: The Battle for Restitution in America's Courts,*[29] I tried to provide an answer to why this third period of Holocaust restitution was born on American soil. I pointed out that "[t]he unique features of the American system of [civil] justice are precisely those factors that made the United States the *only* forum in the world where Holocaust claims could be heard today."[30] Eight factors made Holocaust restitution possible in the United States:

1. The ability of foreign citizens to file suit in the United States for human rights abuses committed in foreign lands.
2. The recognition of jurisdiction over defendants that do business in the United States, even over claims that occurred abroad.
3. The recognition of class action lawsuits.
4. The ability of lawyers to take cases on a contingency basis, thereby giving Holocaust claimants top-notch legal representation when filing suits against European and American corporate giants.
5. A legal culture in which lawyers are willing to take high-risk cases with a low probability of success, in order to test the limits of the law.

6. Fixed and affordable court filing fees when filing a civil lawsuit.
7. The ability to have a jury trial in civil litigation.
8. The existence of an independent judiciary that does not "take marching orders" from the political branches of government.[31]

The United States–centered campaign took the form of four strains, each one acting independently, but at the same time each dependent on each other. These were:

1. The filing of lawsuits in American courts—primarily in federal courts and most as class actions—seeking damages in the millions and billions from European (and also some American) corporations alleged to have profited from the exploitation of Jews and other persecuted minorities during the Nazi era and for theft of Jewish assets, including bank accounts, real estate, and gold. All of the European corporations had, and have, substantial business interests in the United States, and so are subject to jurisdiction in American courts.

2. American public officials, at both the federal and state level, putting a spotlight on theft of Jewish property and use of Jewish and non-Jewish slave labor, with some officials threatening sanctions against European companies as a lever to get the companies to seriously deal with these claims. On a diplomatic level, President Bill Clinton appointed longtime diplomat Stuart Eizenstat as his special representative on Holocaust restitution issues. Nearly two decades later, Ambassador Eizenstat is still involved with the issue and in 2015 helped to effectuate the latest Holocaust restitution settlement with France (see below).

3. Jewish organizations in the United States, particularly the World Jewish Congress (WJC) under its then-head Edgar Bronfman, the Canadian-American liquor magnate, seeking restitution for Jewish theft. After Bronfman's death, the WJC mantle was taken up by Ronald Lauder, the heir to the Estée Lauder cosmetics empire.

4. American media keeping a spotlight on the problem. In our post-Holocaust world, Nazi stories make good news, and stories of Nazi theft and search for loot are even more intriguing.

We can analogize these strains as comprising a four-legged stool, with each leg necessary for the stool to stand. And in this instance, each strain was necessary to bring these long-forgotten financial injustices from the Nazi era into the spotlight and their resolution.

What Did the Lawsuits Accomplish?

The results of the lawsuits were succinctly summarized by Ambassador J. Christian Kennedy, the US State Department Special Envoy for Holocaust Issues, in 2007:

> A combination of court settlements and other U.S.-facilitated agreements resulted in over $8 billion for Holocaust victims and their heirs from Swiss banks, German companies, Austrian companies, and French banks, as well as several large European insurance companies. Most of these agreements were concluded with the participation of European governments and the U.S. Government. As of today, nearly all of the $8 billion from these agreements has been either distributed to survivors and heirs or otherwise obligated for continuing programs to support needy survivors or promote Holocaust education and remembrance.[32]

The fact that American courts for the last decade and a half have dealt with wrongs committed during the Second World War, over a half-century after the events took place, is astounding. In the history of American litigation, these cases represent litigation with the longest window between wrongful acts and the pursuit of litigation arising from such wrongs. However, in evaluating the successes of the Holocaust restitution suits, it is important to remember their limitations.

First, none of these lawsuits went to trial. All ended with settlements; meaning that the victims of the Holocaust or their heirs filing these suits "never got their day in court."

Second, some of these suits ended in complete defeat in court. Just because the European corporations did substantial business in the United States was not enough to hold them liable for acts that took place fifty years later, on another continent, and against victims that were not American nationals at the time. In some instances, however, even when the European defendants won, they did not walk away from the negotiating table but continued to negotiate to reach some kind of settlement. Germany and its corporations, for example, realized that they had not only a legal but a political problem—and a significant public relations headache on their hands. A legal victory still would not keep American politicians from pushing for the Germans to make some kind of compensation. It also could not counter Holocaust victims and their supporters reminding the American consumer that the German products they were buying—whether cars, computers, aspirin, or insurance—were from the same companies that were implicated in some of the most horrific crimes committed in human history.

Third, while each of the settlements in totality involved large sums, some in the billions of dollars, the individual payouts for most survivors and heirs have been small. As an example, a Holocaust survivor working as a slave at Auschwitz for a German company under the most horrific conditions—what the German

Nazis called the "death through work program"—received a one-time payment of approximately $7,500. Non-Jewish forced laborers shipped to Germany from Eastern Europe during the war received $2,500. Survivors of one of the gruesome medical experiments conducted at Auschwitz received less than $10,000 as total compensation for their suffering.[33] Count Otto Lambsdorff, the German government representative to the slave labor negotiations with Ambassador Eizenstat and the American lawyers, testifying before the US Congress, defended the settlement figures: "Believe me, I wish I had greater funds available for distribution. But 10 billion marks [approximately $5.2 billon] is what we got and what was agreed upon by all the participating parties after long and arduous negotiations."[34]

For this reason, at most we can call these payments "symbolic justice." Much more important than the sums received was the recognition by the perpetrators of the wrongs committed against the victims and an issuance of an apology to those victims. As explained by Eva Kor, an identical twin experimented upon at Auschwitz by the infamous Dr. Mengele: "Even though this is a small amount of money, it is a big help to those survivors who are in need of assistance. And more importantly, this shows that Germany has recognized what was done to the victims and has not forgotten their suffering."[35]

Finally, the hidden role of German companies during the Nazi era came to light in the 1990s as these companies opened their archives to Holocaust historians to write reports on their wartime history. American companies have also done the same. The lawsuits also led many European states (Switzerland being the most notable) to reevaluate their wartime history by creating historical commissions to research their archives and thereafter to issue statements of contrition for their wartime behavior. German multinationals likewise retained historians to research their Nazi-era activities in response to revelations that they participated in and benefited from the brutalities of the Nazi regime. The Holocaust restitution movement, therefore, yielded not only money; it also yielded new history and apology.

Art looted by the Nazis and discovered to have been in the collections of the most prominent museums in the world, galleries, and private hands for the last half-century also began to be returned to their rightful owners and heirs at the end of the 1990s, and the process continues to this very day. In 2006, after six years of American litigation and a successful victory before the US Supreme Court a year earlier, Maria Altmann, an elderly survivor from Austria living in Los Angeles, with the assistance of her lawyer Randy Schoenberg, recovered from the Austrian National Gallery five artworks by Gustav Klimt stolen from her family by the Nazis. Altmann and her fellow heirs sold one of the works to Ronald Lauder for a reported $135 million, then the highest price ever paid for a single work of art. The four other Klimts were later sold through auctions for a total of $192 million.[36]

Twenty years after it began with the litigation against the Swiss banks, the Holocaust restitution campaign continues, and most especially with Nazi looted art. In May 2015, Henry Matisse's *Femme Assise* was returned to the Rosenberg family in New York by the German government more than seventy years after its disappearance.[37] The Matisse belonged to Paul Rosenberg, one of the world's leading dealers in modern art, whose collection was looted by the Nazis. The Matisse was part of the accidental discovery by German tax authorities in 2012 of about 1,200 paintings in the small Munich apartment of Cornelius Gurlitt, an elderly recluse and the son of a wartime art dealer Hilderbrand Gurlitt who sold stolen artworks on behalf of the Nazis.[38] German prosecutors seized the paintings, said to be worth over $1 billion. Gurlitt died in 2014 and donated his entire collection to a Swiss museum. The German government, however, held on to the collection to determine the provenance of each painting. The Gurlitt discovery is just the tip of the iceberg. According to the US National Archives, approximately 100,000 works of art looted by the Nazis have yet to be located.[39] The accidental discovery of the Gurlitt hoard demonstrates how little we know about the current whereabouts of the Nazi looted art dispersed around the world.

4. Holocaust Restitution in the Twenty-First Century: The French Railroad Settlement

By the time Barack Obama entered the White House in 2008, it appeared that the only vestige of the Holocaust restitution movement continuing in the twenty-first century was Nazi looted art. The litigation against European banks and insurance companies ended with settlements in 1998 and 2004, respectively (though the $1.25 billion distribution of the Swiss banks class action settlement fund did not end until 2015). The German fund established through the "legal peace" settlement in 2000 with Germany and its corporations by the Clinton administration had within a few years also finished making symbolic payments to former Jewish slaves and non-Jewish forced laborers of German industry and other related claimants. The George W. Bush administration in 2005 settled an action against the United States arising out of the so-called Hungarian Gold Train, a train containing booty stolen from Hungarian Jews captured by the US Army at the end of the war.[40] An announcement in December 2014, therefore, by the Obama administration that it had concluded another Holocaust restitution settlement came as a surprise to all of us following the Holocaust restitution story.

The settlement came out of a class action lawsuit first filed fifteen years earlier alongside the other class action lawsuits filed by American lawyers in the late 1990s. This particular lawsuit, filed in New York federal court, was against SNCF (*Société nationale des chemins de fer français*, or National Society of French Railways), the French state-owned railway company. It arose out of the fact that during the war SCNF transported over 70,000 Jews to concentration camps in Poland.

Germany's invasion of France in 1940 led to a quick German victory. Under an armistice, most of France was occupied by the German forces, but a collaborationist French government was allowed to govern southern France with its capital in the spa town of Vichy. While there was local resistance to the German occupiers, there was also extensive collaboration, both in Vichy France and in occupied France. This shame of collaboration was not fully confronted until 1995 when French President Jacques Chirac acknowledged the role of non-Jewish French citizens in the persecution and murder of Jews. One of the most shameful episodes was the extensive roundup in 1944 of Jewish men, women, and children, undertaken mostly by French police. After imprisonment in transit camps, the Jews were sent to Poland, where most of them were murdered. The mode of transportation was by SNCF cattle cars.

SNCF did not deny that it transported 76,000 Jews to Auschwitz from the Drancy internment camp outside Paris. But it refused to pay restitution, saying it acted under duress, by order of France's German occupiers. The class action lawsuit in the United States, *Abrams v. Société Nationale des Chemins de fer Français,* claimed that SCNF had legal responsibility. According to the complaint:

> SNCF assembled and ran the deportation trains and knew that conditions on those trains would cause thousands to die before the trains reached their destinations. SNCF also knew that the French civilians it delivered to the Nazi death and slave labor camps, in Germany and elsewhere, would be killed or enslaved by the Nazis as part of the Third Reich's policy of genocide. SNCF is therefore liable to Plaintiffs and Plaintiff Class because SNCF knowingly engaged in a course of conduct, and participated in a common plan or conspiracy, both directly and indirectly, to commit war crimes and crimes against humanity.[41]

The lawsuit was initially dismissed by the New York federal judge, heard on appeal multiple times by the Second Circuit of Appeals and once by the Supreme Court, and ultimately dismissed in 2006 for lack of jurisdiction. That year another lawsuit was filed in the United States, *Freund v. Société Nationale des Chemins de fer Français,* but it too was unsuccessful when the Supreme Court in 2011 declined to hear the final appeal by the Second Circuit dismissing that suit also for lack of jurisdiction.[42] A companion case filed in France, *Lipetz et al. v. Prefect of Haute-Garonne and the Société Nationale des Chemins de fer Français,* also was ultimately dismissed by French courts.[43]

Claimants and their American lawyers, however, did not give up. Instead, they approached American federal and state government officials for assistance.

A number of American survivors of these transports contacted the media, which ran stories on the subject. Most prominent among the deportee survivors was survivor Leo Bretholz.[44] In 1942, Bretholz was a young man on a French SNCF train with about 1,000 other Jewish deportees headed to Auschwitz.[45] Bretholz escaped during the journey, prying open with another man loose bars on a small window and then jumping from the moving train. He survived the rest of the war by joining the French resistance. After the war, Bretholz moved to the United States and settled in Baltimore. Quoted in *The Washington Post*, he explained: "All I want is a declaration—a forceful declaration [by SNCF]—of '[w]e did something very wrong, something inhumane. We sent people to their deaths.' "[46]

In Congress, legislators introduced the Holocaust Rail Justice Act, a proposed law that would have specifically granted jurisdiction to federal courts for suits filed against SNCF for its wartime acts. The bill, opposed by both the Bush and Obama administrations, went nowhere. It led, however, to congressional hearings on the issue, with Bretholz as star witness. Testifying before the US House of Foreign Relations Committee, Bretholz recalled the squalid conditions of the SNCF trains:

> For the entire journey, SNCF provided what was one piece of triangle cheese, one stale piece of bread and no water, he said. There was hardly room to stand or sit or squat in the cattle car. There was one bucket for us to relieve ourselves. Within that cattle car, people were sitting and standing and praying and weeping, fighting.[47]

Bretholz was insistent that although SNCF claimed it was coerced into participation, it was still legally responsible. Most critically, the deportations for SNCF was a commercial venture. Apparently, the German authorities paid the company a fee, calculated per head and per kilometer, to transport the deportees to the camps.[48] Until his death at age ninety-three in March 2014, Bretholz continued to advocate for compensation to the surviving victims of the French transports. He died nine months before the settlement was announced.

The breakthrough came when claimants and their lawyers learned that SNCF, through its American subsidiary, Keolis North America, was going to bid on a new lucrative rail construction contract in Maryland. The contract, worth $6 billion, was to be paid over thirty-five years.[49] The Maryland governor and its state legislature began to signal that Keolis might be barred from bidding on such contracts. That did it. In December 2014, the French government issued a surprise announcement that it had agreed to make payments to the former French deportees.[50] Brought back to government service to effectuate the settlement was Ambassador Eizenstat, the godfather of Holocaust restitution. As announced by Eizenstat, the agreement took the form of a bilateral agreement between the United States and France, after (of what we learned later) was a year of negotiations with France undertaken by the Obama administration. Under the agreement, France agreed to create a $60 million fund to be distributed by the US government among a limited group of survivors deported by French trains to German-occupied Poland. Those who returned to France after the war were specifically excluded from the settlement. Eligible were those who settled outside of France. The rationale for limiting the fund to these deportees was that by emigrating abroad after the war, these French survivors were excluded from a 1948 French compensation program set up for returning French Jews. If such deportees are no longer alive, payment can be made to surviving spouses and, in some instances, to the survivors' children or other heirs. Payments are set to begin in 2016–2017, after the 2016 application deadline ends. Eligible claimants are set to receive approximately $100,000 (definitely more than a symbolic payment), depending on the number of claims filed.

The French settlement is the latest example of how the four-legged stool model can bring a small measure of Holocaust justice for the financial crimes of the Holocaust. The class action litigation, though unsuccessful, was the loud knock on the door that brought the issue of SNCF's role in the Holocaust into the forefront. The media kept the issue alive by producing stories on the subject. The Internet also became a valuable tool for disseminating the SNCF story, with the lawyers and claimants forming a group called the Coalition for Railroad Justice (http://holocaustrailvictims.org) publicizing the claims. Bretholz even started a petition on change.org that raised over 165,000 signatures. The winning push came from American legislators. The introduction of bills in the Maryland legislature barring any company involved in the wartime deportation of Jews from being awarded government contracts appears to be the main impetus for the French government wanting to settle the claims. And the agreement by the US government to give "legal peace" to France and its industry by agreeing to oppose any lawsuit arising out of French wartime activities filed in American courts provided the assurance to France and its industry that the settlement would put the issue behind them.

The French railroad settlement also has important symbolic value since trains are a ubiquitous symbol of the Holocaust. Trains transported millions of Jews for "resettlement" to the East: in actuality to their deaths in the death camps that Nazi Germany constructed in occupied Poland. According to historian Alfred Mierzejewski, it took no more than 2,000 trains to perpetuate the Holocaust.[51] The late Holocaust historian Raul Hilberg was obsessed with the use of trains as a critical enabler of the genocide of the European Jews. In his article "German Railroads/Jewish Souls," Hilberg noted that "railways [cannot] be regarded as anything more than physical equipment"—but in the hands of the Germans they "became a live organism which acted in concert with Germany's military, industry, or SS to make German history"[52] and marked "the end of the Jewish people in Europe."[53] One of the most prominent displays at the US Holocaust Memorial Museum is a German boxcar used for deportation of Jews to the killing centers in Poland.

C. WHY DIDN'T THE HOLOCAUST RESTITUTION MODEL WORK FOR OTHER HISTORICAL ATROCITIES?

The perceived successes in the Holocaust restitution litigation led other victim groups to file claims modeled upon these suits. These included: claims against Germany and German companies stemming from the Herero genocide in Southwest Africa at the beginning of the twentieth century; claims against Japan and Japanese industry arising out of the Second World War; claims against multinationals arising out of their business activities in apartheid South Africa; claims for African-American reparations arising from the American slave era; and claims against American and French insurance companies that sold life insurance policies to Armenian citizens of Ottoman Turkey in the pre–First World War era, but which did not honor the policies in the aftermath of the Armenian genocide.[54]

1. Herero Genocide Litigation

On the eve of the centennial of the Armenian genocide in April 2015, Pope Francis called the Ottoman massacres of the Armenians the first genocide of the twentieth century.[55] He was wrong. The first genocide in the modern era was the 1904–1907 genocide of the Herero tribe by Imperial Germany in Southwest Africa, present-day Namibia. As explained by Yale historian Ben Kiernan: "The destruction of the Herero proved to be the opening genocide of the twentieth century."[56] Germany was a latecomer in European colonialism, but in the nineteenth century began playing catch-up with the other European states. It soon became the third-largest colonial power, after France and Britain, with colonies in Africa, China, and the Pacific. One of its colonies was *Deutsch-Suedwestafrika* (German Southwest Africa), established in 1884. Like the Belgians in the Congo, the Germans were not enlightened colonialists. Seeking to exploit the land and other natural resources of the area (gold was supposed to have been plentiful) and the local populace, they expelled the native peoples from their land, forced them to work as slaves, and compelled them to give up their culture and tradition. Coincidentally, the colonial governor of *Deutsch-Suedwestafrika* was Heinrich Ernst Göring, Hermann Göring's father.

In 1904, the Herero rebelled. To quell the uprising, troops of Kaiser Wilhelm II under the command of Prussian general Lothar von Trotha murdered some 65,000 Herero tribe and 10,000 members of the neighboring Nama (also called the Namaqua) tribe, which also rebelled. Survivors were put in concentration camps and forced to work as slaves. Some Herero were forced to undergo medical experiments, and skulls of victims (finally returned in 2011) were brought to Germany for scientific research. Historians today refer to the campaign between 1904 and 1907, the years it took to squash the rebellion, as Germany's first act of genocide, almost four decades before the Holocaust.[57]

While over the years Germany has provided significant amounts of aid to Namibia, it has stopped short of making a formal apology. Its reluctance stems from the fear of exposing itself to billions of dollars in compensation claims from Herero descendants. If the German government can provide compensation for genocide of the Jews, why should it not pay compensation for the genocide of the Herero? Unable to obtain a full apology or reparations from Germany, the Herero descendants did what Jewish claimants did before them: they filed civil suits in the United States. The timing seemed to be right. The year before Germany and its blue-chip companies settled the litigation against them by obtaining what they called "legal peace" in return for a $5.2 billion fund to pay slave and forced laborers and other victims of German industry. They did so even though in 1999 two class action lawsuits were dismissed. Despite their victory, the Germans did not walk away from the negotiating table and continued to negotiate to reach a settlement. Yet, in the Herero litigation, the Germans were not as magnanimous when the two lawsuits filed by the Hereros in the United States failed. The first lawsuit was filed in 2001 by the so-called Herero People's Reparations Corporation against Germany and two German corporations, Deutsche Bank (Germany's largest bank) and the Deutsche Africa-Linien Gmbh & Co (a shipping line that was a successor to the former Woermann Line). Plaintiffs sought damages of $2 billion. Deutsche Bank was alleged to have financed the colonial enterprise in Southwest Africa, and the shipping line was alleged to have used Herero slave labor.[58] The federal trial court dismissed the lawsuit and the D.C. Circuit Court of Appeals affirmed the dismissal in 2004.[59] The Hereros then filed a second lawsuit in federal court in New Jersey in 2005, which was dismissed on the same grounds as the first lawsuit: that American federal courts do not have subject matter jurisdiction over these claims and that the claims were time-barred. The Third Circuit Court of Appeals in 2007 affirmed the dismissal.[60] The fact that the defendant German corporation conducted business in New Jersey was not sufficient to establish jurisdiction.

2. Litigation Against Japanese Industry Arising Out of the Second World War

Over 36,000 American soldiers became Japanese prisoners of war during the Second World War. The Japanese also captured nearly 14,000 American civilians. Approximately 25,000 American prisoners were shipped to Japan and Japanese-occupied Asia to work for private Japanese companies.[61] These companies are now some of the largest corporate entities in the world: Mitsubishi, Mitsui, Nippon Steel, Kawasaki Heavy Industries, and at least forty other Japanese companies. Additionally, the Japanese captured tens of thousands of British, Canadian, Australian, and New Zealander soldiers, who toiled as slave laborers for Japanese industry. These companies also used local Chinese, Korean, Vietnamese, and Filipino civilians as slaves.[62]

The lawsuits against the Japanese multinationals are a direct result of the earlier litigation brought against their European counterparts. Aging victims of Japan's wartime activities began filing their lawsuits in American courts only after witnessing the successes achieved in the Holocaust litigation. In fact, many of the attorneys involved in the Holocaust restitution litigation acted as counsel for claimants in the litigation against the Japanese companies. Nevertheless, this litigation could not emulate the successes of the Holocaust restitution movement.

Former American POW Ralph Levenberg filed the first restitution lawsuit pertaining to Japan against Nippon Sharyo Ltd. and its US subsidiary in March 1999 in federal district court in San Francisco.[63] Other lawsuits followed in various other jurisdictions. Eventually, all such litigation gravitated to California, as a result of a state law enacted in July 1999 permitting any action by a "prisoner-of-war of the Nazi regime, its allies or sympathizers" to "recover compensation for labor performed as a Second World War slave labor victim . . . from any entity or successor in interest thereof, for whom that labor was performed."[64] With this law, the California legislature extended the limitations period for filing such lawsuits until 2010. The legislature passed the statute at the same time that the negotiations with the German companies for wartime slave labor compensation were stalled. Thus, the statute's primary goal was to allow lawsuits against these German companies to proceed in California. As an afterthought, the legislature added language to allow similar suits by POWs captured by "allies or sympathizers" of the Nazi regime, meaning Japan and Italy among others. Ironically, litigants never used the statute for its original purpose because the German companies entered into an all-inclusive settlement of the claims against them. Every attempted use of the statute was made by victims of the Pacific conflict in suits against Japanese companies.

In June 2000, the Japanese cases were consolidated before Judge Vaughn Walker, the federal judge in San Francisco presiding over the *Levenberg* lawsuit. On September 21, 2000, Judge Walker dismissed the lawsuits filed by American POWs and Allied POWs.[65] The judge held that the 1951 Peace Treaty between Japan and its former enemies prohibited the bringing of such lawsuits.[66] Since the United Kingdom and its commonwealth allies had also been parties to this treaty, Judge Walker also dismissed the claims of the British, Australian, and New Zealander POWs. While the judge temporarily left open the claims of Chinese, Filipino, and Korean civilian slaves since these victims did not come from countries which were signatories to the 1951 Peace Treaty, he later also dismissed these claims.[67] The Ninth Circuit Court of Appeals affirmed, agreeing with Judge

Walker that the 1951 Peace Treaty barred the claims. The Ninth Circuit also found that the California statute allowing such suits under California law was unconstitutional, amounting to an improper interference with the federal government's exclusive role in foreign relations.[68] The US Supreme Court refused to review these decisions.

The Herero litigation failed, in large part because the claims concerned atrocities committed over a century earlier in a faraway land, with none of the actual victims still alive to present their claims. In contrast, the Holocaust restitution litigation featured actual survivors as plaintiffs. The presence of individuals like Leo Bretholz to tell their story—in the media, in government hearings, and then in court if the cases ever came to trial—made their claims much more compelling. The litigation against Japanese companies for their participation in Second World War atrocities carried the same favorable factors—and in some ways even more since the plaintiffs were aging GIs who fought in the Pacific War and were part of the Greatest Generation now so beatified in American culture. Why the difference in the results?

One major reason was the different posture taken by Japan and its companies to the litigation involving Pacific War. While the European entities sued in the Holocaust cases were ready for legal and moral closure, and therefore willing to provide a symbolic gesture toward the victims in the form of compensation, Japanese corporations expressed no contrition or willingness to achieve any moral or legal closure. On the eve of his departure from the US government, Stuart Eizenstat, President Clinton's special representative on Holocaust issues, expressed in an interview with the *New York Times* that "one of his regrets was his inability to get Japan to make a similar commitment to Chinese, Korean and others whose assets had been seized or who had been forced into slave labor. The 1951 treaty with Japan clearly foreclosed a lot of options to seek redress, he said, adding, 'In the end we never heard back from the Japanese government or companies.' "[69]

The only avenue for relief left to the victims of Japan and its industry remains, therefore, with the political process and public pressure. The elderly claimants still hope that Japan and its industry some day soon, and perhaps while some of them are still alive, will follow the actions of Germany and its industry, who, even after winning in American courts, still continued negotiating because they desired to bring an end to the claims against them.

On the eve of the seventieth anniversary of Japan's surrender, Prime Minister Shinzo Abe recalled in 2015 that his predecessors expressed remorse for the war and acknowledged that Japan inflicted during its militarist era "immeasurable damage and suffering."[70] But he would not apologize. And he stressed that "we must not let our children, grandchildren, and even future generations to come, who have nothing to do with the war, be predestined to apologize."[71] Japanese industry, however, may be ready to follow German industry. In 2015, Mitsubishi Materials became the first Japanese company to make amends by issuing a formal

Illustration 13 Liberated US prisoners of war, Bilibid Prison, Manila, Philippines, Feb. 8, 1945. Getty Images.

Illustration 14 Hikaru Kimura, Senior Executive Officer of Mitsubishi Materials, bows to offer apology in presence of former POW James Murphy (far right). Rabbi Abraham Cooper, Simon Wiesenthal Center associate dean (middle). July 19, 2015. AP Images.

apology for its wartime activities.[72] The public ceremony took place at the Simon Wiesenthal Center in Los Angeles, dedicated to the memory of the Holocaust and other atrocities, where Mitsubishi senior executive Hikaru Kimura issued the apology and symbolically bowed in the presence of James Murphy, a ninety-four-year-old veteran who was forced to work as a slave in the company's mines during the war, and was one of the few former Pacific War GIs well enough to attend the ceremony.

In 2016, Mitsubishi went one step further: it offered an apology for its use of Chinese slave labor in coal mines during wartime and agreed to pay up to $56 million to victims ($15,000 to each victim) and families as a show of its sincerity.[73]

3. South African Apartheid Litigation

In 2002, victims of apartheid in South Africa began seeking compensation in American courts from American, Swiss, and German companies who did business in South Africa during the apartheid years and directly benefited from the apartheid system. Different groups of American lawyers, aligning themselves with groups of South African lawyers, filed a series of class action lawsuits.[74] Named in the lawsuits as defendants were the Holocaust class action lawyers' old nemeses: Switzerland's UBS and Credit Suisse; Germany's Deutsche Bank, Dresdner Bank, and Commerz Bank; and also American corporate giants Ford Motor Co. and IBM Corp. Plaintiffs asserted that American courts have jurisdiction over these suits because all of the corporate defendants do business in the United States. Additionally, the claimants asserted, apartheid is a universal tort over which American courts should have universal jurisdiction. The lawsuits were consolidated before a federal judge in Manhattan.[75]

If the South African apartheid lawsuits had succeeded, they would have been an example of a historical wrong that did not have to wait fifty years or longer for redress. Unlike the German and other European companies which profited from genocide and then were brought to account almost a half-century later, multinationals benefited from the apartheid system as late as the 1980s (apartheid officially ended in 1991, with the black majority government taking power in 1993). As Lulu Peterson, a plaintiff in one of the apartheid lawsuits, stated: "We want reparations from those international companies and banks that profited from the blood and misery of our fathers and mothers, our brothers and sisters."[76]

After a decade of litigation involving twelve different cases, the last such suit was dismissed by a court of appeals in 2015.[77] As a result of the US Supreme Court's 2013 decision in *Kiobel* (see next section), the last two defendants standing were

American corporations Ford Motor Co. and IBM. Ford was accused of providing military vehicles for South African apartheid security forces and sharing information about anti-apartheid and union activists. IBM, in a throwback to the accusation made for its dealings with Nazi Germany,[78] was accused of supplying South Africa with computer technology as early as 1952 used to perpetuate the system of institutionalized racial discrimination and repression in apartheid South Africa.

In a 3–0 decision, the Second Circuit Court of Appeals held that the plaintiffs did not show that Ford and IBM engaged in enough wrongdoing in the United States from the 1970s to early 1990s to justify lawsuits in American courts over their alleged roles in killings, torture, and other human rights abuses in South Africa. Mere knowledge by the corporate parent in the United States of wrongful activities by their subsidiaries did not make the American company an aider and abettor. As explained by the court: "Knowledge of or complicity in the perpetration of a crime under the law of nations (customary international law)—absent evidence that a defendant purposefully facilitated the commission of that crime—is insufficient to establish a claim of aiding and abetting liability under the ATS."[79]

4. African-American Reparations Litigation

One of the most interesting consequences of the Holocaust restitution litigation in the 1990s was to give fresh impetus to the call for payments to African-Americans for pre–Civil War slavery. Reparation proponents specifically pointed to settlement agreements for the Second World War wrongs as precedent for their cause. If the American legal system can be used to obtain $8 billion in compensation from European entities for slavery and other wrongs committed in another part of the world over a half-century ago, they argued, why can similar compensation not be made for slavery that occurred here in the United States, which ended over a century ago, but whose consequences still reverberate in the African-American community today?

Holocaust survivors and their heirs have been seeking restitution for over fifty years. The African-American slavery reparations movement is well over a century old.[80] Every year since 1989, Michigan Representative John Conyers Jr. has unsuccessfully introduced "H.R. 40" (Conyers uses the number intentionally to represent the "40 acres and a mule" promised by the US government to every freed slave) to study the issue of slavery reparations.[81] Prominent African-American activist Randall Robinson in 1999 published *The Debt*, a bestseller that forcefully argued for slavery reparations.[82] The book's theme, however, did not gain much interest outside the African-American community until Robinson and others began to use the Holocaust restitution movement as a model for their cause. Robinson now was able to entice superstar attorney Johnnie Cochran, of the O. J. Simpson trial fame, to join him in putting together another "dream team" of lawyers and activists to file suit for African-American slavery restitution, formally called the Reparations Movement Coordinating Committee.[83] Michael Hausfeld, one of the lead lawyers in the Holocaust restitution litigation, joined Cochran on the reparations legal team (Cochran died in 2005). Others on the reparations legal "dream team" included Harvard Law School professor Charles Ogletree, Alexander Pires, Jr., who won a $1 billion settlement for African-American farmers for discrimination by the US Department of Agriculture, and Richard Scruggs, who obtained a $368 billion settlement with the tobacco companies for suits filed by various US states.

In 2001, in a first important step signaling the revival of the African-American reparations movement, California enacted a law forcing American insurance companies who sold policies insuring slaves as chattel to disclose information about such policies.[84] In May 2002, following the mandate of the California law, five American insurance companies reported that they insured slaves: Aetna, Inc., American International Group, Inc. (AIG), Manhattan Life Insurance Company, New York Life Insurance Company, and Royal & Sun Alliance.[85] In 2003, in an article published in a Harvard law journal, Ogletree expressly acknowledged the precedent of the Holocaust restitution lawsuits: "All these cases are suits against corporations for their involvement in slavery; the plaintiffs have developed their causes of action on the basis, in part, of the Holocaust litigation model of suing corporations."[86] In another section of his article, titled "Creating Viable Lawsuits: Addressing the Doctrinal Challenges Faced by Reparations Cases," Ogletree laid out a detailed roadmap of how the litigation can succeed.[87] He advised: "Reparations suits are most likely to successful when the broad redress sought can be presented in narrow legal claims."[88]

Another important precedent was the success of the so-called redress movement for the wartime internment of American citizens of Japanese ancestry.[89] The redress movement resulted in the 1998 passage of the Civil Liberties Act,[90] which authorized a one-time lump-sum payment of $20,000 to approximately 60,000 Japanese-American survivors of the wartime internment. Equally significant, President George H. W. Bush in 1990 issued an apology to the Japanese-Americans on behalf of the US government for their wartime imprisonment.

The first African-American reparations lawsuit came in March 2002, against Aetna and two other name-brand corporations, Fleet Boston Financial Corp. and CSX Corp. (the largest railroad on the East Coast), claiming they profited from slave labor. The suit sought unspecified damages, but the plaintiffs' attorneys declared that they would be asking for $1.4 trillion, the figure alleged to represent the current value of unpaid African-African slave labor and interest.[91]

The next month, a second lawsuit was filed, adding as defendants New York Life, investment firm Brown Brothers Harriman & Co, and railroad Norfolk Southern Corporation. Other lawsuits followed. In October 2002, nine lawsuits were consolidated before federal judge Charles Norgle in Chicago.[92] As Ogletree noted in 2003: "The number of reparations lawsuits and legislative initiatives at the local and state level is unprecedented."[93]

Ultimately, the litigation failed, but for reasons having nothing to do with the merits, but rather on the basis of the statute of limitations. Since slavery in the United States ended in 1865, Judge Norgle adjudged that the suits were time-barred. In 2006, the Seventh Circuit Court of Appeals affirmed the dismissal, and the Supreme Court in 2007 declined to hear the case. In addition to the long time gap between litigation and injury, another difficult problem the courts faced is finding the proper class of aggrieved claimants who would have standing in the case. In both the Holocaust restitution and Japanese slave labor lawsuits, the plaintiffs were the actual survivors or slaves, or their immediate heirs. Similarly, in the Japanese-American internment movement, the claimants also were individuals who were actually interned by the US government during the war. No former American slaves are alive today to serve as plaintiffs. Ambassador Eizenstat explained the difference between the two movements: "For slavery *qua* slavery, I think the appropriate remedy is affirmative government action in general, rather than reparations . . . [a]nd if 100 years from now the great-great-grandson of a Holocaust laborer asked for reparations, I don't think that would be appropriate, unless there was some specific property that had been confiscated that they wanted to recover."[94] Passage of time and identification of claimants posed, therefore, the major legal obstacles.

5. Armenian Genocide–Era Litigation

During the Turkish Ottoman Empire, Armenians and other minorities purchased insurance policies from European and American insurance companies, which marketed those policies in the region. Many of the Armenian purchasers perished in the Armenian genocide during and after the First World War. Their relatives, some of whom survived the genocide as young children and are now quite elderly, sought payment from the insurers, claiming that payments were never made on the policies. In 2000, twelve elderly Armenians brought the first lawsuit in Los Angeles federal court against the American insurance giant New York Life Insurance Company. All but one of the claimants resided in the United States. Claimants filed the suit, *Marootian v. New York Life Ins. Co.*[95]

as a class action, similar to the Holocaust restitution litigation, and sought for New York Life to pay on the policies.

New York Life did not dispute that it sold such policies to the Armenian population in Ottoman Turkey. In fact, it combed its archives and located records, including aged insurance cards, for 2,300 Armenian policyholders from that time period. It argued, however, that the suit should be dismissed because all of the policies contained forum selection clauses mandating that if a dispute ever arose about the policies, the parties would resolve such a dispute either before French or English courts. In addition, New York Life argued that, since the policies were written and allegedly unpaid almost a century ago, the lawsuits were time-barred.

California, which has the largest population of residents of Armenian descent in the United States, again came to the rescue. In 2001, the California legislature enacted a statute similar to those it had passed in response to the Second World War–era slave labor litigation. Like the Second World War–related statute, this statute: (1) allowed suits to collect benefits on Armenian genocide–era policies to be heard in California courts, despite the forum-selection clauses in the policies, and (2) extended the limitations (prescription) period of such suits to 2010.[96]

New York Life argued that the statute was unconstitutional, on the same grounds that the Japanese companies challenged the constitutionality of California's slave labor litigation statute. In November 2001, federal judge Christina Snyder in Los Angeles rejected New York Life's arguments and upheld the Armenian insurance policy statute.[97] The Armenian plaintiffs had won a significant victory, but it appeared to be short-lived. Since the Ninth Circuit Court of Appeals in 2003 found the California slave labor unconstitutional, it could likely reach the same result for the Armenian insurance statute once New York Life appealed Judge Snyder's ruling.

It was time to settle, especially since in May 2001, New York Life offered a settlement of $15 million, which the Armenian insurance claimants earlier rejected as inadequate. New York Life, to its credit, continued to negotiate. In January 2004, success was achieved when the parties agreed to settle the Armenian insurance claims against New York Life for $20 million.[98]

The legacy of the Holocaust restitution cases was critical to the success of the settlement reached in the Armenian genocide litigation. Plaintiffs' lead attorney Vartkes Yeghiayan, who initiated the legal campaign against New York Life, explained: " 'For the first time [the Armenian community] has gone beyond lamentation and liturgy to litigation,' from picketing and 'going to church every April 24 [Armenian Day of Remembrance] and mourning' to taking legal action."[99] Paying homage to the Holocaust restitution movement, Yeghiyan noted: " Holocaust victims heirs showed me the way."[100] Unfortunately, later suits arising out of the Armenian genocide all were dismissed, with some, as of this writing in 2016, still on appeal.

6. Shutting the Door on Universal Jurisdiction: The 2013 *Kiobel* Supreme Court Decision

As discussed earlier, a major reason why the Holocaust restitution litigation was taken seriously was because of the precedent established beginning in the 1980s by American courts holding that they have jurisdiction over suits filed by foreigners for human rights abuses committed in foreign lands.[101] The seminal case was *Filartiga v. Pena,* a landmark decision issued in 1980 by the Second Circuit Court of Appeals, in New York, which held that the perpetrator of state-sanctioned torture in Paraguay could be sued in the United States by the relatives of the deceased torture victim.[102] The court of appeals allowed the case to go forward, even though the torture was committed in Paraguay and all the parties were Paraguayan. The decision was a ringing endorsement of the principle of universal jurisdiction, that certain human rights violations are so abhorrent to modern society that their perpetrators can be brought to justice anywhere in the world.[103] And "bringing to justice" means not only criminal prosecution but also civil liability. As Judge Marcus Kaufman, the author of the *Filartiga* opinion explained: "[F]or purposes of civil liability, the torturer [today] has become like the pirate and slave trader before him[:] *hostis humani generis,* an enemy of all mankind."[104]

The jurisdictional basis for *hostis humani generis* litigation was a federal statute enacted by the First Congress of the United States and used by the *Filartiga* plaintiffs to file their suit in Brooklyn.[105] The law is commonly known today as the Alien Tort Statute (ATS).[106] Enacted in 1789, the federal law provides American federal courts with a specific grant of subject matter jurisdiction over civil suits filed by alien (noncitizen) plaintiffs like the Filartigas. However, the ATS only applies for those most serious torts that are also violations of treaties or customary international law, or the term used at the time of the statute's enactment, "the law of nations." From its early days, the ATS provided federal courts with subject matter jurisdiction over such serious international law violations as piracy or attacks on diplomats. Since 1980, the ATS was interpreted under the *Filartiga* precedent to allow foreign victims of such modern-day internationally recognized human rights violations as torture, genocide, and crimes against humanity. The alien plaintiff coming to American shores to sue had to show that the alleged perpetrator (including foreign citizens) was physically located in the United States (or had some other significant ties to justify personal jurisdiction) and had committed a *hostis humani generis* universally condemned tort.

The *Filartiga* plaintiffs were awarded a multi-million-dollar judgment against their *hostis humani generis* defendant Pena-Irala for the death-by-torture committed on their son and brother. However, they could never collect because Pena-Irala was soon back in Paraguay and had no assets in the United States which could be seized to satisfy the judgment. Nevertheless, Dr. Joel Filartiga and his daughter Dolly, the father and daughter plaintiffs of their deceased son and brother, respectively, Joelito Filartiga, obtained an important symbolic victory since an American court solemnly declared that the death-by-torture committed of Joelito was a universal wrong.

And so it went for the next thirty years. Victims of torture and other massive human rights abuses continued to file suits under the ATS against the *hosti* perpetrators found to be in the United States (either living here or passing through momentarily) and then receiving paper judgments (most often in the millions). Most often, the *hosti* would not even participate in the lawsuit after being served, and so the final ruling would be a default judgment assessing monetary damages.

But the ATS plaintiffs' bar was not satisfied with just symbolic victories and paper judgments. In the mid-1990s, a new class of ATS lawsuits appeared targeting multinational corporations that had invested in foreign lands with dictatorial regimes. Suing under the ATS were the local peoples of Third World countries alleging that serious human rights violations were committed against them by their rulers with the connivance of these corporations. While the ATS specifically limits the class of plaintiffs that can sue under the statute—aliens only—it is silent on the class of defendants that can be sued.[107] And so, as explained by law professor Michael Goldhaber: "In the mid-1990s, activist lawyers on both sides of the Atlantic were trying to figure out a way to hold multinational corporations liable for human rights and environmental abuses committed in other nations. Lawyers in the United States primarily chose to use the vehicle of the Alien Torts Statute (ATS)."[108] In 1996, the New York–based Center of Constitutional Rights, the nongovernmental organization that had filed the suit on behalf of the Filartigas two decades earlier, filed an ATS suit against Shell arising from its investment in Nigeria in the 1990s in the oil-rich region of Nigeria called the Ogoni River Delta. In 2009, as the case was about to go to trial, Shell settled for $15.5 million.[109]

The ATS litigation against the multinationals effectively came to a halt in 2013, however, with the US Supreme Court decision in *Kiobel v. Royal Dutch Petroleum Co.*[110] The suit arose out of the same Shell oil exploration project in Nigeria. This suit was filed by another group of locals who claimed that Shell aided and abetted the Nigerian government to commit gross human rights violations in order to promote the drilling for oil in the region. The Supreme Court held that the ATS was not available to the *Kiobel* alien plaintiffs since their suit was against the foreign corporation Shell (albeit doing extensive business in the United States) for alleged wrongs committed in foreign territory. In so doing, the Court interpreted the ATS in a way it had never been interpreted before. Its interpretation was based on the application to the ATS of the judicial doctrine of "presumption against extraterritoriality." The doctrine holds that laws passed by Congress will be interpreted to apply only to conduct within the United States unless Congress specifically states otherwise. Since the language of the ATS is silent on its reach, the Court held that it must necessarily apply only to US-based conduct. As explained by Chief Justice Roberts: "On these facts, all the relevant conduct took place outside the United States. And even where the claims touch and concern the territory of the United States, they must do so with sufficient force to displace the presumption against extraterritorial application. Corporations are often present in many countries, and it would reach too far to say that mere corporate presence suffices. If Congress were to determine otherwise, a statute more specific than the ATS would be required."[111]

The *Kiobel* decision eliminated the vast majority of ATS claims that are based on overseas conduct. While we do not know how lower courts will interpret the decision, it appears that both the majority opinion by Chief Justice John Roberts and main concurring opinion by Justice Stephen Bryer refused to interpret the ATS as authorizing universal jurisdiction by American courts of civil claims based on commission by defendants of international torts *even if* such claims rise to the level of *hostis humani generis* universally condemned conduct. As put by Julian Ku: "All nine justices rejected decades of lower-court precedent and widespread scholarly opinion when they held that the ATS excluded cases involving purely extraterritorial conduct, even if the alleged conduct constituted acts that are universally proscribed under international law."[112]

The *Kiobel* decision marks the death knell of most ATS litigation based on atrocities committed abroad. The only time that such universal atrocity claims could be civilly litigated in the United States—in the absence of a new federal statute passed by Congress (a scenario impossible to imagine today)—is when such atrocities were committed by an American person or an American corporation abroad or when committed in the United States. The disparity with criminal law is startling. Under current federal criminal law, a genocidaire can be criminally prosecuted in the United States for atrocities committed abroad if found on American soil,[113] but after *Kiobel,* cannot be civilly sued under the ATS for the same acts of genocide.

Michael Thad Allen, writing in 2011, concluded: "The Holocaust-era cases of the late 1990s have had few progeny. Despite their spectacular settlements, they are a legal cul-de-sac."[114] With the 2013 *Kiobel* opinion, sadly Allen appears to have been right.

6

Holocaust Denial and the Law

A frequent question raised by anyone faced with the bizarre phenomenon of a person denying the Holocaust is how—in the face of the enormous amount of physical evidence captured from the Nazis, eyewitness testimony by survivors and bystanders, demographic data, and the various confessions of the Nazi perpetrators at both Nuremberg and during other trials—anyone could claim that the Holocaust is a hoax?

This chapter examines the phenomenon of Holocaust denial and the legal response: promulgation of national laws in Europe that make it a crime to deny the Holocaust and/or glorify the Nazi era. Seventeen European countries have promulgated such laws, with Germany in 1960 being the first and Italy in 2016 being the most recent. Seven additional states criminalize denial of genocides in general. And a few have prosecuted Holocaust and genocide deniers under their hate speech statutes. We will then examine the arguments for and against criminalization of Holocaust denial and the future of Holocaust denial legislation.

A. WHAT IS HOLOCAUST DENIAL?

Promotion of the Nazi ideology is easy to recognize. What do we mean, however, by Holocaust denial? Denialists are those individuals who dispute the basic facts of the Holocaust by denying, to use legal parlance, the *mens rea* and the *actus reus* of the crime. The following facts, recognized by all legitimate historians, are rejected by Holocaust denialists: (1) that Hitler and his fellow Nazis intended to wipe out European Jewry and ultimately annihilate the Jewish people; (2) that one means used by the Nazis to accomplish this goal was the use of homicidal gas chambers at Auschwitz and at other concentration camps; and (3) that the ultimate result of these Nazi policies was the murder of approximately six million Jews.

In the denialists' world, all three statements are false. First, claim the denialists (who prefer calling themselves "revisionists"), the Nazis did not desire to exterminate Jews. In *Denying History*,[1] a detailed analysis of the Holocaust denial movement, Michael Shermer and Alex Grobman quote denialist Bradley R. Smith, who summarizes the major creed of the movement: "Revisionists *deny* that the German State had a policy to exterminate the Jewish people (or anyone else) by putting them to death in gas chambers or by killing them through abuse or neglect."[2] Second, according to the denialists, the Nazis built the gas chambers at the concentration camps for delousing of the prisoners' clothing and blankets—not for mass murder. As to the crematoria found at the concentration camps, the denialists claim that they served to efficiently dispose of dead bodies of those who died of "natural causes": disease, starvation, and overwork. Finally, the six million figure, according to the denialists, is a gross exaggeration. Different denialists throw out different figures about how many Jews died during the Second World War, from a few thousand to a few hundred thousand. Shermer and Grobman encapsulate the beliefs of denialists into what they call the three pillars of Holocaust denial: "no gas chambers, no six million murdered, no master plan."[3]

Holocaust deniers come in two categories. First are the so-called hard-core denialists, asserting the mantra of the "3 No's." But there are also soft-core denialists, or distortionists, who will concede that a large number of Jews died during the war, but claim that Hitler did not order the murders and did not know of them.

Other Holocaust deniers aim to instill doubt by mixing truth with lies, providing incomplete or misleading information, and either ignoring incontrovertible documentation or labeling them as forgeries. Eyewitness testimonies of victims and neutral observers are labeled as fabrications. One allegation of many deniers, for instance, is to label *The Diary of Anne Frank* as a forgery. Confessions of the perpetrators are described either as unreliable or obtained under duress. And West Germany's full acknowledgment of the facts of the Holocaust—and making it a crime to publicly assert otherwise—are dismissed as political moves by a defeated nation to ingratiate itself with the Allied nations, rather than as an acknowledgment of truthful facts.

Together with their false claims the denialists and distortionists often add an equivalency argument. The Allies, they claim, killed as many, if not more Germans, during their military campaigns and also engaged in the indiscriminate and unnecessary killing of German civilians. The bombing by American and British planes of Berlin, Dresden, Hamburg, Cologne, and other German cities is usually cited as evidence of such Allied policy.

As part of their antisemitic agenda, another assertion often made by denialists is to turn the victims into perpetrators by claiming that Israel is likewise committing a genocide of the Palestinians. In effect, denialists and their supporters aim to create a moral equivalency between the *Shoah*, the modern Hebrew word for the Holocaust, and the *Naqba* ("the Catastrophe"), the Arab term designating the creation of the State of Israel in 1948. Some Israel-bashers go even further. In July 2007, Hamas leader Khaled Mashaal charged not only that the Holocaust was "exaggerated" but also that "what Israel did to the Palestinians was many, many times worse than what the Nazis did to the Jews."[4] In order to give their claims a cover of legitimacy, denialists refer to their effort as "historical revisionism" or "revisionist research." For example, one of the most active Holocaust denial organizations in the United States calls itself the "Institute for Historical Review" and titles its publication the *Journal of Historical Review*. The publication's format and tone—often containing numerous citations and written in an academic style—mimic mainstream academic publications. However, Holocaust denialists are not legitimate historians. In December 1991, the governing council of the American Historical Association, the largest and oldest professional organization of historians in the United States, unanimously approved a statement condemning the Holocaust denial movement, stating, "No serious historian questions that the Holocaust took place."[5]

Denialists reject the term "Holocaust denial" and, in one instance, brought the matter to court by suing for defamation when branded with this label. The widely publicized trial took place in London in 2000. David Irving, viewed at the time by some as a somewhat respectable British historian, sued American professor Deborah Lipstadt and her publisher, Penguin Books, for defamation. Lipstadt wrote a book in 1994 labeling Irving a Holocaust denier.[6] Irving lost. British High Court Justice Charles Gray found in his decision that "Irving had for his own ideological reasons persistently and deliberately misrepresented and manipulated historical evidence" and that "for the same reasons, he had portrayed Hitler in an unwarrantedly favourable light, principally in relation to his attitude towards and responsibility for the treatment of the Jews."[7] In effect, Irving was found to have committed historical malpractice. As explained by Justice Gray, Irving "treated the historical evidence in a manner which fell far short of the standard to be expected of a conscientious historian. . . . [He] misrepresented and distorted the evidence which was available to him." The judge concluded that Irving was "an active Holocaust denier; that he was anti-Semitic and racist and that he associated with right-wing extremists who promoted neo-Nazism."[8]

A frequently uttered argument of the denialists is that they are merely exercising their free speech rights and providing a missing alternative perspective that should not be dismissed out of hand. Their critics, they charge, are stifling free intellectual inquiry and allowing only the "orthodox" conformist view of the Holocaust to be presented in the academic and public arenas. For example, the denialist Bradley R. Smith calls his US-based group the "Committee for Open Debate on the Holocaust." Former Iranian President Mahmoud Ahmadinejad, in organizing his convocation of deniers in Tehran in 2006, argued that it is impossible in the West to debate the facts of the Holocaust because it is considered sacrosanct. Iran, for that reason, was convening a conference for such a debate.

Holocaust historians, for the most part, refuse to debate Holocaust deniers. Deborah Lipstadt explains why: "[T]he deniers want to be thought of as the 'other side.' Simply appearing with them on the same stage accords them that status."[9] In her *Denying the Holocaust*, the book for which she was sued by Irving, Lipstadt noted that it would be fruitless to respond to each of the deniers' arguments head-on. As she explains: "Time need not be wasted in answering each and every one of the deniers' contentions. It would be a never-ending effort to respond to arguments posed by those who falsify findings, quote out of context, and dismiss reams of testimony because it counters their arguments. It is the speciousness of their arguments, not the arguments themselves, that demands a response. . . . *[A]bove all, it is essential to expose the illusion of reasoned inquiry that conceals their extremist views.*[10]

Shermer and Grobman take the opposite view, pointing out the danger of failing to reply to the denialists in the court of public opinion. As they explain: "We believe that once a claim is in the public consciousness (as Holocaust denial undoubtedly is), it should be properly analyzed and, if appropriate, refuted vigorously in the public arena. . . . Not only is it defensible to respond to Holocaust deniers; it is, we believe, our duty."[11] To counter the deniers' claims, they endeavor to demonstrate the truth of the Holocaust through "convergence of evidence" analysis, meaning that independent facts all lead to the same conclusion. Here are the forms of evidence they marshal for anyone who doubts the veracity of the Holocaust:

1. *Written documents*—hundreds of thousands of letters, memos, blueprints, orders, bills, speeches, articles, memoirs, and confessions.
2. *Eyewitness testimony*—accounts from survivors, Jewish *Sonderkommandos* (who were forced to help load bodies from the gas chambers into the crematoria in exchange for the promise of survival), SS guards, commandants, local townspeople, and even high-ranking Nazis who spoke openly about the mass murder of the Jews.
3. *Photography*—including official military and press photographs, civilian photographs, secret photographs taken by survivors, aerial photographs, German and Allied footage, unofficial photographs taken by the German military.
4. *The camps themselves*—concentration camps, work camps, and extermination camps that still exist in varying degrees of originality and reconstruction.
5. *Inferential evidence*—population demographics, reconstructed from the pre–Second World War era: if six million Jews were not killed, what happened to them all?[12]

For many, Holocaust deniers are viewed with bemusement, as "kooks," on par with flat-Earth advocates and those who believe that Elvis is still alive or that the September 11 tragedy was a US-government plot. The rise of Hitler demonstrates, however, that kooks should nevertheless be taken seriously rather than viewed with amusement as harmless individuals.

B. CRIMINALIZING SPEECH: HOLOCAUST AND GENOCIDE DENIAL LAWS IN EUROPE

In Europe as of 2016, Austria, Belgium, France, Germany, Italy, the Netherlands, and Romania criminalize the denial of the Holocaust and Nazi crimes.[13] Andorra, Cyprus, Hungary, Latvia, Lichtenstein, Lithuania, Luxembourg, the former Yugoslav Republic of Macedonia, Malta, Slovakia, Slovenia, and Switzerland criminally sanction the denial of any genocide. A few others have no specific legislation but have prosecuted deniers under hate-speech statutes.

The terms "Holocaust denial laws" or "genocide denial laws" homogenize what these laws do: making certain kinds of public speech criminal, subjecting the speaker to imprisonment, fine, or both. The European Court of Human Rights has held that criminalization of Holocaust denial (though not criminalization of other genocides) is not incompatible with Article 10 of the European Convention of Human Rights, which guarantees freedom of expression.[14] Criminalization of Holocaust denial would be totally out of place in the United States. Such laws would violate the freedom of speech provisions set out in the Constitution, as interpreted by the Supreme Court. Even if Holocaust denial is considered hate speech, it still cannot be banned. American constitutional law scholar Eugene Volokh makes this clear: "[T]here is no hate speech exception to the First Amendment. Hateful ideas (whatever exactly that might mean) are just as protected under the First Amendment as other ideas. One is as free to condemn Islam—or Muslims, or Jews, or blacks, or whites, or illegal aliens, or native-born citizens—as one is to condemn capitalism or Socialism or Democrats or Republicans."[15] Volokh goes on to explain:

> To be sure, there are some kinds of speech that are unprotected by the First Amendment. But those narrow exceptions have nothing to do with "hate speech" in any conventionally used sense of the term. For instance, there is an exception for "fighting words"—face-to-face personal insults addressed to a specific person, of the sort that are likely to start an immediate fight. But this exception isn't limited to racial or religious insults, nor does it cover all racially or religiously offensive statements.[16]

The United Kingdom, Ireland, Canada, Australia, New Zealand, and the Scandinavian countries roughly follow the American model, though these states never go as far the United States, since certain kinds of speech in those states can be labeled hate speech and thereby made criminal. While Holocaust denial can be found on almost every continent, it is most rampant in those countries that place the fewest restrictions on speech. For this reason, the United States has become a popular safe haven for Holocaust deniers. With the rise of the Internet, deniers are now freely able to transmit their obnoxious ideology worldwide by using servers originating in the United States. As George Soroka aptly observes: "Once furtive pamphleteers, they are now a perpetual Internet presence."[17]

For countries that criminalize denial of the Holocaust, their rationale is "History Matters." Because of their National Socialist past or because they were occupied by Nazi Germany, these countries have chosen to make public denial of the Holocaust a crime. And the trend continues. The most recent countries to ban Holocaust denial were Romania and Italy (both wartime allies of Nazi Germany), enacting such legislation, respectively, in 2015 and 2016. The discussion that follows explores Holocaust denial legislation in the three European states where prosecution has been most prominent—Germany, Austria, and France.

1. Germany

The Federal Republic of Germany remains the country with the strictest legal regime confronting Holocaust denial and glorification of Nazism. And for a good reason. As expressed by Thomas Matussek, the German Permanent Representative to the European Union: "[T]he unprecedented crime of the Holocaust was committed by Germans and in the name of Germany and from that stems our very special responsibility."[18]

Germany has also been in the forefront of using its courts in punishing historical lies about the Second World War. As Robert Kahn notes: "In a society that prides itself on protecting speech, Holocaust deniers are one group that is beyond the pale."[19] Legislation banning the Nazi message and also denial of the Holocaust can be traced back to the original International Military Tribunal trial at Nuremberg beginning in 1945, when the Nazi Party was branded a criminal organization. With the creation of the Federal Republic in 1949, the founders of the new German state enacted legislation prohibiting the existence of political parties directed against the basic democratic order. In 1952, legislation was specifically enacted outlawing the Nazi Party (for further discussion see Chapter 7).

In 1960, the West German parliament, the Bundestag, unanimously enacted the first Holocaust denial law. Section 130 of the German Penal Code, commonly known today in Germany as the *Auschwitzlüge* law, or the Auschwitz Lie Law, prohibits denial or playing down of the genocide committed under the National Socialist regime.[20] The impetus for the law was a rise of antisemitic incidents in West Germany beginning in the 1950s, including attacks on synagogues and Jewish cemeteries. The "last straw" was the dismissal by a lower court judge in Hamburg of charges brought against Friedrich Nieland, a Hamburg businessman, who mailed an antisemitic pamphlet to 2,000 prominent Germans, including every member of the Bundestag. The pamphlets rallied against " 'International Jewry' ('the devils of the Earth') [who are] responsible for the two World Wars, for planning the third and for spreading the 'monstrous lie of a butchery of the six million Jews by the Germans under Hitler.' "[21] In his pamphlet, Nieland also demanded that "[n]o Jew hold any important post whatsoever, be it in the government, be in in political parties or in the banking world or anywhere else."[22] Even though the Federal Supreme Court later banned Nieland's pamphlet on the ground that it contravened the protection of "human dignity" provision of the Basic Law, Nieland's acquittal led the Bundestag to enact the denial law.

The *Auschwitzlüge* denial law (1) criminalized denial of the Holocaust; (2) banned the use of insignia related to Hitler's regime (the swastika, or *Hakenkreuz* in German, being the most prominent example); and (3) made it illegal to publicly disseminate written materials or images promoting the Nazi message.[23] One common-sense exception to the ban on the public display of Nazi imagery was, and still remains, use of such symbols or messages for artistic purposes, such as in art, films or plays.

The law has been amended a number of times since its initial passage in 1960. In its earlier form, Holocaust denial was outlawed as an "insult" (*Beleidigung*) to personal honor (i.e., an "insult" to every Jew in Germany). In a 1985 amendment to the law, the state—rather than individual Jews—could initiate prosecutions against purported deniers. The amendment's underpinning was that the denial of the Holocaust—what the 1985 amendment first called "the Auschwitz Lie" or the denial of the death camps—was an insult not only to the Jews of Germany but also to every German.

In 1994, Holocaust denial became an offense under a general criminal statute prohibiting racial incitement (*Volksverhetzung*). The law states that incitement, denial, approval of Nazism, trivialization, or approval, in public or in an assembly, of actions of the National Socialist regime, is a criminal offense. The 1994 amendment imposed the penalty of up to five years' imprisonment or a fine, where before the maximum penalty under the insult statute was one year. It also extended the ban on Nazi symbols and anything that might resemble Nazi slogans.[24] The law has been interpreted also to ban in public the raising of the arm in a Hitler salute (the so-called "Heil Hitler" salute) and the wearing of a Nazi uniform. Like the amended insult statute of 1960, the 1994 provision continued to make the crime an *Offizialdelikt* that is subject to compulsory prosecution by the state attorneys.

The constitutional basis in Germany for the legality of criminalizing a certain kind of political speech—pro-Nazi statements and denial of the Holocaust—comes from the Basic Law of the Federal Republic of Germany, the *de facto* constitution of Germany. In response to the dictatorship of the Nazis, the Basic Law, in Article 5(1), contains far-reaching provisions guaranteeing the right of free speech and opinion. At the same time, the Basic Law recognizes, in light of the Nazi experience, that such freedoms can be abused and lead to their end. For this reason, the very next article of the Basic Law, Article 5(2), expressly limits these freedoms, stating: "These rights [of freedoms of expression] shall find their limits in the provisions of general laws, in provisions for the protection of young persons, and in the right to personal honor." The German Federal Constitutional Court (FCC) in 1994 held that Holocaust denial was not even protected opinion under Basic Law Article 5(1) since it amounts to not an opinion but false speech. As such, it is outside of the purview of constitutional protection of Article 5(1) protecting "the right [of every person] to express and disseminate his opinions in speech, in writing and pictures." As the FCC explained: "The prohibited statement that there was no persecution of Jews in the Third Reich is an assertion of fact which is proved to be untrue according to innumerable eye witness reports and documents, the verdicts of courts in numerous criminal proceedings, and the findings of history. Taken by itself, an assertion of this content does not, therefore, enjoy the protection of freedom of opinion."[25] German jurisprudence is clear: allegations about the Holocaust that have been proven to be false or that the speaker knows to be false are not protected by freedom of expression.

Moreover, the Basic Law makes another value take precedence over free speech: human dignity, guaranteed in the very first article of the Basic Law.[26] In the Foreword by the Federal President to the year 2012 edition of the Basic Law, former German president Johannes Rau explained: "The most important sentence in the Basic Law will always be Article 1: 'Human dignity shall be inviolable'.... This is not an abstract philosophical concept, but a binding obligation and enduring mission for all those who bear responsibility in our democratic and social state under the rule of law."[27] As interpreted by the FCC, the guardian of the Basic Law, these values of human dignity and personal honor can trump the free speech guarantees of Article 5(1).

Finally, the Germany that emerged out of the ashes of its Nazi years also is anchored on the concept of militant democracy by which those seeking to overturn the democratic order of the nation can be banned by the judiciary from the "marketplace of ideas." With regard to Jew hatred and Holocaust denial, as Kahn points out, "militant democracy has always had a special role in the fight against anti-Semitism. The wave of anti-Semitic incidents that swept across West Germany in the late 1950s led many in the Federal Republic to interpret basic law in a more communitarian fashion—opposing anti-Semitism took precedence over protecting speech."[28]

In 2009, the FCC upheld the law banning the public support of the Nazi regime. The court reasoned that the restriction was necessary to protect public peace and the dignity of the victims of the Nazis, which are "supreme constitutional values." The legislation was originally enacted in 1991 as a response to neo-Nazis assembling for an annual memorial at the gravesite of Rudolf Hess, deputy of the Nazi Party and a close adviser to Hitler. The restriction was repealed in 2000, but in the following years neo-Nazi marches drew thousands of participants, and the legislation was reenacted in 2005.

The criminalization of speech promoting the Nazi message is based on the premise that the Holocaust did not begin with the murder of the Jews but with the antisemitic speeches and writings of Hitler and his fellow Nazis. The sale of Hitler's notorious autobiography, *Mein Kampf* [My Struggle], was banned in Germany until 2016, when the copyright on the book held by the German state of Bavaria ran out.

In addition to Article 130, German prosecutors continue to rely on the slew of penal laws criminalizing "insult" to prosecute deniers. The current German federal criminal code contains twelve such penal sections under Chapter Fourteen ("Insult"), including laws criminalizing "insult," "malicious gossip," "defamation," and "disparaging the memory of deceased persons."[29] Of these, the most commonly used has been Article 185, "outlaw[ing] speech that insults a group."[30]

German prosecutors have been vigilant in prosecuting violations of the anti-Nazis laws. It is safe to say that of all the countries with such legislation, it is most strictly enforced in Germany. A number of examples illustrate the seriousness by which Germany views its Holocaust denial and anti-Nazi criminal prohibitions.

In 2002, a man who came to a carnival in eastern Germany wearing a Hitler mask was prosecuted for violating the anti-Nazi symbol prohibition. The theme of the carnival was to appear in the costume of a political leader, past or present.[31] In September 2006, a German businessman went on trial in Stuttgart for using Nazi symbols, including swastikas, on T-shirts, buttons, and other products that he was selling through a highly profitable mail-order service. In a twist, however, all the products carried an anti-Nazi message. The swastikas, for example, had thick red lines drawn through them representing rejection of Nazism along with the message below it stating: *"We reserve the right to oppose."* The case became a *cause célèbre* of sorts, with much of the German media contending that such a literal interpretation of the law was going too far. The trial judge nevertheless convicted Jürgen Kamm, owner of the mail-order company selling such merchandise, and fined him fine €3,600 (approximately $4,500).[32] In March 2007, the Federal Court of Justice overturned the conviction. A relieved Kamm reacted: "For me it's important that I can use this symbol again. There is no other [means] that shows so precisely that the person wearing it is against Nazism. I cannot imagine what the judge was thinking when he banned the symbol. . . ."[33]

Video games using Nazi imagery have also been banned in Germany. For example, *KZ Manager*, a racist video game developed in the 1990s in which the player operates a concentration camp is banned in Germany. Even games not condoning the Nazi message but only using Nazi imagery have been prohibited. For example, *Commandos: Behind Enemy Lines*, a video game that involves American soldiers on missions to kill Nazi soldiers, has also been banned.

The most vigilance has been shown to enforce Germany's *Auschwitzlüge* law. Germar Rudolf, a forty-two-year-old notorious Holocaust denier earlier deported from the United States to Germany, was convicted and sentenced in 2007 to two and a half years in prison for denying the Holocaust. Rudolf's conviction arose out of a monograph he published in hard copy and distributed over the Internet claiming that Jews were not gassed at Auschwitz. Rudolf's first run-in with the law came in 1995, when a state court in Mannheim found him guilty of breaking laws against denying the Holocaust and sentenced him to fourteen months in prison.[34] Rudolf then fled to the United States, where he sought political asylum. He also married an American citizen and, on that basis, applied for a green card. In 2005, his asylum petition was finally rejected and he was sent back to Germany. In 2006, fresh charges were brought against him, which this time included his Holocaust denial activities in the United States. It was proper to charge him for these American-based activities even though they were legal in the United States since as a German citizen he remained subject to German law. Moreover, under the German Federal Criminal Code, German courts interpreted their anti-denial laws expansively, as having extraterritorial application against German nationals.[35]

Another repeat offender has been Ernst Zündel. Born in Germany in 1939, Zündel emigrated to Canada in 1958 and settled in Toronto. From there, he began disseminating in print form a substantial amount of material denying the Holocaust. In 1974, Zündel published a booklet by a British Holocaust denier entitled *Did Six Million Really Die?* and his own works such as *The Hitler We Loved and Why*. His audience became much larger with the rise of the Internet and through the reach of a website created by his wife and webmaster, Ingrid Rimland. Because of free speech guarantees in the United States allowing Zündel to freely disseminate his views, however vile, the Zundelsite uses a US-based Internet service provider and, as of this writing, is still operational.

Canada twice tried to prosecute Zündel for his activities under their laws criminalizing intentional dissemination of false news. Even though he was twice convicted, Canadian appellate courts both times overturned Zündel's convictions. On appeal of his second conviction in 1988, the Supreme Court of Canada in

1992 declared the False News statute as incompatible with Canada's free speech guarantees and therefore unconstitutional.[36]

Zündel's legal troubles did not end with the cessation of criminal prosecutions in Canada. In 2003, Germany issued an international arrest warrant for Zündel. Pursuant to the warrant, Canadian immigration officials in 2005 deported Zündel back to his native Germany to face trial. In February 2007, a state court in Mannheim found Zündel guilty of Holocaust denial and inciting racial hatred and sentenced him to five years in prison, the maximum sentence allowed under German law for such a crime. He was released early in 2010. Banned by Canadian authorities from returning to Canada, Zündel continues to live in Germany. His German lawyer, Sylvia Stolz, was also convicted of Holocaust denial in 2008, when in the course of representing Zündel she called the murders of European Jews "the biggest lie in world history."[37] The forty-four-year-old attorney also signed a motion during Zündel's trial with "Heil Hitler."[38] Stolz was disbarred following her criminal conviction. Released in 2011, Stolz was imprisoned again in 2015 for twenty months for a speech she made in 2012 again denying the Holocaust.[39]

2. Austria

Austria, as a constituent part of the Third Reich and the original home of many prominent Nazis (Hitler included), likewise takes its anti-denialist law seriously. Austria's denial law, enacted in 1992 as an amendment to a general statute combating Nazism, is simple and direct: "[W]hoever denies, grossly plays down, approves or tries to excuse the National Socialist genocide or other National Socialist crimes against humanity in a print publication, in broadcast or other media [is subject to criminal punishment]."[40] The maximum penalty is ten years' imprisonment.

The most prominent Holocaust denial conviction took place in 2006, with the jailing of British pseudo-historian David Irving. His conviction was based on a speech and an interview he gave in Austria in 1989, in which he disputed the existence of homicidal gas chambers at Auschwitz. In his speeches, he called for an end to the "gas chambers fairy tale."[41] Irving was arrested in 2005 in southern Austria under a 1989 warrant and put on trial in Vienna. He pleaded guilty and asked to be released because he had changed his views from those he held in 1989. He explained: "I made a mistake when I said there were no gas chambers at Auschwitz."[42] Based on repeated statements Irving had been making after 1989 that continued to deny the Holocaust, the judge announced that he did not believe Irving genuinely changed his mind. The Austrian judge sentenced Irving to three years' imprisonment. After thirteen months in jail, Irving was released and allowed to return to Britain. He is barred from ever returning to Austria.

3. France

The French Holocaust denial law, passed in 1990, is formulated differently than in Germany. The law makes Holocaust denial a criminal offense punishable by a year in prison and a fine of €45,000. Known as the Gayssot Law, after the French parliamentarian who introduced the law, the legislation makes it illegal to contest the existence of any of the crimes against humanity as defined by the International Military Tribunal at Nuremberg.[43] In January 2016, the French Constitutional Court upheld the constitutionality of the law. Challenged on the grounds that the law only limited denial of one historical atrocity, the court rejected the challenge by noting that the Holocaust "has in itself a racist and anti-Semitic significance" and that its denial can be banned in France because it was committed in part on French territory.[44]

During the last two decades, approximately twenty individuals were convicted of violating the Gayssot Law, with almost all having to pay a fine. Like in Germany, there are a number of notorious repeat offenders who have made it their mission to deny the facts of the Holocaust. The first conviction was handed down in Paris in 1991 against repeat offender Robert Faurisson, a former professor of literature at the University of Lyon. Faurisson was originally dismissed from his post in the 1980s because of a number of articles he published arguing the "3 No's" (no plan to exterminate the Jews; no gas chambers; no six million). Another repeat offender has been Jean-Marie Le Pen, the founder and longtime leader of the far-right Front National (FN) Party. In 1987, Le Pen made a remark for which he was convicted of racial hatred in 1990 and fined a symbolic one franc. Le Pen appealed the ruling, claiming his freedom of expression was being denied. A court of appeals not only upheld the decision, but increased the fine to 900,000 francs (about $180,000). Le Pen was summoned to stand trial again in 2015 for remarks he made on French television saying that he did not regret his previous statements about the Holocaust. According to Le Pen, the "gas chambers were a detail of the war, unless we accept that the war is a detail of the gas chambers. I continue to hold this view because it is the truth and it should not shock anyone."[45] In response, his daughter Marine Le Pen, the current leader of a seemingly more moderate FN, dismissed him from the party. As of this writing, the rift between father and daughter continues, and his criminal case is still ongoing.

The latest conviction in France was handed out in February 2015, when a criminal court in Normandy sentenced French Nazi ideologue Vincent Reynouard to two years in jail for denying the Holocaust in Facebook postings. Reynouard represented himself in the three-hour trial. The prosecution had asked for a one-year jail sentence. The three-judge panel that convicted him doubled the sentence. In handing out its conviction, the judges considered Reynouard's previous convictions on similar charges. The sentence also reflected the rising concern in France of increasing antisemitism, exemplified most recently by the killings in early 2015 at the satirical weekly *Charlie Hebdo* and a Jewish supermarket in Paris. According to Sorbonne law professor David Chilstein: "'[W]e are in a context of rampant anti-Semitism, and since the January attacks [in Paris] everyone understands the power of words.' The court wants to appear tough on anti-Semitism."[46]

4. European Union–wide Law

Arguments that criminalization of Holocaust denial is incompatible with the European Convention of Human Rights have been rejected by the European Court of Human Rights (ECtHR). A 2015 ECtHR Fact Sheet on Hate Speech summarizes the compatibility of such laws, using its 2003 *Garaudy v. France* decision as example:

> [T]he applicant's remarks had amounted to Holocaust denial, and . . . denying crimes against humanity was one of the most serious forms of racial defamation of Jews and of incitement to hatred of them. Disputing the existence of clearly established historical events did not constitute scientific or historical research; the real purpose was to rehabilitate the National Socialist regime and accuse the victims themselves of falsifying history. As such acts were manifestly incompatible with the fundamental values which the Convention sought to promote, the Court applied Article 17 (prohibition of abuse of rights) and held that the applicant was not entitled to rely on Article 10 (freedom of expression) of the Convention.[47]

For those in favor of laws criminalizing Holocaust denial and banning other hate speech, the patchwork of laws in Europe—all carrying different standards–seemed for a long time not to be entirely effective. As a result, and also as part of the general effort to harmonize laws among the EU member states, countries with Holocaust denial legislation have sought over the years to create a uniform EU law applicable to all members. Germany led the effort for a uniform EU Holocaust denial law but was rebuffed by other member states—the United Kingdom, Denmark, and, for a time, Italy—that had no such laws on their books. The European Union began seriously considering such a law in 2001. The original proposal was modeled on the German law and specifically banned Holocaust denial, promotion of Nazi ideology, and use of Nazi symbols across the European Union. Over the years, however, the proposal was diluted to obtain the necessary unanimous consent of the member states.

In 2005, the German proposal appeared moribund when the European Union's Executive Commission recommended against enactment of such EU-wide legislation. The Commission noted that it would be "unwise" to seek a ban across the then twenty-five-nation bloc, citing the differing views of the countries involved. When Germany took over the rotating six-month EU presidency in January 2007, it made the passage of an EU-wide Holocaust denial law a priority issue. In April 2007, the EU Council of Ministers finally issued a directive that was a far cry from the EU-wide Holocaust denial prohibition law originally envisioned by the Germans.[48] Formally known as "Framework Decision on Racism and Xenophobia," the directive aims to make it a crime in all twenty-eight -member states to engage in "intentional conduct . . . publicly condoning, denying, or grossly trivialising crimes of genocide, crimes against humanity and war crimes . . . [and] directed against a group of persons or a member of such a group defined by reference to race, colour, religion, descent or national or ethnic origin. . . ."[49] The Framework Decision also contains a hate crimes provision by seeking to punish those who "publicly incit[e] to violence or hatred . . . directed against a group of persons or a member of such a group defined by reference to race, colour, religion, descent or national or ethnic origin."[50] The Framework Decision is not an EU law. Rather, the member states agreed to enact domestic legislation within two years to comply with this EU directive and to impose criminal penalties in their legislation "of a maximum of at least between 1 and 3 years of imprisonment."[51]

Supporters of Holocaust denial and genocide denial laws and anti-hate groups, for the most part, were disappointed with the Framework Decision since it contains a number of exceptions and opt-out provisions.[52] The consequence is that the goal of enacting a uniform anti-denial and anti-hate speech law was not achieved. As Michaël Privot of the European Network Against Racism (ENAR) pointed out, "We have ended up with a lowest common denominator law."[53] Since its passage in 2007, very few states have introduced domestic legislation in accordance with the Framework Decision.

The Baltic states, Poland and Slovenia, were also disappointed that the law did not criminalize the denial of Communist-era or "Stalinist crimes." These former Communist states, now EU members, fought hard to add this provision, but the cabinet ministers voting on the final draft rejected this proposal. The members also rejected a Europe-wide ban on the use of Nazi symbols, a provision that appeared in the original 2001 proposal.

In 2015, a new push came to create an EU-wide law with the publication by former British Prime Minister Tony Blair's editorial in the *London Times* calling for such legislation.[54] Blair's editorial came in conjunction with his appointment as chairman of the London-based nongovernmental organization European Council on Tolerance and Reconciliation, which, as part of its mission, seeks to have all European countries adopt laws that criminalize Holocaust denial.

C. SHOULD HOLOCAUST DENIAL BE A CRIME?

What are the arguments for and against criminalization of Holocaust denial?

1. The "Yes" Arguments

1. *Hitler came to power through speech.* If a state allows Holocaust deniers freely to disseminate their message, it is risking the rise of another Hitler and impliedly promotes the resurgence of National Socialism. At least in the early years of the Federal Republic, rife with former Nazis, there was a real fear that West Germany could become a new Weimar. The narrative carried in the new Federal Republic was that the Weimar Republic failed to take strong measures to stamp out Hitler and his followers.

This rationale is especially significant in countries like Germany and Austria, the birthplace of Nationalist Socialism, where any propagation of Nazi ideology is viewed as a threat to the public order. The existence of such laws seeks, using common parlance, to "nip in the bud" the return of Nazism by censoring certain speech of today's neo-Nazis.

2. *Holocaust denial criminalization serves as one of the pillars of postwar German identity.* German journalist Daphne Antachopoulos, speaking in favor of Holocaust denial criminalization in Germany, explains:

> People who deny the Holocaust don't do it by accident. They do it willfully and with a particular aim: to portray the Jews' fate under the Nazi dictatorship as a cock-and-bull story, while connecting it to Germany's alleged exploitation for the benefit of the Jews. Those ideas are consistent with the anti-semitic ideology of the Nazis, who chose the Jews and other minorities as scapegoats. In those days, the majority of Germans' did not bridle against this ideology—some tolerated it and looked away, others backed it. Dealing with German history was a painful process. Nor can it be brought to a close, in view of the dimensions of the Nazis' crimes. Accounting for the past includes legal action against those who have failed to learn any lessons. Remembrance of the victims and their progeny should be protected as should confidence in the constitutional state which will never again allow such atrocities and their adulation.[55]

Lawrence Douglas likewise notes that postwar German identity is based on remembering the horrors of the Holocaust, and so deniers challenge the very basis of the German state that arose out of the horrors of the Second World War. As Douglas explains:

> [B]y criminalizing denial, the German state has confirmed the sacral status of the Holocaust—as the foundational cataclysmic violence out of which the Federal Republic was born. . . . German law . . . demands that no one deny the state's monstrous past. In this manner, the German Federal Republic attempts to redeem its claims of legitimacy through acts of coerced remembering, in which the history of past crimes remains ever present and in which the law serves as the muscle of memory.[56]

German historian Hajo Funke put it more bluntly still: "We can't afford the luxury of the Anglo-Saxon freedom of speech argument in this regard. It's not that I don't understand it, it's just not for us. Not yet. Not for a long time."[57]

3. *Denial of the Holocaust is a manifestation of antisemitism, one of the oldest hatreds in human history*. Douglas explains: "Holocaust denial is an especially invidious form of hate speech. . . . [T]he literature of Holocaust denial presents classic anti-Semitic stereotypes of Jews as conspiratorial, money-hungry internationalists shamelessly attempting to extract advantage from the history of their own alleged victimization. Criminalization of Holocaust denial can thus be seen as part of a larger effort to fight hate speech with the power of the criminal law. . . ."[58]

Permitting Holocaust deniers to erase from historical memory the murder of the Jews at the hands of the Nazis and their supporters opens the door to even more horrid acts of antisemitism. As columnist Hans Rauscher of the Vienna newspaper *Der Standard*, puts it, "Denial of the Holocaust is not an opinion, it is a political act which tries to bring Nazi thought into the mainstream."[59]

4. *Denial of the Holocaust attacks one of the cornerstones of post-Holocaust Western civilization*. The Holocaust changed the very foundation of Western thought by exposing the capability of our supposedly civilized culture to commit heretofore unimagined brutalities. The result has been the creation of a new post-Holocaust consciousness about the capacity of human beings to exterminate each other. Those who seek to erase the event from Western history are therefore attacking not only the targeted victims of the event—the Jews—but are attacking all of Western society and its post-Holocaust belief system. This is also the reason why until recently denial of only this genocide was made a crime, and why the French Constitutional Court in 2016 recognized the singularity of the Holocaust to France. The

European Court of Human Rights in 2015 did the same (see discussion below).

5. *Denial of genocide is recognized by many scholars as the final stage of genocide.* Elie Wiesel, Holocaust survivor and Nobel Peace Prize laureate, considers the "denial of genocide" as the "final stage" of the genocide.[60] Elaborating on what he means, Wiesel says that the denial of genocide slays the dignity of the survivors—a double killing—by destroying the remembrance of the crime. Denial defames the dead and insults the living survivors. French classicist Pierre Vidal-Naquet, in his analysis of Holocaust denialists, labels them "assassins of memory."[61]

Criminalizing denial of the Holocaust carries a special motivation since the Nazis psychologically tormented their Jewish victims by telling them that no one would believe them. Legal responses to Holocaust denial safeguards this past from what Geoffrey Hartman has termed "an encroaching anti-memory." In the next decade or so, we will reach a time when there will be no living witnesses to the Holocaust. In this new post-survivor era we are about to enter, "the law is asked to protect the past."[62]

6. *Criminalization of Holocaust denial works to reduce this ugly phenomenon.* Public trials and conviction of Holocaust deniers helps deter Holocaust denial, according to a 2006 report by the US-based David S. Wyman Institute for Holocaust Studies. The study contends that although "some civil libertarians decried the use of laws prohibiting Holocaust-denial, but there was a noticeable decline in denial activity following the jailing of the movement's best-known figure, David Irving, in Austria, and the prosecution of prominent activists Ernst Zündel and Germar Rudolf in Germany."[63] The report added that Irving's release from prison that year, after serving one-third of his three-year sentence, was "likely to reinvigorate the denial movement in the year ahead."[64]

7. *The growing threat of antisemitism and extremism in Europe requires that Holocaust denial be banned.* Supporters of the Holocaust denial laws note that despite the passage of time, hatred of Jews in Europe has not dissipated. In some respects, it is even growing. In 2013, 1,275 antisemitic incidents were recorded in Germany, and the number has never gone below the 1,000 mark, with 2006 recording the highest number at 1,809.[65] In France, antisemitic incidents are also on the rise, climbing 84 percent in 2015.[66]

Supporters also argue that continuing criminalization, even expansion, is necessary since the transborder dissemination through the Internet of the Holocaust denier message in the current era of globalization has increased the power of the message exponentially. Social media has also increased exposure to neo-Nazi messages, which are freely posted on Facebook, Twitter, and Instagram. YouTube also hosts videos that promote Nazi propaganda. Up to 10,000 Internet users access neo-Nazi blogs and platforms every day according to *jugendschutz.net*, a German nongovernmental organization that seeks to combat extremism in cyberspace targeted to children and youth.[67] The skinhead movement is alive and well not only in Germany but throughout Europe, and most of the suspects implicated in neo-Nazi crimes in Europe are under twenty-one years old.

The danger that the Nazi message may become more attractive over time is ever-present, as indicated by the rising popularity of far-right extremist parties in European politics. Princeton historian Harold James, in a 2016 opinion piece in *Reuters* titled "There Are Good Reasons Why Europe's Jews Are Worried," speaks of "an intellectual contagion, in which native far-right radicals often use anti-Israel and anti-American slogans that proliferate in the Middle East as part of their anti-Semitic arsenal."[68]

2. The "No" Arguments

1. *Holocaust denial criminalization is counterproductive, turning deniers into free speech martyrs and leading to further dissemination of their falsehoods.* Critics oppose Holocaust denial criminalization laws on practical grounds, following Voltaire's observation: "It is the characteristic of the most stringent censorships that they give credibility to the opinions they attack."

Criminalizing Holocaust denial gives power to the vile views it seeks to suppress. Censoring Holocaust deniers creates the impression that their message has some credibility and power, and that is why the state does not allow them to propagate it. Civil libertarians take up their cause, so their ugly message is lost and what is most remembered is the result of a denier being imprisoned simply for speech. As Charles Haynes explains: "[S]tate censorship doesn't work. Putting people like David Irving in prison only makes them martyrs of the extreme right. Attempting to silence [deniers] only makes them media magnets and pushes them to more outrageous behavior"[69] and helps them to publicize their views. Holocaust denial and related laws simply have not been effective in stemming anti-Jewish hatred. Alec Brandon posits the following scenario:

> [Consider] a society in which a Holocaust denier isn't thoroughly rebutted on a television news show, or made a fool of by even the stupidest of pundits, but in which he is carted off to jail. First, the denier starts to be viewed

as a victim and martyr to some, which makes the act of Holocaust denial sympathetic. Second, the fact that the state would go to such great lengths to squelch denial only grants legitimacy to those who deny the truth (not to mention that it stokes Jewish conspiracy theories that often go hand-in-hand with Holocaust denial). Third, decreeing the "fact" that the Holocaust happened causes Holocaust remembrance groups to rely on the state's punishment to achieve their aim as opposed to taking the airwaves and trying to convince people, rather than threaten them.[70]

Libertarians quote the words of US Supreme Court Justice Louis Brandeis: "Sunlight Is the Best Disinfectant."[71]

2. *Seventy years after the end of the war, there is no chance of the return of the Nazis to power in Germany.* One can understand the need for Holocaust denial legislation in the early years of the Federal Republic, when the memory of Nazism was still fresh and many former Nazis quickly were returning to their positions of wealth and power. The publication of books like *The New Germany and the Old Nazis*[72] in 1961, arguing that Nazism in Germany was far from dead because so many former Nazis held positions in the government and military and postwar Germans still holding antisemitic views, stoked these fears. Seventy years after the end of the Second World War, these laws seem to be vestiges of a bygone era, with the threat of Nazism or another authoritarian takeover no longer credible. Some in Germany make this argument and call for a reevaluation of both sets of laws: those banning vestiges of Nazism and those criminalizing denial or trivialization of the Holocaust.

Today's Europe is not the Europe of the 1930s, when antisemitism emanated from government authorities and sprouted from the mouths of leaders. Today's elites of Europe uniformly condemn any manifestation of antisemitism or racism. At a rally in 2013 against antisemitism, German Chancellor Angela Merkel said: "Anyone who hits someone wearing a skullcap is hitting us all. Anyone who damages a Jewish gravestone is disgracing our culture. Anyone who attacks a synagogue is attacking the foundations of our free society."[73]

3. *Criminalizing Holocaust denial threatens free speech—the "slippery slope" argument.* Once you criminalize public denial of the Holocaust, what other speech will you criminally punish? The criminalization for Holocaust denial has led to a movement to criminalize the denial of other genocides and other mass atrocities, with no end in sight. In 2004, Sweden convicted a Swedish Pentecostal pastor of "hate speech" for preaching a sermon against

homosexuality.[74] Although the Swedish Supreme Court eventually reversed the conviction, the trial provoked worldwide concern about the use of hate-speech laws to limit freedom of speech and religion.[75] In an editorial objecting to the jailing by Austria of David Irving in 2006, Michael Shermer observed: "Freedom is a principle that must be applied indiscriminately. We have to defend Irving in order to defend ourselves. Once the laws are in place to jail dissidents of Holocaust history, what's to stop such laws from being applied to dissenters of religious or political histories, or to skepticism of any sort that deviates from the accepted canon?"[76]

The passage of such laws by liberal democracies also sets a bad example to totalitarian-minded regimes, which likewise enact such laws but then use them to stifle opposition. In other words, by giving the state the power to ban the offensive speech of a few, we give the state the power to limit the fundamental rights of us all. In 2005, Turkish novelist Orhan Pamuk was put on trial for questioning the official version of the mass killing of Armenians. After intense international pressure, an Istanbul judge halted the trial. But if we protect Pamuk's right to speak, then we must also protect the right of Holocaust deniers to do the same.[77]

4. *Criminalization of Holocaust denial attempts to regiment history by legislating an "Official Truth"*. Concomitant with the effort to criminalize denial of the Holocaust is the effort to criminalize the denial of other genocides. If denial of the Holocaust is made a crime in Europe, why should not other atrocities receive similar treatment? Ukraine, for example, seeks to have the Holomodor, the Stalin-imposed 1932–1933 famine, recognized as a genocide by other states and by international bodies. Within the country, it is a crime to publicly assert that the Holomodor was not a genocide. In 2015, Ukraine went a step further by making it a crime to deny the "criminal nature" of the Soviet regime.

Ukraine is not alone, as other post-Communist states seek to equate Communism with Nazism. As of 2015, in addition to Ukraine, the Czech Republic, Hungary, Latvia, Lithuania, and Poland have enacted such equivalency statutes. Other states formerly behind the Iron Curtain are certain to follow. Such equivalency is even taking place at the pan-European level. In 2008, the European Parliament declared August 23, the date when the Soviets and the Germans signed the Molotov-Ribbentrop Nonaggression Pact—which cleared the way for Hitler to invade Poland as Germany and the Soviet Union divided up Poland between them—as the European Day of Remembrance of Victims of Stalinism and Nazism, and currently called the European Day of Remembrance for Victims of Totalitarian Regimes.

Those arguing for the uniqueness of the evil of the Holocaust go apoplectic upon passage of such laws, since they minimize the horrors of Nazism. As these critics point out, the Soviets, no matter how horrid, never sought to eradicate a group of people.[78] Critics also argue that linking the two movements in Eastern Europe is a way to exculpate the local populations of Nazi crimes.

And the trend is continuing. Most of the new denialist laws have been enacted in the past two decades, after the fall of the Iron Curtain. A number of European states now make it a crime to deny the Armenian genocide. Armenian-American journalist Garin Hovannisian dissents to his brethren's widespread support of the French law (later declared unconstitutional by the Council of State) that criminalized denial of the Armenian genocide. He explained: "Genocide deniers insult us. Yet in any decent society, their rights are the most vital, precisely because they are the most difficult to respect. Here's the test of true democracy: Do we tolerate another's view when it is thoroughly repulsive? France has failed the test. . . . Like that of the Holocaust, the cause of bringing greater recognition to the Armenian genocide is best served through total freedom of speech, in which historians can argue the deniers into silence. We should long for a society where those who deny documented crimes against humanity will not be fined or jailed, but worse, be exposed, humiliated, and condemned to oblivion."[79]

5. *Laws limiting freedom of speech are unevenly applied.* In the wake of the Paris terror attack in January 2015 on the satirical paper *Charlie Hebdo,* large rallies were held throughout France in support of free speech, including the right of the newspaper to lampoon the Prophet Mohammed, with many carrying signs proclaiming *Je suis Charlie* ("I am Charlie"). Over one million Parisians participated in the march. Keeping the Holocaust denial Gayssot Law on the books appears to some to be a betrayal of the march. Advocates of free speech see this as an example of "cherry picking" in the application of laws surrounding speech. Karin Deutsch Karlekar of Freedom House, an NGO which specializes in freedom of the press, observes: "What I would say is on occasion those laws are unevenly applied. [C]ertain people are charged, or arrested or prosecuted under the laws and others are not."[80]

6. *Seeking to control the content on the Internet stifles democratic movements. It is also a failed effort.* The Internet, and especially social media outlets like Facebook, Twitter, and Instagram, has become an important tool for dissidents to fight "Official Truth". China, Ukraine, and the Arab Spring revolutions are prime examples of the positive use of social media as a tool of democracy. For this reason, free speech advocates decry elaborate efforts by China to keep selective Internet content out of reach of its citizens (i.e.,a

search of the term "Tiananmen Square" aims to block all Western content dealing with the 1989 political events). Most of the same advocates, however, remain silent to efforts by Germany to keep antisemitic and other racist speech from reach by its citizens via the Internet.

Besides, efforts to erect firewalls or to scrub cyberspace clean of loathsome content are doomed to fail, whether attempted by China or anti–Holocaust deniers. In 2000, the French anti-racist group *Ligue contre le racisme et l'antisémitisme et Union des étudiants juifs de France* (LICRA) sued Yahoo! in France and in the United States seeking to ban the sale of Nazi memorabilia through its server. LICRA relied on the French Penal Code provision making it illegal to "wear or exhibit" in public Nazi uniforms, insignias, and emblems. It prevailed. The French courts ordered Yahoo! to take all appropriate measures to prevent access to auctions of Nazi memorabilia on its site by French residents. The court also ruled that Yahoo! Inc. must comply with the injunction within three months or face a fine of 100,000 francs (approximately $20,000) per day. The Ninth Circuit in the United States refused to block the injunction, ruling that First Amendment guarantees do not reach out beyond American borders.[81] If France wants to block speech within its territory constitutionally protected in the United States, American courts are powerless to stop it. Silicon Valley–based Yahoo! nevertheless complied with the injunction lest it be banned from doing business in France. LICRA's efforts, however, were all for naught. Today, Nazi memorabilia can be freely purchased in France through other servers and anonymous websites accessible through the Darknet.

In 2015, the Shurat HaDin Israel Law Center filed a class action lawsuit in the United States against Facebook seeking to force it to remove all pages containing clear incitement to violence and those seeking to link terrorists with one another—both real and serious problems in need of a solution. Columnist Jay Michaelson called the suit "a 20th-century solution to a 21st-century problem . . ."[82] And the same goes for efforts to legally force the Internet to screen Holocaust denial and related content. In a world where technology advances exponentially within a matter of months, it simply will not work.

3. Which Way Is Best?

In his comparative study of Holocaust denial trials, Robert Kahn expresses his frustration with the shape of the debate about whether denial of the Holocaust should be criminalized. As he explains: "Suing Holocaust deniers was either good or bad, for all places and times. There was no middle ground. . ."[83] Kahn correctly points out that criminalization of Holocaust denial does not fit into the "all good/all bad" dichotomy. Rather, it depends on the historical context where those laws are enacted and the weight that each country assigns, in light of its history, to two competing values: the right to speak out versus the right to human dignity. In the United States, freedom of speech is enshrined in the First Amendment to the Constitution. In the German Constitution, Article 1 protects not speech but human dignity. A general treatise on German law explains: "The primary position of this Article demonstrates the importance given to it. . . . This is not surprising bearing in mind the experience of the atrocities under the Nazi dictatorship and the contempt with which human dignity was treated in the Third Reich. . . . Against the background of the Holocaust, which not only infringed the right to life but also negated respect for humans as individual beings, this formula makes sense."[84]

Ultimately, laws limiting speech must be examined in their context. In the United States, the display of Nazi symbols may not need to be criminalized since the Holocaust did not take place on American soil. However, public display of hate symbols exclusive to the United States—such as cross burning—can be criminalized, according to a 2003 decision of the US Supreme Court,[85] because of the potent symbol which a burning cross has played in the persecution of African Americans since the end of the American Civil War and abolition of slavery. As explained by Justice O'Connor: "The First Amendment permits Virginia to outlaw cross burnings done with the intent to intimidate because burning a cross is a particularly virulent form of intimidation."[86] Another such potent symbol of a hateful past is the noose, representing lynching of African Americans in the South. More than 5,000 people were lynched in the United States between 1882 and 1951. Whenever there appears a spate of noose displays, there is call for criminalization of such symbolic speech, with some states already making it a crime to display a noose when done with intent to harass or intimidate.[87]

The United States is not the only liberal democracy to impose special limits on free speech in instances where the particular history of that country calls for an exception to the general rule. German historian Christian Meier relies on this rationale to justify his support for Germany continuing criminalization of Holocaust denial.

> In principle I cannot approve of placing any historical fact under the protection of the courts. And I must admit that I am particularly struck in my heart of hearts when the "right" holds it against me that one cannot tell "the truth" about Auschwitz without being hailed before a judge. I propose flatly to challenge any false allegations about the NS [National Socialist] crimes, any attempts to deny, diminish or set them off against other crimes. But the reference to a judge causes me some embarrassment. I manage, however, to overcome that feeling as well, since there are sufficient grounds for the

> pertinent legislation.... This therefore must remain an exception. It can find its justification only in the uniqueness of the NS crime.[88]

We return therefore to the uniqueness of the Holocaust for Europe as the rationale for the use of the criminal sanction on the denial of these unique events. In the United States, Holocaust denial is not viewed as a threat. The same goes for Canada. Even North American Jews are loath to prosecute Holocaust deniers, for fear of giving them a national (and international) spotlight and making them appear as martyrs. Yet, even the libertarian London-based *Economist* recognizes the distinction between criminalizing Holocaust denial in Germany and Austria and the lack of need of such laws in states like the United Kingdom. In arguing against an EU-wide ban on Holocaust denial, it explains: "Holocaust denial laws are wrong whoever imposes them. But they are at least understandable in countries where Nazism had indigenous roots."[89]

D. THE FUTURE OF DENIAL LAWS

Freedom of speech will continue to forestall prosecutions of Holocaust deniers in the United States. Holocaust deniers disseminating their message from America will be completely free to insist that the Holocaust was a hoax and will be allowed to promote the Nazi message. With the emergence of the Internet as the information superhighway, the United States will continue to be the place from where Holocaust denial and neo-Nazi and other hate and racist websites will emanate. And so the Westboro Baptist Church can freely picket the funerals of gay men who died of AIDS or were murdered in hate crimes and of soldiers killed in Iraq and Afghanistan. It can also host websites such as jewskilledjesus.com and godhatesfags.com. According to the Supreme Court in 2010, it is even shielded from civil tort liability for its outrageous conduct.[90]

Europe, however, will continue to criminalize Holocaust denial. In Western European countries like Germany, Austria, and France, where these laws have been on the books for decades, no movement exists to repeal these laws. Even calls for repeal of the Holocaust denial laws after the *Charlie Hebdo* terrorist attack in January 2015 quickly lost their steam with the multiple terrorist attacks in Paris in November 2015. Public statements by such a prominent figure in the Holocaust denial fight as Deborah Lipstadt that Holocaust deniers should not be criminally punished, has not struck a chord in Western Europe.[91]

For Germany especially, having Holocaust denial criminal laws on the books and a vigorous enforcement of those laws plays an important role in the self-identity that Germans have of themselves as a people that have come to terms with their Nazi past. In late 2015, eighty-seven year-old Ursula Haverbeck, characterized by leading media outlets as a "Nazi grandma," was sentenced to ten months in prison for publicly denying the Holocaust. Haverbeck's conviction stemmed from her picketing in 2014 the trial of former SS Auschwitz guard Oskar Gröning, who testified that Auschwitz was a death camp (see Chapter 4). In a TV interview at the time, Haverbeck claimed that "the Holocaust is the biggest and most sustainable lie in history." At trial, she challenged the Hamburg judge who convicted her to prove that Auschwitz was a death camp. He replied that he wouldn't debate "someone who can't accept any facts. Neither do I have to prove to you that the world is round."[92]

With the increasing use of the Internet, however, it is doubtful whether the laws on the books and the use of such laws will prevent the dissemination of Nazi ideology from reaching the public in those countries, and especially the youth. While Zündel was sitting in a German jail, his Zündelsite remained accessible to any German with a computer and access to the Internet. The aura of being in jail and his views being criminal can make his message appear more attractive, especially to computer-savvy youth, who can easily access anything found on the Internet, even if banned in their country.

It is also clear that deniers will not stop preaching their ideology even if they are jailed for it. While Irving may have told the judge that he now believes that there were homicidal gas chambers at Auschwitz, as soon as he was out of jail and in the free speech zone in his native country, he was able to state with impunity that he in fact still holds to his original views. Specific deterrence for deniers just does not work. In 2015, Irving began hosting trips to Treblinka and Sobibor and Hitler's "Wolf's Lair" headquarters in Europe, offering his own version of history to the paid participants.[93]

What about general deterrence? Will jailing the likes of Irving and Zündel prevent others from continuing to make claims of Holocaust denial? Just like there will be those who will believe that the Earth is flat, or that the 9/11 terrorists attacks were directed by the CIA, there will always be a small number of individuals who will believe that the Holocaust was a hoax. Criminalization and prosecution of Holocaust denial may make their message more muted (they are unlikely to write editorials or make public speeches in those countries with a ban on Holocaust denial), but they nevertheless will be able to publicly disseminate their views.

Ultimately, the major benefit of criminalization and prosecution—rather than toleration of the Nazi message and Holocaust denial claims—is to make it socially unacceptable to utter those views. By continuing to criminalize Holocaust denial, countries like Germany, Austria, and France and those that follow their lead are sending the message that such views are unacceptable in their culture and society.

What about the future of laws criminalizing denial of other genocides and mass atrocities? Such "us too" laws seem to be multiplying in Europe. In 2015, however, the Grand Chamber of the European Court of Human Rights

(ECtHR) in *Perinçek v. Switzerland*[94] put a damper on such laws by striking down a Swiss law criminalizing the public denial of the Armenian genocide. After taking into account all relevant factors, the appellate chamber concluded that the Swiss government's interference with the right to freedom of expression by criminally punishing those who deny the Armenian genocide in Switzerland was not necessary in a democratic society.

The Grand Chamber balanced the free speech interest found in Articles 10 and 17 of the European Convention on Human Rights against the legitimate interest of European states to prohibit speech that promotes or justifies violence, hatred, xenophobia, or other forms of intolerance.[95] In its previous case law concerning the denial of Holocaust, including statements denying the existence of gas chambers or describing the Holocaust as sham or myth, the ECtHR found that such denialist statements regarding the Nazi period necessarily amounted to speech that promoted hatred and intolerance toward Jews and disdain toward the victims of the Holocaust.[96] However, in this case, the Grand Chamber distinguished the criminalization of Holocaust denial with criminalization of denials of other genocides. Why? According to the court, the Holocaust was an event indigenous to Europe, and so the denial of the Holocaust can be particularly dangerous in countries that have experienced the Nazi horrors, which may demand special moral responsibility to outlaw such denial. No such moral imperative existed with regard to the Armenian genocide since, in the court's words, there was no "direct link between Switzerland and the events that took place in the Ottoman Empire in 1915 and the following years."[97] In distinguishing its earlier case law of upholding criminalization of Holocaust denial, the Grand Chamber decision appears to be the death knell to the movement to criminalize denial of other genocides, atrocities, and the "official view" of certain historical events. But while the Grand Chamber put in doubt the legality of the genocide denial laws in Europe, it strongly affirmed the legality of the criminalization of the denial of the Holocaust and related acts. As the court explained:

> The [ECtHR] has always been sensitive to the historical context. . . .
>
> This is particularly relevant with regard to the Holocaust. For the Court, the justification for making its denial a criminal offence lies not so much in that it is a clearly established historical fact but in that in view of the historical context in the States concerned—the cases examined by the former Commission and the Court have thus concerned Austria, Belgium, Germany and France—its denial, even if dressed up as impartial historical research, must invariably be seen as connoting an antidemocratic ideology and anti-Semitism. *Holocaust denial is thus doubly dangerous*, especially in States which have experienced the Nazi horrors, and which may be regarded

> as having a special moral responsibility to distance themselves from the massive atrocities that they have perpetrated or abetted by, among other things, outlawing their denial.[98]

For the Grand Chamber to find in 2015 that Holocaust denial is "doubly dangerous" sends a clear signal that criminalization in Europe of the denial of the facts of the Holocaust and the glorification of the Nazi regime are here to stay. Because post–Holocaust Europe—Ground Zero for the Holocaust—continues to grapple seventy years later with the extermination of its Jews, its laws will continue to reflect this reality.

7

The Impact of the Holocaust on Post-Holocaust Legal Philosophy

Christian and Jewish theology faced a devastating crisis as the gates of the concentration camps and death camps were opened and the full horrors inside revealed. How could God allow this happen? Or put it another way: Where was God during the Holocaust? These questions are still being asked seventy years later with a new generation of theologians pondering the subject.[1] The parallel question for legal scholars is: Where was law during the Holocaust? Chapter 1 revealed the answer: Law was busy facilitating mass murder. Distinguished philosopher and ethicist John K. Roth, reflecting on his lifetime of work trying to understand the role of philosophy during the Nazi era, came to the conclusion that "philosophy can expedite genocide."[2] We in the legal profession must likewise acknowledge that *law can expedite genocide.* And this statement includes that branch of law called jurisprudence, or legal philosophy. German law professor Arthur Kaufmann warns those in the legal academy: "It appears, and this is fatal, that a career in jurisprudence renders one incapable of recognizing and opposing injustice. . . . Jews and other 'artfremde' [aliens] were deprived of their rights, with the full cooperation of many legal minds."[3] And, as we will see below, many fine legal minds.

This chapter examines the impact of the legal pathology that took place in Nazi Germany upon postmodern legal philosophy. We first focus on Carl Schmitt, the so-called "Crown Jurist of the Third Reich" and a leading representative of Germany's legal pathology. We will then look at efforts by legal philosophers after the war to make sense of what happened to law between 1933 and 1945. This in turn leads to the question of the nature of law itself: What is *law?* Trying to deconstruct *law* for these postwar legal academicians had a utilitarian purpose. If law can expedite genocide, can we inoculate law so that next time it will not so readily become an agent of would-be tyrants? Or to put it more directly and personally, if jurists behaved so badly during the Nazi era, can steps be taken to prevent a repeat of such horrid, so that next time jurists do not become agents of tyrants? Kaufmann's German law colleague Michael Stolleis believes not, affirming that "professors of jurisprudence were average individuals with average reactions, and that their connivance with the [Nazi] regime only casts a dark shadow where ideal and reality met."[4] I disagree. German jurists could have done better. As American law professor Vivian Curran points out, examining the behavior of German judges during the Hitler era can assist us in "determining if there *may* be ways . . . *to increase the likelihood* that judges in times of political and social crises will resist the temptation of abandoning constitutional, democratic principles and values."[5]

Finding an antidote to legal pathology has important implications. Israeli Holocaust historian Yehuda Bauer reminds us that the Holocaust "happened because it could happen. . . . And because it happened once, it can happen again"[6]—at some other place, at some other time, and to another group of victims. Yale historian Timothy Snyder in his 2015 book, *Black Earth: The Holocaust as History and Warning,* issues the same counsel, but puts it in more concrete terms: "As Hitler demonstrated during the Great Depression, humans are able to portray a looming crisis in such a way as to justify drastic measures in the present. . . . A global problem that seems otherwise insoluble can be blamed upon a specific group of human beings. . . . Jews can again be seen as a universal threat. . . . So might Muslims, gays, or other groups that can be associated with changes on a worldwide scale."[7] If Snyder is right, will jurists again become genocidaires or join the ranks of anti-genocidaires?

The last part of the chapter deals not with a "looming crisis" but a present one: terrorism. In the post-9/11 world, law and lawyers are playing a leading role in deciding how liberal democracies should confront Al-Qaeda and ISIS-style Islamic extremism. The challenge is a legal one. On the one hand, the threat of the next terrorist attack requires passage of laws giving government further police powers so it can protect us.[8] On the other hand, there is the continued need for preservation of our civil liberties against excessive government encroachment. How to balance these two interests?

A. CARL SCHMITT AND THE STATE OF EXCEPTION

Just as there was no shortage of lawyers and judges beginning in 1933 eager to become members of the *Bund Nationalsozialistischer Deutscher Juristen* (the Association of the National-Socialist German Jurists), the legal academy likewise eagerly joined the Nazi movement. As in the United States today, Jewish law professors formed a significant segment of the legal academy in Weimar Germany. The purge of these Jewish law professors after 1933 provided a convenient opportunity for career advancement to their non-Jewish junior colleagues.

The scholarly output of the remaining German law professors now consisted of books and articles explaining and glorifying *die Führerprinzip* (the Führer principle): that Hitler was both the supreme lawmaker and the highest appellate single-judge court in every legal case. Arthur Kaufmann tells us that the "majority of legal philosophers not only did not oppose National Socialism, they firmly and unequivocally supported almost all of the important goals of the new *völkische bewegung* (popular movement), including their racial policies."[9]

Foremost among these philosophers was political theorist and distinguished university professor Carl Schmitt. During the Weimar Republic, Schmitt already enjoyed much fame as a result of his publication in 1927 of *The Concept of the Political*—still his best-known work. The work explained that politics is ultimately based on the recognition of the distinction between friend and enemy, and such a distinction is at the very heart of politics. "[A]ll political concepts, images, and terms have a polemical meaning," he wrote, and so "the result (which manifests itself in war or revolution) is a friend-enemy grouping. . ."[10] For Schmitt, a people can be a polity only to the extent that they share common enemies. All politics is a struggle, based on hard-nosed confrontation between opponents. It is here that he coined another of his famous phrases: "Tell me who your enemy is, and I will tell you who you are."[11] In his own milieu, Schmitt's enemy was personified by Hans Kelsen, a prominent Austrian philosopher of Jewish background, who was a defender of positivism and the liberal state and who grounded democracy in the power of judicial review.

When the Nazis came to power, Schmitt was a law professor at the University of Bonn and a bestselling author. American political philosopher Paul Gottfried in 2015 describes Schmitt as "a literary and scholarly star [who] operated on a different level from the professional posts he held."[12] Prior to Hitler's rise to power, Schmitt enjoyed the support and companionship of many Jewish colleagues. He was also a vocal opponent of the National Socialists, even publicly calling for banning of the Nazi Party. This always made him suspicious in the eyes of the other Nazis.

Hitler was appointed German chancellor on January 30, 1933. Within months, Schmitt began kowtowing to the Nazis. It was not difficult for him to become a National Socialist since his authoritarian-leaning political theories fit neatly within Nazism. In March 1933, Schmitt formally joined the Nazi Party and started to cut ties with his Jewish colleagues, including mentors who earlier had helped his career. Nazi Party membership by such a well-known public intellectual brought Hitler much needed respectability and legitimacy. It also brought Schmitt innumerable benefits. He was given a professorship at the prestigious University of Berlin. He became editor-in-chief of the *Deutsch Juristen-Zeitung*, the leading legal magazine of the day, and was named president of the Association of National-Socialist Jurists. Schmitt plunged into National Socialism with gusto, which he manifested through both virulent antisemitism and public adulation of Hitler. After the "Night of the Long Knives"—when Hitler orchestrated in a period of three days in summer 1934 the assassination of nearly one hundred political opponents—Schmitt wrote a famous article titled "The Führer Protects Justice" in which he defended Hitler's extrajudicial killings:

> The Führer protects justice against the worst abuse when he in the moment of danger by force of his leadership status as highest judicial authority creates justice directly . . . The real Führer is always a judge. Out of Führerdom flows judgeship. One who wants to separate the two from each other or puts them in opposition to each other would have the judge be either the leader of the opposition or the tool of the opposition and is trying to unhinge the state with the help of the judiciary.[13]

"The Führer's action," Schmitt added, "was true judging. It is not subject to law but is in itself the highest justice."[14] Schmitt's article came out shortly after Hitler made a speech to the Reichstag on July 13, 1934, nine days after the purge, calling himself, as he put it, "the supreme judge of the German people."

Over the next few years, Schmitt authored some forty articles supporting Nazi changes to the law, including the expulsion of the Jew from the body politic. One of those expelled was Kelsen, forced to flee Germany to make a new home in the United States. For Schmitt, the Jew became the specific enemy identified in general terms in his political philosophy. Schmitt publicly greeted the Nuremberg anti-Jewish decrees with enthusiasm, calling them "the constitution of freedom, the core of our present-day German law."[15]

In October 1936, Schmitt organized and chaired a notorious legal conference entitled "Judaism in Legal Studies." There Schmitt joined with other prominent antisemitic scholars in presenting a plan to purge German jurisprudence of Jewish thought. In his speech at the conference, he maintained that this was necessary in order to protect students from becoming confused by the fact that "on the one hand we keep pointing to the necessary fight against the Jewish spirit," while on the other "a seminar library in legal studies looks as if the greater part of the legal literature is being produced by Jews."[16]

Schmitt's political prominence within the Third Reich was short lived. By 1937, as a result of infighting with Himmler's SS, Schmitt was dismissed from his government and party positions. He did, however, maintain his prestigious chair at the University of Berlin until the end of the war. Returning to full-time academia in the second half of the Nazi era, Schmitt began publishing articles on international law. This included a defense of German expansionism, arguing that it was in conformance with international law. He also argued that suspension of the rules of warfare on the Eastern Front was necessary because of the great evil of Communism that was threatening Germany.

Schmitt's fame led to his arrest by the Americans in 1945. He was brought to Nuremberg, interrogated, and seriously considered as a defendant. Eventually Schmitt was released, but was permanently barred from returning to academia. He returned to Plettenberg—the place of his birth—to lead a mostly secluded life. However, even in semi-seclusion, Schmitt became through his writings "a key conversation partner for an entire generation of political thinkers."[17] Until his death in 1985 at age ninety-six, Schmitt refused to admit that he had done anything wrong. "[T]he conduct I am held responsible for [consists] essentially only in the publication of explanations which were intended to be academic . . . and which led to a number of fruitful academic disputes."[18]

Many Germany philosophers who became ardent Nazis were discredited after the war and died in oblivion. But not Schmitt. Raphael Gross observes that "[t]he extraordinary impact of Schmitt's writings has not been lessened by either his Nazi or antisemitic engagement."[19] A 2015 review of the most recent biography of Schmitt points out that his books *Concept of the Political; Legality, and Legitimacy; Dictatorship; Law of the Earth*; and *Political Ideology* "continue to be read because of their conceptual depth and stylistic brilliance."[20] Harvard law professor Noah Feldman considers Schmitt so important that he teaches a semester-long seminar on Schmitt.[21] And in a 2013 editorial in the *New York Post*, Feldman introduced Schmitt to the masses, calling him "the most important political theorist you've never heard of. . ."[22]

The fact that Harvard Law School offers a seminar dedicated to Schmitt's legal philosophy raises the question whether Schmitt's rabid antisemitism can be disengaged from his thought. Gross argues that it cannot. He explains:

> At present in Europe and North America, many efforts are evident in the academic fields of legal studies . . . to make his ideas fruitful by simply excising their openly racist and antisemitic dimension. . . . [S]uch exclusion is not possible . . . [T]he question of the significance of the Jews and "the Jewish" had defining importance for Schmitt's works as whole. As his ideas developed, his response to this question became increasingly foundational for his legal theory. The postwar reception of his work is not coincidental but the laborious process of denial.[23]

But, as the saying goes, a Jew can enjoy Wagner's music despite Wagner's virulent antisemitism. Gross rejects the analogy: "If someone were a very good cook and at the same time a committed antisemite, one might then say: I will continue to use his cookbooks, because his hatred has no effect on the recipes. But is this a serious possibility in the case of a legal thinker, a theoretician of political philosophy?"[24] Gross points out that Schmitt's "antisemitism is more abstract and more dangerous than simple distaste. For one thing, it can be directed at endless images of the enemy: Bolshevism, Marxism, Liberalism, Freemasonry. For another, it can very concretely legitimate a program of murder, offering itself like a mania—an uncorrectable delusion—as the explanation and solution to every evil in this world."[25]

The continued appeal of Schmitt's thought comes from his theories on political power in a modern state during times of crisis. Liberal democracies constitute themselves on the basis of eliminating one person as a sovereign. Instead, sovereignty is placed with different branches of government, each with limited powers. The different branches govern through checks and balances. A set of constitutional norms is either posited in written law, as in the United States, or in an unwritten constitution, as in Britain. These constitutional norms are supreme. All must follow them—even the head of state.

In Schmitt's political cosmology, however, every government of the modern nation state will eventually find itself in an emergency, what he calls the "state of exception," when decisive action must be taken. Any government, including a constitutional government, must be aware of "exceptional circumstances" in order to function even in normal times. And since times of crisis will eventually arise, a modern state cannot exist without predetermining a sovereign authority who will decide (1) whether such an extreme situation is at hand, and (2) what actions to take during such time of crisis. Schmitt argued that the existence of a single sovereign-as-person is necessary to the continued existence of any state, and this is due to the impossibility of anticipating exceptional circumstances that trigger the need to restore order.

In Schmitt's view, Western liberal democracies—whether parliamentary or presidential—can never effectively cope during the state of exception because of their diffusion of authority. Only a strong dictator can effectively confront the danger posed to the nation by taking decisive action that best embodies the will of the people. As Schmitt put it, in arguably his most famous aphorism, "He is sovereign who decides the exception." "The exception," he went on to explain, "which is not codified in the existing legal order, can best be characterized as a case of extreme peril, a danger to the existence or the like. But it cannot be circumscribed factually and made to conform to a preformed law." In such case, Schmitt argued, it is for the executive—not the judiciary or the legislature—not only to declare the exception but then to step outside the rule of law in order to continue the existence of the state. Laws of the state, claimed Schmitt, cannot limit actions of its sovereign since the sovereign is at once within and outside the legal order and cannot be properly sovereign unless he has the power to suspend such law.

For Schmitt, every government capable of decisive action must include a dictatorial element within its constitution. A sovereign "decides whether there is an extreme emergency as well as what must be done to eliminate it."[26] For this reason, Schmitt maintained: "The exception is more interesting than the rule. The rule proves nothing; the exception proves everything. . . . In the exception the power of real life breaks through the crust of a mechanism that has become torpid by repetition."[27] In the end, "rule is of men and not of law—or rather that the rule of men must always existentially underlie the rule of law."[28]

As a quintessential anti-liberal, to Schmitt a world consisting of peaceful liberal states sharing universal human values based on equality of all human beings is an impossibility.[29] Or, as Schmitt put it in another of his aphorisms, "Whoever says humanity, wants to deceive."[30] According to Schmitt, every liberal state eventually will reach the sorry condition of the Weimar Republic, when equality, pluralism, and tolerance toward "the Other" cannot be accommodated. Political clashes will follow, government will come to a standstill, and a dictator, who rules outside the law, must emerge to save the day.

In the field of political philosophy, Schmitt remains the most well-known expounder of illiberalism, and so must be confronted head-on by every serious defender of a constitutional liberal democracy.[31] And because Schmitt provides the most serious critique of liberal democracy when confronting times of stress, his theories of state power have become in vogue in our current "Age of Terrorism." After 9/11, academics and policymakers continue to pay increasing attention to Schmitt in their efforts to analyze and critique how liberal states respond to emergencies.[32] We return to this in the last part of the chapter.

B. KARL LOEWENSTEIN AND POSTWAR GERMANY'S MILITANT DEMOCRACY

The most prominent critic of Schmitt's reliance on an authoritarian executive as a guardian of the state and its people was Hans Kelsen, the intellectual enemy of Schmitt. Their very public confrontation took place in law articles and speeches, each published in pre-Hitler Weimar. Kelsen was a strong advocate of the principle of judicial review, with the judiciary as the ultimate guardian of the constitution. In 1931, he wrote a scathing reply to Schmitt's "The Guardian of the Constitution" in his essay, "Who Should Be the Guardian of the Constitution?" There he rallied against Schmitt's excessive form of an executive authoritarian government, putting his trust instead in the courts to defend the constitution, and especially in a specialized constitutional court. According to Sandrine Baume, "Kelsen defended the legitimacy of the constitutional court by combating the reasons that Schmitt cites for assigning the role of the guardian of the Constitution to the President of the Reich. The dispute between these two lawyers was about which body of the state should be assigned the role of guardian of the German Constitution. Kelsen thought that this mission ought to be conferred on the judiciary, especially the Constitutional Court."[33] After the war,

Kelsen's view prevailed: the German Federal Constitutional Court (FCC) has the last say on all constitutional matters, while the German president is merely a figurehead.[34]

But having a strong constitutional court, Kelsen's solution, was not enough. The lesson that the founders of the Federal Republic of Germany took from how the Nazis came to power is that the very rights provided by democracies can be misused to destroy the democracy itself. As Nazi propagandist Joseph Goebbels famously observed: "It will always remain one of the best jokes of democracy that it provides its own deadly enemies with the means with which it can be destroyed."[35] Schmitt saw the same. According to Schmitt, because liberalism fails to distinguish between friends and enemies, liberal states render themselves vulnerable to internal enemies to whom membership has been extended, but who do not in reality belong to the state. Schmitt's answer was to acknowledge and create a dictatorial sovereign. Liberals found another solution.

The counterweight to Schmitt's philosophy was the adoption of a peculiar concept called "militant democracy" (*wehrhafte Demokratie*).[36] In practical terms, the creation of a militant democracy in the nascent Federal Republic meant that this time Germany would equip itself with institutional tools that it could use to defend itself against forces aiming to destroy the republic. Haunted by the failure of the Weimar Republic, these self-defense mechanisms would now be utilized when a threat to the constitutional order arose. At the same time, they could not be misused by anti-democratic forces to destroy the constitutional order itself. As noted in Chapter 6, one manifestation of militant democracy was the criminalization of both Holocaust denial and glorification of the Nazi era.

The founding father of militant democracy is Karl Loewenstein, another German Jewish philosopher who fled to the United States after Hitler came to power.[37] Loewenstein argued that in the Weimar Republic democracy had failed because of absence of militancy against forces that sought to destroy it.

> Democracy and democratic tolerance have been used for their own destruction. Under cover of fundamental rights and the rule of law, the anti-democratic machine could be built up and set in motion legally. Calculating adroitly that democracy could not, without self-abnegation, deny to any body of public opinion the full use of the free institutions of speech, press, assembly, and parliamentary participation, fascist exponents systematically discredit the democratic order and make it unworkable by paralyzing its functions until chaos reigns.[38]

The tolerant features of democracy became "the Trojan horse by which the enemy enters the city."[39] And so "fire should be fought with fire."[40] Loewenstein's prescription: "Democracy must become militant."[41] Loewenstein, of course, was not the first to invoke the principle of "no liberty for the enemies of liberty."[42] However, as a fellow German, Loewenstein's views resonated with the postwar founders of the Federal Republic who sought to construct a new constitutional order after the double disasters of Weimar and Nazism.

On May 23, 1949, the Parliamentary Council of the Federal Republic of Germany met at Bonn and confirmed the *Grundgesetz* (Basic Law). Bonn was the temporary capital of the West German state, and the Basic Law was a provisional constitution. At the time of the future reunification of Germany, the capital would be moved to a reunified Berlin and a permanent constitution would be established. The first happened; the second did not. After reunification in 1990, the German parliament (Bundestag) opted to keep the Basic Law rather than draft a new constitution.

The Basic Law was meant to correct the deficiencies that supposedly led to the failure of the Weimar Republic. To this end, a number of its provisions are specifically targeted at impeding anti-democratic groups from seizing power. The most conspicuous feature of a militant democracy is a ban on anti-democratic parties. Article 21 states: "Parties that, by reason of their aims or the behavior of their adherents, seek to undermine or abolish the free democratic basic order or to endanger the existence of the Federal Republic of Germany shall be unconstitutional."[43] The FCC invoked this clause in 1952 when it outlawed the Socialist Reich Party of Germany, as well as in 1956 when it declared the Communist Party of Germany to be illegal.[44] Like all liberal state constitutions, the Basic Law guarantees such basic rights as the freedoms of expression, assembly, and association. However, these rights are subject to forfeiture when abused. Article 18 states: "Whoever abuses the freedom of expression . . . in order to combat the free democratic basic order shall forfeit these basic rights." Declaring such a forfeiture is also under the purview of the FCC. Article 20 is another unique militancy feature, giving all Germans the right to "resist any person seeking to abolish the constitutional order" so long as no other remedy is available.[45]

The most important provision of the Basic Law is Article I, protecting a value never mentioned in the American Constitution: human dignity. It reads: "Human dignity shall be inviolable. To respect and protect it shall be the duty of all state authority. The German people therefore acknowledge inviolable and inalienable human rights as the basis of every community of peace and of justice in the world."[46] In contrast to the rights enumerated in of the US Constitution, which are negative rights, the Basic Law places an affirmative burden on the German government to respect and protect human dignity and the other basic rights.

Last, the Basic Law is not politically neutral. Postwar Germany rejected Hans Kelsen's value-neutral model of pluralist democracy whereby all political positions are given equal rights of expression and participation in the public space. Instead, it makes the decision that the state will always operate on the basis of a "free democratic basic order" (*Freiheitlich demokratische Grundordnung*). The term appears six times in the Basic Law.[47]

The fact that liberal democracy "took" in postwar Germany is a surprising development, considering the absence of a strong liberal tradition in German society prior to the Second World War. How much of this success is to be attributed the militancy provisions in the Basic Law? Arguably, the postwar German economic miracle, European integration, and American guarantee of Germany's national security through NATO were more important factors. Some believe that the militancy provisions haven been unduly glorified. According to American law professor Russell Miller, "Germany's militant democracy has been very rarely and only symbolically implemented."[48] Nevertheless, the militant democracy experiment in Germany is viewed as a huge success. With the fall of Communism, many of the former Eastern European people's republics sought to emulate Germany and introduced militant democracy provisions in their constitutions. These were meant to protect their new and seemingly fragile democratic order. The European Court of Human Rights has also recognized militant democracy principles, most notably in upholding party bans and national laws criminalizing Holocaust denial.

In the Age of Terrorism, some scholars and policymakers have argued that other liberal democratic states should follow Germany's example and adopt militant democracy provisions to tackle Islamic fundamentalist terrorism. German philosopher Jürgen Habermas asserts: "If a democratic state does not wish to give itself up, then it must resort to intolerance towards the enemy of the constitution, [including] today's terrorists."[49] Australian academic Svetlana Tyulkina, in her 2015 study of militant democracy, observes: "[M]ilitant democracy is by no means a concept that is 'withering away,' but is still seen in many nations as an important tool for protecting democracy [from terrorism]."[50]

C. GUSTAV RADBRUCH AND THE HART-FULLER DEBATE: WHAT IS LAW?

Can the term "law" be applied to rules as immoral as the enactments of the Nazis? This question confronted legal philosophers after the Second World War. Seventy years later, law scholars worldwide still debate the question in conferences and in their writings. In the Justice Trial at Nuremberg, the defendant German judges and Justice Ministry officials offered as their lead defense the argument that they were now being prosecuted for acts that were perfectly legal under German law.[51] The American judges hearing the case rejected that argument, finding that Nazi Germany was a criminal state whose Nazi-inspired laws could not be given the label of legality. (See Chapter 3.) Nevertheless, this jurisprudential conundrum—that everything done by lawyers, governmental officials, and judges was in accordance with existing German law and procedure and so could not be criminal—was not put to rest by the American judges presiding at the Justice Trial. It still poses a dilemma for each generation of legal scholars trying to reconcile how the Holocaust could simultaneously have been both legal and criminal.

The first legal philosopher to tackle the subject was Gustav Radbruch, one of the most influential German legal minds of the twentieth century. Before the war, Radbruch was known as a positivist, adhering to the dominant jurisprudential philosophy at the time. Positivists hold that law derives its legitimacy from being posited, that is, being brought legally into existence by a supreme legislative power. As the story is told, Radbruch abandoned positivism after the war.[52] The legal lesson that Radbruch took away from the Nazi era is that blind obedience to written laws duly enacted by the government in power—represented by the positivist slogan "The Law is the Law" (*Gerecht als Gerecht*)—was one of the reasons that Nazi "criminality through law" was able to take hold so easily in Germany. The chastened Radbruch now argued that in some instances a state-promulgated rule is so unjust that it loses its status of valid law. In deciding a case where such a rule is implicated, judges can set aside that positive rule and decide the case on the basis of unwritten moral norms. This became known as the Radbruch Formula (*Radbruchsche Formel*).[53] Robert Alexy simplifies the formula as follows: "Extreme injustice is no law."[54] He also adds the observation, "Whoever supports this thesis has ceased to be a positivist."[55]

Morality as a source of law is represented by the legal theory known as natural law, which predated positivism.[56] The great British eighteenth-century jurist William Blackstone explained the dominance of natural law over man-made law.

> This law of nature, being coeval with mankind, and dictated by God himself, is of course superior in obligation to any other. It is binding over all the globe in all countries, and at all times: no human laws are of any validity, if contrary to this; and such of them as are valid derive all their force and all their authority, mediately or immediately, from this original.[57]

Radbruch's turnabout was radical, not only because of his prestige as a legal scholar but because positivism had effectively replaced natural law as the dominant legal theory in Western thought. For the postwar West German judiciary, his identification of the culprit as *a theory of law* posed much attraction, since guilt could no longer be personal but could be blamed on "the system." German jurists became genocidaires because the system made them, or at least allowed them, to do it. German judges in the Federal Republic now began to apply natural law theory in their decisions to ameliorate perceived Nazi-era injustices.[58]

A paradigm case showing West Germany's return to natural law was the so-called Case of the Grudge Informer.[59] In 1944, a woman wishing to be rid of her husband denounced him to the authorities for insulting remarks he had made about Hitler while home on leave from the German army. The husband's remarks were in violation of a Nazi-era statute making it illegal to make statements critical of the Third Reich and its leaders. The husband was arrested and sentenced to death. Fortunately, he was not executed but instead sent to the front, and later returned. In 1949, the wife was prosecuted in a West German court for an offense best described as illegally depriving a person of his freedom (*rechtswidrige Freiheitsberaubung*). This was punishable as a crime under the German Criminal Code of 1871, in force during the Nazi years. In defense, the wife pleaded that her husband's imprisonment was pursuant to the Nazi statutes. Hence, she committed no crime. The trial court accepted the wife's argument but a court of appeal reversed and found her guilty. It held that the wife could not rely on the Nazi-era statutes because the wartime statute "was contrary to the sound conscience and sense of justice of all decent human beings" and so null and void.

A 1952 Federal Court of Justice decision laid out most directly Radbuch's "natural law in cases of extreme injustice" formula to be applied to unjust Nazi era laws.

> Rules that do not even attempt to achieve justice, deliberately disavow equality, and clearly violate elementary standards of humanity common to all civilized people, have no claim at all to legal status; deeds done on this basis lack, therefore, legal justification. In fact, authoritative measures that grossly and patently offend against the fundamental tenets of justice and humanity are to be regarded as void from the outset.[60]

Radbruch's ultimate conclusion was that the experience of the Third Reich should turn us all into natural lawyers. As he explained:

> We must hope that the denial of the fundamentals of law and justice that occurred under Hitler will remain isolated and not-to-be-repeated aberration of the German people in the state of temporary derangement. Yet to be prepared for every eventuality we must arm ourselves against the return of such a state of affairs. *To do this we must thoroughly overcome the positivistic legal philosophy that rendered impotent every possible defense against the abuses of the National Socialist regime.*[61]

Note how Radbruch's resort to arms ("we must arm ourselves against the return of such a state of affairs") echoes Loewenstein's military terminology. Each was proposing a different arsenal to guard against the return of Nazism.

The subject of Nazi law in the context of positive law versus natural law came to America through the famous Hart-Fuller debate of the 1950s–1960s. [62] British Oxford legal scholar H. L. A. Hart and his American counterpart Harvard law professor Lon Fuller were among the foremost legal theorists of the twentieth century. In a series of 1958 articles in the *Harvard Law Review*[63] and later in their individual books,[64] Hart and Fuller used the Nazi legal conundrum as the background to argue their opposing views of the meaning of law. Hart was a positivist par excellence, who argued that the inquiry into the existence of law and the wisdom of that law are separate considerations, thereby separating the law as it is and the law as it ought to be. Consequently, even the most morally reprehensible Nazi laws, in Hart's view, were *law*, possessing valid legal character.[65] In other words, the Nazi statute's validity is not dependent on its credentials as just or otherwise morally acceptable.

Fuller, on the other hand, was a firm proponent of the notion that every law must be examined through the filter of morality. Without morality, a group of robbers exerting their will over their victims has the same legal effect as a law passed by a government of a free people. According to Fuller, for a law to be *law* it must have a minimum degree of "inner morality."[66] To Fuller, Nazi laws were immoral both in their content and in their form and so could not be granted the status of *law*. As Fuller explained in his 1958 reply to Hart:

> To me there is nothing shocking in saying that a dictatorship which clothes itself with a tinsel of legal form can so far depart from the morality of order, from the inner morality of law itself, that it ceases to be a legal system. When a system calling itself law is predicated upon a general disregard by judges of the terms of the laws they purport to enforce, when this system habitually cures its legal irregularities, even the grossest, by retroactive statutes, when it has only to resort to forays of terror in the streets, which no one dares challenge, in order to escape even those scant restraints imposed by the pretense of legality—when all these things have become true of a dictatorship, it is not hard for me, at least, to deny to it the name of law. [67]

Hart disagreed, conceding that laws may be immoral but that their immorality does not disqualify them from being law. In his initial *Harvard Law Review* article, Hart specifically raised the Case of the Grudge Informer to illustrate his point. He argued that the German courts were wrong in convicting the woman by annulling the Nazi-era law. Hart contended that because the woman had committed no crime under the positive law of the state at the time, the only legally valid way of punishing her would be to enact a piece of retroactive legislation.[68] Hart defends this method, although unjust in itself, as the least unjust route of imposing punishment—the lesser of two evils.[69] Fuller disagreed, and asserted that the Nazi law under which the woman acted was so evil, and also so disfigured of its ordinary meaning by the Nazi judges who resorted to it to convict the husband, that it could not be considered a valid law.[70]

Robert Alexy calls the conflict over positivism "a conflict with no end, and that means it is a philosophical debate."[71] He observes: "In such disputes which are at once endless, acute and stubborn, one can surmise that all the participants are right in one or other aspect or in regard to one or other assumptions."[72] British jurist Tony Honoré describes it in more extravagant terms: "Decade after decade positivists and natural lawyers face one another in the final of the World Cup. Victory goes now to one side, now to the other. The legal theorist can only cheer or jeer, label his opponent a moral leper or a disingenuous romantic."[73]

The current argument whether Nazi law was *law* or *notlaw* has been taken by up by Australian law professor Kristen Rundle, the intellectual heir to Lon Fuller. In her excellent *The Impossibility of an Exterminatory Legality*,[74] Rundle contends that the anti-Jewish decrees and their application by the German judiciary was *law*, but the later legal measures used to exterminate the Jews, discussed in Chapter 1, cannot be law but amount to pure terror. Implicitly, she adopts the Radbruch Formula: the later decrees are not law because they are so extremely unjust. [75]

For Rundle, the demarcation criterion seems to hinge on who is enforcing the anti-Jewish measures. If it is the regular state bureaucracy, including courts, then we are in the world of law. The Jews still are considered legal subjects. Once the SS takes over, those measures against Jews no longer can be classified as *law*, and the Jews against whom the SS measures are applied cannot be considered agents of law. She explains:

> [T]he Nazi legislative program against the Jews was . . . a system, at least until the assumption of the primary jurisdiction over Jewish affairs by the SS. . . . By functioning through means of official action mediated by rules, this system necessarily recognized and relied upon the capacities of its subjects for self-direction, and, in doing so, granted those [Jewish] subjects a certain room to manoeuvre within an otherwise oppressive social order. It is for these reasons . . . that I am willing to lend the early phase of the Nazi legislative program against the Jews the title of "law."[76]

But is this conclusion important to anyone other than legal theorists?

Let's return briefly to the example of Leo Katzenberger, the Jewish head of the Nuremberg community sentenced to death by Judge Oswald Rothaug, for "racial pollution" (see Chapter 3). As discussed, Rothaug commandeered the case to be moved to a special court, where he could mete out the death sentence. It mattered not to Mr. Katzenberger that he was executed pursuant to a system of *law* rather than a system of pure terror. Or another example: the 1941 "Night and Fog" Decree (*Nacht-und-Nebel-Erlass—NN*) that authorized extraordinary measures in all occupied territories. Under this decree, political suspects would simply "disappear" to special detention facilities where, following a summary court proceeding, they would face the death penalty or, if fortunate, imprisonment. It is noteworthy that the Justice Ministry lawyers in Berlin worked with their military counterparts at the German General Staff (OKW) on the drafting of the NN decree and rules for its implementation. It would be hard to argue that the NN decree that these civilian and military lawyers had drafted was *notlaw*.

Finally, a bright-line demarcation that any SS decree or order from Himmler or his subordinates was not law would also be incorrect. The SS operated through its own internal system of laws. It even had its own legal department, the *Hauptamt SS-Gericht* (SS Court Main Office), and operated its own courts. The most well-known jurist working in the *Hauptamt SS-Gericht* was SS Judge Konrad Morgen, who testified at Nuremberg and later in the Frankfurt Auschwitz trial. As discussed in Chapter 1, Morgen's legal task was to investigate and prosecute corruption and thievery of SS commandants and other SS personnel inside the concentration camps. Under the SS system of law, extermination of the Jews and stealing from them on orders of superiors was not a crime. Keeping the loot was.[77]

D. THE STATE OF EXCEPTION AFTER 9/11

The traditional contest between positivism and natural law has provided armchair philosophers an excellent vehicle by which to frame the debate about the nature of law. In the current Age of Terrorism, however, it is not positivism versus natural law but Schmitt's "state of exception" that is most relevant for our times. The challenge that liberal democracies face today in protecting civil liberties while confronting threats of terrorism has made Schmitt's focus on the "state of exception" a "hot topic" in political and legal discourse. Schmitt's predictions posthumously challenge us to confront the threat of terror without resorting to the extralegal solution offered by him.

Fortunately, liberal democracies, for the most part, have met the challenge of preserving individual liberties in the face of terror. Much of the credit must be given to judges who have shown that maintaining the independence of the judiciary from politics is a critical component of preventing legalized barbarism. On four different occasions in the post-9/11 era, the US Supreme Court has issued critical rulings striking down as unconstitutional a series of national security measures enacted by the George W. Bush administration, even when such measures have been confirmed by Congress.

In *Rasul v. Bush*,[78] the Court held in 2004 that US courts have jurisdiction to consider challenges to the legality of the detention of foreign nationals captured abroad and incarcerated at Guantánamo Bay on the orders of the president. In a 6–3 decision, the majority opinion by Justice Stevens held that Shafiq Rasul, a British national, had a statutory right to appeal to a judge for release under the 1868 federal habeas corpus statute. Because the United States exercises exclusive jurisdiction and control over the base at Guantánamo Bay, federal law applied in Guantánamo. In a companion case, *Hamdi v. Rumsfeld*,[79] the same Court majority held that the president does not have the power to hold a US citizen indefinitely in violation of the due process clause. Yaser Esam Hamdi was born in Louisiana and moved to Saudi Arabia with his family as a child, at all times retaining his American citizenship. In 2001, Hamdi went to Afghanistan, where he was captured by the anti-Taliban forces and turned over to the American military. The military classified him as an enemy combatant and eventually transferred him to Guantánamo. The Bush administration maintained that since Hamdi was captured in a zone of active combat in a foreign theater of conflict, the decision of the president, as commander in chief, to label Hamdi as an enemy combatant could not be challenged in court. War is the prerogative of the political branches and not the court. Eight of the nine justices disagreed. In her plurality opinion, Justice Sandra Day O'Connor explained: "We have long since made clear that a state of war is not a blank check for the President when it comes to the rights of the Nation's citizens."[80] She continued:

> Whatever power the United States Constitution envisions for the Executive in its exchanges with other nations or with enemy organizations in times of conflict, it most assuredly envisions a role for all three branches when individual liberties are at stake. Likewise, we have made clear that, unless Congress acts to suspend it, the Great Writ of habeas corpus allows the Judicial Branch to play a necessary role in maintaining this delicate balance of governance, serving as an important judicial check on the Executive's discretion in the realm of detentions. [. . .] it would turn our system of checks and balances on its head to suggest that a citizen could not make his way to court with a challenge to the factual basis for his detention by his government, simply because the Executive opposes making available such a challenge. Absent suspension of the writ by Congress, a citizen detained as an enemy combatant is entitled to this process.[81]

Two years later, in *Hamdan v. Rumsfeld*,[82] the Court ruled that the president does not have authority to establish special military commissions for enemy detainees at Guantánamo Bay without congressional authorization. Congress fixed that problem by the passage of the Military Commissions Act of 2006[83] (MCA). However, in *Boumediene v. Bush*,[84] the Court struck down parts of the MCA because the law stripped regular federal courts of jurisdiction over habeas petitions filed by foreign citizens detained at Guantánamo. The 5–4 majority held that the MCA's suspension of habeas corpus was likewise barred by the US Constitution. The detainees had a constitutional right to challenge their detention in federal court. In his opinion, Justice Kennedy assessed the situation as follows:

> The Constitution grants Congress and the President the power to acquire, dispose of, and govern territory, not the power to decide when and where its terms apply. Even when the United States acts outside its borders, its powers are not "absolute and unlimited" but are subject "to such restrictions as are expressed in the Constitution."[85] To hold that the political branches have the power to switch the Constitution on or off at will . . . would lead[] to a regime in which Congress and the President, not this Court, say "what the law is."[86]

Scott Horton has rightly called *Boumediene* "a setback for [Schmitt's] the state of exception" because the Supreme Court for the fourth time rejected the contention that the president's commander-in-chief powers give him unfettered authority in national security matters.[87]

All four were bold decisions and follow in the tradition of the great *Ex parte Milligan*,[88] where the Supreme Court held in 1866 that President Abraham Lincoln had violated the Constitution by suspending the right of habeas corpus during the Civil War in areas where the civilian courts were still operating. Much credit should go to Justice Anthony Kennedy, the decisive "swing vote" on the Court. In his opinions, Kennedy has held firm against the argument that the extraordinary situation that the country faces in the post-9/11 era provides a reason for the political branches of the government to suspend civil liberties protected by the Constitution.[89]

Lest Americans pat themselves on the back, it must be acknowledged that the exceptional insecurity after 9/11 led to some horrid conduct by the United States.[90] In the name of national security, the National Security Agency violated the Fourth Amendment by collecting and then storing private data belonging to millions of Americans. The Defense Department incarcerated prisoners in Guantánamo indefinitely. The CIA undertook "extraordinary rendition," the transfer without legal process of a detainee to foreign dictatorial governments with a likelihood of mistreatment—but using the excuse that the receiving country gave its assurance that the transferee would not be mistreated. Thousands of individuals were detained and held without charges, some of them for months without judicial review in the immediate days after 9/11.[91]

But the most shameful conduct, going against the core values of all liberal democracies (militant or not), has been the torture by the CIA of suspected terrorists. The Convention Against Torture, to which the United States is a party, permits no exemptions.[92] No human being can ever be tortured. No reason or excuse is permitted.[93] Prosecutor Telford Taylor explained in his opening statement at the Doctors' Trial at Nuremberg (see Chapter 3): "To kill, to maim, and to torture is criminal under all modern systems of law."[94]

The temptation to torture after 9/11 was great. On the morning of September 11, 2001, terrorists from the Islamic group Al-Qaeda attacked the Unites States and killed 2,976 individuals, more deaths than at Pearl Harbor. The immediate concern was to prevent a second wave of attacks. President Bush and other senior officials received a daily "threat matrix," a document listing every possible impending threat directed at the United States. According to CIA Director George Tenet, "You simply could not sit where I did, and [reading the threat matrix] be anything other than scared to death about what it portended."[95]

Captured Al-Qaeda members were thought to have had the best information about any impending attacks—whether the next day, next month, or next year. The CIA proposed an interrogation program for these detainees. The program was modeled after the so-called SERE (Survival, Evasion, Resistance, and Escape) program used by the military during the Cold War designed to prepare downed American pilots to withstand interrogation by torture by the Russians or the Chinese. It would now be reverse-engineered and used on the suspected terrorists with the aim of obtaining the most accurate information and in the shortest period of time. The torture by the CIA of suspected terrorists was hidden under the euphemism of "enhanced interrogation techniques" (EITs). The most notorious among them was waterboarding, a method of interrogation for which Japanese soldiers were tried and convicted as war criminals at the end of the Pacific War.[96]

Sadly, the torture was made possible through involvement of lawyers. The CIA interrogators wanted immunity from prosecution before engaging in torture. The plan would go forward only after it was approved by the US Department of Justice (DOJ). The interrogators and their CIA superiors asked DOJ lawyers for the so-called Golden Shield: A Get Out of Jail Free card stating that these techniques were lawful. They got it. The DOJ's Office of Legal Counsel (OLC) delivered to the Department of Defense memoranda in August 2002 opining that the EITs about to be conducted upon the detainees were lawful both under American law and international law.[97] And so the US government began torturing people.[98] Rather than committing these "enhanced interrogation techniques" in the United States, the CIA established secret "black sites" abroad to commit the torture. Inevitably, the slippery slope appeared. Once the torture began, the CIA interrogators went beyond the techniques for which they received the Golden Shield from the DOJ lawyers.

In December 2014, the Senate Intelligence Committee publicly released a 528-page summary of its still-classified report on the CIA's detention and interrogation program. Issued more than eight years after the program was shut down, the summary erased any lingering doubt that the EITs were not only immoral but also illegal. It called the so-called EITs by their rightful name: torture.[99] Earlier, in 2005, CIA agents destroyed ninety-two videotapes documenting the harsh interrogations of two Al-Qaeda suspects in CIA detention. According to the *New York Times*, "The tapes were destroyed as Congress and the courts were intensifying their scrutiny of the agency's detention and interrogation program."[100]

The Convention Against Torture, which the United States ratified in 1994, obligates state parties to prosecute individuals responsible for acts of torture conducted at the behest of a government. The War Crimes Act of 1996 contemplates such prosecutions. In December 2014, the *New York Times* called for such criminal prosecution.[101] And in our post-Holocaust world, the Nazi analogy invariably arose. In "When Lawyers Are War Criminals," Scott Horton refers to the prosecution of jurists at the Justice Trial at Nuremberg as precedent that the government lawyers that created 9/11 law should be prosecuted.[102] Horton explains:

> That case stands for some simple propositions. One of them is that lawyers who dispense bad advice about law of armed conflict, and whose advice predictably leads to the death or mistreatment of prisoners, are war criminals, chargeable with potentially capital offenses. Another is that cute lawyerly evasions and gimmicks, so commonly indulged in other areas of the law, will not be tolerated on fundamental questions of law of armed conflict relating to the protection of civilians and detainees. In other words, lawyers are not permitted to get it wrong.[103]

I reject Horton's resort to the Nazi analogy. Unlike during the Nazi period, the post-9/11 emergency was real. Jews, Poles, and other Nazi victims did not pose a danger to Germany. The same cannot be said today about Al-Qaeda and ISIS. The state of extreme insecurity existing at the time that the torture took place and the legal memoranda were issued is crucial. As described by one lawyer working at the OLC in the immediate period after 9/11: "[T]o use sort of a technical term, everyone was freaked out about it, because they thought we really were going to suffer a significant attack. And it was in the context of that and a relatively recent capture of a particular individual [who might have valuable information] that the sort of great urgency arose. . . . because a lot of people are going to die if we don't prevent this attack."[104] In the same vein, in December 2014, James Mitchell, one of the CIA interrogators, stated in a December 2014 television interview:

> [T]he situation that I found myself in personally was one where it was clear that we had been attacked, it was clear that there was a second wave coming . . . and there was all this pressure not just from the CIA, but from Washington and everywhere they were saying, "the gloves are off. We have to take extraordinary measures." . . . [A]nd it was in the context of that that they were putting this program together.[105]

President Obama upon taking office in January 2009, in one of his first acts, banned EITs. He also signaled at the same time that there would be no prosecutions.[106]

In his historical study, *All the Laws but One*,[107] published in 2000, before the United States began to fight the so-called War on Terror, former US Supreme Court Chief Justice William Rehnquist anticipated the current debate on how to balance civil liberties and national security. Rehnquist cited some notorious examples: President Lincoln's suspension of habeas corpus during the Civil War; the strict First World War censorship laws under President Woodrow Wilson; and the US Supreme Court's willingness to uphold President Franklin Roosevelt's order to intern Japanese Americans during the Second World War. Rehnquist explained:

> In any civilized society the most important task is achieving a proper balance between freedom and order. In wartime, reason and history both suggest that this balance shifts to some degree in favor of order—in favor of the government's ability to deal with conditions that threaten the national well-being. It simply cannot be said, therefore, that in every conflict between individual liberty and governmental authority the former should prevail.[108]

Exhibiting prescience about the challenges faced by the Bush and Obama administrations in the Age of Terrorism, Rehnquist noted:

> [T]here is no reason to think that future wartime presidents will act differently from Lincoln, Wilson, or Roosevelt, or that future justices of the Supreme Court will decide questions differently from their predecessors. . . . [T]here's every reason to think that the historic trend against the least justified of the curtailments of civil liberty in wartime will continue in the future. It is neither desirable nor is it remotely likely that civil liberty will occupy as favored a position in wartime as it does in peacetime. But it is both desirable and likely that more careful attention will be paid by the courts to the basis for the government's claims of necessity as a basis for

> curtailing civil liberty. The laws will thus not be silent in time of war, but they will speak with a somewhat different voice.[109]

With the threat of future 9/11-type attacks still looming large, a final evaluation cannot be made about whether judges and other legal actors in today's liberal democracies will continue to handle themselves more responsibly than did German legal actors during 1933–1945. Remembering the horrid behavior of German judges, lawyers, and law professors, however, can play an important role in reminding their contemporary counterparts of the critical role they play in assuring that today's democracies do not transform themselves into legal tyrannies.

What is the practical lesson to be learned by today's legal theorists from the Nazi era? Arthur Kaufmann concludes that "almost all philosophical and legal doctrines can be abused for purposes foreign, or even contradictory to law—which is why no one should imagine that he is in a possession of a so-called 'operational safe' theory."[110] The legal philosopher Ilmar Tammelo put it more harshly: "[J]urisprudence plays the role of a whore, by cloaking oppression, degradation, even genocide. Among legal philosophers, contortionists can be found, who could twist their thoughts to conform to the political order of the day, who tried to wrap their thoughts in a philosophical cloak, however much moral perception was outraged by the reality."[111] In other words, no theory of law can inoculate jurists from doing evil. Ultimately, it comes down to the values held by the individual legal actors. Kaufmann has a practical answer for today's lawyers seeking to learn from the Nazi era: "There is only one path to follow: Keep your eyes open and your mind alert."[112]

PART THREE

The Holocaust as a Catalyst for Modern International Criminal Justice

8

Nuremberg's Legacy

The UN Tribunals for Yugoslavia and Rwanda and the International Criminal Court

With the onset of the Cold War, the Nuremberg legacy was dead.[1] The only remnant was the set of seven Nuremberg Principles that the UN International Law Commission adopted in 1950. These, however, soon were largely forgotten.[2] Standard international law texts used in American law schools only summarily covered the history of the prosecution of Nazi war criminals at Nuremberg and elsewhere. If they did, it was only just that, as a historical event never to be repeated again. The same was taking place in Europe.[3]

The memory of Nuremberg, however, was kept alive for over a half-century, coinciding with the years of the Cold War, by human rights nongovernmental organizations (NGOs) and by scholars of international law who held on to the notion that the principles established at Nuremberg could serve as the foundation for the future accountability of political leaders and other actors for state crimes. With the sudden collapse of the Soviet Union in December 1991 and realignment of the entire political order, it became possible for the first time since Nuremberg to speak about international prosecutions and to involve diplomats and jurists in the process. Even as late as the 1990s, however, it was not at all clear that the Nuremberg precedent had any value for how to deal with perpetrators of mass atrocities. In an essay in 1993 in the *New York Review of Books* titled "Misjudgment at Nuremberg," prominent historian István Deák argued that "the lesson of the Nuremberg trials is that there should be no other trials following the model of the Nuremberg trials."[4] As the rest of this chapter illustrates, Deák was completely off the mark.[5]

The end of the Cold War did not bring an end to mass atrocities. Soon the Security Council faced two new crises. The breakup of multiethnic and multireligious Yugoslavia in 1991–1992 brought some of the horrors of the Holocaust back on European soil. Until the Dayton Peace Accords ended the war in 1995, the Yugoslav conflict left 100,000 people dead and 2.2 million others homeless. One of the iconic images from that time period was graphic television footage of emaciated, shirtless Bosnian Muslim male prisoners behind a barbed wire in the Omarska and Trnopolje camps run by Bosnian Serbs.[6] These images, reminiscent of the images of concentration camp prisoners following liberation of the Nazi-run camps, were broadcast worldwide and shamed the Security Council to take action. US Secretary of State Madeleine Albright describes how those images reminded her "of other faces, photographed on their way to other unfamiliar hard-to-spell places, such as Auschwitz, Treblinka and Dachau."[7] In December 1992, the UN General Assembly issued a resolution citing "the existence in Serbian and Montenegrin controlled areas [of Bosnia of] concentration camps and detention centres in pursuit of the abhorrent policy of 'ethnic cleansing', which is a form of genocide."[8] In our post-Holocaust world, the international community (and especially the West) could not stand by idly in the face of concentration camps once again being established in Europe. When the Security Council unanimously voted for the establishment of the International Criminal Tribunal for the former Yugoslavia (ICTY) on February 22, 1993, Albright observed: "There is an echo in this chamber today. The Nuremberg principles have been reaffirmed."[9]

The ICTY, with its seat in the Dutch capital The Hague, was the first international war crimes tribunal established since the Nuremberg and Tokyo tribunals. Like its predecessors, the ICTY was a temporary international court, established on an ad hoc basis to prosecute individuals who had committed genocide, war crimes, and crimes against humanity on the territory of the former Yugoslavia in the 1990s.

The atrocities in the former Yugoslavia were soon overshadowed by an even greater human tragedy. On April 6, 1994, the fragile peace between the majority Hutu and minority Tutsi tribes in Rwanda was shattered when the Rwandan president's plane was shot down as it was about to land in the capital Kigali.[10] Immediately thereafter, Hutu extremist militias began an organized killing program to destroy the entire Tutsi population of Rwanda. The massacres ended one hundred days later when a Tutsi rebel army defeated the Hutu extremist regime in early July. By that time, an estimated 800,000 men, women, and children were murdered. The daily rate of death for those three months exceeded the daily murder rate of the Holocaust, with the simple machete being the primary tool of mass murder. The Hutu extremists killed those whom they called "cockroaches," usually by hacking them to death. As shocking was the fact that the United Nations had peacekeepers on the ground when the killings began, but the UN leadership in New York ordered the UN commanders not to intervene, leaving the helpless civilian Tutsi victims to fend for themselves. Two decades later, the United Nations still has not fully confronted this blunder. The immediate reaction in 1994 was to create a second ad hoc tribunal. The Security

Council established the International Criminal Tribunal for Rwanda (ICTR) on November 8, 1994, through Resolution 955. With its seat in the city of Arusha, in neighboring Tanzania, the mandate of the ICTR was to prosecute individuals who committed genocide, war crimes, and crimes against humanity on the territory of Rwanda between January 1 and December 31, 1994. The establishment of these international criminal tribunals (ICTs) led to additional mixed ad hoc courts for Sierra Leone, East Timor, and Cambodia,[11] and ultimately provided momentum for the adoption of the Rome Statute and the creation of the permanent International Criminal Court in 1998.

The ICTs are Nuremberg's progenies. As Guénaël Mettraux, defense counsel before the ICTs, has noted: "When the time came to give political and moral legitimacy to the idea of international criminal justice and to build a new house for it, Nuremberg gained renewed relevance. The political creators of the new war crimes tribunals saw fit to anchor the new courts and tribunals within the tradition of their forebear and to model those after their venerable ancestor."[12] And as Timothy Snyder reminds us, "It was Lawrence Eagleburger, the first President Bush's last secretary of state, who promised Yugoslav ethnic-cleansers 'a second Nuremberg.' "[13]

Nothing more attests to the Nuremberg legacy than the statement of Louise Arbour, former chief prosecutor for the ICTs: "Collectively, we're linked to Nuremberg. We mention its name every single day."[14] Legal scholars today hail the Nuremberg proceedings as the beginning of the "judicialization of World War II atrocities in Europe"[15] and "legalism's greatest moment of glory."[16] Giving credit in particular to two of the Allies, Gary Jonathan Bass notes: "In the end, [at Nuremberg] America and Britain managed to produce something extraordinary. We have created nothing to compare with it since."[17]

The Nuremberg paradigm has become the "gold standard" by which any significant domestic prosecution of state actors for international crimes is evaluated. It is impossible to put someone on trial today for war crimes, crimes against humanity, and genocide (even though it was not one of the crimes enunciated at Nuremberg) without invoking the legal norms developed at Nuremberg. Every recent significant domestic legal proceeding of state leaders or for international crimes, whether it is the trial of Saddam Hussein for crimes against humanity and genocide or the current military tribunal trials at Guantánamo under the Military Commissions Act of 2009, are invariably compared to the standards of Nuremberg.

A. BUILDING A BETTER NUREMBERG

Nuremberg held the authors of great crimes accountable under international law. The ICTs built on the virtues of Nuremberg. The architects of the ICTs, however, did not want just to reproduce the process employed at the International Military

Tribunal at Nuremberg (IMT), but to improve upon it. Since no international criminal trials had taken place in the period between the end of the Second World War and the end of the Cold War, what little jurisprudence that came out of the IMT in 1945 remained the most relevant precedent for the ICTs fifty years later.[18] Nevertheless, some new norms—either through international human rights treaties or as customary international law—came into being in the interim years. These new norms were either incorporated initially into the ICT statutes or were enunciated later in the court opinions issued by the ad hoc tribunals.

The most important criticism of Nuremberg, widely voiced at the time and ever since, is that it violated the fundamental legal principle of ex post facto by holding the German defendants accountable for acts that had not been designated in advance as crimes. Crimes against humanity was also novelty in international law. At Nuremberg, only war crimes—such as the killings of prisoners of war or civilians beginning in 1939—involved the application of previously established international law norms. The ICTs do not suffer from the ex post facto defect. The crimes that fall within their jurisdiction are all well established in international law. They are violations of international humanitarian law, of which the most important are the provisions of the Third and Fourth Geneva Conventions of 1949 and of Protocol I of 1977 specifying that certain acts are "grave breaches," or war crimes.[19] Violations of the Genocide Convention, which entered into force in 1951, are also part of the jurisdiction of the ICTs. Also, the ICTs have the authority to try the accused for crimes against humanity, a crime uniformly today accepted in international law. Nuremberg's great contribution in establishing that certain crimes, when committed on a large-scale and systematic basis against particular racial, religious, or political groups, would be considered crimes against humanity under international law continues with the ICTs.

The second major criticism of Nuremberg was that it constituted "victor's justice." That is not the case for the ICTs. None of the judges came from a country that was a party to the conflicts that took place in the former Yugoslavia and Rwanda. Instead jurists from over twenty different countries have sat as judges on the ICTs. A corollary criticism was that the victorious Allies themselves committed many acts during the war which they accused the defendants of committing (the "you too" or *tu quoque* argument). The most egregious were the wars of aggression that the Soviet Union undertook against Poland, the Baltic states, and Finland after signing the nonaggression pact with Nazi Germany in 1939. Moreover, the systematic bombing by British and American forces of German cities with no military value (Dresden and Hamburg being the most egregious examples) were war crimes under the Fourth Hague Convention of 1907, which bars the "bombardment, by whatever means, of towns, villages, dwellings or buildings which are undefended."[20] The Allies, of course, did not stand trial for such bombings. In contrast, those who sat in judgment at the ICTs have no connection with the crimes committed in the former Yugoslavia and Rwanda.

Other advantages that the ICTs have had over Nuremberg include:

1. The modern-day unacceptability by most nations of the death penalty as punishment, no matter how grave the crime committed by the defendant. For this reason, the highest punishment that can be meted out by the ICTs is life imprisonment.

2. At Nuremberg, Martin Bormann was tried *in abstentia*. Today, trials *in abstentia* are no longer considered procedurally proper. For this reason, those indicted by the ICTs must be apprehended and appear in person before the court. At the outset, each indictment was publicly announced, which led to the suspected defendant going into hiding. As a result, later ICT prosecutors issued indictments under seal and then unsealed them upon the defendant's capture. This rule was adopted by the International Criminal Court (ICC): the ICC does not try individuals unless they are present in the courtroom. As discussed below, because the majority of defendants under ICC indictment are still at-large, few trials have taken place so far.

3. Nuremberg did not have an appellate tribunal, with the judgment issued by the IMT judges being final. In contrast, the three-judge tribunal judgments before the ICTs are appealable to a joint five-judge Appeals Chamber, which hears appeals from both the ICTY and ICTR Trial Chambers.

In contrast to Anglo-American jurisprudence, the prosecution can appeal an acquittal verdict after a trial on the basis that the Trial Chamber based its acquittal on an incorrect application of the law. In the latest example of such a reversal of an acquittal, the Appeals Chamber in December 2015 reversed the acquittals of Serb military officers Jovica Stanišić and Franko Simatović and sent the case back down for a retrial.[21]

4. Additional due process guarantees are afforded to the defendants at the ICTs that were not available to defendants at Nuremberg.[22] Procedural trial fairness is the foremost goal of international criminal justice, and the Nuremberg tribunal was in some ways thin in this area. In contrast, the statutes of the ICTs provide extensive due process guarantees to the accused. One of those is the right of the accused to self-representation, a right not recognized at Nuremberg.[23]

The flip side of such extensive guarantees to the accused is that the trials became quite long, with some lasting a number of years. In contrast, the IMT concluded its proceedings against the leading Nazis in just eleven months. More than two decades later, the ICTs are still prosecuting defendants. In a 2015 interview, Judge Theodor Meron, president of the Appeals Chamber, responded to this criticism:

> I think that there is an answer to it. In Nuremberg, the allies benefited from an incredible paper trail. The Nazis were great archivists. They kept records of everything. In principle, every person who arrived in Auschwitz was registered in some kind of a way. In the former Yugoslavia, maintaining archives and records was not a national pastime. There was very few of that. So you had to produce witnesses, bring them to The Hague from several thousand kilometers away. . . . In contrast to Nuremberg, we did not have a police, a military police [that] we could send anywhere . . . to seize evidence, to subpoena witnesses, to bring them to the court. We were totally dependent on the cooperation of states."[24]

5. Provisions giving voice to the victims during the trials, with a special "Victims and Witnesses Section" created for that purpose.[25] As discussed earlier, while the Nuremberg trials featured testimony of some victims, it was not until the Eichmann trial in Israel that victim testimony became a leading feature of a mass atrocity trial. This embracement of a "victim-centred" approach continues with the ICC, where so-called "Legal Representatives of Victims" have a seat at the counsel table alongside counsel for the prosecution and the defendants.

6. One last improvement cannot be ignored: bringing diversity to the international bench and bar. Nuremberg was an all-male affair, with almost all the principal players coming from Europe or the United States. Not so with the ICTs, the mixed tribunals, or ICC. Women and people of color have played a critical role in modern-day international criminal justice. The current ICC chief prosecutor, Fatou Bensouda, is a female barrister from Ghana. The former and first ICC prosecutor was Argentinian Luis Moreno Ocampo. Richard Goldstone of South Africa, the first ICTY and ICTR prosecutor, though of East European Jewish heritage, proudly calls himself an African. Goldstone was followed by two female chief prosecutors, Louise Arbour of Canada and Carla Del Ponte of Switzerland.[26] And one of the first judges appointed to the ICTY bench, and who later served as president of the court, was Gabrielle Kirk McDonald, a retired federal African-American jurist from Texas. In 1993, Secretary Albright explained that "the United States government is determined to see that women jurists sit on the tribunal and that women prosecutors bring war criminals to justice."[27] That goal has been accomplished.

The new procedural guarantees made the ICT trials more fair than those conducted at Nuremberg. The two biggest challenges for the upstart courts was lack of sufficient funding and getting countries to cooperate in arresting suspects indicted by the ICT prosecutors. At the outset, Serbia would not cooperate with the ICTY. Seeking integration into the European community, Serbia later changed its stance and began to cooperate. The three top ICTY Serb defendants were eventually all arrested by Serbian authorities and flown to The Hague to face charges before the ICTY: Serbian president Slobodan Milošević in 2001, after being toppled by a "people's power" movement in 2000; Bosnian Serb political leader Radovan Karadžić in 2008, after spending thirteen years on the run and hiding under a new identity as a "faith healer"; and Bosnian Serb General Radko Mladić in 2011, who disappeared after Milošević's arrest ten years earlier. Croatia and Bosnia did the same for their suspects when faced with similar pressure. Likewise, a number of ICTR suspects discovered to be living in Africa, Europe, Canada, and the United States were arrested and handed over to the ICTR for trial in Arusha, Tanzania. This is in stark contrast to the current lack of cooperation by many African countries with indictments issued by the ICC (see below).

Illustration 15 Judge Theodor Meron. Courtesy of ICTY.

When we speak of the ICTs, one jurist stands out: American law professor Theodor Meron. In 1993, as a longtime professor of international law at New York University (NYU) Law School, Meron was one of the first academics to call for the establishment of an international war crimes tribunal for Yugoslavia.[28] In 2001, Meron was appointed as a judge to the ICTY and served as president of the tribunal on two occasions, in 2003–2005 and again in 2011–2015. Both ICTs have issued a number of significant opinions clarifying the law of genocide and other crimes subject to the jurisdiction of the ICTs. For many of these decisions, Meron was presiding judge and author of the opinions. In recognition of his critical role, the UN Security Council in 2012 appointed Meron as president of the residual Mechanism for International Criminal Tribunals, the successor "cleanup" court to the ICTY and ICTR.

Meron's personal and professional life follows in the footsteps of the two most significant international law scholars from the Nuremberg and immediate post-Nuremberg era: Raphael Lemkin and Hersch Lauterpacht. Like his predecessors, Meron is a Jew born in prewar Poland. Hailing from a middle-class Jewish family in the small town of Kalisz in central Poland, Meron was nine years old when war came to Poland in 1939. The Germans murdered almost all of the 20,000 Jews of Kalisz, destroying an ancient Jewish community going back to the twelfth century. One of the survivors was the young Meron. Herded with his family into a series of ghettos and then forced-labor camps, Meron survived the war while many of his family members, including his mother, perished.

In 1945 at age fifteen, Meron came to Mandate Palestine. Educated at the Hebrew University in Jerusalem, Cambridge, and Harvard, Meron served as the Legal Advisor for the Israeli Foreign Service and later as the Israeli ambassador to Canada. In 1978, he restarted his life for a second time by emigrating to the United States. At age forty-eight, Meron became a full-time American academic, teaching international law for many years at NYU. In 1998, Meron served on the American delegation to the Rome Conference on the Establishment of an International Criminal Court, where he was involved in drafting the ICC's provisions on war crimes and crimes against humanity. Like Lemkin and Lauterpacht, the Second World War motivated much of Meron's work. As he explains:

> [T]he imprint of the war made me particularly interested in working in areas which could contribute to making atrocities impossible and avoiding the horrible chaos, the helplessness, and the loss of autonomy which I remembered so well. . . . My World War II experience was never far away.[29]

It is significant that the jurist most responsible in the last decade for creating the case law of genocide is a Holocaust survivor born in Poland.[30]

B. CREATING THE CASE LAW OF GENOCIDE

Until the decisions issued by the ICTs, the crime of genocide was an empty shell since no one had ever been prosecuted for genocide. After adoption of the Genocide Convention in 1948, no court had a chance to actually apply its text to particular situations. The most difficult challenge confronted by the ICT judges was how to apply the general definitions of genocide as enunciated in the Convention to the specific acts committed by defendants at the dock.

The ICT judgments filled the empty shell of genocide by adjudging criminal cases unprecedented in scope and scale and involving acts rarely prosecuted on a national level. International criminal law's understanding today of genocide comes from these actual prosecutions before the ICTs. In short, the authoritative legal answer to the question raised in Chapter 2—*What is genocide?*—is found today in the legal opinions issued by the ICTs (the ICC as of 2016 not yet having tried anyone for genocide). Here is how the Appeals Chamber in 2004 in the *Krstić* case in an opinion by Judge Meron—the case that judicially recognized that genocide was committed against Bosnian Muslims in Srebrenica by the murder of 8,000 men and boys—explained the crime:

> The gravity of genocide is reflected in the stringent requirements which must be satisfied before this conviction is imposed. These requirements—the demanding proof of specific intent and the showing that the group was targeted for destruction in its entirety or in substantial part—guard against a danger that convictions for this crime will be imposed lightly. Where these requirements are satisfied, however, the law must not shy away from referring to the crime committed by its proper name. By seeking to eliminate a part of the Bosnian Muslims, the Bosnian Serb forces committed genocide. They targeted for extinction the forty thousand Bosnian Muslims living in Srebrenica, a group which was emblematic of the Bosnian Muslims in general. They stripped all the male Muslim prisoners, military and civilian, elderly and young, of their personal belongings and identification, and deliberately and methodically killed them solely on the basis of their identity. The Bosnian Serb forces were aware, when they embarked on this genocidal venture, that the harm they caused would continue to plague the Bosnian Muslims. The Appeals Chamber states unequivocally that the law condemns, in appropriate terms, the deep and lasting injury inflicted, and calls the massacre at Srebrenica by its proper name: genocide. Those responsible will bear this stigma, and it will serve as a warning to those who may in future contemplate the commission of such a heinous act.[31]

One lesson learned through these actual prosecutions was the discovery of how difficult it is to prosecute someone for genocide, and especially establishing beyond a reasonable doubt the *mens rea* of the crime: the specific intent to destroy a protected group in whole or in part.[32] As discussed in Chapter 2, perpetrators do not reveal their state of mind through written documents (the Nazis being the rare exception) or through an explicit genocidal order ("Exterminate all Tutsis!") or a confession ("I admit that I sought to exterminate all members of the Tutsi tribe"). As a result of the genocide prosecutions before the ICTs, we now have about a dozen decisions providing significant case law as to what is necessary to prove the *mens rea* of genocide and its related crimes.

1. Joint Criminal Enterprise and Genocide

A significant and controversial innovation not specifically set out in the Genocide Convention was the recognition by the ICTs that a defendant may be guilty of genocide by participating in a joint criminal enterprise (JCE) to commit the crime.[33] JCE is mentioned nowhere in the Genocide Convention or in the ICTs' statutes. Rather, it is solely a construct of the ICT judges—and especially the ICTY's first activist president Antonio Cassese—who held that it derived from customary international law, similar to the way the Nuremberg judges found crimes against humanity to be derived from international custom. At Nuremberg defendants could be found guilty for the acts of their co-conspirators, but those convicted at least had to actually know the object of the conspiracy. Not so, as we shall see below, with JCE.

Complicity via JCE is applicable not only to genocide but also to war crimes and crimes against humanity. As William Schabas explains:

> "[J]oint criminal enterprise" complicity [is] a way of imputing guilt to a person who participates in a form of collective criminal activity. The accused can be convicted not only for the crimes that he or she actually committed, with intent, but for those committed by others that he or she did not specifically intend but that were a *natural and foreseeable consequence of executing the crime that formed part of the collective or common purpose or enterprise.*[34]

Schabas goes on to explain: "Since the theory of 'joint criminal enterprise' was first mooted by the [Appeals Chamber] Tribunal, in *Tadić* in July 1999 [the first case prosecuted by an ICT before a panel presided by Judge Cassese[35]] it has become the magic bullet of the Office of the Prosecutor."[36] Prosecutors repeatedly have turned to JCE to prove the *mens rea* of genocide.

Participating in a JCE to commit genocide carries a greater penalty than aiding and abetting genocide. This gradation concept has given much-needed flexibility to the judges when confronting real-life perpetrators of the crime rather than just words on paper. The most complicit genocidaires are given a life sentence; JTE genocidaires are meted out a lesser sentence (ranging from twenty to thirty-five years); and aiders and abettors to genocide sentenced to an even lesser term (usually ten to fifteen years). On the other hand, it is hard to differentiate the JTE accomplice from the non-JCE aider and abettor. While on paper the former may be more blameworthy than the latter, this is just a construct created by the judges with no real distinction between these two concepts.

More problematic is the tribunals' recognition of an extended form of joint criminal enterprise dubbed JCE III and encapsulated by the last portion of Schabas's quote. Under JCE III, an individual is criminally culpable for the acts of others even if he or she did not know their intent but should reasonably have known of such intent from the circumstances (in the language of the ICTY, should have known because the result was the "natural and foreseeable consequence" of the common plan). For genocide, for example, if a collective of individuals jointly decides to destroy a protected group, an actor who helps that collective but does not share that intent to destroy can be liable for liable under JTE III if he or she should reasonably have known that the destruction of the protected group was the natural and foreseeable consequence of the acts of the actor's compatriots.

All criminal systems recognize that individuals can be guilty for the acts of another. There is no problem *if* the actor *shared the same intent* to commit the criminal act with those who actually committed the act (JCE I). There is also no objection *if* the actor does not share the intent of his or her acting compatriots *but knew* of their intent *and* still colluded with them (JCE II). Under JCE III, however, an actor can be found guilty for the acts of others *even if* the actor (1) *did not have the intent* that these acts be committed and (2) *did not know* that these acts would be committed. JCE III thus appears to violate the basic fairness principle of individual criminal responsibility. Yet, as Bachmann and Fatić point out in their 2015 study of the ICTs: "Each and every [ICTY] leadership case was based on Type 3 JCE, because it allowed the prosecution to implicate politicians and higher military officers in crimes they had not committed, if they had agreed to a common plan, whose 'natural and foreseeable consequence' had been the said crimes. There was even no need to prove that the participants in a JCE had belonged to the same power structure or institution."[37] Fortunately, the JCE III prosecution strategy did not always work, and if it did work before a trial chamber, the decision was reversed on appeal. At this point, it is unclear whether JCE III will stick. It was rarely used by the ICTR prosecutors during the twenty-one years of that tribunal's existence and has not been successful before the Extraordinary Chambers in the Courts of Cambodia (ECCC), the mixed Cambodia tribunal. To date, it is not part of ICC jurisprudence.

2. Public Incitement to Commit Genocide

The ICTR convictions for public incitement to commit genocide, an inchoate crime, was also a critical development in ICT jurisprudence, illustrating that the incitement crime in the Genocide Convention is not just a theoretical construct.[38] At the IMT at Nuremberg, the Nazi newspaper editor Julius Streicher was convicted of crimes against humanity while Nazi radio chief Hans Fritzsche was acquitted of the same charge. The antithetical holdings left us unsure whether public incitement through speech is criminalized by international law. We now definitively know that individuals can be convicted for genocide simply through words. We also know that incitement to genocide is an inchoate crime, with the crime completed with the dissemination of the genocidal message, even if does not lead others to taking action against a protected group. As Richard Wilson explains: "A direct call for the destruction of a group protected by the 1948 UN Genocide Convention in a public setting, even if utterly ignored by its intended audience, is a criminal act. This type of 'genocidal speech' is a crime *per se*, by virtue of what it itself does."[39]

In Rwanda, the two instruments of death were the machete (used to kill the victims) and the radio (used to incite the perpetrators and broadcast the location of the victims). As one prosecution witness explained: "In the case of the 1994 genocide in Rwanda, the effect of language was lethal . . . hate media . . . played a key role in the instigation of genocide."[40] In the *Nahimana* case, the leading ICTR genocide incitement case, the Trial Chamber observed: "Without a firearm, machete or any physical weapon, he [Nahimana] caused the deaths of thousands of innocent civilians."[41] Known as *The Media Case*, the trial involved three defendants. Two were founders of the notorious RTLM radio station, referred to as Radio Machete, that broadcast messages urging Hutus to kill Tutsis and even gave specific locations where the victims could be located. The third defendant was owner of an extremist newspaper that also called for the murder of Tutsis. All three were convicted of genocide, conspiracy to commit genocide, and incitement to genocide (and also crimes against humanity through persecution and extermination). In 2007, the Appeals Chamber partially reversed their convictions.[42] It acquitted all three defendants of conspiracy to commit genocide and all genocide charges relating to RTML, including incitement. Simply being owners of media outlets that broadcast or published incitement messages, the appellate court ruled, was not sufficient for conviction of genocide incitement. Actual evidence of these defendants actually ordering their journalist employees to incite the murder of Tutsi was missing. Thus, while the court found that the actual messages transmitted by the radio station did amount to incitement to genocide, it could not tie these statements directly to the defendants sufficient for a criminal conviction. As for the newspaper owner, the appellate court found that certain articles published in 1994 did constitute incitement to genocide and could be tied to the defendant, and so affirmed the incitement conviction.

In 2006, the ICTR sentenced Joseph Serugendo to six years in prison for direct and public incitement to commit genocide and persecution as a crime against humanity. Serugendo was the technical director of Radio RTML. After fleeing Rwanda, he was arrested in Gabon and turned over to the ICTR. Under a plea agreement, the ICTR prosecutor dropped the more serious charges of genocide, conspiracy to commit genocide, and complicity to commit genocide, in exchange for Serugendo's guilty plea for incitement. Serugendo died a month later. And in 2000, RTLM on-air presenter Georges Ruggiu, after being arrested in Kenya and turned over to the court, pled guilty to one count of crimes against humanity through persecution in connection with his broadcasts during the genocide and sentenced to twelve years' imprisonment. Flown to Italy in 2008 to serve out the remainder of his sentence, he was released a year later. Ruggiu, originally from Belgium, was the only white broadcaster on the radio station and was the only non-Rwandan to be convicted by the ICTR.

In 2005, the ICTR prosecutor charged Rwanda's most popular singer Simon Bikindi, known as Rwanda's Michael Jackson, with incitement to genocide. At trial, Bikindi was acquitted of incitement through his anti-Tutsi songs but convicted of incitement for statements he made at a public rally calling Tutsis "snakes" and exhorting his audience to kill Tutsis. The trial court found specifically that Bikindi "abused his stature by using his influence to incite genocide"[43] and sentenced him to fifteen years' imprisonment. In 2010, the Appeals Chamber affirmed the conviction and sentence.

3. Command Responsibility and Genocide

ICT jurisprudence has confirmed that genocide is a difficult crime to prosecute, even with JCE as an aid. One outcome is to make it harder to convict military and political leaders of genocide through command responsibility. The most recent appellate chamber case law appears to hold that being a commander of armed forces does not automatically make the commander guilty for acts committed by his troops. Required is proof beyond reasonable doubt that the commander had actual knowledge of the crimes. JCE III complicity is not enough.

Critics say that these latest decisions have weakened the Nuremberg precedent holding commanders and political leaders responsible. Critics also argue that the case law of the ICTs has been inconsistent, acquitting top commanders of serious charges, while minor defendants in the earlier trials have been convicted on far lesser counts. Supporters of these acquittals make the point that because of the egregious criminality and horrific nature of the crime of genocide, it is reasonable for a court to apply a standard of proof higher than for a normal common crime or for the lesser crimes committed by the initial minor defendants prosecuted before the ICTs.

As noted above, the modern-day Justice Marshall of the law of genocide has been Judge Meron, who through the decisions he authored has stamped his personal imprint on the parameters of the law of genocide. Meron has been a strict constructionist of the crime, writing significant decisions reversing convictions of individuals convicted by the trial chambers based on command responsibility and JCE III. In doing so, he has corrected the punitive tendency in some of the trials to convict *someone* for the horrible acts presented at these trials, even if evidence against the *actual defendants* on the dock may be shaky.[44]

In February 2012, the ICTY Appeals Chamber presided by Judge Meron acquitted Momcilo Perisić, the former Yugoslav army chief of staff, along with Serbian State Security Service Chief Jovica Stanisić and his deputy Franko Simantović, holding that as military commanders these men were not responsible for crimes committed by their subordinates.

A more significant acquittal came in November 2012, when the appellate chamber with Judge Meron presiding reversed the convictions for crimes against humanity and acquitted two Croatian generals Ante Gotovina and Mladen Markać for their role in the 1995 massacres of Serbs in Croatia. Gotovina was the commander of the Croatian military in the southern Krajina region during "Operation Storm" in 1995, when army units drove Serbian troops, along with hundreds of thousands of Serbian civilians, out of Croatia. Markać was the head of the special police forces in the area. Prosecutors argued that Gotovina and Markać had participated in a meeting with Franjo Tudjman, then president of Croatia, at which they all planned to drive out the state's Serbian population. The prosecution further argued that this was carried out through indiscriminate shelling and that both men bore "command responsibility" for murders, plunder, and cruelty committed during the operation. In 2011, the Trial Chamber found both men guilty, sentencing Gotovina to twenty-four years in prison and Markać to eighteen years. The Appellate Chamber found the entire prosecution to be a mistake, the problem being lack of solid evidence. Meron's decision rebuked the trial judges for relying on "circumstantial evidence" on which "no reasonable Trial Chamber" should have based a conviction.

In December 2011, the ICTR Appeals Chamber with Judge Meron presiding reduced the sentences of Colonel Théoneste Bagosora and Colonel Anatole Nsengiyumva, both of whom had been sentenced to life in prison by the ICTR for genocide, crimes against humanity, and war crimes on the basis of command responsibility. Bagosora was accused of being one of the masterminds of the

Rwandan genocide. When the genocide started, Bagosora was the *directeur de cabinet*, or executive assistant, to the Minister of Defense. After the plane crash that killed the president of Rwanda, Bagosora positioned himself as the *de facto leader* of the country by taking control over the civil defense posts. In that capacity, he established paramilitary *Interahamwe* "self-defense" units across the country and supplied them with machetes as well as deploying the militias at killing points. Despite holding both defendants liable, the Appeals Chamber presided by Judge Meron reduced the sentence to thirty-five years in prison for Bagosora and to fifteen years for Nsengiyumva.

Similarly, in February 2014, the ICTR Appeals Chamber with Judge Meron presiding acquitted Rwandan gendarmerie (police) General Augustin Ndindiliyimana of genocide. In 2011, The Trial Chamber convicted Ndindiliyimana and sentenced him to eleven years' imprisonment. Even though Ndindiliyimana was head of the gendarmerie, the appellate judges found that he could not be held legally responsible for the killings committed by his police officers because by the time the mass killings began he had ceded control of most of the police to the Rwandan army. Ndindiliyimana consequently became one of the most senior figures to be acquitted by the ICTR. The same Appeals Chamber also reversed the conviction of former army major François-Xavier Nzuwonemeye for conspiracy to commit genocide, crimes against humanity and war crimes. Nzuwonemeye was head of an army battalion involved in the killing of Rwandan Prime Minister Agathe Uwilingyimana and Belgian peacekeepers guarding her in the opening days of the Rwandan genocide in April 1994. He was sentenced for twenty years' imprisonment by the trial judges. The Appellate Chamber reversed, ruling that Nzuwonemeye could not have known that some of his men on their own initiative would assist in the murder of the prime minister or that they would attack and murder the peacekeepers.

On the other hand, Judge Meron was the presiding judge in the appeal in the *Krstić* case,[45] which in 2004 recognized that the 1998 massacre of approximately 8,000 Bosnian Muslim men and boys in Srebrenica by the Bosnian Serb forces was a genocide—the first legally established genocide on European soil since the end of the Second World War. At trial, defendant General Radislav Krstić received a prison sentence of forty-six years for his role as commander of the Bosnian Serb unit that attacked the safe haven enclave of Srberenica. On appeal, the appellate panel headed by Judge Meron reduced his sentence to thirty-five years' imprisonment, finding that Krstić could be found guilty of aiding and abetting the genocide (and crimes against humanity through extermination and persecution) but not, as the Trial Chamber found, of direct participation in the genocide.

In September 2014, the Appeals Chamber affirmed the life sentences for two former heads of the ex-ruling party in Rwanda, convicted of genocide in

2011. Matthieu Ngirumpatse and Edouard Karemera, the former chairman and deputy chairman of Rwanda's then-ruling National Revolutionary Movement for Development, were both handed life terms by the Trial Chamber. And in April 2015, the Appeals Chamber, with Judge Meron presiding, affirmed the life sentence of Zdravko Tolimir. The Bosnian Serb general was convicted in December 2012 of genocide with regard also to the massacres in Srebrenica.[46] Tolimir was General Mladić's chief aide and intelligence chief of the Bosnian Serb army's main headquarters.[47] As these words are being written in early 2016, the ICTY is still proceeding with its two most important cases: of former Bosnian Serb president Radovan Karadžić and top Bosnian Serb military commander General Ratko Mladić. Both of these "big fish" went into hiding and were not caught until the ICTY was well underway and by which time it had already issued its first genocide conviction in 2004 for Srebrenica.[48]

The ICTs also have made significant contributions to crimes against humanity and war crimes. Crimes against humanity is no longer a crime that can only committed in connection with a war. The ICTs established that an individual can be convicted of crimes against humanity for acts committed in peacetime, a proposition not accepted at the IMT judgment. With regard to war crimes, the ICTY in its first case, *Prosecutor v. Tadić*,[49] established that war crimes can also be committed in internal armed conflicts.

Like Nuremberg, the ICT prosecutions have also created a detailed court record of the crimes. The ICTY's last chief prosecutor, Serge Brammertz, speaking about the atrocities committed in the former Yugoslavia, notes: "Without the tribunal there wouldn't be a database of seven million documents which very clearly gives the history of the conflict."[50]

The last accomplishment of the ICTs has been the relatively large number of defendants that have been brought to trial—despite the fact that the ICTs do not have police powers to arrest individuals. When the tribunals first started operating in the early 1990s their future looked bleak, described by one scholar as "twin petri dishes for the international criminal project writ large."[51] Their rocky start, however, was followed by increasing support for the courts, demonstrated not just through words but through deeds: the consistent turnover by various countries of perpetrators who came to their shores to seek safe haven. It is remarkable that every individual indicted by the ICTY has been arrested. In all, 126 individuals have been prosecuted before the tribunal. The reason for this success was the EU use of the carrot and stick approach with the former Yugoslav states. The European Union would not consider these states for membership or European aid until they gave up their war criminals to the ICTY. Unlike the unhappy experience so far with the ICC (see discussion below), countries for the most part eventually cooperated in turning over suspects to The Hague or Arusha.

In the Rwandan case, after the genocidal government was overthrown, the accused fled and ended up in about twenty-six countries. These countries, including some African states, were willing to abide by their obligations to the UN Charter and extradited suspects to Arusha. As a result, the ICTR's numbers are similar. By December 31, 2015, when the ICTR closed, it had indicted close to one hundred individuals, with almost all brought to trial. Eight still remain at large, with the latest capture taking place in December 2015, when the Democratic Republic of Congo arrested top suspect Ladislas Ntaganzwa, a former Rwandan mayor who was on the run for twenty-one years. Ntaganzwa is accused of crimes against humanity by allegedly instigating the killing of thousands of Tutsis. Since the ICTR is now closed, Ntaganzwa is expected to be turned over to Rwanda for trial.[52]

C. CRITICISMS OF THE ICTS

1. Slow Start

Both tribunals had a rocky start. Much credit for the tribunal's continued existence goes to the ICTY's first president (chief justice), Antonio Cassese, and first prosecutor, Richard Goldstone. Both adroitly navigated the UN bureaucracy to keep the tribunals moving forward. Cassese was the most prominent jurist on the ICTs. A distinguished Italian international law scholar, in 1993 he accepted the UN appointment as the first president of the ICTY. Judge Cassese sat on the ICTY until 2000. He died in 2011 at age seventy-four. Judge Cassese's most notable achievement on the ICTY was simply to keep the tribunal going, when in the initial years there was little support for the court, financial or otherwise, and much opposition. Without his and Goldstone's persistent promotion of the ICTs, they would have likely died in their infancy.

Cassese credits Madeleine Albright, US Ambassador to the United Nations and later secretary of state, as one of the critical supporters of the court in its early years. Judge Cassese himself admitted that he was an activist judge, working with Goldstone to go after the major perpetrators after starting the initial trials with the low-level hanging fruit defendants.

> I asked Goldstone how many people he thought had committed genocide in the former Yugoslavia. He said about 200,000 people. And I said, all right, so we cannot try 200,000 people. We can only try maybe 100. And these 100 must not be [all minor] people like Tadić and Nikolić.[53]

Goldstone, a respected South African jurist and the first chief international prosecutor since Justice Jackson, concurred.[54] In July 1995, Goldstone's office indicted Radovan Karadžić and Radko Mladić, the political and military leaders of the Bosnian Serbs.

2. Inconsistent Jurisprudence

The most major substantive criticism of the ICTs has been that they have produced an inconsistent jurisprudence, with various panels interpreting the text of the Genocide Convention and the law of war crimes and crimes against humanity according to the judges' own proclivities and understanding of the law. Before the IMTs, there was no existing case law interpreting the words of the Genocide Convention or set definitions for war crimes and crimes against humanity. The IMT judgment, as discussed in Chapter 3, had little law in it. The judgment of the International Military Tribunal for the Far East in Tokyo also did not have much helpful legal analysis. The judgments issued by the twelve NMT tribunals and the occupation courts set up by other Allies provided helpful case law for prosecuting war crimes and crimes against humanity; however, these decisions also suffered from inconsistent judgments. No one had ever been prosecuted for genocide before. The ICT judges in Arusha and at The Hague were the first to tackle the difficult problem of what the prosecution must prove for an individual to be found guilty of this crime of crimes. It was inevitable that different panels would come up with different conclusions.

3. Inconsistent Quality of Jurists

The various jurists appointed to the ICTs—representing over twenty countries—have been of varied quality, with some being excellent jurists and others bordering on mediocrity. Appointments were made by the United Nations based on regional diversity and just plain horse-trading, with not the best and the brightest always being appointed to the bench.[55] A bigger problem was lack of bench experience. As one ICTY defense counsel has pointed out: "[I]t has not been uncommon to have diplomats and professors, with no real trial or appellate experience, appear in court for the very first time and embark on a new career, that of a 'professional' international judge. . . . The unintended consequence of appointing clever diplomats and bright professors is that some of them are utterly unfit to sit on the bench—at least for their first trial."[56]

4. Punitive Tendency

The ICTs have been criticized by some as having a punitive tendency. Faced with horrible crimes, there is an urge to convict *someone* of the crimes, even if the evidence against the actual defendant on the dock is shaky. Bachmann and Fatić, in their study, explain this culture of conviction.

> There is also a general picture that emerges from the ICTY's and ICTR's legal innovations: all of them . . . were directed to making the ICL [international criminal law] more punitive, to increase the number of convictions, to ease the burden of the prosecution and to make the defence's task more difficult.[57]

On the other hand, some of the light verdicts handed out (coupled with early releases), especially to repentant defendants, demonstrate a leniency by the judges. The recent spate of acquittals discussed above, authored by Judge Meron, also show a pushback against the ICTs' punitive tendency.

5. Cost and Pace of Trials

On the procedural side, the two major criticisms of the ICTs have been their cost, averaging around $400 million per year for each tribunal, and the slow pace of the trials, with some taking years to complete. The longest proceeding lasted over nine years, and it is still not finished.[58] In contrast, the IMT completed its work in eleven months. As Karen Naimer, a former staff lawyer on the ICTs, observes: "Somehow between Nuremberg and the emergence of the new international legal order in the 1990s, we lost the ability to try cases as quickly or as efficiently as they were able to do back then, for better or for worse."[59]

Beginning with the first trial, *Prosecutor v. Tadić*, ICT prosecutors both *overprosecuted* (charging a multitude of counts that all must be proved) rather than pruned the indictment to the most significant crimes and *overtried* their cases (for example, bringing in multiple witnesses when one would be sufficient). Sadly, the judges for the most part allowed the prosecutors to do so. Unlike at the IMT trial, there was no Sir Geoffrey Lawrence at the ICTs to control the courtroom, a skill of experienced trial judges that almost none of the ICT judges-academicians possessed.

The prosecutors and judges are not the only ones to blame. Defense attorneys also sought on many occasions to sabotage the proceedings by bringing multiple unwarranted motions, and then seeking appeals of rulings that went against them. They too also overtried their cases. The nadir of efficiency was reached during the Milošević trial, which went on for four years before coming to an unseemly end in the midst of the trial with Milošević's fatal heart attack in 2006. As one commentator noted: "[B]y trying to prove Milošević guilty of everything under sun, the Prosecution was required to present a parade of witnesses that never seemed to end. Furthermore, many of these witnesses had little to contribute other than second-hand knowledge of alleged crimes."[60] Lawrence Douglas lays much blame on "crucial missteps [made] by the court and the prosecution."[61] He explains:

> Early on, the court, with little objection from the prosecution, acceded to Milošević's demand that he be allowed to present his own defense. . . . [This right of self-representation does] not include a right to insult the dignity of the court. Yet this is exactly what Milošević got away with, time and time again. Almost from the start, the court found itself hostage to the defendant's tendentious, time-consuming and yet not unresourceful harangues. . . . The prosecution also made an early, fateful misstep in tendering an overly broad and ambitious [sixty-six count] indictment . . . [which] . . . slowed the trial, [and] made for an unfocused and confusing presentation of evidence. . . .[62]

Douglas's characterization of the Milošević trial could just as well apply to many other ICT proceedings. And then there are the overly long opinions that have come out of the ICTs, with some judgments numbering over a thousand pages. What is the impact of this snail pace justice? Naimer explains:

> [T]he length of these cases and the corresponding cost reinforce the notion that justice is very slow, and it's very costly, and so as a result is only going to capture very, very few people who even get there. As a result a deep amount of cynicism has set in and more people are trying to explore alternative opportunities for meting out justice at least at the local level.[63]

After twenty-one years, the ICTR closed its doors on December 31, 2015, after delivering its forty-fifth and final judgment. The ICTY is set to close by the end of the 2017 upon completion of its ongoing prosecutions. As noted, the Security Council in 2010 created a wind-down successor court, the Mechanism for International Criminal Tribunals (MICTs), to adjudge the appeals from both tribunals after their closing. The MICT consists of twenty-five standby judges and one full-time judge, Judge Meron as its president.[64] To cut down on costs for the successor tribunal, the stand-by judges are compensated only when they are hearing cases. The MICT is based in Arusha, with the ICTR's former on-the-ground resources taken over by the MICT.[65]

6. The Ivory Tower Syndrome

Another criticism has been about the lack of connection of the ICTs to their most important stakeholders: the people of the region where the atrocities took place.

Physical distance is a major contributing factor. The ICTY sits in The Hague and the ICTR sat in Arusha, Tanzania. The successor MICT court will be sitting in Arusha. As a consequence, the ICTs have been accused of being inflicted with the Ivory Tower Syndrome: more interested at how international legal scholars view their work than the local Serbs, Croats, Bosniaks,[66] Kosovars, and Rwandans. Refic Hodzić, a former spokesperson for the ICTY, while still remaining a supporter of the court, put it this way in a 2013 blog post titled "ICTY: Not Our Court":

> [T]o the vast majority of judges and lawyers who shaped its development and jurisprudence . . . the only people they saw themselves accountable to were the policymakers in New York, Washington, Berlin and other key capitals. . . . [T]he Tribunal's judges have been and will always be more interested in what international law journals have to say about their judgments than the people to whose lasting peace they are supposed to be contributing.[67]

7. Failure to Prevent

The last criticism is that prosecutions before the tribunals, and international prosecutions in general, have not stopped genocides and other mass atrocities. Referring to the ICTs, Bloxham and Pendas assert that "neither ever stopped anyone from committing a single crime."[68] Of course, they are right. The hundreds of international prosecutions to date have not stopped self-appointed ISIS caliph and genocidaire Abu Bakr al-Baghadadi and his followers from committing their mass brutalities in Iraq and Syria. However, prevention is not their job. Rather, their primary task is to bring perpetrators of mass atrocities to face justice. As David Scheffer explains:

> War crimes tribunals were created to pursue justice and, over the long term, influence the attitudes of would-be perpetrators and targeted victim populations. It is preposterous to assume that they would have significant short-term impacts on warring parties. Diplomacy, economic sanctions, and military action have been far more important for the immediate pursuit of peace and stability. But the tribunals began a process that steadily produced indictments (which shame, delegitimize, and sideline criminals), prosecutions, and historical records, all of which help build the peace over time.[69]

In 2014, Judge Meron summarized the accomplishments of Nuremberg's "children":

> The ad hoc Tribunals' achievements, grounded on customary law, are manifold. They have created a set of evidentiary and procedural rules that the

> Nuremberg tribunals did not bequeath, as well as a corpus of substantive law expressed in detailed jurisprudence and hundreds of judicial decisions. They have also enshrined individual criminal liability for an increasing number of norms previously only applied to states as a matter of civil responsibility. Most fundamentally, they have laid to rest the age-old question of whether international law really is law. The direct application of international law to individuals by international courts and tribunals leaves no doubts that it is.[70]

Meron's statement is an excellent academic summary of the many ways that the ICTs have strengthened international criminal law by carrying on (and improving upon) the legacy of Nuremberg. The ICTs have shown that *some* perpetrators of international crimes in *some* instances will be punished for their actions. In the end, however, "[t]here are too many graves containing the bones of all ethnicities for international justice to cope with."[71] Given finite resources, international justice will always "discriminate[] against victims in favor of perpetrators."[72]

D. NUREMBERG AND THE INTERNATIONAL CRIMINAL COURT

The ICTs are temporary tribunals. The ICTR closed down on December 31, 2015. The ICTY is set to close sometime in 2017 when it completes the trials already underway. The dream of the founders of Nuremberg was not just to convene a temporary tribunal to prosecute the leading Nazis but to create a permanent international court. Leading perpetrators of mass atrocities could be judged by this court for grave breaches of international law. Article VI of the 1948 Genocide Convention specifically contemplates the creation of such a tribunal for the crime of genocide. It provides for alleged genocidaires to "be tried by a competent tribunal of the State in the territory of which the act was committed or by such international penal tribunal as may have jurisdiction."[73] In his 1949 Final Report on the NMT trials, Telford Taylor called for the establishment of "a permanent international penal jurisdiction . . . to enforce the Nuernberg principles."[74]

Even though there were no shortages of atrocities for which perpetrators could be prosecuted, the Cold War made the project impossible. Soon after adoption of the Genocide Convention, members of the UN General Assembly did ask the newly established International Law Commission (ILC) to study the possibility of establishing an international criminal court. From 1949 to 1954, the ILC drafted a series of draft statutes for such a court. But the Cold War cut the process short, as both the Soviet Union and the Western countries failed to put much stock in the effectiveness of such a tribunal. As a result, the UN General Assembly effectively abandoned the effort.

As Cold War tensions dissolved, the world community showed a renewed interest in creating a permanent international criminal tribunal. On December 4, 1989, the General Assembly adopted a resolution that instructed the ILC to return to the project. Four years later, the General Assembly called on the ILC to commence the process of drafting a statute for the court. The draft statute was presented in 1994. The following year a preparatory committee was established to further review the substantive issues regarding the creation of a court based on the ILC report.

The International Criminal Court (ICC) was established by the Rome Statute of the International Criminal Court on July 17, 1998, when 120 states participating in Rome at the "United Nations Diplomatic Conference of Plenipotentiaries on the Establishment of an International Court" adopted the statute. The ICC statute sets out the court's jurisdiction, structure, and functions and provides for its entry into force sixty days after sixty states have ratified or acceded to it. This took place on July 1, 2002, sixty days after the sixtieth instrument of ratification was deposited with the Secretary-General, with ten countries simultaneously deposited their ratifications. On March 11, 2003, the ICC, seated in The Hague, began its work.

The ICC became the first ever permanent, treaty-based, international criminal tribunal created to ensure that the gravest international crimes do not go unpunished. Its establishment was a monumental achievement of a long overdue dream. The Rome Statute gives the ICC jurisdiction to prosecute perpetrators of genocide, war crimes, and crimes against humanity. Anyone who commits any of these crimes after July 1, 2002, when the ICC began operations, became potentially liable for prosecution by the court. Though not a UN court, like the ICTs, it operates alongside the United Nations; the Security Council can refer cases to it, as it has already done twice in the cases of Sudan and Libya.[75]

The court operates under the principle of complementarity, meaning that its jurisdiction is complementary and subsidiary to the jurisdiction of national criminal courts. Only if a state is unable or unwilling to take on the prosecution of these international crimes can the ICC take on the prosecution.

In order to avoid the possibility of a rogue prosecutor operating on his or her own personal agenda, independent action by Office of the Prosecutor (OTP) is highly circumscribed. The ICC prosecutor may act on instructions by the Security Council or at the request of individual states that are parties to the court and on whose territory the treaty-enunciated crimes may have occurred or whose nationals participated in the alleged crimes. The prosecutor may also take action on his or her own initiative, but is subject to strict oversight by a pre-trial chamber. Additionally, the prosecutor must obtain that chamber's authorization before beginning investigations that are not requested by the Security Council or an impacted state party on its territory. Like the ICTs, the ICC has no executory powers; it must rely on the party states to enforce its measures.

In 2003, the first set of eighteen multinational ICC judges was elected. That same year, the Assembly of States Parties, the formal executive body of the ICC, elected Luis Moreno Ocampo of Argentina as the first chief prosecutor of the ICC, with Fatou Bensouda of Gambia as chief deputy prosecutor. Moreno Ocampo stepped down in 2012 and Bensouda took over the chief prosecutor post.

As of early 2016, 139 states have signed the ICC Statute, with 123 of those ratifying the treaty and becoming members of the court. Among the notable holdouts: the United States (which signed the treaty but did not ratify it), Russia, and China. To date, the ICC has indicted thirty-six individuals and has held two trials. All those indicted have come from Africa, with the charges likewise based solely on atrocities committed on that continent.[76]

In 2006 came the first arrest, when the Democratic Republic of Congo turned over Thomas Lubanga Dyilo to the ICC. Lubanga was a former warlord who had been charged by the ICC with commission of war crimes and crimes against humanity in connection with the civil conflict in the gold-rich Ituri region of Congo. The brutal conflict took place in Congo from 1996 to 2007 and claimed approximately 60,000 lives. Its intensity significantly decreased with the presence of UN peacekeepers in 2003. Lubanga was flown to The Hague and later that year appeared at the first public hearing by the ICC, when he was formally indicted and pleaded not guilty. The Congolese government later turned over two more rebels to the ICC connected with the Ituri conflict, Germain Katanga and Mathieu Ngudjolo Chui.

The civil war in Congo is little known outside the immediate region. Much more prominent, due to the CNN effect and NGO activism, are the mass murders and other atrocities taking place in the Darfur region of Sudan. As a result of focused initiatives by a multitude of NGOs in the West, Darfur became popularly known as the first genocide of the twenty-first century. As discussed in Chapter 2, the United States under the George W. Bush administration characterized the atrocities as genocide, though a later-established UN-based fact-finding commission labeled them as crimes against humanity. Following the Darfur report, the Security Council in 2005 referred the Darfur situation to the ICC, with the United States—though a vocal opponent of the court—not vetoing the referral. With the Darfur situation now formally under the ICC's jurisdiction, the pretrial chambers confirmed in 2007 the OTP's issuance of arrest warrants for the Sudanese Minister for Humanitarian Affairs and former Deputy Minister of the Interior Ahmed Harun, and for Ali Kushayb, a Janjaweed militia commander. The Janjaweed are local Arab militias operating with the support of the central Arab government in Khartoum. In June 2008, ICC prosecutor Moreno Ocampo went after his first "big fish" when he requested the issuance of an arrest warrant against the sitting president of Sudan, Omar Hassan Ahmad Al-Bashir, charging him with crimes against humanity, war crimes, and genocide in Darfur.[77]

In the first decade of its existence, the court showed much promise. When Belgium turned over to the ICC another former warlord, Jean-Pierre Bemba Gombo of the Central African Republic in 1998, William R. Pace, head of the multi-NGO Coalition for the International Criminal Court, observed:

> With the growing global reach of the Rome Statute, there are fewer safe havens for perpetrators of massive crimes. Exactly ten years after the adoption of the Rome Statute, this Court embodies the promise of seeing individuals held responsible for the gravest crimes they committed, regardless of their position. We are, we believe, at the beginning of a new age when the establishment of these kinds of militias that commit crimes against humanity is no longer a corridor to power, but a pathway to prison.[78]

In 2012, the prosecutors secured their first conviction when Lubanga was found guilty of crimes against humanity and war crimes connected with the forcible use of child soldiers. The court sentenced him to fourteen years' imprisonment. Recognizing its Nuremberg legacy, among those giving closing arguments for the prosecution was ICC special prosecution co-counsel Benjamin Ferencz, the last living Nuremberg prosecutor at the spry age of ninety-two.[79]

In 2014, the prosecution secured its second conviction, of former Congolese rebel Germain Katanga. The conviction arose out of a 2003 massacre in the village of Borogo in the Ituri region, when approximately two hundred villagers were murdered and many women raped and forced into sexual slavery. Katanga was given a twelve-year sentence.

The Katanga verdict led to much debate about the prosecutor's office handling of the case. Moreno Ocampo originally painted Katanga as one of the masterminds of the Botobo massacre, but the court, in a 2–1 decision, found that Katanga was primarily responsible for supplying guns and logistical support to the actual killers and so could not be found guilty as a participant. The majority decision found him guilty of being an accessory to war crimes and crimes against humanity. The dissenting judge argued that the court's changing of the charge from principal to accessory denied Katanga a fair trial. All three judges acquitted Katanga of directing rapes, sexual slavery, and use of child soldiers. His co-defendant Mathieu Chui was acquitted of similar charges in 2012 and released. Katanga wisely chose not to appeal his conviction, since he had already been in custody for seven years and would be credited with time served. A year later, in November 2015, the ICC judges granted Katanga an early release, making him the first ICC convict to be freed.

In December 2014, the ICC dropped its case against the Kenyan President Uhuru Kenyatta, stunning many in the international community. The case collapsed amid claims of sabotage and lack of cooperation by the Kenyan government, with the ICC prosecutor announcing that she was withdrawing charges against Kenyatta who, along with Vice-President William Ruto and broadcaster Joshua Sang, were charged with orchestrating crimes against humanity during Kenya's 2007–2008 post-election violence. In April 2016, came the death knell of the Kenya case when a three-judge ICC Pre-trial Chamber, in a 2-1 ruling, granted defense motions filed by Ruto and Sang at the conclusion of the prosecution's case-in-chief to "terminate" the trial. The case fell apart when several prosecution witnesses recanted their testimony. The majority rejected ICC prosecutor Fatou Bensouda's argument that while the loss of witnesses weakened the case, there still remained enough evidence to proceed with the trial. Technically, the Kenya case is still ongoing, since Bensouda appealed the court's granting of the defense's no-case-to-answer motion. Also, the Pre-trial Chamber rejected defendants' application to acquit, meaning that the prosecutor could refile the charges with stronger evidence ("t]he charges against the accused are vacated and the accused discharged without prejudice to their prosecution afresh in future.") Nevertheless, the first such pre-trial dismissal in the ICC for lack of sufficient evidence came as another blow to a court whose prestige was already waning.

The fact that to date only Africans have been indicted and prosecuted has led some African leaders and local activists to accuse the ICC of having an anti-Africa bias. The criticism of the ICC being Afro-centric is strange since Africa widely hailed in 1994 the creation the ICTR for the prosecution of the Rwandan genocidaires. In fact, before the ICTR's creation, the West was accused of *ignoring* African atrocities by establishing an ad hoc tribunal for Yugoslavia but not for Rwanda. The charge was of racism: black African lives are considered less worthy than white European lives. And so, as Alex Whiting has pointed, out, the former criticism for not paying enough attention to Africa has now turned into the current criticism of paying *too much attention* to Africa.[80] Whiting correctly explains:

> The problem is not that the ICC is "targeting" Africa. Rather, the problem is that the Court lacks jurisdiction over many parts of the world where international crimes are occurring, such as in Syria and Iraq today . . . [T]hose attacking the ICC for an Africa bias should redirect their criticisms towards those countries that have refused to join the ICC or to find other means to achieve accountability for international crimes, either through domestic processes or other international or regional courts. They should also redirect their criticisms towards the UN Security Council, which referred the cases of Sudan and Libya to the ICC, but to date has failed to refer Syria or to establish an alternative justice mechanism for the massive crimes being committed in that country. The problem is not that accountability is sought in Africa for crimes committed against Africans. That is a good thing. The problem is that there is a failure to pursue accountability in other places where crimes

> are also being committed. That is a failing not of the ICC but of the international community, and that's where critics should direct their attention.[81]

The "only Africa" situation changed in early 2016, when an ICC pre-trial chamber gave prosecutor Bensouda authority to formally open an investigation into atrocities possibly committed during the three-month-long conflict in 2008 in the Russian-supported breakaway province of South Ossettia in the Republic of Georgia.[82] The regular Georgian army sent troops to quash the rebellion, and Russia sent forces to help the rebels. Since Georgia became a member of the ICC in 2003, atrocities committed on its territory by any party come within jurisdiction of the court.

As of this writing in early 2016, and with close to two decades of existence, the ICC has become a beleaguered institution, not of its own doing. Lack of proper and timely cooperation by governments and by the Security Council is the main culprit. Frustrated by the international community's lack of assistance on Sudan, ICC Chief Prosecutor Bensouda (herself an African, from Ghana) announced in December 2014, after a decade of no progress, that she was formally suspending the criminal case against the still-sitting President al-Bashir and his fellow Sudanese defendants.[83] Addressing directly the UN Security Council, she lamented:

> It is indeed an understatement to say that we have failed the Darfur victims. . . . Given this Council's lack of foresight on what should happen in Darfur, I am left with no choice but to hibernate investigative activities in Darfur as I shift resources to other urgent cases. . . . What is needed is a dramatic shift in this Council's approach to arresting Darfur suspects.[84]

In June, 2015, the prosecutor again warned of her "deep concern about the negative consequences for the court in case of non-execution of the warrants by member states."[85]

Unlike the situation with the ICTs, states have been much less cooperative with the ICC. Whiting explains:

> The ICC's experience has been very different [than of the ICTs]. The Court's first prosecutor also sought to generate support for his investigations, but the resources allowed and the responses from other actors have not been the same. . . . [S]pecific support for the prosecution's investigations has been very uneven and often nonexistent, either because of a lack of sustained interest or because of lack of leverage over situation countries. While many factors account for both the successes and failures at the ICC, a lack of consistent support for the Court's work has contributed to the prosecutor's inability to push a number of cases forward beyond the charging stage.[86]

In summer 2015 came another embarrassment when al-Bashir took yet another trip outside Sudan to attend an African Union summit in South Africa. Even though South Africa is a signatory to the ICC, it did not arrest al-Bashir. Following al-Bashir's departure back to Sudan, the *LA Times* published a lead editorial with the tag line: "The International Criminal Court has proved to be expensive and so far ineffective."[87] The editorial pointed out that "after more than a dozen years and $1 billion, the ICC has brought just 22 cases and has obtained just two convictions. . . . The victims of inhumanity deserve better."[88] That same year, Duncan McCargo critiqued the entire project of international criminal justice and concluded: "By and large, the international community should get out of the business of 'putting people on trial.' "[89]

And so as of this writing, the pendulum swing is against international criminal justice. But the pendulum is bound to swing back. As Whiting asked and answered in 2015: "[I]s the ICC dead and buried or alive and kicking? It is, in fact, a mistake to think that the ICC is or will meet either of these destinies, emerging as a total failure or a complete success."[90] Rallying against this binary division of "all good" or "all bad," Whiting added: "The Court is here to stay, it is a reality, and over time it will experience both highs and lows, triumphs and setbacks. And that has been precisely the history of the international criminal justice project starting with Nuremberg and throughout the life of the modern tribunals. Each time it seemed that the international criminal justice project was dead, it rose again to achieve new successes."[91] Using his own experience on the ICTY, he explained:

> I was a prosecutor at the ICTY when Slobodan Milošević died in 2006 after four years of trial. Many thought that the Court would not survive the premature end of its signature case and that the UN would quickly pull the plug and wind down the tribunal. In truth, some of the ICTY's best work came afterwards, particularly with the apprehension and trials of Ratko Mladić and Radovan Karadžić, and nearly nine years after Milošević's death the Court is still moving forward.[92]

We all await a reversal fortune for the ICC, but the *sine qua non* is increased cooperation by individual states, including the United States. As of this writing in 2016, the United States is still not a party to the ICC, though its cooperation with the tribunal increased significantly during the Obama administration. As Judge Cassese eloquently put it as president of the ICTY: "International courts have been bestowed with the sceptre and the gavel, not however with the attendant sword. It follows that they can only operate as long as sovereign states are prepared to lend them a helping hand."[93]

With the UN ad hoc tribunals now closing shop, the ICC has become the sole international tribunal responsible for prosecutions of suspected genocidaires and other international outlaws. While domestic prosecution of such outlaws can always take place before national courts, a bias-free, competent and highly regarded permanent international tribunal can play an important function in delivering justice to those committing the most serious international crimes. Conviction of a *hostis humani generis* by an international tribunal carries a stronger message of revulsion and rejection of impunity than a conviction by a domestic court. Trials of captured ISIS leaders, for example, would carry much more gravitas if conducted before the ICC than before courts of Syria, Iraq, or even the United States, France, or Britain.[94] International prosecutions may be expensive, but in the end they are worth it. It would be a major blow to the principle of international criminal justice first recognized seventy years ago at Nuremberg if the ICC failed.

9

Prosecuting Genocide

A limited number of individuals have been found guilty of genocide, the gravest state crime known to humankind, and branded with the most repugnant label to be placed upon a criminal: genocidaire. This chapter discusses some of the notable prosecutions.

A. INTERNATIONAL PROSECUTIONS

The Genocide Convention, adopted by the United Nations on January 12, 1951, gave states the right to prosecute the crime of genocide as an international crime. Article I of the Genocide Convention provides that state parties shall "undertake to . . . punish [the international law crime of genocide]." Article VI provides that persons charged with genocide "shall be tried [1] by a competent tribunal of the State in the territory of which the act was committed or [2] by such international penal tribunal as may have jurisdiction with respect to those Contracting Parties which shall have accepted its jurisdiction."

The International Criminal Tribunal for the former Yugoslavia (ICTY) and the International Criminal Tribunal for Rwanda (ICTR) are the first international courts to try individuals for genocide.[1] The statutes for both tribunals adopt verbatim the definition of genocide from the Genocide Convention.[2] In all, of the sixty-one defendants convicted by the ICTR, fifty-three were convicted of genocide or genocide-related crimes. At the ICTY, five defendants were convicted of genocide or genocide-related crimes out of the total eighty convicted by the tribunal.[3]

1. ICTR Prosecutions

The world's first international conviction for genocide took place in 1998, when the ICTR found Jean-Paul Akayesu, the former Hutu *bourgmestre* (mayor) of

Taba, guilty on October 2, 1998, of both genocide and incitement to genocide. Approximately 2,000 Tutsis were murdered by Hutus and scores of Tutsi women were raped in the Taba region between April and June 1994.[4] Akayesu's criminal responsibility was based on his direct participation in acts of genocide and on his position as a superior in command of the other perpetrators. The incitement conviction arose out of a public gathering where Akayesu urged the killing of Tutsi tribesmen by his fellow Hutus.

In addition to being the first genocide conviction by an international court, the *Akayesu* decision is also significant for finding that mass rape can constitute an act of genocide as part of a plan to destroy a group.[5] The *Akayesu* Trial Chamber also set out the widely quoted description of genocide as "the crime of crimes." The ICTR Trial Chamber sentenced Akayesu to life imprisonment. In June 2001, the ICTR Appeals Chamber upheld his conviction.[6] Akayesu is serving his sentence in a prison in Mali.

On September 4, 1998, two days after finding Akayesu guilty, the same ICTR Trial Chamber sentenced Jean Kambanda, former prime minister of Rwanda, also to life imprisonment. Kambanda was found guilty of (1) genocide, (2) conspiracy to commit genocide, (3) incitement to commit genocide, (4) complicity in genocide, (5) crimes against humanity (murder), and (6) crimes against humanity (extermination). At the trial stage, Kambanda did not contest his charges and pled guilty. On appeal, he claimed ineffective assistance of counsel, but the ICTR appellate chamber rejected this charge and upheld his conviction. As a result, Kambanda technically remains, to date, the only head of state to plead guilty to genocide. Kambanda is also serving his sentence in Mali.

In another significant conviction, an ICTR trial panel found a Roman Catholic priest guilty of genocide. Father Athanase Seromba, a Hutu, was in charge of a parish church where some 2,000 Tutsis sought refuge from rampaging Hutus. Seromba ordered the bulldozing of the church and the killing of all those who tried to escape. Approximately 1,500 Tutsis sheltered inside were murdered. In 2006, the Trial Chamber sentenced Seromba to fifteen years' imprisonment. In 2008, the Appeals Chamber quashed Seromba's conviction for the lesser crime of aiding and abetting genocide and found him guilty instead of the more serious charge of committing genocide by being a direct perpetrator. As a result, Seromba's sentence was increased to life imprisonment. Seromba became the first cleric to be convicted for genocide. He is serving his sentence in Benin along with eight others.

Of the total ninety-three individuals indicted by the ICTR during its two-decade existence, sixty-one were found guilty, with approximately two dozen found guilty of genocide or some other genocide-related crimes.[7]

2. ICTY Prosecutions

The first person convicted of genocide before the ICTY was Bosnian Serb General Radislav Krstić. In 2001, Krstić, in his role as commander of the Drina Corps of the Bosnian Serb Army (*Vojska Republike Srpske*, or VRS), was found guilty of genocide arising out of the Srebrenica massacre in 1995 where 8,000 men and boys of Bosnian Muslim descent were murdered. This was the largest mass murder on European soil since the end of the Second World War. The Trial Chamber sentenced Krstić to forty-six years in prison for his role in the genocide.[8] On appeal, the ICTY Appeals Chamber overturned his conviction as a direct perpetrator of genocide on the grounds that he lacked sufficient intent to commit genocide. Instead, he was found guilty of the lesser crime of aiding and abetting genocide. The Appeals Chamber explained:

> [A]ll that the evidence can establish is that Krstić [as commander of the separate Drina Corps of the VRS] was aware of the intent to commit genocide on the part of some members of the VRS Main Staff, and with that knowledge, he did nothing to prevent the use of Drina Corps personnel and resources to facilitate those killings. *This knowledge on his part alone cannot support an inference of genocidal intent.* Genocide is one of the worst crimes known to humankind, and its gravity is reflected in the stringent requirement of specific intent. *Convictions for genocide can be entered only where that intent has been unequivocally established.* There was a demonstrable failure by the Trial Chamber to supply adequate proof that Radislav Krstić possessed the genocidal intent. Krstić, therefore, is not guilty of genocide as a principal perpetrator.[9]

However, conviction of the lesser crime of aiding and abetting genocide was proper.

As the Appeals Chamber explained: "Krstić knew that by allowing Drina Corps resources to be used *he was making a substantial contribution to the execution of the Bosnian Muslim prisoners*. Although the evidence suggests that Krstić was not a supporter of that plan, as Commander of the Drina Corps he permitted the Main Staff to call upon Drina Corps resources and to employ those resources. The criminal liability of Krstić is therefore more properly expressed as that of an aider and abettor to genocide, and not as that of a perpetrator."[10] Krstić is serving his thirty-five-year sentence at a jail in the United Kingdom.

The latest ICTY genocide conviction case upheld on appeal as of this writing was in January 2015, when the Appeals Chamber dismissed the appeals of five more officers in the Bosnian Serb Army involved in the Srebrenica massacre. Two of the officers—Vujadin Popović and Ljubiša Beara—were found to be direct participants in a genocide and so sentenced to life imprisonment. They were transferred to Germany in late 2015 to serve their sentences. Popović was the chief of security of the Drina Corps of the VRS, and Beara was chief of security on the Main Staff of the VRS. Others received sentences ranging from thirty-five to five years. One of them, Drago Nikolić, was convicted of a genocide-related crime, aiding and abetting genocide, and given the thirty-five-year sentence.

The top individual to be charged with genocide by the ICTY was Slobodan Milošević, the former Yugoslav and Serbian president. In 1999, while still in power, Milošević was charged with genocide, along with war crimes and crimes against humanity in connection with the wars in Bosnia, Croatia, and Kosovo. After resigning following a disputed election in 2000, Milošević was arrested by Serbian authorities and flown on a Serb helicopter to a NATO military base in Bosnia. He was then transported by an American military plane to The Hague and placed in a holding cell to await trial. Milošević's trial began in 2002. Four years later, the trial was still ongoing. It came to an abrupt end when Milošević was found dead in in his jail cell in March 2006. A victim of a heart attack at age sixty-four, it turned out that he was not taking his prescribed medications.[11]

As of this writing in early 2016, the prosecutions of the remaining "big fish" before the ICTY—Bosnian Serb president Radovan Karadžić and Bosnian Serb army chief General Ratko Mladić—have not been fully concluded. Both were on the run for many years, hiding out in Serbia, before finally being arrested by Serbian authorities. Educated as a psychiatrist, Karadžić as a fugitive created for himself a new identity as a practitioner of alternative medicine, sporting a long beard and a ponytail prior to his arrest in Belgrade in 2008. Mladić was arrested three years later, found to be living in a Serbian village under an assumed name. Both were accused of masterminding the Srebrenica massacre and other crimes arising out of the war in Bosnia. The pair were both charged with genocide, war crimes, and crimes against humanity, and tried separately. With the death of Milošević, Karadžić and Mladić remained the highest-ranking defendants to be tried for the international crimes arising out of the Yugoslav conflict.

After five years of hearings, during which nearly 600 witnesses gave testimony and over 11,000 exhibits were introduced, the trial phase in *Prosecutor v. Karadžić* ended in October 2014. The three-judge panel issued its judgment in March 2016, seventeen months later. Karadžić was found guilty of genocide, war crimes, and crimes against humanity and sentenced to forty years in prison. The genocide conviction was limited to Karadžić's role in the murder of 8,000 unarmed Muslim men and boys at Srebrenica, but not to killings in other parts of Bosnia during the war. In so doing, the Karadžić Trial Chamber followed rulings by previous ICTY chambers that the only place where genocide took place during the

1992–1995 Yugoslav conflict was in Srebrenica. Karadžić's crimes and crimes against humanity convictions were based on his involvement in the killing and expulsion of Bosnian Muslims from Srebrenica and other parts of Bosnia that the Bosnian Serbs claimed as their territory. The court also found that Karadžić was instrumental in the shelling and sniping campaign during the siege of Sarajevo, the capital of Bosnia, conducted by Bosnian Serb military forces from the hills surrounding Sarajevo between April 1992 and February 1996.

The *New York Times* labeled the Karadžić trial as "the most important in the 23-year history of the [ICTY], and a defining test for the entire system of international justice."[12] The judgment is on appeal to an Appeals Chamber. Since it is the Appeals Chamber that will ultimately decide whether these convictions and the acquittal will stand, *the* defining test has yet to take place. We can also question why Karadžić, the political leader of the Bosnian Serbs, received a forty-year sentence and not life imprisonment; some lower-ranking Bosnian Serb leaders were given life terms. If the sentence stands on appeal, the seventy-year-old Karadžić will be eligible for early release after serving two-thirds of his sentence—with credit for the eight years' imprisonment during the trial—meaning that around age ninety he could be a free man.

Mladić's trial for genocide and other mass crimes is still ongoing, with a verdict expected in 2017, followed by the expected appeal. As such, the final chapter of the ICTY prosecutions may not take place until 2018 or 2019.

3. ICC Prosecutions

Article II of the Genocide Convention is incorporated into the statute of The Hague–based International Criminal Court (ICC), which since 2002 has stood ready to try individuals for genocide, war crimes, and crimes against humanity. As of this writing in early 2016, the ICC has yet to hold its first genocide trial.

The only case to date before the ICC to charge genocide has been the unsuccessful prosecution (so far) of Sudanese president Omar al-Bashir and his cohorts over the decade-old atrocities in Darfur. The violence in the Darfur region of Sudan began in 2003 and has been variously characterized as a "slow motion genocide" (because the killings have now been going on over a decade) and "the first genocide of the 21st century."[13] Over 300,000 have been killed and over two million displaced. The victims have been local non-Arabic African tribes (Fur, Masalit, and Zaghawa) murdered, raped, and displaced at the hands of militias (locally known as the *Janjaweed*, or "devils on horseback") under the control of the central Arab government in Khartoum.[14] The local Darfuri tribes, among whom are militias fighting the central government, certainly fit the definition of a protected ethnic group under the Genocide Convention.

The disagreement has been over *mens rea*: Do the rulers in Khartoum have the necessary genocidal intent to destroy in whole, or in substantial part, these local tribes? Genocide law scholar William Schabas rejects the use of the term for the Darfur tragedy based on lack of intent. His conclusion is based largely on a blue-ribbon study commissioned by former UN Secretary-General Kofi Annan and chaired by the late eminent Italian jurist Antonio Cassese that recommended in 2005 for the Darfur events to be referred to the ICC as constituting crimes against humanity—but concluding that " the Government of Sudan has not pursued a policy of genocide."[15] Two leading human rights nongovernmental organizations (NGOs), Amnesty International and Human Rights Watch, have also declined to date to characterize the violence in Darfur as genocide, instead calling them crimes against humanity and war crimes. Other NGOs, however, like World Without Genocide and Jewish World Watch, readily accept the characterization of genocide. The US Holocaust Museum's Center for the Prevention of Genocide likewise labels the killings in Darfur as genocide.

Luis Moreno Ocampo, the first ICC prosecutor, after receiving the referral of the Darfur situation from the Security Council disagreed with the Cassese Commission study. In 2010, Moreno Ocampo succeeded in convincing a pre-trial ICC panel that al-Bashir should be charged with genocide, alongside with crimes against humanity. However, the Darfur prosecution is now stalled. Al-Bashir, the first head of state to be indicted by any international court for genocide, remains ensconced as president of Sudan and travels freely to other states without being arrested. Of course, the political situation in the Sudan may change, with President Al-Bashir becoming at any time ex-President Al-Bashir, and extradited to The Hague like Milošević.

Will the ICC prosecutor be able to obtain a genocide conviction? Andrew Cayley, former chief prosecutor at the Cambodia tribunal, doubts it. He contends:

> The crimes perpetrated by Al Bashir's regime are proven facts. Serious disagreement remains, however, as to whether Al Bashir and the Sudanese government intended actually to destroy, in part, the Fur, Masalit and Zaghawa peoples of Darfur. Some have termed this mere speculation. It is difficult to cry government-led genocide in one breath and then explain in the next why 2 million Darfuris have sought refuge around the principal army garrisons of their province. One million Darfuris live in Khartoum where they have never been bothered during the entire course of the war. As Rony Brauman of Medecins sans Frontieres points out, "Can one seriously imagine Tutsis seeking refuge in areas controlled by the Rwandan army in 1994 or Jews seeking refuge with the Wehrmacht in 1943?"[16]

On the other hand, the Srebrenica precedent from the ICTY, where the targeting of only a small portion of the Bosnian Muslim group for destruction—Srebrenica-area Bosnian Muslim males only—was found to be a genocide may lead an ICC tribunal to adjudge the same for Darfur.

B. DOMESTIC PROSECUTIONS

As noted above, Article VI provides for national prosecutions of genocidaires, stating that perpetrators shall be tried "by a competent tribunal of the State in the territory of which the act was committed." Though this text appears to limit jurisdiction only to courts of those states where the acts of genocide were committed, customary international law recognizes that genocide is a crime of universal jurisdiction. Genocidaires are outlaws against all mankind—*hostis humani generis*—and so can be prosecuted by any tribunal granted jurisdiction to prosecute such individuals under domestic law. This means, in the words of the European Court of Human Rights, that national courts have "jurisdiction for crimes [of genocide] committed outside the State's territory by non-nationals against non-nationals of that State and which are not [even] directed against the State's own national interests."[17]

Soon after the Genocide Convention came into being in 1951, signatories to the Convention began promulgating domestic legislation criminalizing genocide under their national laws. But legislation was not followed by prosecution. Despite an imperfect but workable set of mechanisms for prosecutions of genocide, most perpetrators have gotten off scot-free. Impunity for genocide seems to be the norm, and prosecution and punishment the exception. And we are not speaking about impunity only for those who physically carried out the actual murders—the killers, whether they be soldiers of a regular state army or members of a ragtag paramilitary group—but also the desk murderers who actually planned the policy of genocide and set the genocidal behavior into motion.

The first domestic prosecution of an individual for the crime of genocide did not take place until 1961 when Adolf Eichmann was tried in Israel under its "Nazi and Nazi Collaborators" law. One of the articles of the Israeli law, as noted earlier, includes "crimes against the Jewish people" committed during the Nazi era, which in effect means genocide committed against Jews.[18] Eichmann was found guilty by Israel of the genocide of European Jews even though his crimes were committed (1) before the State of Israel came into existence in 1948 and (2) before the promulgation of the Genocide Convention in 1951. As more fully discussed in Chapter 4, the Israeli courts found Eichmann's acts to be crimes of universal jurisdiction, and so "vest[ing] in every State the authority to try and punish those who participated in their commission"[19]—even states that did not exist at the time of their commission. Another Israeli law, the Crime of Genocide (Prevention and

Punishment) Law,[20] punishes genocide committed against other groups by incorporating the language of the Genocide Convention into Israeli domestic law. While Eichmann was not convicted under Israel's general genocide penal statute, his conviction for "crimes against the Jewish people" under the specific Nazi and Nazi Collaborators (Punishment) Law in effect makes him the first person to be convicted by any court for genocide.

Other individuals have been convicted of genocide by domestic tribunals under their local statutes, but the number is small. The European Court of Human Rights observed in 2007 that "there have been only very few cases of national prosecutions of genocide."[21] That statement is still true as of this writing in 2016. Here are some notable and not-so-notable (but interesting) instances.

In 2001, a court in Lithuania convicted ninety-three-year-old Kazys Gimzauskas of genocide. As a member of the Lithuanian Security Police, Gimzauskas participated in the murder of the Jews during the Nazi occupation.[22] To date, Gimzauskas has been the only person found guilty of genocide by a Lithuanian court. The court, however, did not imprison Gimzauskas due to his poor health, and he died shortly after the end of his trial.

In neighboring Latvia, local courts convicted three individuals between 1995 and 2001 of genocide, including a former KGB officer. The convictions were based on acts committed during the Soviet era[23] and so were meant to signal the distaste of the newly independent Latvia for crimes committed during Communist rule.

Other domestic prosecutions charging genocide likewise appear to reflect a desire by the local authorities to demonstrate their opprobrium toward the acts committed by the defendants or against the former regime. For this reason, the indictment often charges genocide rather than a common crime like murder, or even crimes against humanity or war crimes. These convictions rarely explain how the defendant possessed the necessary *mens rea* of genocide or how the necessary acts of genocide under the Genocide Convention were committed. On Christmas Day 1989, for example, the just-deposed longtime dictator of Romania, Nicolae Ceausescu, and his wife Elena were put on trial for genocide. After a secret trial lasting a few hours at a makeshift courtroom at a military base, they were found guilty and then immediately shot.

Latin American countries also have a proclivity for charging their former rulers with genocide, but such genocide convictions are likewise dubious.[24] A more credible genocide prosecution is that of former Guatemalan dictator Efrain Rios Montt in 2013. During his seventeen-month reign in 1982–1983, the Guatemalan military systematically targeted the indigenous native Mayan population in the Quiche region of Guatemala. The conviction and eighty-year sentence was thrown out by an appellate tribunal on a technicality. As of this writing Rios Montt is being retried, but a court has already ruled that the eighty-nine-year-old former dictator cannot be sentenced if convicted because he suffers from dementia.

In 2006, an Ethiopian court convicted *in abstentia* former dictator Mengistu Haile Mariam of genocide and sentenced him to life in prison. During his "Red Terror" regime, tens of thousands of Ethiopians were either murdered, went missing, or starved to death from a famine exacerbated by Mengistu's policies. Mengistu at the time of his trial was living in exile in Zimbabwe. Another headline-grabbing prosecution for genocide by a domestic court was that of Saddam Hussein and his fellow Baathist leaders before the Iraqi High Tribunal. In April 2006, the special tribunal charged the ex-president and his cousin, Ali Hassan al-Majid, also known as "Chemical Ali," with genocide. Saddam and his cousin were accused of attempting to annihilate the ethnic Kurds in northern Iraq in 1988. During the so-called Anfal military campaign, the Iraqi army, through the use of chemical weapons, among other means, killed at least 50,000 civilians and destroyed thousands of Kurdish villages. For Saddam, the case for genocide never reached a verdict, since he was executed in 2006 on earlier charges for crimes against humanity arising from the Dujail murders committed by his forces. "Chemical Ali" was found guilty of genocide for the Anfal murders and also for his part in crushing a Shia revolt that came after the 1991 Gulf War. He received death sentences for both and was hanged in 2010.

1. Nikola Jorgić: The First Person Convicted of Genocide?

The above national prosecutions for genocide are of some dubious legality. The first clear conviction of anyone for genocide took place in 1997 when the German state supreme court of North Rhine-Westphalia found fifty-one-year-old Nikola Jorgić, a Bosnian Serb leader of a paramilitary group, guilty of genocide committed in Bosnia-Herzegovina. What makes this genocide conviction flawless is that in this instance the perpetrator did not commit his acts in the country that tried him. Moreover, unlike the Eichmann trial, there was no connection between the prosecuting state and the victim group.

The Federal Republic of Germany became a party to the Genocide Convention in 1954. A year later, the Bundestag (parliament) added § 220a to the German penal code, making genocide a crime under German law and defining the elements of the crime by tracking the language of Article II of the Genocide Convention.[25] It also recognized genocide as a crime of universal jurisdiction by permitting prosecutions by its domestic courts of non-Germans and allowing for prosecution even if the criminal acts were committed outside Germany. As noted in Chapter 4, Germany prosecuted its Nazi war criminals under the German penal code's normal homicide statutes covering murder and manslaughter, rather than any post-1945 law (like § 220a) that might violate the prohibition against ex post facto prosecution. Jorgić became the first person to be charged with genocide under § 220a.

Born in 1946 in the Bosnian republic of Communist Yugoslavia, Jorgić emigrated to Germany in 1969. He married a German woman, had a daughter, and worked as a locksmith in Düsseldorf.[26] He and his family apparently visited Yugoslavian Bosnia over the years, and he even bought a house there.[27] With the start of the interethnic conflict in Bosnia, Jorgić returned to Bosnia in 1992 to fight along with his fellow Bosnian Serbs against Croats and Muslims. He became a commander of a Serb paramilitary unit in the Doboj region of Bosnia, from where he hailed. Jorgić's unit became involved in the campaign to expel Bosnian Muslims from the region from May to September 1992. Specifically, Jorgić "participated in the arrest, detention, assault and ill-treatment of male Muslims of three villages in Bosnia in the beginning of May and June 1992. He had killed several inhabitants of these villages."[28] Jorgić was also charged with the killing of twenty-two inhabitants of the village of Grabska, which included the shooting of women, disabled individuals, and the elderly. In another military operation, Jorgić led his group in "chasing [out of] some forty men from their home village and had ordered them to be ill-treated and six of them to be shot. A seventh injured person had died from being burnt with the corpses of the six people shot."[29] A few months later, in September 1992, Jorgić killed a prisoner in the Doboj prison "with a wooden truncheon in order to demonstrate a new method of ill-treatment and killing."[30]

On December 16, 1995, Jorgić flew back to Germany. He was arrested upon arrival at the Düsseldorf airport.[31] Then something unusual happened. The local prosecutor charged Jorgić with genocide under § 220a. Because of the serious nature of the crime, the trial was held before a five-judge Trial Chamber of the state supreme court, the Court of Appeal [*Oberlandesgericht*] of North Rhine-Westphalia located in the state capital city of Düsseldorf. After a seven-month trial that began on February 28, 1997, the court issued its judgment on September 26, 1997, finding Jorgić guilty of eleven counts of genocide, twenty-nine counts of murder (twenty-two in one location and seven in another location), and several other counts of assault and false imprisonment.[32] Finding his guilt to be of particular gravity, the court sentenced Jorgić to life imprisonment. In reading out the judgment, presiding judge Günter Krantz noted that "[w]hoever hoped . . . events like the Nazi genocide of Jews could never be repeated is bitterly disappointed after the events in the former Yugoslavia."[33]

In 1999, the *Bundesgerichtshof*, the Federal Court of Justice of Germany, the federal supreme court, affirmed Jorgić's genocide conviction, but combined the eleven counts of genocide into one omnibus genocide count for intending to destroy a part of the Muslim group in Bosnia. It also found Jorgić guilty of thirty counts of murder.[34] The supreme court faced two important issues on appeal, both involving important questions of international law: (1) whether the principle of universal jurisdiction applies to the crime of genocide, so that Jorgić could be prosecuted in Germany even though he was not a German national (he never obtained German citizenship despite living in Germany for thirty years), did not target Germans, and committed his crimes abroad; and (2) whether genocide is not limited to physical destruction, but can involve targeting the group as a social unit. The court answered both questions in the affirmative.

With regard to jurisdiction, the court rejected the defense argument that Germany lacked jurisdiction to prosecute the non-German Jorgić for acts committed abroad and against non-Germans. Rather, it found that German courts had jurisdiction to prosecute Jorgić for genocide committed in Bosnia based on the international customary law principle of universal jurisdiction, enshrined in Article 6(1) of the German penal code (*StB*). Article 6(1) specifically set out that the crime of genocide in § 220 of the *StB* is prosecutable in Germany even if the acts were committed abroad and against non-Germans. With regard to the all-important element of *mens rea* of genocide, the supreme court held that the intent does not necessarily have to be to physically destroy a protected group but "that it was sufficient to intend its destruction as a social unit."[35]

Jorgić filed a constitutional complaint with the German Federal Constitutional Court (FCC), which rejected his appeal in 2000.[36] The FCC agreed with the federal supreme court that international law allows Germany under principles of universal jurisdiction to prosecute the foreigner Jorgić for acts committed against other foreigners in foreign territory. It also found that Germany's prosecution of Jorgić did not in this instance violate the international law principle of nonintervention (*Interventionsverbot*) because Bosnia never sought his extradition.[37] Last, the FCC agreed with the supreme court that "the intent to destroy the group . . . extends beyond physical and biological extermination. . . . The text of the law does not therefore compel the interpretation that the culprit's intent must be to exterminate physically at least a substantial number of the members of the group. . . ."[38]

Jorgić then appealed to the European Court of Human Rights (ECtHR). The ECtHR in 2007 unanimously upheld the conviction and life sentence. First, the ECtHR confirmed that the crime of genocide falls under the principle of universal jurisdiction even though Article VI of the Genocide Convention only provides for national prosecution by courts of the territory where "the act was committed." On its face, therefore, Article VI did not grant Germany jurisdiction to try Jorgić for genocide because his acts were not committed on German territory. Nevertheless, the ECtHR found that most states in their domestic penal statutes make genocide a crime of universal jurisdiction, "at least if the defendant was found to be present on its territory."[39] The international criminal tribunals have also accepted that genocide is a crime of universal jurisdiction, allowing courts other than those named in Article VI to try accused genocidaires. As such, the ECtHR accepted Germany's argument that Article VI "laid down minimal requirements in respect of the duty to prosecute genocide, [but] did not prohibit the tribunal of a State other than the one in the territory of which the act was committed from prosecuting genocide."[40]

The ECtHR had a more difficult time with Germany's proposition that destruction of the protected group is not limited to physical destruction. Most legal scholars recognize that the perpetrator's "intent to destroy" must be intent to *physically* destroy the group (see Chapter 2). More serious, in 2001, the ICTY Trial Chamber in *Prosecutor v. Krstić* specifically rejected by name the FCC's earlier-discussed wide interpretation in *Prosecutor v. Jorgić* in 2000 that "intent to destroy" did *not* cover only physical destruction.[41] The ECtHR nevertheless upheld Jorgić's conviction in Germany for genocide by recognizing its limited power of the review. According to the European court, as long as Germany's decision to interpret its domestic genocide statute to also include nonphysical destruction was reasonable, the ECtHR had to accept that decision. As the court put it: "Consequently, the applicant's acts, which he committed in the course of the ethnic cleansing in the Doboj region with *the intent to destroy the group of Muslims as a social unit*, could reasonably be regarded as falling within the ambit of the offence of genocide."[42]

In 2004, Jorgić died at age sixty-eight while still in prison. Under German law, he would have been eligible for parole in 2012, after serving fifteen years of his life sentence.[43] Since the Jorgić conviction, three other Serbs living in Germany have been convicted of genocide or genocide-related crimes by German courts for acts in Bosnia.

Was justice served by convicting the lowly Jorgić of genocide and sentencing him to prison for life? Jorgić's fate can be compared to the much more lenient punishment meted out by the ICTY to Duško Tadić, the first person to be tried and convicted by the ICTY. The likewise lowly Tadić holds the dubious honor of being the first person prosecuted by an international tribunal since Nuremberg. Tadić's journey to prosecution mirrored in some ways that of Jorgić. Like Jorgić, Tadić also emigrated to Germany, but came later, in 1993 during the Yugoslav conflict. He settled in Munich and started a new life. Recognized on a Munich street by Bosnian Muslim refugees who were inmates in the notorious Omarska prison run by the Bosnian Serb military, Tadić was arrested by German police. The arrest took place on February 13, 1994, a year earlier than Jorgić's arrest. Since the ICTY had no defendants in custody, it requested Germany to transfer Tadić to The Hague, which Germany did on April 25, 1995. When Jorgić was arrested in Germany in December 1995, Tadić was already sitting at the ICTY jail and awaiting trial. The ICTY prosecutor, busy preparing for the Tadić trial, did not seek Jorgić's extradition. Jorgić was put on trial in Germany—and the Düsseldorf prosecutor charged genocide.

At The Hague, the ICTY prosecutor did not charge genocide. Rather, Tadić was charged with war crimes and crimes against humanity for crimes allegedly committed in the Prijedor region of Bosnia, including at the Omarska prison. Tadić made his first appearance in court on April 26, 1995, and his trial at The Hague overlapped Jorgić's trial. On May 7, 1997—four months before Jorgić's verdict was announced—an ICTY Trial Chamber found Tadić guilty of both crimes and sentenced him to twenty years' imprisonment. In October 2000, after exhausting his appeal to the appellate chamber, Tadić was transferred to Germany to serve his sentence in a Munich prison. The Appeals Chamber ordered that Tadić must serve at least ten years of his sentence, to end no earlier than July 14, 2007. On July 18, 2008, the ICTY granted Tadić's early release petition. By that time, Tadić had already served more than two-thirds of his sentence. Tadić came to Serbia, which granted him citizenship in 2006, and where he apparently still lives.

Both Tadić and Jorgić were mass murderers, killing scores of Bosnian Muslims around the same time but in different regions of Bosnia. It seems incongruous, however, that one should receive twenty years and the other a life sentence. Tadić had the good fortune to be transferred to a court that leans toward leniency, while that same court, which likewise had the right to do so, declined to prosecute Jorgić for administrative reasons. Another incongruity is the judicial treatment received by Jorgić in Germany as compared to the sentences meted out to by German courts to their Nazi war criminals. Some of the Nazis were prosecuted at the same time as Jorgić and received much lesser prison terms. German judges have no compunction putting foreign *hostis humani generis* in prison for life, but are much less willing to do the same for their brethren.

2. Rwandan Genocidaires

Eighteen years after Jorgić's conviction, a German court issued its first genocide conviction arising out of the Rwandan genocide. In December 2015, a court in Frankfurt found fifty-eight-year-old Onesphore Rwabukombe guilty of genocide in Rwanda and sentenced him to life in prison.[44] Rwabukombe was the mayor of the town of Muvumba during the mass killings in 1994. He was accused of ordering an attack on a church on April 11, 1994, in the nearby town of Kiziguro, where hundreds of Tutsis were seeking refuge. In 2002, Rwabukombe came to Germany as a refugee and settled in Frankfurt. He was arrested in 2010, after Rwanda issued an international arrest warrant for him. The German authorities decided to try him in Germany, concluding that he would not receive a fair trial in Rwanda. The ICTR did not seek his extradition. After a three-year trial where over one hundred witnesses testified, the state supreme court in Frankfurt in 2014 found Rwabukombe guilty as an accessory to genocide. The court found that while Rwabukombe did not kill anyone with his own hands, he oversaw and assisted in the murder of over 450 men, women, and children in the church compound. He apparently even used his own pickup truck to drive militiamen to the massacre site and then ordered the men to "go do your work."[45] Rwabukombe's original sentence was fourteen years in prison. The prosecution appealed the sentence to the Federal Court of Justice, arguing that there was sufficient evidence for him to be convicted as a perpetrator and not just an accomplice. The federal supreme court agreed and asked the trial court to reconsider the case. This time, after a five-day trial, the trial judges ruled that Rwabukombe had indeed possessed special intent to commit genocide against the entire Tutsi ethnic group. According to the ruling, Rwabukombe "knowingly and willingly, along with other authorities, prepared, organized, commanded and set in motion the massacre [on the church grounds]."[46] Explained presiding judge Josef Bill: "This was an unimaginable bloodbath. The accused stood there covered in a pool of blood reaching up to his ankles while he continued to give the orders [to kill.]"[47]

Rwandan genocidaires have scattered around the world, and so prosecutions have taken place in France, Belgium, Sweden, and Norway. In France, serious prosecutions of Rwandans involved in the 1994 massacres only began after 2012, when a special war crimes unit was set up in France. The first conviction was of Pascal Simbikangwa, the fifty-four-year-old former intelligence chief in the Hutu presidential administration. A paraplegic since a car accident in the 1980s, Simbikangwa was accused of arming Hutu militias and organizing road blocks, where militia members slaughtered fleeing Tutsi men, women, and children. Witnesses testified that he ordered some victims to bow down, so he could smash them from his wheelchair. Simbikangwa went into hiding after the massacres in 1994. He was arrested in 2008 on the French island of Mayotte in the Indian Ocean, where he had been hiding for three years. After a six-week trial featuring fifty-three witnesses, Simbikangwa was found guilty on March 14, 2014 of genocide and complicity in crimes against humanity and sentenced to twenty-five years' imprisonment.[48]

In a similar vein, Canada put on trial in 2007 a Rwandan who fled to Canada ten years earlier. Desiré Munyaneza was the son of a shopkeeper in the town of Butare and ran the store when the killings began in 1994. He was accused in a Montreal court of committing murder, sexual violence, and psychological terror against Tutsi victims. In addition to genocide, the forty-two-year-old Munyaneza was charged with crimes against humanity and war crimes. Witnesses from Rwanda testified how Munyaneza had raped women and girls, participated in the killings at roadblocks, pillaged Tutsi-owned businesses, and encouraged others to do the same. The court also found that he used sticks to beat to death children who were tied up in sacks.

Munyaneza entered Canada in 1997 under a fake Cameroon passport and was arrested in 2005 when immigration officials discovered his links to the killings. He became the first person in Canada tried under the Crimes Against Humanity and War Crimes Act, enacted by the Canadian parliament in 2000 after Canada joined the International Criminal Court. After a two-year trial that began in March 2007 before the Quebec Superior Court, Munyaneza was found guilty in May 2009 of all seven counts against him, including genocide, crimes against humanity, and war crimes. The trial cost Can$4 million and included the entire court traveling to Butare to take live testimony.[49] He was sentenced to life in prison, the harshest penalty possible under Canadian law. Trial judge Andre Denis observed: "The accused, an educated and privileged man, chose to kill, rape and pillage, in the name of supremacy of his ethnic group."[50] (Munyaneza held a master's degree in economics). In December 2014, Munyaneza exhausted his appeals after the Canadian Supreme Court affirmed his conviction and upheld the constitutionality of the 2000 War Crimes Act. Munyaneza becomes eligible for parole in 2030.

While the US Congress promulgated a domestic statute criminalizing genocide in 1988,[51] no one has been prosecuted for genocide to date in the United States. In a repeat of the fate of Nazis and collaborators who found refuge in America after the war, federal prosecutors instead are charging suspected Rwandan genocidaries of making false statements in their naturalization papers. In addition to being stripped of US citizenship, the defendants are prosecuted for visa fraud. To date, two sisters, one living in Rhode Island and one in Boston—Beatrice Munyenyezi and Prudence Kantengwa—have been convicted of visa fraud and are serving their sentences in federal prison.[52]

Conclusion

Can Genocide Be Prevented?

By focusing on the connections between criminal and civil justice, on the one hand, and the Holocaust and genocide, on the other, this volume has been backward looking. Criminal justice focuses on the prosecution and punishment of individuals for crimes after they have already taken place. Civil justice likewise seeks to compensate victims for past wrongs. The goals of Justice Robert Jackson and the other Nuremberg lawgivers and of Raphael Lemkin, however, were not merely to look backward and punish all those who had committed international crimes. Just as important was the desire to prevent such crimes from being repeated in the future. It is often forgotten that the full name of the Genocide Convention is "*The Convention on the Prevention* and Punishment of the Crime of Genocide"—with the goal of prevention preceding punishment.

Prevention is also a major theme to come out of the Holocaust. One of the most memorable phrases in the post-Holocaust world is the cry of "Never Again!" What does the phrase mean? First and foremost, it is the commitment that never again would the wholesale murder of the Jewish people be allowed to happen. This vigilance against another Holocaust is one of the major beliefs by many Israelis and Jews around the world. The cry of "Never Again" is therefore an important motivation for action by Israel when it feels threatened by outside forces. Israeli author and journalist Tom Segev explains:

> The Holocaust has in recent years become a very central element of Israeli identity. There is not a single day in the Israeli media, for example, without some reference to the Holocaust. The Israelis carry the Holocaust in themselves very much and that is also true for Israelis who do not even come from European origins.[1]

However, "Never Again" today is usually understood as not just applying to preventing another genocide of the Jews, but preventing genocide of or mass atrocity against any other group. It means that humanity cannot just stand idly by while another genocide of any peoples takes place, or danger signs appear that a genocide anywhere is about to happen.[2]

The "Never Again" cry is codified in the Genocide Convention. Article I commits state parties to "undertake to prevent and to punish" genocide. Article VIII authorizes state parties to "call upon the competent organs of the United Nations to take such action under the Charter of the United Nations as they consider appropriate for the prevention and suppression of acts of genocide."

Under the postwar international legal system created around the United Nations, the UN competent organ given the mandate to "take such action" is the Security Council. Chapter V, Article 24(1) of the UN Charter reads:

> In order to ensure prompt and effective action by the United Nations, its Members confer on the Security Council primary responsibility for the maintenance of international peace and security, and agree that in carrying out its duties under this responsibility the Security Council acts on their behalf.

Chapter VII sets out the actual mechanics for the maintenance of international peace and security. Titled "Action with Respect to Threats to the Peace, Breaches of the Peace, and Acts of Aggression," it contains the following "action clauses":

- Article 39: "The Security Council shall determine the existence of any threat to the peace, breach of the peace, or act of aggression and shall make recommendations, or decide what measures shall be taken in accordance with Articles 41 and 42, to maintain or restore international peace and security."
- Article 41 gives the Security Council the power to "decide what measures not involving the use of armed force are to be employed to give effect to its decisions, and it may call upon the Members of the United Nations to apply such measures."
- Article 42: "Should the Security Council consider that measures provided for in Article 41 would be inadequate or have proved to be inadequate, it may take such action by air, sea, or land forces as may be necessary to maintain or restore international peace and security."

On paper at least, the UN founders in 1945 created in Chapter VII a detailed plan to carry out the Genocide Convention's goal of the "prevention and suppression of acts of genocide."

Unfortunately, the hope of "Never Again" since the end of the Second World War has turned out to be a myth. As forcefully explained by Gregory Stanton, founder of *Genocide Watch* and former president of the International Association of Genocide Scholars:

> When the Genocide Convention was passed by the United Nations in 1948, the world said, "Never again." But the history of the twentieth century instead proved that "never again" became "again and again." The promise the United Nations made was broken, as again and again genocides and other forms of mass murder killed 170 million people, more than all the international wars of the twentieth century combined.[3]

David Kader, referring to Lemkin's original dream, makes a similar point. Though his words were penned in 1991, they unfortunately remain as true today.

> Lemkin's ambition to fashion an edifice of law by which the emerging mid-century world community could begin to punish and prevent genocide remains. This ambition continues, simply because it has not been realized . . . This double failure—the reality of both the crime and the impotent response—mirrors the themes in the writings on law and genocide, from the earliest writings to the most recent.[4]

A sad confirmation of the failure of the signatories of the Genocide Convention to abide by its obligations to prevent and suppress genocide through Chapter VII was that the Security Council *never* invoked it for this purpose for over a half-century after the Convention came into existence. The first formal reference came in 2004, with the United States explicitly invoking the Genocide Convention in urging the United Nations to take action under Chapter VII in response to the mass atrocities in Darfur.[5]

Taking into consideration the tragic reality of post-Holocaust genocides and other mass atrocities, civil society activists in the West have moved from the general obligation of "Never Again" on the part of states and the United Nations to the more specific goal of putting the responsibility on each individual to take action in reaction to an ongoing or impending genocide. The kickstart of this twenty-first-century grassroots anti-genocide awareness movement was Darfur. In 2007, actors and activists George Clooney, Brad Pitt, Matt Damon, and Don Cheadle (the latter played the lead role in the film *Hotel Rwanda*) launched Not On Our Watch, an organization to stop the ongoing atrocities in Darfur and to bring attention to other atrocities worldwide. Massive demonstrations, letter-writing campaigns to politicians, and ads in the print media have played a critical role in making sure that Darfur is not ignored and has led to action by both individual countries and such international organizations as the United Nations, the European Union, and the African Union. As of this writing in early 2016, while the Darfur atrocities have not completely ceased since the peak of violence in 2005, they have at least diminished. On the negative side, the Sudanese government under President Al-Bashir has expanded the killings into the Sudanese states of South Kordofan and Blue Nile, where another rebel movement has sprung up. In response, the Sudan Consortium (formerly known as the Darfur Consortium), a coalition of about fifty nongovernmental organizations (NGOs) focusing on the human rights situation in Sudan, has created the South Kordofan Blue Nile Coordination Unit (SKBN CU) to monitor and report monthly on developments in the region.

The worldwide response to the atrocities in Sudan is the best illustration how in the age of civil society Western NGOs focusing on genocide prevention abound. In addition to the aforementioned Not On Our Watch, a multitude of other NGOs (Genocide Watch, World Without Genocide, Enough, The Sentinel Project, United to End Genocide, and others) have sprung up in the last decade with an exclusive focus on genocide prevention. Universities in the West have created centers focusing on genocide studies, and the scholarly field now has two associations: the International Association of Genocide Scholars and the International Network of Genocide Scholars.[6]

At a quasi-governmental level, the US Holocaust Memorial Museum has a standing Committee on Conscience and a Center for the Prevention of Genocide, both focusing on how to best respond to threats of genocide. In 2007, the Committee joined with the American Academy of Diplomacy and the United States Institute of Peace to form a "Genocide Prevention Task Force." The Task Force, co-chaired by Clinton-era cabinet members former Secretary of State Madeleine Albright and Secretary of Defense William Cohen, aimed to generate practical recommendations for the US government on how best to respond to emerging threats of genocide and mass atrocities. The report generated by the Albright-Cohen task force, *Preventing Genocide: A Blueprint for U.S. Policymakers*,[7] became the blueprint for the Obama administration's creation of the Atrocity Prevention Board (APB).

A decade earlier, the Clinton administration in 1997 created a new post in the US State Department, the US Ambassador-at-Large for War Crimes Issues, with a mandate to focus on genocide and other large-scale international criminal law violations. The creation of the post has, at most, a negligible effect on the task of genocide prevention. Nevertheless, David Scheffer, the first holder of this post, in an address at my university in 2012 boldly spoke of "new reality, namely, that impunity is on the losing side of history now."[8] According to Scheffer, the new reality began with in the 1990s with the creation by the UN Security Council of the ad hoc tribunals for Yugoslavia and Rwanda. In this new world, "we now have the beginning of the end of impunity . . . [and] so it is becoming more normal than abnormal to achieve accountability, at least through a level of indictment, if not ultimately a prosecution."[9]

In 2011, President Obama took genocide prevention as American policy up a notch by establishing, through the Presidential Study Directive (PSD) 10, the APB. The new interagency is composed of representatives from eleven agencies, and was part of the Obama administration's stated aim to making deterrence of genocide and mass atrocities "a core national security interest and a core moral responsibility."[10] PSD 10 charged the APB with coordinating a "whole-of-government approach to preventing mass atrocities and genocide."[11] At an address at the US Holocaust Memorial Museum announcing the creation of the APB, the president said that with its establishment we are "making sure that the United States government has the structures, the mechanisms to better prevent and respond to mass atrocities."[12] The APB meets at least monthly to develop and oversee the implementation of atrocity prevention and response policies by the United States.

In May 2016, President Obama issued Executive Order (EO) 13729. EO 13729 solidified the structure and functions of the APB and directed US agencies to take on a broader atrocity prevention strategy. The EO's "all hands on deck" approach aimed to institutionalize the APB, with the goal of making it more likely that the Board will continue to operate after Obama leaves office.

One concrete positive outcome that the APB helped to shape was Obama's decision in the summer of 2014 to order airstrikes against ISIS troops about to attack 40,000 Yazidis trapped on the peaks of Mount Sinjar in Iraq. As was reported at the time, the word "genocide" was uttered in the White House Situation Room.[13] Most of the trapped Yazidis were freed from their mountaintop refuge through American military intervention by air and Kurdish forces on the ground. Yet, the continuing atrocities in Syria and Iraq have cast a pall over the board's work.

At the international level, UN Secretary-General Kofi Annan in 2004 took a stab at the task of genocide prevention by creating the position of "Special Adviser on the Prevention of Genocide and Mass Atrocities" and appointing Juan Mendez, a respected law professor, human rights advocate, and former political prisoner from Argentina, to the post. Mendez resigned after a few years, having seen little progress from the work he was doing as the United Nations' point man on genocide prevention. In May 2007, he was replaced by Francis Deng, appointed by the new Secretary-General Ban Ki-moon. Deng, a respected Sudanese law scholar and diplomat, also brings decades of experience to this post. However, he has not brought any more success to the job than his predecessor. Rwanda, Darfur, and now Syria show that prevention of genocide is a job not very well done, either by the international community or by individual nations.

Scholars from numerous disciplines have followed in Lemkin's footsteps by offering their own individualized prescriptions for how to best prevent genocide.[14] The solutions they offer are based on the common understanding that genocide is never a spontaneous act but is reached in predictable steps. Genocide is best prevented, all agree, when action is taken during these pre-genocide stages. When mass atrocities are already taking place—whether in Nazi-occupied Europe, Rwanda in 1994, or Darfur in 2003–2008—suppression of an ongoing genocide becomes a much more complex, or practically insurmountable, task since it requires military action that the international community, either through the United Nations or a regional body like NATO or the African Union, is almost always not willing to undertake. As Matthew Smith of the NGO *Fortify Rights* explains:

> We often associate gas chambers and mass killing to situations of genocide, but elevating the crime to the most extreme examples is not necessarily helpful, and it's not required by the law of genocide. Waiting for the appearance of gas chambers is precisely the mentality that has contributed to our world's repeated failures to prevent atrocities.[15]

In the 1970s, Israel Charny and Chanan Rapaport devised the Genocide Early Warning System (GEWS), an analytic process by which to recognize preludes to genocides, so that effective action can be taken before the events on the ground escalate into a full-blown genocide.[16]

In the 1980s, Leo Kuper, an internationally recognized University of California, Los Angeles, sociologist and scholar whose research on genocide set benchmark guidelines in the field, wrote what is still considered a landmark work, *Genocide: Its Political Use in the Twentieth Century*.[17] In it, Kuper used careful empirical research to provide theories seeking to explain the phenomenon of genocide. He also introduced the theme of "the odious scourge" that has carried over into other works on the subject. In his 1985 follow-up study, *The Prevention of Genocide*,[18] Kuper blamed the United Nations and the major powers for failing to enforce the organization's Genocide Convention prevention goal, especially in Africa—where both then and now intrastate tribal violence is a major problem. Going beyond pure scholarship, Kuper founded in 1986 International Alert, a London-based NGO designed to provide early warnings of ethnic violence within states with the aim of facilitating peaceful resolution of disputes. In 2014, International Alert, still going strong, began to focus on the internal crisis in Syria.

In the 1990s, Stanton addressed the same issue as Charny and Rapaport and Kuper by giving us an important tool by likewise identifying the signposts on the road to genocide. Stanton explains that "[g]enocide is a process that develops in eight stages that are predictable but not inexorable. At each stage, preventive measures can stop it. The process is not linear. Logically, later stages must be preceded by earlier stages. But all stages continue to operate throughout the process."[19] In 1996, Stanton published a paper entitled *The Eight Stages of Genocide*—later changed to ten stages— that he presented to the US State Department. Stanton describes the ten stages as follows: (1) *classification*: viewing people in terms of "us and them"; (2) *symbolization*: giving names to or distinguishing groups of people by symbols such as colors or dress; (3) *discrimination*: using laws, customs, or political power to deny the rights of other groups; (4) *dehumanization*: denying the humanity of another group; (5) *organization*: organizing groups to commit crimes against the other group; (6) *polarization*: employing propaganda to drive the groups apart; (7) *preparation*: planning to systematically eliminate the other group; (8) *persecution*: identifying and separating out the other group; (9) *extermination*: killing members of the group on a large scale; and (10) *denial*: covering up evidence of the genocide and shifting blame on the victims.[20]

How can reaching Stage Nine be prevented? At the nongovernmental level, his group issues "Genocide Alerts," bringing awareness of impending genocides. Other NGOs have done the same. The US Holocaust Memorial Museum has gone one step further with what it describes as "a first-of-its-kind tool" which it calls the Early Warning Project. The museum describes how it works: "The Early Warning Project is unique. Our system analyzed over fifty years of historical data and dissected the conditions present prior to mass atrocities. We use that historical base to recognize contemporary warning signs in countries around the world and to rank those most at risk."[21] It adds: "[T]his tool measures, tracks, and analyzes known risk factors that could lead to a future instance of mass atrocities. The data, along with real-time analysis from regional and genocide experts, generate a forecast. The results allow us—and other organizations—to focus our resources and attention on the countries most at risk."[22]

In 2015, for the second year in a row, the Project's statistical assessments identified Myanmar (also known as Burma) "as the country most susceptible to the start of a new episode of state-led mass killing."[23] It explained:

> This year's assessments come at a time when many advocates and other observers are warning loudly about the imminent risk of genocide in Myanmar in response to discriminatory policies targeting the Rohingya [Muslim] minority [by the Buddhist-majority nation].[24]

Genocide Watch in 2015 also issued a Genocide Alert for Myanmar. And in January 2016, Nicholas Kristol of the *New York Times*, after visiting the limited areas where the Rohingya are allowed to live, wrote of "concentration camps" in

Myanmar and concluded that "the systematic destruction of the Rohingya remains one of the 21st century's most neglected human rights catastrophes."[25]

Stanton, however, had a greater concern. In congressional testimony on December 9, 2015, on the sixty-seventh anniversary of the Genocide Convention, he urged that the United States recognize that "ISIS is committing genocide" against Yazidis, Christians, Shi'a Muslims, Turkmen, Shabaks, and other religious groups that ISIS labels "infidels" or "apostates."[26] According to Stanton: "[T]he Islamic State in Iraq and Syria (ISIS) . . . is the greatest threat to civilization since Nazism and Stalinist and Maoist Communism. Like those movements, ISIS has a millenarian, utopian ideology that turns mass murder into an ideological duty, and worse, a religious virtue."[27] Stanton seeks to formalize the genocide alert process by the creation at the United Nations of "a Genocide Prevention Center to support the work of the Special Advisor and to provide a focal point for the efforts of many organizations around the world that are working to prevent genocide."[28] A critical division of this UN Genocide Prevention Center would be an "Early Warning Unit" that would identify "situations at risk of genocide," communicate that information to a "Political Unit" composed of respected UN diplomats, whose aim is to prevent the impending genocide through the political process and, failing that, bring into action the "Missions and Operations Unit," whose task would include urging the Security Council to sending UN troops to stop the genocide. Despite the wariness of many, Stanton maintains that the United Nations remains the best hope for prevention of genocide.[29]

As explained in Chapter 2, Northwestern University law professor David Scheffer, the first US Ambassador-at-Large for War Crimes Issues, offers another proposal to make genocide prevention more effective. Scheffer correctly points out that the legal definition of genocide, as found in the Genocide Convention, has acted as a constraint to genocide prevention because it provides both the United Nations and individual nations a ready-made legal excuse for not taking action by claiming that the acts being committed, while horrible, have not (yet) risen to the level of genocide as set out in the legal definition. As Scheffer puts it: "[T]he prospect of the term genocide arising in policy-making too often puts an intimidating brake on effective responses."[30] David Bosco, senior editor of *Foreign Policy* magazine, agrees. Explaining the negative impact of relying on the existence of a genocide as a call to action, Bosco points out how the United Nations' decision not to label the atrocities in Darfur as a genocide led to a popular belief that no action was necessary.

> In considering whether and where to intervene, one question has assumed talismanic significance: Is it genocide? . . . Intended as a clarion call, the term itself has become too much of a focal point, muddling the

> necessity for action almost as often as clarifying it. . . . Looking to the genocide label to motivate international intervention . . . overlooks two sad truths: Widespread slaughter can demand intervention even if it falls outside of the genocide standard. And the world is quite capable of standing by and watching even when a genocide is acknowledged.[31]

In 1953, Lemkin noted: "The [General] Assembly felt strongly that cases of genocide would require speedy action because preservation of human life and stopping human suffering are paramount and must supersede any protracted search for legal niceties."[32] But legal niceties are what we have focused on rather than speedy action. As discussed in Chapter 2, while the genocide in Rwanda was ongoing, the Clinton administration shied away from calling the events a "genocide" since use of the "G-word," it was believed, required action. During the height of the crisis in Darfur, a verbal duel was being waged between the United States and the United Nations as to what to call this latest man-made catastrophe in Sudan. The George W. Bush administration and the entire US Congress repeatedly labeled the events as genocide.[33] Pinning the genocide label on Darfur did not lead, however, to the United States taking any military action to stop the genocide even after three years of failed diplomatic efforts and a mounting death toll. The United Nations and its human rights and humanitarian agencies, for its part, refuses to use the term, employing the less shocking "war crimes" and "crimes against humanity."[34] This verbal sideshow—which Bosco characterizes as a "warped diplomatic parlor game (who will say the G-word first?)"[35]—distracts the international community from its real task: how best to respond to the crisis in order to stop the human catastrophe. William Schabas came to the same conclusion, noting that "the sterile debate about whether the Darfur atrocities are genocide or 'merely' crimes against humanity did not enhance justice, it did the opposite" by delaying action on the part of the international community.[36]

Governments and international institutions are not the only ones notorious for playing word games with the term "genocide." Some NGOs, in an effort to mobilize public opinion and at times as a means to increase financial support for their work, employ the term when its use appears improper. In contrast to politicians and diplomats, who tend to shy away from using the term, human rights activists tend to overuse it. As Samantha Power, before she became the US Ambassador to the United Nations, explained: "We outside government have spent far too much time arguing for the brand of genocide to be employed in the real-time to describe the atrocities underway."[37]

Ultimately, however, we must concede that no matter how many international legal norms are enacted criminalizing and punishing genocide, and regardless of what terms we employ, law and language on their own can do little to stop genocide. Lack of law is not the problem. As David Kader pointed out more than two decades ago: "Although legal norms against genocide have existed for over twenty years, necessary will to apply these norms is still lacking. Enforcement is frozen, not out of the law's inadequacy as an instrument, but because of the political and moral paralysis of the national actors. Law does not create order, it is order that permits law."[38] Holocaust historian Omer Bartov makes the same point: "[T]he act of actually codifying genocide did not mean that it would be prevented. It has to be enforced, and it cannot be enforced without the international community actively doing so."[39]

How to best prevent genocide and make "Never Again" a reality? Bartov goes back to the grassroots answer:

> [T]he most important point to be made is that it is really up to citizens, particularly in democratic states to make their voices heard and say that this is their own national interest to stop such events from occurring, even in countries that are very far from them, happening to people with whom they do not speak. . . . Governments, after all, it takes them quite a while to recognize [genocide], but they depend on the will of the people. . . . This is not just people in the street; this has to do with the media, this has to do with academia, this has to do with anyone who has some access to public opinion, and when that happens, then policy can change. If it does not happen, it does mean that people do not care, and if they do not care then their governments will not act.[40]

In 2012, on the day of the establishment of the APB, his interagency anti-genocide group, President Obama echoed Bartov's words in an address delivered at the US Holocaust Memorial Museum, but also stressed new technology as a tool of prevention:

> "Never again" is a challenge to societies. We're joined today by communities who've made it your mission to prevent mass atrocities in our time. The museum's Committee of Conscience, NGOs, faith groups, college students, you've harnessed the tools of the digital age — online maps and satellite and a video and social media campaign seen by millions. You understand that change comes from the bottom up, from the grassroots. You understand—to quote the [Albright-Cohen] task force convened by this museum—"preventing genocide is an achievable goal." It is an achievable goal. It is one that does not start from the top; it starts from the bottom up.[41]

Eight years earlier, Obama's UN Ambassador Samantha Power, author of the Pulitzer-Prize-winning study of genocide *A Problem from Hell*,[42] noted that while political pressure from the bottom is critical for leaders to begin paying attention to genocide prevention, the leaders themselves need to take initiative. At a lecture delivered at the same museum, Power explained:

> [L]eadership is not really coming to this building once a year and regretting the occurrence of the Holocaust; leadership means a genocide presidential decision, leadership means contingency military planning, leadership means consultation with allies or, in the case of today, retrieval of allies and then consultation with allies. Leadership means the beginning of a public conversation that leads beyond "Never again" and to the "what" and the "how."[43]

In 2008, Power left the world of academia to join the Obama administration, first working within the White House and as US Ambassador to the United Nations. In 2012, Power got her wish with the creation of the interagency APB, the "Problem from Hell" Taskforce with genocide prevention on its weekly

Illustration 16 US Ambassador to the United Nations Samantha Power, speaking at 2014 UN Commemoration in Memory of the Victims of the Holocaust. Courtesy of the United Nations, photograph 578034.

agenda. Genocide prevention acquired a higher priority under Obama than under any other American president. Yet it appears to have made little difference as the carnage around the world continued. More disappointing, the inertia took place on the watch of Samantha Power as US Ambassador to the United Nations. In her previous role as "one of us"—a respected outsider academic and human rights advocate—Power castigated the United States for its repeated indifference to the "problem from hell." In one of her strongest statements in *Problem from Hell,* Power boldly asserted the need for American boots on the ground to prevent genocide: "Given the affront genocide represents to America's most cherished values and to its interests, the United States must also be prepared to risk the lives of its soldiers in the service of stopping this monstrous crime."[44] Such blunt statements made her "an atrocities prevention rock star," according to Simon Adams, director of the NGO Global Center for the Responsibility to Protect.[45]

Yet after becoming an insider and policymaker, Power seemed unable to convince President Obama that military action should be taken to stop the problems from hell taking place in Syria. Even after Syrian President Assad crossed Obama's "red line" by using chemical weapons against his opponents in June 2012, no military response was forthcoming. Instead, it was Russia's Vladimir Putin who brokered an agreement to dispose of Syria's chemical arms. In 2015, when Assad again resorted to use of chemical weapons, this time using chlorine dropped in canisters into rebel areas by the Syrian air force, no punitive action was taken against him.

What happened? One answer favored by many is that Power had the misfortune to serve under a president much more cautious in intervention than she is. In April 2014, Obama explained his philosophy: "There are going to be times where there are disasters and difficulties and challenges all around the world, and not all of those are going to be immediately solvable by us."[46] And the hands-off approach was not adopted by Obama in a vacuum. Rather, Obama was elected to the presidency on an anti-interventionist platform, in reaction to the *uber* interventionist president George W. Bush.

This did not preclude deep disappointment within the human rights community, seeing one of our own unable to stop the mass atrocities. David Rothkopf, the editor of *Foreign Policy,* comments on Power's experience "on the inside":

> Here is the person who wrote the best-reported, analyzed *cri de coeur* on genocide, in an Administration that has effectively said, in the face of humanitarian disasters, We're going to do very little, whether it is the continuing catastrophe in the Democratic Republic of Congo or Syria or the brewing problem with Rohingya [Muslims persecuted in Myanmar]. We will periodically do something, like send in helicopters to look for two

> hundred missing schoolgirls, or blow up somebody on the Horn of Africa. But this has not been the antidote to Rwanda that she may have wanted.[47]

It well may be that those of us in the human rights world have undue expectations about Obama, Power, and the APB. As Power herself acknowledged: "Serving in the executive branch [of the most powerful country on earth] is very different than sounding off from an academic perch."[48] As for Syria, Power argued that President Obama, unlike his predecessors, has employed every tool in the atrocity prevention toolbox, except one: ground troops. According to Power, the risk of what such military engagement might produce is "substantial" and "off the charts" and "what we are not doing is going to war to bring about the end of the [Assad] regime."[49] But she admits: "ISIL keeps me up at night. Assad keeps me up at night."[50]

Sarah Sewall, Power's Harvard colleague who joined the Obama administration as Undersecretary for Civilian Security, Democracy, and Human Rights at the State Department, in a March 2015 address before the Council of Foreign Relations met head on the disappointment of many as she defended the administration's deep concern about atrocities occurring in many part of the world:

> Some observers have expressed dissatisfaction with the Obama Administration's commitment to prevent mass atrocities across the globe. I understand their perspective. The APB has not halted violence worldwide; in its three years of existence, it has not protected every civilian from governments, insurgents and terrorists. As imperfect as our current efforts are, they represent undeniable progress—both in symbolism and in concrete results. . . . President Obama took a bold step in 2012 by elevating concern about mass atrocities as a foreign policy priority. Atrocity prevention, he said, is not just a matter of values but also an issue of national security. The President acknowledged that "It can be tempting to throw up our hands and resign ourselves to man's endless capacity for cruelty," but he reminded us that Elie Wiesel and other Holocaust survivors chose never to give up. Nor can the United States of America.[51]

Commitment is the key. At a symposium I co-hosted in Los Angeles on November 20, 2015, marking the exact day seventy years earlier when Sir Geoffrey Lawrence banged his gavel to start the trial at Nuremberg, our keynote speaker was Benjamin Ferencz. At age ninety-six, Ben Ferencz is the last living Nuremberg prosecutor. When asked by a student for one piece of advice on how to create a world that he and the other Nuremberg founders dreamed of, Mr. Ferencz gave us a three-word answer: "Never Give Up."[52]

Notes

Introduction

1. *Quoted in* "Darfur Genocide Charges for Sudanese president Omar al-Bashir," *The Guardian*, July 14, 2008.
2. Omer Bartov, *Germany's War and the Holocaust: Disputed Histories* (2003), 192.
3. See http://www.holocaustremembrance.com (official page of International Holocaust Remembrance Alliance—IHRA).
4. See http://holocaustmemorialyear2014.gov.hu (official page of the Hungarian Holocaust 2014 Memorial Committee).
5. John C. Torpey, *Making Whole What Has Been Smashed: On Reparation Politics* (2006), 37.
6. Ibid.
7. Ibid., 40.
8. International Crimes Tribunal—1, Bangladesh, *available at* http://www.ict-bd.org/ict1/ (italics added).
9. For "[c]ommitting genocide by killing professionals and intellectuals, . . . accused Motiur Nizami . . . as president of the Islami Chhatra Sangha and head of Al-Badr Bahini, an auxiliary force [of the Pakistani Army], that committed said atrocities all over Bangladesh. . . . [these two organisations] mounted Gestapo-like attacks to devoid Bangladesh of professionals and intellectuals, amongst others." Chief Prosecutor v. Motiur Rahman Nizami, Judgment, para. 285 (Int'l Crimes Trib. Bangl. Oct. 29, 2014).
10. Timothy Snyder, *Black Earth: The Holocaust as History and Warning* (2015), xii, 144–177.
11. John K. Roth, *The Failures of Ethics: Confronting the Holocaust, Genocide and Other Mass Atrocities* (2015), 49.
12. See Michael J. Bazyler and Frank M. Tuerkheimer, *Forgotten Trials of the Holocaust* (2014), 2–3, 303–312.
13. See Michael J. Bazyler, *Holocaust Justice: The Battle for Restitution in America's Courts* (2003); *Holocaust Restitution: Perspectives on the Litigation and Its Legacy* (Michael J. Bazyler and Roger P. Alford eds., 2006); see also www.swissbankclaims.com (official court site of the Swiss Banks settlement).
14. John Hagan, *Justice in the Balkans: Prosecuting War Crimes in The Hague Tribunal* (2003), 18.

15. *Quoted in* Marshal Zeringue, "Gavriel D. Rosenfeld's, '*Hi Hitler!*,'" *The Page 99 Test*, Nov. 30, 2014. Rosenfeld is incorrect to place Snyder as a critic of uniqueness of the Holocaust. In his latest study, Snyder states: "The Holocaust was different from other episodes of mass killing or ethnic cleansing because German policy aimed for the murder of every Jewish child, woman and man." Timothy Snyder, *Black Earth: The Holocaust as History and as Warning* (2015), 327.
16. *Is the Holocaust Unique?* (Alan S. Rosenbaum, ed., 3rd ed., 2009).
17. Ibid., 223.
18. See Gavriel D. Rosenfeld, *Hi Hitler!: How the Nazi Past is Being Normalized in Contemporary Culture* (2015), 78–121 (debating the Holocaust's uniqueness).
19. Yehuda Bauer, *Rethinking the Holocaust* (2001), 2.
20. Ibid., 3.

Chapter 1

1. For discussion of the debate about whether the Holocaust was conducted within the framework of the law or was extralegal, see Chapter 7. The two opposing views are best presented in David Fraser, *Law After Auschwitz: Towards a Jurisprudence of the Holocaust* (2005) (legal), and Kristen Rundle, "The Impossibility of an Exterminatory Legality: Law and the Holocaust," 59 *U. Toronto L. J.* 65 (2009) (extralegal).
2. Richard L. Rubenstein, *The Cunning of History: The Holocaust and the American Future* (1975), 87.
3. Raul Hilberg, *Perpetrators, Victims, Bystanders: The Jewish Catastrophe* 1933–1945 (1992), 71.
4. *Nazi Crimes and the Law* (Nathan Stoltzfus and Henry Friedlander, eds., 2008), 8 (footnote omitted).
5. Margaret Buber-Neumann, "Hitler or Stalin: Which Was the Worst?" 74 *Amer. Mercury* 74 (1952), 79; see also Margarete Buber-Neumann, *Under Two Dictators: Prisoner of Stalin and Hitler* (Edward Fitzgerald, transl., 1949).
6. Nigel Foster and Satish Sule, *German Legal System and Laws* (4th ed., 2010), 36.
7. In the early part of the twentieth century, European racial theorists began categorizing humans into biologically distinct races and used the term "Aryan race" to refer to white Europeans. This terminology was appropriated by the Nazis to refer to Western European Caucasians of non-Jewish descent.
8. Marinus van der Lubbe, an unemployed bricklayer from Holland, allegedly was found inside the burning Reichstag building and supposedly confessed to setting the blaze. He was executed on January 10, 1934. In 2008, seventy-four years after his execution, the German Federal Prosecutor announced that van der Lubbe's conviction was null and void, and he was posthumously rehabilitated.
9. Dachau housed approximately 200,000 prisoners from over thirty countries, one-third of them Jews. At least 32,000 died of starvation, disease, and the gruesome medical experiments conducted on the prisoners. After its liberation in April 1945, Dachau became the site of the first trial of German perpetrators held under American military command. See Michael J. Bazyler and Frank M. Tuerkheimer, *Forgotten Trials of the Holocaust* (2014), 75–99.
10. Excerpt from the decision in *U.S.A. v. Altstoetter*, "The Justice Case," *in Trials of War Criminals Before the Nuernberg Military Tribunals under Control Council Law No. 10*, v. III (1951), 1014, 477.

11. The translation of "Reich" is "empire."
12. France and Britain's motivation for agreeing to cede Czechoslovakian territory to Germany was to avoid another catastrophic war in Europe. British Prime Minister Neville Chamberlain, returning from Munich to triumphant crowds, declared that he had achieved "peace in our time." Winston Churchill, warning against this policy of appeasement, countered: "You were given the choice between war and dishonour. You chose dishonour and you will have war." Stephen J. Lee, *Aspects of British Political History, 1914–1995* (2005), 154.
13. These four stages of destruction were identified by the late Holocaust historian Raul Hilberg, one of the pioneers of Holocaust historians, in his classic volume first published in 1961. See Raul Hilberg, *The Destruction of the European Jews* (1961, 3rd ed., 2003).
14. Sarah Gordon, *Hitler, Germans, and the "Jewish Question"* (1984), 125. For further discussion, see Michael J. Bazyler, "The Thousand Year Reich's over One Thousand Anti-Jewish Laws," *in The Routledge History of the Holocaust*, (Jonathan C. Friedman, ed., 2012).
15. "Kindred blood" (*artverwandten Blutes)* meant white, non-Jewish, and non-Roma persons. Such persons were technically eligible to become citizens of the Reich under the Nuremberg laws. Later, Slavic peoples were also excluded from the category "kindred blood."
16. Over time, the situation of the *Mischlinge* became more precarious. As Annegret Ehmann concludes: "Had the Nazis won the war, the Mischlinge would have shared the fate of the Jews." Annegret Ehmann, "Mischlinge," *in The Holocaust Encyclopedia* (Walter Laqueur, ed., and Judith Tydor Baumel, assoc. ed., 2001), 425.
17. *Quoted by* Ingo Müller, *Hitler's Justice: The Courts of the Third Reich* (Deborah Lucas Schneider, transl., 1991), 100–101 (italics added). This still remains one of the best studies of the legal system of Nazi Germany.
18. The Jewish Black Book Committee, *The Black Book: The Nazi Crime Against the Jewish People* (1946), 97.
19. The Jewish Black Book Committee, *The Black Book*, 97. The Germans enacted the measure at the behest of the Swiss government, which wanted to differentiate German Jews from non-Jews seeking to cross the border into Switzerland. While non-Jewish Germans could enter Switzerland, German Jews, seeking refuge and whose identity was now clearly marked on their passports, were barred from crossing the border. In 1998, Switzerland paid compensation to those Jews still alive who were barred entry. Michael J. Bazyler, *Holocaust Justice: The Battle for Restitution in America's Courts* (2003), 36.
20. For further discussion of this topic, see Götz Aly, *Hitler's Beneficiaries: Plunder, Racial War, and the Nazi Welfare State* (Jefferson Chase, trans., 2005). According to Aly's thesis, Nazism secured the support of the German people in large part by redistribution of the possessions taken from the victims, first from German and Austrian Jews, and then from Jews and others in the conquered territories.
21. The state initially wanted to collect all the insurance payments owed to the Jewish policyholders, but ultimately let the insurance firms wiggle out of paying almost all their obligations to anyone. The regime pocketed a little over 1 million reichsmarks, Jews were allowed to deduct a small portion of their foregone insurance claims from the fine imposed upon them, and the firms walked away largely unscathed. See

Gerald D. Feldman, *Allianz and the German Insurance Business 1933–1945* (2001), 195, 206.

22. "Discussions by the Authorities Following Kristallnacht: Stenographic Report of the Meeting on the Jewish Question held under the Chairmanship of Field Marshal Göring in the Reich Air Ministry at 11 A.M. on November 12, 1938," *in Documents on the Holocaust: Selected Sources on the Destruction of the Jews of Germany and Austria, Poland, and the Soviet Union* (Yitzhak Arad, Yisrael Gutman, and Abraham Margaliot, eds., 6th ed., 1996), 108, 112–114.
23. The German word Hitler used was *die Vernichtung*. The entire speech was filmed and broadcast around the world. A transcript and video are available on the United States Holocaust Memorial Museum website. https://www.ushmm.org/wlc/en/media_fi.php?MediaId=3108.
24. Gerald Reitlinger, "The Truth About Hitler's 'Commissar Order': The Guilt of the German Generals," *Commentary*, July 1, 1959, *quoting Trials of War Criminals Before the Nuernberg Military Tribunals under Control Council Law No. 10*, v. X (1951), 1138.
25. Diemut Majer, *"Non-Germans" under the Third Reich: The Nazi Judicial and Administrative System in Germany and Occupied Eastern Europe, with Special Regard to Occupied Poland 1939–1945* (Peter Thomas Hill, Edward Vance Humphrey, and Brian Levin, transl., 2003), 447–448.
26. Ibid., 453.
27. Justice Ministry lawyers worked with their legal counterparts at the German General Staff (OKW) on the drafting of the decree and rules for its implementation. These highly particularized rules specified how political detainees were to be treated upon arrest, their ability to make wills and write final letters of farewell, how their death would be recorded, and what should be done with their children. Other lawyers drafted orders creating special secret courts and detention facilities for those interned under the *Nacht-und-Nebel-Erlass* (Night and Fog) Decree.
28. Majer, 453.
29. Ibid., 313.
30. The most complete study of the *Judenrat* is found in Isaiah Trunk, *Judenrat: The Jewish Councils in Eastern Europe Under Nazi Occupation* (1979).
31. Hilberg, *Destruction*, v. 1, 219.
32. Yisrael Gutman, "Poland" (Introduction)" *in Documents on the Holocaust: Selected Sources on the Destruction of the Jews of Germany and Austria, Poland, and the Soviet Union* (Yitzhak Arad, Yisrael Gutman, and Abraham Margaliot, eds., 6th ed., 1996), 169–170.
33. Daniel Marc Segesser and Myriam Gessler, "Raphael Lemkin and the International Debate on the Punishment of War Crimes (1919–1948)," 7 *J. Genocide Research* 460–461 (Dec. 2005).
34. Michael Ignatieff, Transcript of "The Legacy of Raphael Lemkin," Lecture at US Holocaust Memorial Museum, Dec. 13, 2000.
35. See Bibliography in this book.
36. A good collection of Nazi-era documents translated into English that includes legal measures taken against Jews in German-occupied Poland and the Soviet Union can be found in *Documents on the Holocaust* (Yitzhak Arad, Yisrael Gutman, and

Abraham Margaliot, eds., 1999). For France, see the excellent study by Richard H. Weisberg, *Vichy Law and the Holocaust in France* (1996). For the Low Countries, see J. N. M. E. Michielsen, *The "Nazification" and "Denazification" of the Courts in Belgium, Luxembourg and The Netherlands* (2004).

37. Majer, xvii (Preface to the English-Language Edition) (italics in original).
38. Ibid., at 450.
39. Ibid., 450 (citing Martin Broszat, *Nationalsozialistische Polenpolitik* (1961) (footnotes omitted).
40. Ibid.
41. Justice Case, *in Trials of War Criminals Before the Nuernberg Military Tribunals under Control Council Law No. 10,* v. III (1951), 1064 (italics in original).
42. Majer, 933.
43. Majer, 282.
44. Timothy Snyder, "Hitler's Logical Holocaust," *N.Y. Review of Books,* Dec. 20, 2012, 3.
45. Valerie Hébert, *Hitler's Generals on Trial: The Last War Crimes Tribunal at Nuremberg* (2010), 116–117.
46. Directives for the Treatment of Political Commissars, June 6, 1941, *available at* <http://germanhistorydocs.ghi-dc.org/pdf/eng/English58.pdf>.
47. Hébert, 100.
48. Saul Friedländer, "Ideology and Extermination: The Immediate Origins of the Final Solution," *in Lessons and Legacies: The Holocaust and Justice,* v. 5 (Ronald Smelser, ed., 2002), 34–35 (emphasis in the original).
49. Hilary Earl, *The Nuremberg SS-Einsatzgruppen Trial, 1945–1958: Atrocity, Law and History* (2009), 122. For discussion of "legitimation of genocidal violence" preached by Himmler and his SS officers to the SS cadres, see Christian Ingrao, *Believe & Destroy: Intellectuals in the SS War Machine* (Andrew Brown, transl., 2013), 152–160, 203–208, 254–259.
50. For general discussion of judges as conduits for genocide and other massive human rights abuses, see Hans Petter Graver, *Judges Against Justice: On Judges When the Rule of Law Is Under Attack* (2015).
51. Timothy Snyder, "Hitler's Logical Holocaust," *N.Y. Review of Books,* Dec. 20, 2012 (*quoting* Christoph Dieckmann, *Deutsche Besatzungspolitik in Litauen 1941–1944 [German Occupation Policies in Lithuania, 1941–1944]* (2012)). The postwar trial in West Germany of members of one of these German murder squads in Lithuania, the so-called Ulm trial, is discussed in Chapter 4.
52. The full text is available at http://www.yadvashem.org. Rumkowski's sacrifice of the children did not work. In August 1944, two years later, the ghetto was liquidated and the surviving residents, including Rumkowski, sent to Auschwitz. By that time, the Germans knew that they would lose the war.
53. Roderick Stackelberg and Sally A. Winkle, eds., *The Nazi Germany Sourcebook: An Anthology of Texts* (2002), 340.
54. Valerie Genevieve Hébert, *Hitler's Generals on Trial: The Last War Crimes Tribunal at Nuremberg* (2010), 277, n.121.
55. Gordon, *Hitler, Germans,* 137. Himmler committed suicide soon after being captured by the British, and so was never questioned about his involvement in the extermination of the Jews.

56. Ibid.
57. Ibid., 138–139.
58. Testimony of Rudolf Höss, Apr. 15, 1946, *Trial of the Major War Criminals Before the International Military Tribunal*, v. XI (1947), 398.
59. Gordon, *Hitler, Germans*, 140.
60. Foundation Memorial to the Murdered Jews of Europe, Auschwitz Decree, *available at* <http://www.stiftung-denkmal.de/jugendwebsite/r_zoom/e_zoom_ausc_e.html>.
61. The Kurt Gerstein Report, *available at* http://www.holocaustresearchproject.org/ar/gersteinreport.html.
    For further details, see Valerie Hébert, "Disguised Resistance?: The Story of Kurt Gerstein," 20 *Holocaust & Genocide Studies* (2006), 1–33.
62. Interrogation of Konrad Morgen, Oct. 11, 1946, *quoted in* Herlinde Pauer-Studer, "Law and Morality under Evil Conditions: The SS Judge Konrad Morgen," 3 *Jurisprudence* 367, 383 (2012). See also Herlinde Pauer-Studer and J. David Velleman, *Konrad Morgen: The Conscience of a Nazi Judge* (2015).
63. R. J. Rummel, *Death by Government* (1994), 111, 113. At the end of the war, eight million people were also displaced throughout Europe.
64. Wolfgang Benz, "Death Toll," *in The Holocaust Encyclopedia* (Walter Laqueur, ed., and Judith Tydor Baumel, assoc. ed., 2001), 145.
65. Harry S. Truman, *Memoirs: Year of Decisions*, v. 1 (1955), 341.

Chapter 2

1. For a comprehensive history, see Ben Kiernan, *Blood and Soil: A World History of Genocide from Sparta to Darfur* (2007). See also David M. Crowe, *War Crimes, Genocide and Justice: A Global History* (2014).
2. Raphael Lemkin, *Totally Unofficial: The Autobiography of Raphael Lemkin* (Donna-Lee Frieze, ed., 2013), 1.
3. Lemkin, *Totally Unofficial, cited and quoted in* "From the Guest Editors: Raphael Lemkin: The 'Founder of the United Nation's Genocide Convention' as a Historian of Mass Violence," 7 *J. Genocide Research* 447 (2005), 448.
4. Lemkin, *Totally Unofficial, cited and quoted* in Samantha Power, *"A Problem from Hell": America and the Age of Genocide* (2002), 19.
5. The principle of universal jurisdiction is set out in the Restatement (Third) of Foreign Relations, Sec. 404 (2006).
6. Lemkin's proposal in Madrid also included a second crime of universal jurisdiction, which he called "vandalism" and which made criminal acts aimed at destruction of "cultural or artistic works" of a collectivity. The full proposals are available at <http://www. preventgenocide.org>.
7. Michael Ignatieff, "The Unsung Hero Who Coined the Term 'Genocide,'" *New Republic*, Sept. 21, 2013.
8. Raphael Lemkin, *Axis Rule in Occupied Europe: Laws of Occupation; Analysis of Government; Proposals for Redress* (1944), 79.
9. Ibid.
10. Books and Authors, *N.Y. Times*, Nov. 17, 1944, 17.
11. William A. Schabas, "Origins of the Genocide Convention: From Nuremberg to Paris," 40 *Case Western Reserve J. Int'l Law* 41 (2007), 41.

12. Lemkin was in London, working with the American team of lawyers drafting the London Charter for the upcoming trial of the senior Nazi leaders before the International Military Tribunal at Nuremberg. His presence on the committee charged with drafting the portion of the indictment dealing with war crimes led to the appearance of the term "genocide" in the London Charter.
13. *Nuremberg Trial Proceedings Vol. 1 Indictment: Count Three* (italics added).
14. In a section titled "Proof of the defendant's atrocities and other crimes," Jackson's Planning Memorandum included: "*Genocide* or destruction of racial minorities and subjugated populations by such means and methods as (1) underfeeding; (2) sterilization and castration; (3) depriving them of clothing, shelter, fuel, sanitation, medical care; (4) deporting them for forced labor; (5) working them in inhumane conditions." Report of Robert H. Jackson, United States Representative to the International Conference on Military Trials (1949), 68 (italics added).
15. Hilary Earl, "Prosecuting Genocide Before the Genocide Convention: Raphael Lemkin and the Nuremberg Trials, 1945–1949," 15 *Journal of Genocide Research* 317 (2013), 319.
16. GA Res. 96(I) (1946).
17. Ibid.
18. *Quoted in* Tanya Elder, "What You See Before Your Eyes: Documenting Raphael Lemkin's Life by Exploring his Archival Papers, 1900–1959," 7 *J. Genocide Research* 469, 484 (2005).
19. Lemkin was twice nominated for the Nobel Peace Prize, the first time by Winston Churchill in 1950 and then again in 1952.
20. Ignatieff, "Unsung Hero."
21. William A. Schabas, *Genocide in International Law: The Crimes of Crimes* (2nd ed., 2009), 11. The phrase "crime of crimes" comes from opinions issued in two trials before the International Criminal Tribunal for Rwanda.
22. *Watchers of the Sky*, a superb 2014 documentary, tells the story of Lemkin's life and his legacy.
23. Omer Bartov, "The Legacy of Raphael Lemkin," (Interview with Jerry Fowler), Voices on Genocide Prevention, US Holocaust Memorial Museum Podcast, Mar. 8, 2007, *available at* http://web.archive.org/web/20070525165226/http://www.ushmm.org/conscience/analysis/details.php?content=2007-03-08.
24. *Quoted in* William Korey, *An Epitaph for Raphael Lemkin* (2001), 25. At about the same time Lemkin learned that almost all his relatives perished in the Holocaust. The only surviving family members were his brother Elias and his family, who had spent the war years in a Soviet forced-labor camp.
25. The full text of the Nuremberg Charter defines crimes against humanity as follows: "namely, murder, extermination, enslavement, deportation, and other inhumane acts committed against any civilian population, before or during the war, or persecutions on political, racial or religious grounds in execution of or in connection with any crime within the jurisdiction of the Tribunal, whether or not in violation of the domestic law of the country where perpetrated."
26. IMT Judgment (italics added), *in Trial of the Major War Criminals before the International Military Tribunal*, v. XXII (1948), 498.
27. The poswar United Nations should not be confused with the wartime "United Nations"—the name used to describe the alliance fighting Nazi Germany,

Italy, and Japan. Dan Plesch explains the term's origin: "On the morning of 29 December 1941, Winston Churchill was in the bathroom of his room at the White House when he heard Franklin Roosevelt calling him. He emerged, a naked pink cherub, drying himself with a towel and without a stich on, to find the President waiting in a chair. The President pointed at Churchill and exploded, 'United Nations.' As so the United Nations was born. . . . The two politicians had wrestled with the need for a catchy name for the proposed alliance, 'Associated Nations' being a term offered by the US State Department but discarded as boring. . . . The Declaration by the United Nations [was announced] on New Year's Day 1942." Dan Plesch, *America, Hitler and the UN: How the Allies Won World II and Forged a Peace* (2011), 1.

28. The US Constitution set out the procedure by which the United States could become a party to a treaty: "[The President] shall have Power, by and with the Advice and Consent of the Senate, to make treaties, provided two thirds of the Senators concur." U.S. Constitution, Article II, Section 2.
29. The same argument is made today by those who oppose the United States becoming a party to the International Criminal Court.
30. Civil Rights Congress, *We Charge Genocide: The Historic Petition to the United Nations for Relief from a Crime of the United States Government Against the Negro People* (Civil Rights Congress, 1951).
31. The editorial was published as a long letter to the editor, with Lemkin identified as "the founder of the world movement to outlaw genocide." "Letter to the Editor, Nature of Genocide: Confusion with Discrimination Against Individuals Seen," *N.Y. Times*, June 14, 1953, E10 (letter dated June 12, 1953).
32. 18 U.S.C. § 1091. During the presidency of George W. Bush, the law was expanded to add non-US citizens who committed genocide abroad but reside in the United States as prosecutable in federal court for genocide.
33. Convention on the Prevention and Punishment of the Crime of Genocide, 78 U.N.T.S., v. 78, p. 277 (1948), Article II. Currently, the more common term for the adjective "ethnical" is "ethnic." The use of either term is proper.
34. "The Uses and Abuses of the G-Word; Genocide," *Economist*, June 4, 2011.
35. William A. Schabas, "The 'Odious Scourge,' Evolving Interpretations of the Crime of Genocide," 1 *Genocide Studies and Prevention* 93 (2006), 97.
36. William A. Schabas, *Genocide in International Law*, 11.
37. GA Res. 96 (1946). The Israeli judges in the *Eichmann* case in 1962 explained how the *actus rea* of genocide differs from homicide, the killing of a human being: "[T]he criminal act itself (actus reus) is different in its nature from the sum total of all the murders of individuals and the other crimes perpetrated during its execution. The people, in its entirety or in part, is the victim of extermination which befalls it through the extermination of its sons and daughters." The Attorney-General v. Eichmann, Judgment, Dist. Ct. of Jerusalem, para. 190.
38. In 1999 and 2000, the German Supreme Court and the constitutional tribunal in the *Jorgić* case held that destruction need not be physical but can be social. See Chapter 9 discussion. However, the ad hoc tribunals have rejected this view. Thus, the Appeals Chamber of the International Criminal Tribunal for the former Yugoslavia (ICTY) in *Krstić* explained: "The Genocide Convention, and customary international law in

general, prohibit only the physical or biological destruction of a group." Prosecutor v. Krstić, Appeals Chamber, Apr. 19, 2004, para. 25.

39. In so finding, the ICTR Trial Chamber found that rape in the course of the Rwandan genocide was often a prelude to the killing of the victim. Prosecutor v. Akayesu, Trial Chamber, Judgment, Sept. 2, 1998, para. 731. Rape is specifically set out as constituting a crime against humanity in the Statutes of the ICTR and the ICTY. See Article 3, ICTR Statute and Article 5, ICTY Statute. In 2001, the ICTY found that acts of rape can constitute both war crimes and crimes against humanity. It also found that sexual enslavement was a crime against humanity and can also constitute a war crime. See Prosecutor v. Kunarać, Trial Chamber, Judgment, Feb. 22, 2001, para. 531.
40. Martin Shaw, *What Is Genocide?* (2nd ed. 2015), 19.
41. Elder, 487, n.62 (*quoting* Lemkin from "Background paper: United States Statement on the Civil Rights Congress Publication 'We Charge Genocide,'" Box 4, Folder 7, American Jewish Archives, Powers, 75).
42. <http://www.CNN.com/US/9908/19/furrow.indictment>.
43. John G. Heidenrich, *How to Prevent Genocide: A Guide for Policymakers, Scholars, and the Concerned Citizen* (2001), 3. The ICTY also hypothesized that a "lone wolf" could commit genocide: "[T]he drafters of the [Genocide Convention] did not deem the existence of an organization or a system serving a genocidal objective as a legal ingredient of the crime. In so doing, they did not discount the possibility of a lone individual seeking to destroy a group as such." Prosecutor v. Jelisić, Judgment, Trial Chamber, Dec. 14, 1999, para. 100.
44. As Schabas points out, "The United States delegation worried about 'broadening' the concept of genocide to cases where 'a single individual was attacked as a member of a group.'" Schabas, *Genocide in International Law,* 275 (*citing* Genocide Convention drafting history).
45. Ibid., 276. Schabas provides an excellent discussion of this numerical debate. Ibid., 273–287.
46. Rome Statute of the International Criminal Court, Preamble.
47. Irving Louis Horowitz, *Taking Lives: Genocide and State Power* (4th ed., 1997), 12.
48. Prosecutor v. Jelisić, ICTY Trial Chamber, Judgment, Dec. 14, 1999, para. 100. For a critique of the view that state action should not be required for the commission of genocide or other international crimes, see William Schabas, "State Policy as an Element of International Crimes," 98 *J. Crim. L & Criminology* 953 (2007–2008).
49. John Quigley, *The Genocide Convention: An International Law Analysis* (2006), 139.
50. For a good discussion, see Carola Lingaas, "Defining the Protected Groups of Genocide Through the Case Law of International Tribunals," ICD Brief 18 (December 2015).
51. Prosecutor v. Akayesu, ICTR Trial Chamber, Judgment, paras. 170–171.
52. Quigley, 153–156.
53. Prosecutor v. Jelisić, ICTY Trial Chamber, Judgment, para. 70.
54. Schabas points out that "the subjective approach seems to function effectively virtually all the time." Schabas, *Genocide in International Law,* 128.
55. Ibid., 154 (*citing* UN debates on Genocide Convention).

56. Ibid., 158.
57. Ibid., 160. Schabas also rejects the view that the Soviet Union is most to blame for the eventual exclusion of political groups from the Convention's protections since Stalin and his cohorts feared that they might be branded as genocidaires for their brutal repression of political opponents. "The Soviet views were shared by a number of other States for whom it is difficult to establish any geographic or social common denominator: Lebanon, Sweden, Brazil, Peru, Venezuela, the Philippines, the Dominican Republic, Iran, Egypt, Belgium and Uruguay." Ibid., 160 (citations omitted).
58. For a good discussion, see Beth Van Schaak, "The Crime of Political Genocide: Repairing the Genocide Convention's Blind Spot," 106 *Yale L.J.* 259 (1997).
59. The following states have added political groups to the list of groups protected from destruction in their domestic genocide penal statute: Colombia, Ethiopia, Ivory Coast, Panama, Poland, and Switzerland. The Polish Penal Code is illustrative: "Any person who, with the intent to destroy, in whole or in part, a national, ethnic, racial, political or religious group or a group of persons with a definite philosophical conviction, kills a member of the group or causes serious harm to the health of a member of the group, shall be punished with imprisonment for a time not shorter than twelve years, with imprisonment for twenty years, or with imprisonment for life." Penal Code of the Republic of Poland, Law of 6 June 1997, Art. § 118(1), reproduced in <http://www.preventgenocide.org>.
60. Consolidated Statutes of Canada, S.C. 2000, c. 24 Sec.4 & Sec. 6, *cited and quoted in* Quigley, 18.
61. Steven R. Ratner and Jason S. Abrams, *Accountability for Human Rights Atrocities in International Law: Beyond the Nuremberg Legacy* (2001), 34. The UN Draft Declaration on the Rights of Indigenous Peoples (Aug. 26, 1994), specifically uses the term "cultural genocide." Earlier, in 1981, UNESCO (the United Nations Educational, Scientific and Cultural Organization) issued a declaration equating the terms "cultural genocide" and "ethnocide." ("We declare that ethnocide, that is, cultural genocide, is a violation of international law equivalent to genocide . . .").
62. Webster's definition of genocide includes cultural genocide: "the deliberate and systematic destruction of a racial, political, or cultural group." *Merriam-Webster Dictionary*, http://www.merriam-webster.com/dictionary/genocide.
63. Note that the acts of the majority group must be intentional. Unintended assimilation over time of a minority culture into a majority culture cannot be genocide since the *mens rea* element of genocide is missing.
64. Schabas, "The 'Odious Scourge,'" 97.
65. In May 2015, Supreme Court of Canada Chief Justice Beverley McLachlin labeled the forced assimilation of indigenous children into the European culture practiced by the Canadian government for over two centuries as "cultural genocide." A few weeks later, Canada's Truth and Reconciliation Commission issued a landmark report concluding that the country's decades-long policy of forcibly removing indigenous children from their families and placing them in state-funded Christian schools amounted to "cultural genocide." The first schools opened in 1883. The last one closed in 1998. During that time period, over 150,000 Canadian indigenous

children were sent away from their families to be Christianized and thereby rid of their connection to their native cultures, including their native languages.

66. As will be discussed in Chapter 8, almost all discussion of genocide by the ad hoc tribunals has focused on the *mens rea* element of the crime.
67. The drafters of the Genocide Convention could have been more artful in their draftsmanship of the Article II subparagraphs by specifically noting that each of the acts criminalized in these subparagraphs must be committed intentionally. They did so for subparagraph (c) by inserting the word "deliberately" ("deliberately inflicting on the group conditions of life calculated to bring about its physical destruction in whole or in part") but failed to do so for the other subparagraphs.
68. In the *Akayesu* case discussed above, the first international conviction for genocide, the ICTR confirmed the *mens rea* requirement of the "specific intent to commit genocide" in order to secure a conviction for genocide. Prosecutor v. Akayesu, ICTR Trial Chamber, Judgment, para. 498.
69. Prosecutor v. Jelisić, ICTY Trial Chamber, Judgment, para. 66.
70. Quigley, 10 (*citing* Otto Triffterer, "Genocide, Its Particular Intent to Destroy in Whole or in Part the Group as Such," 14 *Leiden J. Int'l L.* 399 (2001)).
71. Quigley, 10.
72. Lemkin, Axis Rule, 79.
73. What was the Nazis' ultimate intent is still a matter of conjecture. One indicator that the Nazis intended to eradicate all Jews everywhere was their plan to build a "Central Museum of the Extinguished Jewish Race" in Prague at the conclusion of the war to house Jewish artifacts plundered from their Jewish victims. Another is that the Nazis intended to apply the same measures to the Jews of North Africa and the Middle East, including in British Mandate Palestine, if they had succeeded in conquering those territories. From every territory that the Nazis conquered—including the British Channel Islands—Jews were segregated, arrested, and sent to extermination camps.
74. Quigley, 139.
75. Ibid.
76. 18 U.S. Code Section 1093(8).
77. Prosecutor v. Kayishema, ICTR Trial Chamber, Judgment, paras. 96–97.
78. Prosecutor v. Krstić, ICTY Trial Chamber, Judgment, para. 634. The Krstić Appeals Chamber agreed with that view. See Prosecutor v. Krstić, ICTY Appeals Chamber, Judgment, paras. 6–8.
79. Ibid., 106, n.37 (*quoting* legal scholars Jordan Paust and Leila Sadat).
80. Prosecutor v. Krstić, Appeals Chamber, para. 12.
81. The United States Code criminalizes not only genocide but also publicly inciting others to commit genocide, attempted genocide, and conspiracy to commit genocide. 18 U.S.C. § 1091 (c) and (d). As with the basic offense of genocide, no one has yet been prosecuted for these crimes.
82. Contrary to the indictment, where conspiracy was charged alongside all of the three substantive crimes, the Nuremberg judges of the International Military Tribunal found only those defendants who were found guilty of "crimes against peace" also guilty of a "conspiracy to commit crimes against peace" (in other words, a concrete plan by the Nazi leaders to engage in an aggressive war). No one was found guilty

simply of conspiracy. Also, no one was found guilty of "conspiracy to commit war crimes" or "conspiracy to commit crimes against humanity." See Chapter 3 for further discussion.

83. See ICTY Statute, Article 4(3)(b) ("Conspiracy to Commit Genocide"); ICTR Statute, Article 2(3)(b) ("Conspiracy to Commit Genocide").
84. The Statute of the Rome Treaty creating the International Criminal Court (ICC) does not recognize the separate crime of conspiracy. It well may be, therefore, that as international criminal law is further developed though ICC jurisprudence, conspiracy as an inchoate crime or even as a separate crime alongside the substantive offenses of genocide, war crimes, or crimes against humanity may disappear.
85. Schabas, *Genocide in International Law,* 320–323.
86. Nazi propagandist Julius Streicher was convicted at Nuremberg of crimes against humanity and sentenced to death for his repeated calls for the murder of Jews.
87. As explained by the ICTR, "mere vague or indirect suggestion" will not do. Prosecutor v. Akayesu. Trial Chamber, Judgment, para. 557. On the other hand, euphemisms or coded language to kill would qualify as express incitement if the listeners understand the true meaning of the coded language. As example, at the Wannsee Conference held by the Nazi leaders to discuss the physical extermination of the Jews of Europe, "resettlement to the East" was widely known to refer to the transfer of Jews to the death camps of Eastern Europe where they would be murdered. During the Rwanda genocide, inciters told their cohorts to "take care of the problem" or "do your job." Both the speaker and listener knew what that meant.
88. Schabas points out that *Black's Law Dictionary* defines "abet" to also mean "to incite." Schabas, *Genocide in International Law,* 325.
89. For a discussion of attempted genocide, see Schabas, *Genocide in International Law,* 334–339.
90. Ibid., 339.
91. A separate crime of complicity, therefore, is unnecessary in British-derived legal systems, and is the reason why the United Kingdom, in incorporating the Genocide Convention in its domestic law, did not include Article III complicity in the domestic version of the law. As explained by one of the drafters of the UK domestic legislation, "Complicity in genocide has not been included in Clause 2(1) [because] we take the view that the sub-heading in Article III is subsumed in the act of genocide itself in exactly the same way as, under our domestic criminal law, aiding and abetting is a situation in which a person so charged could be charged as a principal in relation to the offense itself." Statement of Parliamentary Secretary Elystan Morgan, *cited and quoted in* Schabas, *Genocide in International Law,* 347.
92. United States v. Alstotter, et al. ("Justice Trial") (1948) 6 LRTWC (1948), 62, *cited and quoted in* Schabas, *Genocide in International Law,* 356.
93. Schabas, *Genocide in International Law,* 340.
94. Prosecutor v. Krstić, Appeals Chamber, para. 140.
95. Ibid., paras. 137–141.
96. Ibid., para. 140.
97. Quigley, 134–136.
98. Geoffrey Robertson, Was There an Armenian Genocide, Geoffrey Robertson Q.C.'s Opinion, April 12, 2009 (footnotes omitted). In *Akayesu,* the ICTR Trial Chamber

stated that "genocidal intent [may] be inferred from the physical acts and specifically the massive and/or systematic nature of the atrocity." Prosecutor v. Akayesu (ICTR Trial Court Judgment) (1998), *quoted in* Prosecutor v. Jelisić (ICTY Appeals Chamber Judgment) (2006). Moreover, "even in the absence of a confession from the accused, his intent is inferred from . . . the perpetration of other culpable acts systematically directed against that same group, whether these acts were committed by the same offender or by others." Ibid.

99. UN Economic and Social Council, 2nd Sess., Draft Convention on the Crime of Genocide, Report of Secretary-General (June 26, 1947), UN Doc. E/447 (1947), *cited and quoted in* Quigley, 91.
100. In 2015, the Confront Genocide campaign of the US Holocaust Memorial Museum issued a genocide warning on the plight of the Rohingya, who comprise 5 percent of the population of Burma. Numbering approximately 1.3 million people, the Rohingya are concentrated primarily in western Burma. See US Holocaust Memorial Museum, *They Want Us All to Go Away: Early Warning Signs of Genocide in Burma* (2015).
101. Quigley, 92.
102. Rome Statute of the International Criminal Court, Art. 66(3).
103. ICTY Rules of Procedure and Evidence, Rule 87 and ICTR Rules of Procedure and Evidence, Rule 87.
104. Art. IV.
105. Art. VI.
106. ICC Statute, Arts. 17 and 53
107. John Torpey, "Beyond Recognition: Truth, Reparations, and the Armenian Genocide," paper presented at USC symposium International Law and the Armenian Genocide, 2007.
108. Michael Ignatieff, The Legacy of Raphael Lemkin, Lecture at US Holocaust Memorial Museum, Dec. 13, 2000.
109. Alain Destexhe, *Rwanda and Genocide in the Twentieth Century* (1995), 6.
110. William Schabas, *Unimaginable Atrocities: Justice, Politics, and Rights at the War Crimes Tribunals* (2012), 99. Canadian law professor Payam Akhavan laments about the "the fetishistic invocation of this privileged abstraction . . . in the arena of competitive suffering." Payam Akhavan, *Reducing Genocide to Law: Definition, Meaning, and the Ultimate Crime* (2012), 199.
111. Schabas, *Unimaginable Atrocities*, 102–103.
112. Richard Fuchs, "Armenian Genocide—German Guilt?", *DW*, Apr. 3, 2015.
113. Ignatieff, Lecture at US Holocaust Memorial Museum.
114. David Bosco, "Crime of Crimes: Does It Have to Be Genocide for the World to Act?," *Wash. Post*, Mar. 6, 2005.
115. Payam Akhavan, *Reducing Genocide to Law*, 3 (italics in original).
116. Philip Gourevitch, *We Wish to Inform You that Tomorrow We Will Be Killed with Our Families: Stories from Rwanda* (1998), 152.
117. See Rebecca Hamilton, "Inside Colin Powell's Decision to Declare Genocide in Darfur," *Atlantic*, August 17, 2011.
118. Akhavan, 3.
119. Ibid.

120. David Scheffer, "Genocide and Atrocity Crimes," 1 *Genocide Studies & Prevention* 230 (2006).
121. Ibid. See also David Scheffer, "The Merits of Unifying Terms: 'Atrocity Crimes' and 'Atrocity Law,'" 2 *Genocide Studies & Prevention,* 91 (2007).
122. And the term "deportation" does not fairly describe what the Armenians were forced to endure. As Schabas explains: "The treatment of the Armenians by the Turkish rulers in 1915 provides the paradigm for the provision [of subsection (c)] dealing with imposition of conditions of life. These crimes have often been described as 'deportations'. But they went far beyond mere expulsions or transfer, because the deportation itself involved deprivation of fundamental human needs with the result that large numbers died of disease, malnutrition and exhaustion." Schabas, *Genocide in International Law,* 192–193.
123. Robertson, 12 (*quoting* Henry Morgenthau, *Ambassador Morgenthau's Story* (1918), 333–338, 342) (italics in original).
124. For a discussion of this statement by Hitler, see Kevork B. Bardakjian, *Hitler and the Armenian Genocide* (1985). Hitler is sometimes quoted as saying, "Who still talks nowadays of the extermination of the Armenians?"
125. For Lemkin's writings on the massacres of the Armenians, see Raphael Lemkin's *Dossier on the Armenian Genocide* (manuscript from Raphael Lemkin's Manuscript Collection, American Jewish Historical Society) (Vartkes Yeghiayan, ed., 2008).
126. According to Turkey's Ministry of Foreign Affairs website, the Armenian deaths were due to the effects of "inter-communal conflict" and a world war when 2.5 million Muslims also perished.
127. Donald Bloxham, *The Great Game of Genocide* (2007), 92. For another well-researched study, see Ronald Grigor Suny, *"They Can Live in the Desert But Nowhere Else": A History of the Armenian Genocide* (2015). The title comes from a pronouncement made by Talaat Pasha, Ottoman Minister of Interior, considered the primary architect of the Armenian genocide. The book of notes from Talaat's private papers documenting the actions against the Armenians is now available in English. See *Talaat Pasha's Report on the Armenian Genocide, 1917* (Ara Sarafian, ed., 2011).
128. Carol J. Williams, "As Centenary of Armenian Massacre Nears, 'Genocide' Dispute Sharpens," *L.A. Times,* Apr. 20, 2015.
129. To date, the governments of twenty-four nations, either through their legislature or through an executive branch pronouncement, have issued public proclamations or statements recognizing the Armenian genocide. In the United States, forty-three states have acknowledged the Armenian massacres as a genocide. At the federal level, the US House of Representatives has on various occasions passed resolutions to this effect. A good discussion of the Armenian genocide recognition campaign can be found in Thomas de Waal, *The Great Catastrophe: Armenians and Turks in the Shadow of Genocide* (2015).
130. President Reagan's use of the G-word in 1981 officially came during a presidential proclamation for commemoration of the Holocaust. The reference was put in by Reagan's Armenian-American speechwriter, Ken Khachigian.
131. Another holdout is the United Kingdom. As of 2016, the United Kingdom still declines to apply the term "genocide" to the massacre of the Armenians, though it

do not oppose the term being used by others or having British diplomats attend Armenian genocide commemoration ceremonies.

132. Michael Bobelian, *Children of Armenia: A Forgotten Genocide and the Century-Long Struggle for Justice* (2009).
133. Whatever objections one may have to the ICTY finding the events in Srebrenica constituted a genocide, or the decision by the International Court of Justice not to find Serbia responsible for genocide, or the ICTR finding the murders in Rwanda in 1994 to be a genocide, at least we can concede that these decisions were made by judges whose task is to leave politics out of their decision process.
134. The starvation campaign of the Bolsheviks under Stalin against those Ukrainians resisting collectivization in the 1920s led to over one million Ukrainians being murdered. However, because the Bolsheviks only targeted political opponents of the Soviet regime, the Holomodor cannot be considered a genocide under the Genocide Convention since political opponents are not a protected group under the Convention.
135. For further discussion by an Israeli academic of this phenomenon, see Yair Auron, *The Banality of Denial: Israel and the Armenian Genocide* (2004).
136. "Russia-Turkish Standoff: Russian Lawmakers to Consider Penalizing Armenian Genocide Denial," http://armenianow.com, Nov. 26, 2015.
137. Thomas de Waal, "The G-Word: The Armenian Massacre and the Politics of Genocide," *Foreign Affairs*, Jan./Feb. 2015. See also de Waal, *The Great Catastrophe* for an excellent discussion of the century-old dispute between the Armenians and Turkey of the narrative regarding what happened to the Ottoman Armenians.

Chapter 3

1. For some notable book-length accounts of the Nuremberg trials, see Victor Bernstein, *Final Judgment: The Story of Nuremberg* (1947); Peter Calvocoressi, *Nuremberg: The Facts, the Law, the Consequences* (1948); James Owen, *Nuremberg Evil on Trial* (2006); Whitney Harris, *Tyranny on Trial* (1999); Telford Taylor, *The Anatomy of the Nuremberg Trials* (1992); Joseph Persico, *Nuremberg: Infamy on Trial* (1994); Ann Tusa and John Tusa, *The Nuremberg Trial* (1984); Bradley F. Smith, *Reaching Judgment at Nuremberg* (1977); Robert E. Conot, *Justice at Nuremberg* (1984); Michael Marrus, *The Nuremberg War Crimes Trial* (1997); Arieh Kochavi, *Prelude to Nuremberg: Allied War Crimes Policy and the Question of Punishment* (1998). See also Gary Jonathan Bass, *Stay the Hand of Vengeance: The Politics of War Crimes Tribunals* (2003) for an excellent summary. For a recent study, *see* Kim Christian Priemel, *The Betrayal: The Nuremberg Trials and German Divergence* (2016).
2. The nine countries were Belgium, Czechoslovakia, France, Greece, Luxembourg, Norway, the Netherlands, Poland, and Yugoslavia.
3. See Arieh J. Kochavi, "The Moscow Declaration, the Kharkov Trial, and the Question of a Policy on Major War Criminals in the Second World War," 76 *History* 401 (1991).
4. *Quoted in* Ann Tusa and John Tusa, 24.
5. Bass, 186.

6. Henry Stimson, Secretary of War, Memorandum to President Roosevelt, September 5, 1944, *quoted in* Bass, 163.
7. *International Law Collected Papers of Hersch Lauterpacht, Disputes, War and Neutrality*, v.5, parts IX–XIV (Sir Elihu Lauterpacht, ed., 2004), 492.
8. Sheldon Glueck, "By What Tribunal Shall War Offenders Be Tried?," 56 *Harv. L. Rev.* 1059, 1082 (1943) (footnotes omitted).
9. A. N. Trainin, *Hitlerite Responsibility Under International Law* (Andrew Rothstein, transl., 1945). The book was also translated into French and German. Trainin explained: "The State cannot be freed from responsibility from crimes in wartime. . . . Criminal responsibility for crimes committed, however, must be borne by concrete physical persons who are guilty of the crimes which they have committed." Trainin, 72. For Trainin's numerous contributions to Nuremberg jurisprudence—still widely unrecognized—see Francine Hirsch, "The Soviets at Nuremberg: International Law, Propaganda, and the Making of the Postwar Order," 113 *Am. Hist. Rev.* (2008), 705–713.
10. *Quoted in* Bass, 188. The British missive stated "that it would be preferable that the Nazi leaders should be declared world outlaws and summarily put to death as soon as they fell into Allied hands."
11. Bass, 196.
12. Richard Severo, "Telford Taylor, Who Prosecuted Top Nazis at the Nuremberg Trials, Is Dead at 90," *N.Y. Times*, May 24, 1998.
13. "Rule of Law Among Nations," Speech of Associate Supreme Court Justice Robert H. Jackson before the American Society of International Law, Washington, D.C., Apr. 13, 1945.
14. Without a trial "Germany will simply have lost another war. The German people will not *know* the barbarians they have supported, nor will they have any *understanding* of the criminal character of their conduct and the world's judgment upon it." Murray Bernays, "Memorandum on Trial of European War Criminals, 15 September 1944," *quoted in The American Road to Nuremberg: The Documentary Record 1944–1945* (Bradley Smith, ed., 1982), 36 (emphasis in original).
15. *Quoted in* Conot, 12.
16. See Murray C. Bernays, "Legal Basis of the Nuremberg Trials", 35 *Survey Graphic* 5 (1946).
17. Whitney Harris, *Tyranny on Trial* (1999).
18. Kirsten Sellars, "Imperfect Justice at Nuremberg and Tokyo," 21 *Eur. J. Int'l. L.* 1085, 1086 (2010).
19. "The Nuremberg Trials," PBS American Experience, television broadcast, Jan. 30, 2006. *Transcripts available at* http://www.pbs.org/wgbh/amex/nuremberg/filmmore/pt.html
20. Bradley F. Smith, *Reaching Judgment at Nuremberg* (1977), 102.
21. *Quoted in* Stephan Landsman, *Crimes of the Holocaust: The Law Confronts Hard Cases* (2005), 9.
22. Seventy years later, the Palace of Justice still operates as the central courthouse of Nuremberg, and Courtroom 600 is still a working courtroom. One floor up is the Nuremberg Trials Memorium, an exhibition of the Nuremberg proceedings opened in 2010.

23. The full transcript is available at Yale Law School's Avalon Project website: <http://www.avalon.law.yale.edu>.
24. "The Nuremberg Trials," *PBS American Experience*, television broadcast, Jan. 30, 2006, *Transcripts.*
25. Article 19 of the Charter abrogated the application of "technical rules of evidence" and directed the court to "admit any evidence which it deems to have probative value."
26. IMT Transcript, vol. 3, 543.
27. The prosecution relied less on documents during the concentration camp and slave labor stages of the trial.
28. *Quoted in* Lawrence Douglas, The *Memory of Judgment: Making Law and History in the Trials of the Holocaust* (2005), 18.
29. Rebecca West, *A Train of Powder* (1955), 3.
30. *Quoted in* Lawrence Douglas, "Film as Witness: Screening of *Nazi Concentration Camps* Before the Nuremberg Tribunal," 105 *Yale L.J.*, 449 (1995).
31. Douglas, *Memory of Judgment*, 20, 23.
32. *Quoted in* Douglas, *Memory of Judgment*, 21.
33. Ibid.
34. The Soviets, during the course of their case, likewise presented a film showing atrocities in the East.
35. Doug Linder, *The Nuremberg Trials* (2010), *available at* <http://law2.umkc.edu/faculty/projects/ftrials/nuremberg/nurembergACCOUNT.html>.
36. After Nuremberg, Wisliceny was turned over to the Czechs for trial, found guilty, and then hanged.
37. Höss suffered the same fate as Wisliceny. He was turned over to the Poles for trial. Found guilty, he was hanged on the grounds of Auschwitz.
38. An additional 140 witnesses provided evidence for the defense through written interrogatories.
39. See, e.g., James Owen, *Nuremberg: Evil on Trial* (2006),132: "[F]atally from the beginning Jackson's line of questioning was too vague and too passive, seemingly seeking to engage Goering in elevated moral debate rather than to pin down his involvement in specific crimes;" Conot, *Justice at Nuremberg*, 338: "[Jackson's] questions wandered hither and yon, bouncing sometimes like a marble in pinball machine from the pointless to the irrelevant. Their impreciseness gave Goering the opportunity to expatiate at length, causing Jackson to express greater and greater irritation."
40. John Barrett, Jackson's biographer, has a more nuanced and accurate view: "The press, like Jackson himself, has a sort of prize fight mentality about the event that they were watching. They expected another knockout, a crushing blow, a collapse, a confession, something of that dramatic order. Instead what they saw was a great lawyer running into a great powerful and brilliant witness and a combative examination that was something of a draw whenever they tried to talk about the great topics of the ultimate questions." PBS, Transcript, *Nuremberg Trials* documentary.
41. *Quoted in* Jacqueline George, *Göring Cross-Examined* (2014), 88.
42. Conot, *Justice at Nuremberg*, 343.
43. George, 194–195.

44. Soviet judge Nikitchenko dissented from the main verdict. He would have found all defendants and all organizations charged as guilty and would have sentenced Rudolf Hess to hang rather than life imprisonment.
45. Justice Jackson's Report to the President on Atrocities and War Crimes, June 7, 1945.
46. Charles WyzanskiJr., "Nuremberg—A Fair Trial?," *Atlantic Monthly*, Apr. 1946, 67. For detailed discussions of arguments made by proponents and opponents of charging the Nazi leaders with crimes against peace, see Kirsten Sellars, *Crimes Against Peace and International Law* (2013), 132–136.
47. As George Finch, editor-in-chief of the *American Journal of International Law* wrote, norms of customary international law could not be established merely "by placing interpretations upon the words of treaties which are refuted by the acts of the signatories in practice, [or] by citing unratified protocols or public and private resolutions of no legal effect." George Finch, "The Nuremberg Trial and International Law," 41 *Am. J. Int'l. L.* 20, 28 (1947).
48. The Llandovery Castle Case, *Annual Digest 1923–1924*, Case No. 235, Full Report, 1921 (CMD. 1450).
49. Hersch Lauterpacht, "The Law of Nations and the Punishment of War Crimes" (1944), *reprinted in Perspectives On the Nuremberg Trial* (Guénaël Mettraux, ed., 2008), 4. David Luban similarly explained forty-three years later that because political leaders can be put on trial for waging an aggressive war only if they are beaten on the battlefield, the only kind of justice possible is victor's justice. David Luban, "The Legacies of Nuremberg" (1987), *reprinted in* Mettraux, 658 ("Only victors' justice is possible").
50. Article 18 of the Nuremberg Charter declared: "The Tribunal shall (a) confine the Trial strictly to an expeditious hearing of the issues raised by the charges, (b) take strict measures to prevent any action which will cause any unreasonable delay, and rule out irrelevant issues and statements of any kind." The words "strict" and "strictly" were meant to prevent the defendants from raising in court any Allied misdeeds.
51. The *Pre-trial Indictment* speaks in Count 1 (titled "The Common Plan or Conspiracy") of the conspirators' "program of relentless persecution of the Jews, designed to exterminate them," and concludes: "[I]t is conservatively estimated that 5,700,000 have disappeared, most of them deliberately put to death by the Nazi conspirators. Only remnants of the Jewish population remain." Justice Jackson's opening statement contained the following: "The most savage and numerous crimes planned and committed by the Nazis were those against the Jews . . . The avowed purpose was the destruction of the Jewish people as a whole . . . History does not record a crime ever perpetrated against so many victims or one ever carried out with such calculated cruelty." Opening Statement of Robert H. Jackson, Nov. 21, 1945.
52. Robert Chandler, "Translator's Introduction," *in* Vasily Grossman, *Life and Fate* (Robert Chandler, trans., 1985), xiii–xiv.
53. Reizman also testified that in order to prevent the transports of Jews from discovering, as soon as they arrived there, that Treblinka was a death camp, the Germans erected a façade of a regular railroad station, although the camp had no rail connections aside from the train leading to it. Signs were posted on the station indicating that it was on the route to Vienna and other points.

54. A portion of Sutzkever's testimony, which he gave standing as a tribute to the Jewish victims, is available on YouTube.
55. Testimony of Severina Smaglevskaya, Feb. 27, 1946, *available at* <http://avalon.law.yale.edu/imt/02-27-46.asp>.
56. Testimony of Marie Claude Vaillant-Couturier, Jan. 28, 1946, *in Trial of the Major War Criminals before the International Military Tribunal,* v. VI, 214–216 (1947).
57. Closing Address of Hartley Shawcross, July 27, 1946, *in Trial of the Major War Criminals before the International Military Tribunal,* v. XV, 501 (1948).
58. Shawcross's summation can be viewed on the US Holocaust Memorial Museum website. *Quoted in* Michael Bazyler and Frank Tuerkheimer, *Forgotten Trials of the Holocaust* (2015), 4–5.
59. *Nazi Conspiracy and Aggression: Opinion and Judgment* (1947), 77–82, *available at* <http://www.loc.gov/rr/frd/Military_Law/pdf/NT_Nazi-opinion-judgment.pdf>.
60. Charles Wyzanski Jr., "Nuremberg in Retrospect," *Atlantic Monthly,* Dec. 1946, 57.
61. Raul Hilberg, *The Politics of Memory: The Journey of a Holocaust Historian* (1996), 71–72.
62. See Kevin Heller, *The Nuremberg Military Tribunals and the Origins of International Criminal Law* (2011). Heller's work offers the most comprehensive treatment of the trials. The other comprehensive study, in article form, is Matthew Lippman, "The Other Nuremberg: American Prosecutions of Nazi War Criminals in Occupied Germany," 3 *Indiana Int'l. Comp. L. Rev.* 1 (1992–1993). The US Government Printing Office published between 1949 and 1953 a fifteen-volume set of the trials, *Trials of War Criminals before the Nuernberg Military Tribunals under Control Council Law no. 10, Nuernberg 1946–April 1949.* These are commonly referred to as the "Green Series" because of the books' green covers. Today, materials from the trials are available online through various sources.
63. Ibid., 435.
64. Strictly speaking, the NMT, unlike the IMT, was not applying the Nuremberg Charter. Rather, it was "an international tribunal established by the International Control Council, the high legislative branch of the four Allied powers . . . controlling [occupied] Germany. . . . The Tribunal administers international law." Flick Judgment, vol. VI, 1188.
65. Between 1946, with the end of the IMT tribunal and April 1949, when prosecutions were abandoned as the Federal Republic of Germany came into being, American military tribunals issued 185 indictments of second-tier Germans. The US Army also tried 1,700 Germans, of which about 300 were convicted. This is in addition to the over 500 military tribunals constituted in former concentration camps like Dachau liberated by the Americans. These tribunals indicted close to 2,000 individuals, not only Germans but also concentration camp personnel of other nationalities who were prisoners and appointed by the Germans in some supervisory capacity. Of these 1,517 were convicted, with 324 sentenced to death and 247 given life imprisonment.
66. In a rare joint session of all the presiding judges, the NMT held that conspiring to commit war crimes and crimes against humanity was not covered by CCL10 and so dismissed that count on the ground that they had "no jurisdiction to try any defendant upon a charge of conspiracy considered as a separate substantive offense." The count was then dropped after the first three multidefendant cases.

67. Heller, 400.
68. Ibid.
69. Robert Servatius, who represented Brandt, was chosen by Adolf Eichmann to represent him a decade and a half later in Jerusalem. See Chapter 4.
70. United States v. Altstoetter, *Trials of War Criminals Before the Nuernberg Military Tribunals under Control Council Law No. 10* (hereinafter *Justice Case*), Indictment.
71. *Justice Case*, Judgment, 985 (*quoting* Indictment).
72. Lippman, "The Other Nuremberg," 1, 69.
73. Ibid., 70.
74. Heller, 55.
75. Telford Taylor, *Final Report to the Secretary of the Army on the Nuernberg War Crimes Trials Under Control Council Law No. 10.* (1949),169.
76. *Justice Case*, Judgment, 324.
77. *Quoted in* Matthew Lippman, "The Prosecution of Josef Altstoetter *et al.*: Law, Lawyers and Justice in the Third Reich," 16 *Dick. J. Int'l L.* 343, 414.
78. Rothaug then went to explain: "It is the fault of the Jews that this war happened. Those who have contact with the Jews will perish. . . . Racial defilement is worse than murder, and poisons the blood for generations. It can only be atoned by exterminating the offender." Extracts of Testimony of Defendant Rothaug, *quoted in* Lippman, "The Prosecution of Josef Altstoetter," 414.
79. *Justice Case*, Judgment, 1161.
80. Taylor, Final Report, 169.
81. See *The Law in Nazi Germany: Ideology, Opportunism and the Perversion of Justice* (Alan E. Steinweiss and Robert D. Rachlin, eds., 2013), Appendix I, The Fate of Markus Luftglass: Excerpt from the Record of the Nuremberg Justice Case.
82. *Justice Case*, Opinion and Judgment, 1087.
83. Ibid., 1082.
84. Taylor, Final Report, 109–110.
85. Affidavit and Testimony of Friedrich Flick, Green Series, v. 6, 394.
86. Ibid.
87. Ibid., 187.
88. For comprehensive discussion, see Florian Jessberger, "I.G. Farben on Trial," 8 *J. Int'l Crim. Just.* 783 (2010).
89. Taylor, Final Report, 196.
90. For a good discussion, see Jonathan A. Bush, "The Prehistory of Corporations and Conspiracy in International Criminal Law: What Nuremberg Really Said," 109 *Colum. L. Rev.* 1094 (2009).
91. *United States v. Wilhelm List, Trials of War Criminals Before the Nuernberg Military Tribunals under Control Council Law No. 10*, v. XI (hereinafter *Hostage Case*), Judgment, 1249.
92. Ibid., Judgment, 1255, 1257.
93. Valerie Hébert, *Hitler's Generals on Trial: The Last War Crimes Tribunal at Nuremberg* (2010), 197.
94. RuSHA Indictment, *Trials of the War Criminals before the Nuernberg Military Tribunals under Control Council Law No. 10, v.IV*, 609–610, para. 2.

95. For a study of the *Einsatzgruppen Case,* see Hillary Earl, *The Nuremberg SS-Einsatzgruppen Trial, 1945–1958: Atrocity, Law and History* (2009). See also Michael Bazyler and Frank Tuerkheimer, *Forgotten Trials of the Holocaust* (2015), 159–194.
96. Ibid., 180
97. The speech was filmed and can be viewed at the US Holocaust Memorial Museum website.
98. Taylor, Final Report, 181.
99. Ibid., 183–184 (*quoting* trial transcript).
100. For a study of the *High Command Case,* see Hébert, *Hitler's Generals on Trial.*
101. *High Command Case,* Judgment, 489, *quoted in* Lippman, "The Other Nuremberg," 49.
102. *High Command Case,* Judgment, 507–508.
103. Heller, 6.
104. Heller, 47, n.30.
105. Taylor, Final Report, 92.
106. Heller, 5.
107. *Quoted in* Valerie Hébert, "The Politics of Punishment," *in After Fascism: European Case Studies in Politics, Society, and Identity Since 1945* (Matthew Paul Berg and Maria Mesner, eds., 2009), 111.
108. Ibid.
109. Ibid.
110. The Americans executed 278 Germans at Landsberg, 259 by hanging and 29 by firing squad.
111. Hébert, The Politics of Punishment, 113. To be fair, McCloy never succumbed to the pressure to grant a full amnesty to the Nuremberg defendants. While most did not serve the full sentences imposed by them by the NMT tribunals, they still left their jail cells as convicted criminals.
112. The prison facility was turned over to the Bavarian government, which uses it as a prison to this day.
113. The words come from the speech outside the gates of Landsberg by Gebhard Seelos of the Bavaria Party. His speech was met by applause. Smaller counterprotests were met with hostility and sometimes with outright violence.
114. Hébert, *Hitler's Generals,* 199.
115. *Quoted in* Sharon A. Williams, "Laudable Principles Lacking Application: The Prosecution of War Criminals in Canada," *in The Laws of War Crimes* (Timothy McCormack and Gerry J. Simpson, eds., 1997), 152.
116. Bloxham, *Genocide on Trial,* 162–163.
117. Telford Taylor, "The Nazis Go Free," *The Nation,* Feb. 24, 1951, 170.
118. Heller, 5.
119. Hébert, "The Politics of Punishment," 121.
120. Heller, 4.
121. *Quoted in* Lawrence Douglas, "Genocide on Trial: War Crimes Trials and the Formation of Holocaust History and Memory," 18 *Holocaust & Gen. Stud.* (Spring 2004), 135.
122. Heller, 400.
123. Ibid., 372.

124. Ibid., 401.
125. *High Command Case*, Judgment, 508.
126. *Einsatzgruppen Case*, Judgment, 462.
127. United States v. Ernst von Weizaecker, *Trials of War Criminals Before the Nuernberg Military Tribunals Under Control Council Law No. 10*, v. XIV ("*Ministries Case*"), Judgment, 527.
128. Ferencz, who for the last half-century unsuccessfully sought to make crimes against peace (or its modern name "crimes of aggression") at least a full partner with genocide, crimes against humanity, and war crimes in the panoply of the most serious violations of international law, has given up. He now seeks to make the waging of aggressive war a crime against humanity. See Benjamin B. Ferencz, "The Illegal Use of Armed Force as a Crime Against Humanity," 2 *J. Use of Force & Int'l L.* 1 (2015). The International Criminal Court currently has no remit to adjudge crimes of aggression, though it is set to take up the issue after January 1, 2017.
129. Heller, 3 (paragraph break deleted).
130. David Glazier, "Kevin Jon Heller and the Historical Legacy of the U.S. Nuremberg Military Tribunals (NMT)," *Opinio Juris*, Oct. 31, 2011.

Chapter 4

1. United Nations War Crimes Commission, History of the UNWCC and the Development of the Laws of War (1948), 376–380.
2. For discussion, see *A Nation of Victims?: Representations of German Wartime Suffering from 1945 to the Present* (Helmut Schmitz, ed., 2007).
3. For further information on Bauer, see Fritz Bauer Institute, http://www.fritz-bauer-institut.de/.
4. *Quoted in* Volker Wagener, "Auschwitz Trial Ensured that Germany Would Never Forget," *Deutsche Welle*, Aug. 18, 2015.
5. Rebecca Wittmann, "Punishment," *in The Oxford Handbook of Holocaust Studies* (Peter Hayes and John K. Roth, eds., 2010), 534.
6. BGH, NJW 22 (1969), 1181.
7. *Quoted in* Annette Weinke, "Between Demonization and Normalization: Continuity and Change in German Perceptions of the Holocaust as Treated in Post-War Trials," *in Holocaust and Justice: Representation and Historiography of the Holocaust in Post-War Trials* (David Bankier and Dan Michman, eds., 2010), 203, n.22.
8. See Ben Knight, "Reinhard Strecker, The Man Who Exposed German Judiciary's Nazi Past," *Deutsche Welle*, Jan. 26, 2015.
9. David Cesarani, "War Crimes," *in The Yale Holocaust Encyclopedia* (Walter Laqueur, ed. and Judith Tydor Baumel, assoc. ed., 2001), 680.
10. Central Office of the Land Judicial Authorities for the Investigation of National Socialist Crimes, Information Sheet, Dec. 31, 2013, 7.
11. Weinke, 208. Hermann Göring was sometimes also added to the list, making it a four-man grand crime.
12. According to § 211: "A murderer is someone who kills a human being out of bloodthirst, for the satisfaction of sexual desires, for greed or any other base motives, in a cunning or cruel manner or by means causing common danger, or to make possible or conceal another felony."

13. See, e.g., Convention on the Non-Applicability of Statutory Limitations to War Crimes and Crimes against Humanity, adopted 26 November 1968; European Convention on the Non-Applicability of Statutory Limitations to Crimes and Against Humanity and War Crimes and Crimes against Humanity, adopted on 25 January 1974.
14. Jörg Friedrich, *Die kalte Amnestie: NS-Täter in der Bundesrepublik* (1984), 377.
15. H. Ostendorf, "Die—widerspüchlichen—Auswirkungen der Nürnberger Prozesse auf die westdeutsche Justiz" in *Strafgerichte gegen Menscheitsverbrechen, zum Völkerstrafrecht 50 Jahre nach den Nürenberger Prozesse* (Gerd Hankel and Gebhard Stuby, eds., 1995), 81.
16. The most comprehensive discussion of the Ulm trial can be found in Patrick Tobin, Crossroads at Ulm: Postwar Germany and the 1958 Ulm Einsatzkommando Trial (Dissertation, UNC-Chapel Hill, 2013).
17. Tobin, 18–22.
18. See http://www.jewishvirtuallibrary.org/jsource/Holocaust/jaegerreport.html. The tallies were sent to Jäger from commanders in the field, including those from EK Tilsit. Jäger lists one hundred executions in seventy-one locations in Lithuania. This tally was sent to Berlin and is known as the Jäger Report. Of the five copies sent to Berlin, one survived. Jäger was captured after the war, but committed suicide while in custody.
19. Tobin, 108.
20. Ibid.
21. See Katharina von Kellenbach, *The Mark of Cain; Guilt and Denial in the Post-War Lives of Nazi Perpetrators* (2013).
22. *Quoted in* Tobin, 211.
23. Ibid., 278.
24. Ibid., 244.
25. Ibid., 251.
26. Ibid., 244.
27. Ibid., 244.
28. Ibid., 259.
29. Ibid., 226–227.
30. Ibid., 227–228.
31. No transcript of the trial was taken.
32. Tobin, 267.
33. Ibid., 228.
34. Ibid., 258, *quoting* article in *Schwäbische Donau-Zeitung*, May 13, 1958.
35. Ibid., 218.
36. Ibid., 263
37. Ibid., 264.
38. Ibid., 267.
39. Ibid., 279.
40. Ibid., 281.
41. "Nazi Officer Admits Participation in Killing 813 Lithuanian Jews," *JTA*, July 14, 1958.
42. Tobin, 281.
43. "Nazi Officer Admits Participation," *JTA*.

44. Ibid.
45. Tobin, 285. The witness Hartl, one of the shooters, in answer to the question why he did not make known his opposition to the orders to kill innocent civilians, answered, "I was too cowardly." Tobin, 272–273.
46. Ibid., 289.
47. Ibid., 300.
48. Caroline Sharples, *West Germans and the Nazi Legacy* (2012), 35. See also Devin O. Pendas, "'I Didn't Know What Auschwitz Was': The Frankfurt Auschwitz Trial and the German Press, 1963–1965," 12 *Yale J.L. & Human.* 397 (2000) (1,400 articles in seventy newspapers about the trial).
49. Tobin, 26.
50. Sharples, 34 (*quoting* German historian Ulrich Brochhagen).
51. In 1940, Schüle was drafted into the Wehrmacht to fight on the Eastern Front. Captured by the Red Army in 1945, he remained a POW until released in 1950, when he returned to West Germany to resume his legal career.
52. "German Hunter of Nazis Admits He Was a Storm Trooper as Youth," *JTA*, Feb. 19, 1965.
53. For two excellent studies on the Frankfurt Auschwitz trial, see Devin O. Pendas, *The Frankfurt Auschwitz Trial, 1963–1965: Genocide, History and the Limits of Law* (2006), and Rebecca Whitmann, *Beyond Justice: The Auschwitz Trial* (2005). See also Michael J. Bazyler and Frank M. Tuerkheimer, *Forgotten Trials of the Holocaust* (2014), 227–245.
54. This was the third major trial of Auschwitz personnel. In 1947, the Poles held two Auschwitz trials before the Polish National Tribunal, a specially created war crimes court. The first trial had a single defendant, Auschwitz commandant Rudolf Höss. Later that year, the same court convicted twenty-one former Auschwitz staff, including commandant Arthur Liebhenschel. Twenty were executed, including Liebhenschel. Poland and West Germany held other trials of lesser Auschwitz personnel. Some Auschwitz staff were tried by the Allies in their respective occupation zones. According to one source: "In total no more than 15% of the Auschwitz concentration camp staff ever stood before the bar of justice in any country. Yet the percentage tried because of their work at Auschwitz is significantly larger than at any other camps, perhaps owing to the emblematic nature of Auschwitz as the epicenter of the Holocaust." Auschwitz Trials Summary, *available at* <http://www.jewishvirtuallibrary.org/jsource/Holocaust/auschtrial.html>.
55. Both survived the war and were recognized by Yad Vashem in 1980 as "Righteous Among Nations," non-Jews who saved Jews. Ella Lingens died in 2002. Her Auschwitz memoir, *Prisoners of Fear*, published in 1947, was reissued in 2015.
56. *Quoted in* Ben Knight, "Why the Gröning Trial Matters," *Prospect*, April 30, 2015.
57. For further discussion, see Michael S. Bryant, *Eyewitness to Genocide: The Operation Reinhard Death Camp Trials 1955–1956* (2014).
58. David Cesarani, *Becoming Eichmann: Rethinking the Life, Crimes, and Trial of a "Desk Murderer"* (2006), 1. Some other notable works on the trial are Bettina Stangneth, *Eichmann Before Jerusalem: The Unexamined Life of a Mass Murderer* (2014); Haim Goury, *Facing the Glass Booth: The Jerusalem Trial of Adolf Eichmann* (2004);

Hannah Yablonka, *The State of Israel vs. Adolf Eichmann* (2004); Sergio Minerbi, *The Eichmann Trial Diary: A Chronicle of the Holocaust* (2011); Harry Mulisch, *Criminal Case 40/61, the Trial of Adolf Eichmann: An Eyewitness Account* (2009); and Deborah Lipstadt, *The Eichmann Trial* (2011). See also excellent chapter accounts in Stephen Landsman, *Crimes of the Holocaust: The Law Confronts Hard Cases* (2005); Lawrence Douglas, *The Memory of Judgment: Making Law and History in the Trials of the Holocaust* (2001); and Tom Segev, *The Seventh Million: Israelis and the Holocaust* (1993). Chief Prosecutor Gideon Hausner also wrote his account of the trial. See also Gideon Hausner, *Justice in Jerusalem The Trial of Adolf Eichmann* (1966) (memoir of chief Eichmann prosecutor).

59. Arendt arrived in Israel on April 9, 1961, two days before the trial began. She was present for prosecutor Gideon Hausner's opening statement. She was also in court during some additional sessions. On May 6, Arendt wrote to her husband in New York that she was leaving Jerusalem the next morning for Switzerland to visit Swiss-German philosopher Karl Jaspers. She apparently returned to Israel and could have been in court (this according to Lipstadt) when Eichmann first took the stand on June 20, 1961. She was not there during any of Eichmann's cross-examination. Eichmann left the stand on July 24, 1961.
60. Hannah Arendt, *Eichmann in Jerusalem: A Report on the Banality of Evil* (rev. and enlarged ed., 1965). For a point-by-point deconstruction of Arendt's arguments and response, see Jacob Robinson, *And the Crooked Shall Be Made Straight: The Eichmann Trial, the Jewish Catastrophe, and Hannah Arendt's Narrative* (1965). For more recent critiques, see *Hannah Arendt in Jerusalem* (Steven E. Ascheim, ed., 2001).
61. For many years, *Eichmann in Jerusalem* was near taboo in Israel, not for Arendt's banality of evil thesis but for her castigation of the *Judenräte,* the Jewish ghetto leaders who compiled names for deportation and then enforced the Nazi deportation orders. "To a Jew," she wrote, "this role of the Jewish leaders in the destruction of their own people is undoubtedly the darkest chapter of the whole dark story." Arendt, 117. And then came the most stinging words: "Wherever Jews lived, there were recognized Jewish leaders, and this leadership, almost without exception, cooperated in one way or another, for one reason or another, with the Nazis. The whole truth was that if the Jewish people had really been unorganized and leaderless, there would have been chaos and plenty of misery but the total number of victims would hardly have been between four and a half and six million people." Ibid., 125. With these words Arendt was tarnishing the victimhood of the Jewish "martyrs"—a word that is still part of the official name of Yad Vashem. Arendt's narrative of the Holocaust emphasized Jewish guilt and de-emphasized Nazi guilt. In effect, it blamed the Jews for their own destruction. Strangely, Arendt wasn't saying anything new. The "sheep-to-the-slaughter" belief already permeated Israeli culture before Eichmann in Jerusalem, and so the denunciation of Arendt (not only in Israel but in America) for pointing out the meekness of the Jews seemed out of place. It was not until 2000 that *Eichmann in Jerusalem* was finally translated and published in Hebrew.
62. Arendt, 54.
63. Ibid., 276. Normality, however, does not mean innocence. In Arendt's eyes, Eichmann was "one of the greatest criminals of that period." Ibid., 288.

64. Arendt, 46. Auschwitz commandant Rudolf Höss recalled that during one of Eichmann's visits to camp, Höss "confided to Eichmann that upon seeing Jewish children herded into the gas chambers his knees quivered. Eichmann rejoined that it was precisely the Jewish children who must be first sent into the gas chambers in order to ensure the wholesale elimination of the Jews as a race. Richard Wolin, "The Banality of Evil: The Demise of a Legend," *Jewish Rev. of Books*, Fall 2014.
65. *Quoted in* Stangneth, 304.
66. Christopher R. Browning, *Collected Memories: Holocaust History and Postwar Testimony* (2003), 3. Browning borrows this formulation from Yaacov Lozowick, *Hitler's Bureaucrats: The Nazi Security Police and the Banality of Evil* (2002), 277–279.
67. Lipstadt, 164.
68. Stangneth, xvii.
69. Ibid. The Arendt/Eichmann controversy heated up again in 2014 with the publication in English of Stangneth's *Eichmann Before Jerusalem*.
70. Eichmann Trial, Session No. 17, April 26, 1961. Eichmann's success in Vienna lead to the establishment of other such central offices in Berlin and Prague.
71. http://remember.org/eichmann/timeline.
72. Ibid.
73. Testimony of Dieter Wisliceny, Jan. 3, 1946, IMT Trial.
74. Prosecution Opening Statement, Session 7, Apr. 17, 1961.
75. Leon Poliakov, "Eichmann: Administrator of Extermination, The Definitive Solution of the Jewish Problem," *Commentary*, May 1, 1949.
76. "We have already mentioned another hypothesis: profiting by his knowledge of Hebrew and of Jewish life in general, he may have passed as a Jew escaped from a concentration camp. Perhaps he is now in a displaced-persons camp, or he may even have succeeded in emigrating under his new identity, perhaps even to Palestine. . . . Eichmann was in a position to supply himself with a thoroughly credible identity, and he had the knowledge required for an expert impersonation." Ibid.
77. After Eichmann's capture, Vera Eichmann returned to Germany with two of the four Eichmann sons, leaving her two eldest sons in Argentina. She died in 1993. In 2015, Israel revealed that Vera was allowed to visit Eichmann in jail two months before he was executed.
78. Stangneth, 265.
79. Ibid., xxii.
80. According Israeli journalist Tom Segev, Wiesenthal informed Israeli authorities in 1953, seven years before the Mossad caught up with Eichmann, that the Nazi criminal was in Argentina, but his memo was filed away in an archive. Tom Segev, *Simon Wiesenthal: The Life and Legends* (2010), 106.
81. Following Eichmann's capture, the Soviet Union intimated that it might call for reconvening the Nuremberg tribunals, as was its right. It never did so.
82. See Michael J. Bazyler and Julia Y. Scheppach, "The Strange and Curious History of the Law Used to Prosecute Adolf Eichmann," 34 *Loy. L.A. Int'l & Comp. L. Rev.* 417 (2012). See also Michael J. Bazyler and Frank Tuerkheimer, *Forgotten Trials of the Holocaust* (2014), 195–225. Eichmann was also charged with the international law crimes of "crimes against humanity" and "war crimes," the crimes enunciated at Nuremberg. Last, he was charged with "membership in a hostile organization,"

referencing the SS, the SD, and the Gestapo, all of whom had been declared criminal organizations by the IMT at Nuremberg.

83. Nowhere did the Nazi and Nazi Collaborators Law define "collaborator" and how that individual is to be distinguished from a Nazi. In effect, by failing to distinguish between Nazis and collaborators, the NNCL conflated the behavior of both groups and appeared to equate their behavior.
84. Bazyler and Sheppach, 429 (*citing* Orna Ben-Naftali and Yogev Tuval, "Punishing International Crimes Committed by the Persecuted: The Kapo Trials in Israel," 4 J. *Int'l Crim. Just.* 128, 129 (2006)).
85. Segev, *Seventh Million*, 262 n.21.
86. Arendt, xviii.
87. Ibid.
88. Stephen Landsman, "The Eichmann Case and the Invention of the Witness-Driven Atrocity Trial," 51 *Colum. J. Trans. L.* 69, 79 (2012).
89. One specific charge made against Hausner is why he continued to ask witnesses why they did not resist. It wasn't an accusation. Hausner wanted people to recognize that not resisting was the most practical response that the Jews could make. As Deborah Lipstadt explains: "Some people felt this question was insensitive. I don't think so. I think Hausner had absorbed how impossible it was to stand up to the Nazis. This was his way of telegraphing the message just how hard resistance was." Aaron Howard, "50 Years After the Eichmann Trial, A New Assessment, *Jewish Herald Voice*, Mar. 10, 2011.
90. Eichmann Trial, Session 6, Apr. 17, 1961.
91. Ibid.
92. Ibid. The opening address can be viewed on YouTube: https://www.youtube.com/watch?v=B7oSox54weU.
93. Hausner, 177.
94. Eichmann Trial, Session 21, May 1, 1961.
95. Eichmann Trial, Session 27, May 4, 1961.
96. Eichmann Trial, Session 100, July 18, 1961.
97. "Eichmann Tells His Own Damning Story," *Life*, Nov. 28, 1960. He added: "It would be as pointless to blame me for the whole final solution of the Jewish problem as to blame the official in charge of the railroads over which the transports traveled. . . ." In January 2016, Israel released a recently discovered clemency petition written by Eichmann to Israeli President Yitzhak Ben-Zvi. In the two-page handwritten letter, dated May 29, 1962, Eichmann repeats his "little cog" defense. He explains: "It is not true that I was personally of such a high rank as to be able to persecute, or that I myself was a persecutor in the pursuit of the Jews . . . I never served in such a high position as required to be involved independently in such decisive responsibilities. Nor did I give any order in my own name, but only ever acted 'by order of.' . . . I was not a responsible leader, and as such do not feel myself guilty." Paul Vale, "Adolf Eichmann Letter Reveals Nazi Pleading Not to Be Executed as He Was 'Only Following Orders," *The Huffington Post UK*, Jan. 27, 2016. The Israeli president denied the request. Two days later, Eichmann was hanged.
98. As explained by the Israeli Supreme Court: "The Appellant was overjoyed at preventing the rescue of Jewish children, for that was the most effective blow against the

physical survival of the nation, and against the physical survival of the nation, and against the emigration he fought everywhere." State of Israel v. Eichmann, 36 ILR 333.

99. Judgment, para. 221.
100. Judgment, para. 243.
101. These criticisms are well summarized in William Schabas, "The Contribution of the Eichmann Trial to International Law," 26 *Leiden J. Int'l L.* 667, 668–669 (2013).
102. Leora Bilsky, "The Eichmann Trial: Towards a Jurisprudence of Eyewitness Testimony of Atrocities," 12 *J. Int'l Crim. Just.* 27, 28 (2014).
103. Ibid.
104. See Gary J. Bass, "The Adolf Eichmann Case: Universal and National Jurisdiction," *in Universal Jurisdiction: National Courts and the Prosecution of Serious Crimes Under International Law* (Stephen Macedo, ed., 2002). See also Amnesty International, *Eichmann Supreme Court Judgment: 50 Years On, Its Significance Today* (2012).
105. Eichmann Trial, Session 81, June 28, 1961.
106. Attorney General v. Eichmann, para. 25.
107. Schabas, "The Contribution of the Eichmann Trial," 667, 670.
108. See Hanna Yablonka, "The Eichmann Trial: Was It the Jewish Nuremberg?," 34 *Loy. L.A. Int'l & Comp. L. Rev.* 301 (2012).
109. *Quoted in* Schabas, "The Contribution of the Eichmann Trial," 667, 675, n.47.
110. State of Israel v. Eichmann, Appeal, Israel Supreme Court, para. 6 (May 29, 1962).
111. Arendt, 286.
112. Landsman, "The Eichmann Case and the Invention of the Witness-Driven Atrocity Trial," 71. For a contrary view, see Bilsky, "The Eichmann Trial: Towards a Jurisprudence of Eyewitness Testimony of Atrocities," 27.
113. Landsman, "The Eichmann Case and the Invention of the Witness-Driven Atrocity Trial," 69.
114. Schabas, "The Contribution of the Eichmann Trial," 670.
115. Another infamous Nazi to join Eichmann in Argentina was Joseph Mengele, the Auschwitz doctor notorious for performing grotesque pseudo-medical experiments on prisoners—children and adults alike—especially those who were twins. Using the same Vatican-enabled escape route as Eichmann, Mengele lived openly under his own name in Buenos Aires. Upon Eichmann's capture, he fled to Paraguay and then to Brazil. For more than two decades, Mengele was the most infamous Nazi thought to be still alive. The search for Mengele ended in the 1990s when it was determined that in 1979 he drowned at a Brazil resort as a result of suffering a stroke while swimming. See "In the Matter of Josef Mengele: A Report to the Attorney General of the United States," Office of Special Investigations, U.S. Dept. of Justice (Oct. 1992).
116. Eric Litchtbau, *The Nazis Next Door: How America Became a Safe Haven for Hitler's Men* (2014). See also Richard Rashke, *Useful Enemies: John Demjanjuk and America's Open Door Policy for Nazi War Criminals* (2013).
117. For British prosecutions, see Bazyler and Tuerkeimer, 275–301. For Australian prosecutions, see David Fraser, *Daviborschch's Cart: Narrating the Holocaust in Australian War Crimes Trials* (2011).
118. United States v. Hajda, 963 F. Supp. 1452, 1457 (N.D. Ill. 1997).

119. Canada switched to the American system after its Supreme Court declared such criminal prosecutions unconstitutional. See Sharon A. Williams, "Laudable Principles Lacking Application: The Prosecution of War Criminals in Canada," *in The Laws of War Crimes* (Timothy L.H. McCormack and Gerry J. Simpson, eds., 1997), 151.
120. For post–World War II cases, an individual can be prosecuted for the separate crime of immigration fraud under a new statute, 28 U.S.C. § 1425. Thus, in 2013, a federal judge in New Hampshire sentenced Beatrice Munyenyezi to ten years' imprisonment for lying about her role in the 1994 Rwandan genocide when she applied for and received US citizenship a decade earlier. Like the Nazi persecutors before her, Munyenyezi entered the United States as a refugee. See Chapter 9.
121. Fedorenko v. United States, 449 U.S. 490 (1981). For discussion of the *Fedorenko* proceedings, see Bazyler and Tuerkheimer, 247–273.
122. Rinkel even had a plot waiting for her in a Jewish cemetery next to her husband's, who apparently never knew of her Nazi past.
123. Lawrence Douglas, *The Right Wrong Man: John Demjanjuk and the Last Great War Crimes Trial* (2015).
124. United States Department of Justice, Criminal Division, Human Rights and Special Prosecution Section, *available at* <http://www.justice.gov/criminal-hrsp/about-hrsp>.
125. Roman Lehberger, "Demjanjuk War Crimes Conviction Caps 30-year Battle," CNN, May 12, 2011.
126. Michelle Martin, "'Bookkeeper of Auschwitz' Found Guilty by A German Court," *Reuters*, July 15, 2015.
127. Of the estimated 6,500 SS personnel stationed at Auschwitz, less than fifty were ever convicted. Klaus Wiegrefe, "Why the Last SS Guards Will Go Unpunished," *Spiegel*, Aug. 28, 2014 (citing German historian Andreas Eichmüller).
128. Matthias Geyer, "An SS Officer Remembers: The Bookkeeper from Auschwitz," *Spiegel*, Aug. 19, 2005.
129. *Quoted in* Knight, "Why the Gröning Trial Matters."
130. *Quoted in* Michele Mandel, "Last Nazi Trial," *Toronto Sun*, June 16, 2016.
131. A designation Zuroff reserves to "a person who assisted in the persecution of innocent civilians during World War II, in the territory of or in collaboration with the forces of Nazi Germany." Alan S. Rosenbaum, *Prosecuting Nazi War Criminals* (1993), 8 (*quoting* Efraim Zuroff).
132. Donald McKale, *Nazis After Hitler: How Perpetrators of the Holocaust Cheated Justice and Truth* (2012), For another recent study with a similar theme, see Gerard Steinacher, *Nazis on the Run: How Hitler's Henchmen Fled Justice* (2012).
133. McKale, 345.
134. Rosenbaum, 8 (quoting Efraim Zuroff).
135. Mark A. Drumbl, *Atrocity, Punishment and International Law* (2007), 48.

Chapter 5

1. Michael R. Marrus, *Some Measure of Justice* (2009), 3. I use the term "restitution" to designate both the actual return of properties (real and personal) and financial compensation. The term thus encompasses payments made to Jews who toiled as

slaves and non-Jews as forced laborers for Nazi Germany; Jewish and non-Jewish victims of Nazi Germany's medical experiments; Jewish survivors of Nazi concentration camps, in ghettoes and in hiding; payments made on unpaid insurance policies and confiscated and dormant bank accounts; and other instances where money was paid to victims or heirs of mass atrocities. For further discussion of the terminology of "restitution" and the related term "reparations," see *The Oxford Handbook of Reparations* (Pablo de Greiff, ed., 2006), and Regula Ludi, *Reparations for Nazi Victims in Postwar Europe* (2012).

2. Elie Wiesel, Foreword to Stuart E. Eizenstat, *Imperfect Justice: Looted Assets, Slave Labor, and the Unfinished Business of World War II* (2003), ix.
3. Peter Hayes, "Plunder and Restitution," *in The Oxford Handbook of Holocaust Studies* (Peter Hayes and John K. Roth, eds., 2010), 544. Hayes continues: "In the succeeding years, the regime may have raked in as much as half of the remainder through additional impositions, the mandatory conversions of sums in blocked accounts into war bonds, and the terms of the Eleventh Decree to the Reich Citizenship Law, which declared that the property of German Jews 'fell' to the state at the moment they exited the country, whether through emigration or deportation." Ibid.
4. Herlinde Pauer-Studer and James David Velleman, *Konrad Morgen: The Conscience of a Nazi Judge* (2015).
5. Saul Friedländer, *The Years of Extermination: Nazi Germany and the Jews, 1939–1945* (2007), 544.
6. *Quoted in The Decent One,* Vanessa Lapa's 2014 Himmler documentary based on discovered Himmler letters. Himmler used similar language in his October 4, 1943, infamous speech to a group of senior SS deputies at Posen: "We have taken from them what wealth they had. . . . We have the moral right, we had the duty to our people to do it—to kill this people who wanted to kill us. But we do not have the right to enrich ourselves with even one fur, with one Mark, with one cigarette, with one watch, with anything. That we do not have. Because at the end of this, we don't want—because we exterminated the bacillus—to become sick and die from the same bacillus."
7. Gold stolen by Nazi Germany from state treasuries of countries they conquered was high on the list of assets to be returned. Much of this gold was deposited in neutral Switzerland. In 1946, under the Washington Accords, Switzerland agreed to return a portion of the gold. See Michael J. Bazyler, *Holocaust Justice: The Battle for Restitution in America's Courts* (2003), 2–3. Art and cultural objects stolen from state museums was another high-priority restitution item. Ibid., 202–203. The 2014 Hollywood film *The Monuments Men,* directed by and starring George Clooney, dramatized the efforts of the US Army to find and return such art.
8. Hayes, "Plunder and Restitution," 541.
9. See Benjamin B. Ferencz, *Less Than Slaves: Jewish Forced Labor and the Quest for Compensation* (1979). For an excellent recent discussion, see Michael Meng, *Shattered Spaces: Encountering Jewish Ruins in Postwar Germany and Poland* (2011), 29–59.

10. The problem lingers seventy years later. Poland has yet to pass a comprehensive restitution law dealing with seizure of property lost during the Nazi and Communist eras. It is the only East European country that has failed to pass such a law.
11. Israel Ministry of Foreign Affairs, *Documents Relating to the Agreement between the Government of Israel and the Federal Republic of Germany, Signed on 10 September 1952 at Luxembourg* (1953).
12. Karen Heilig, "From the Luxembourg Agreement to Today: Representing a People," 20 *Berkeley J. Int'l L.* 176, 179 (2002).
13. http://www.jewishvirtuallibrary.org/jsource/Holocaust/reparations.html.
14. Ibid.
15. Heilig, 180.
16. Nehemiah Robinson, *Ten Years of German Indemnification* (1964), 8.
17. *Quoted in* The Conference on Jewish Material Claims Against Germany, *60 Years of the Claims Conference* (2012), 3. http://forms.claimscon.org/Claims-Conference-60-Years.pdf.
18. Elazar Barkan, *The Guilt of Nations: Restitution and Negotiating Historical Injustices* (2000), xxiv.
19. See Daniel E. Rogers, "Restoring a German Career, 1945–1950: The Ambiguity of Being Hans Globke," 31 *German Stud. Rev.* 303 (2008).
20. Jeffrey Herf, "Germany," *in Oxford Handbook of Holocaust Studies*, 641.
21. *60 Years of the Claims Conference*, 6.
22. Kurt Schumacher's anti-Nazi credentials were even stronger than Adenauer's. Schumacher served in the Reichstag during the Weimar Republic, was arrested by the Nazis, and spent ten years in a concentration camp. Unlike Adenauer, who opposed the Nuremberg trials, Schumacher was one of the prosecution witnesses. Schumacher was a firm believer that Germany had to face up to its Nazi past, including the mass murder of the Jews. He rejected the myth that most Germans did not know what was going on around them. In a 1945 speech he stated that Germans "saw with their own eyes with what common bestiality the Nazis tortured, robbed and hunted the Jews." *Quoted in* Herf, 638. Speaking an unspoken truth, Schumacher added: "Not only did they remain silent, but they would have preferred that Germany had won the Second World War, thus guaranteeing them peace and quiet and also a small profit." Ibid. Schumacher died suddenly in August 1952, shortly after appearing on the cover of *Time* magazine, and so sadly did not live to see the actual signing of Germany's treaty with Israel.
23. For some, the discomfort with Germany continues. In 2016, Israeli Tourism Minister Yariv Levin announced that he would not attend a major tourism expo because it was being held in Berlin. Levin explained: "I see great importance in the relationship between Israel and Germany. Within that context, I have met with German officials more than once here in Israel. However, I do feel uneasy visiting Germany." "Israeli Tourism Minister Refuses Germany Visit, Citing Country's Nazi Past," *Jerusalem Post*, March 14, 2016. That same year Transportation Minister Yisrael Katz also declined to visit Germany. "As a son of survivors, I do not travel to Germany," Katz explained. "My father escaped on a train from Budapest, and my mother was imprisoned in seven concentration camps in Germany and Poland by the time she was 15." Ibid.

24. Tom Segev, *The Seventh Million: The Israelis and the Holocaust* (1991), 241.
25. Ibid., 249.
26. See Susan Slyomovics, *How to Accept German Reparations* (2014), 19. For general studies, see Christian Pross, *Paying for the Past: The Struggle over Reparations for Surviving Victims of the Nazi Terror* (1998); Ronald W. Zweig, *German Reparations and the Jewish World: A History of the Claims Conference* (2nd ed., 2001); Marilyn Henry, *Confronting the Perpetrators: A History of the Claims Conference* (2007).
27. Uriel Helman, "$70 Billion on, Claims Conf. Marks 60 Years of Reparations from Germany," *JTA*, July 11, 2012.
28. Segev, 196.
29. Michael J. Bazyler, *Holocaust Justice: The Battle for Restitution in America's Courts* (2003).
30. Ibid., p. xii (italics in original).
31. Ibid., xii–xiii. For another view of why Holocaust restitution litigation succeeded in American courts, see Leora Bilsky, Rodger D. Citron, and Natalie R. Davidson, "From Kiobel Back to Structural Reform: The Hidden Legacy of Holocaust Restitution Litigation, 2 *Stan. J. Complex Litig.* 139 (2014).
32. *Address before the House Foreign Affairs Committee: Subcommittee on Europe, Holocaust Survivors in America: An Overview of Outstanding Holocaust Issues* (statement of J. Christian Kennedy, Special Envoy for Holocaust Issues) (United States House of Representatives, Oct. 3, 2007).
33. Ibid.
34. *Hearing of the Committee on Banking and Financial Services*, 106th Cong. 6 (Feb. 9, 2000) (Otto Lambsdorff).
35. Conference on Jewish Material Claims Against Germany, <http://www.claimscon.org/?url=medex/payment2> (statement of Eva Kor).
36. The story is told well in the 2015 Hollywood film *Woman in Gold*, with Helen Mirren playing Mrs. Altmann and Ryan Reynolds as Randy Schoenberg.
37. Melissa Eddy, "Matisse from Gurlitt Collection Is Returned to Jewish Art Dealer's Heirs," *N.Y. Times*, May 15, 2015.
38. See Susan Ronald, *Hitler's Art Thief: Hildebrand Gurlitt, the Nazis, and the Looting of Europe's Treasures* (2015); Catherine Hickley, *The Munich Art Hoard: Hitler's Dealer and His Secret Legacy* (2015).
39. Elizabeth Campbell Karlsgodt, "Why Are Museums Holding on to Art Looted by the Nazis," *Newsweek*, May 10, 2015.
40. For discussion of the Hungarian Gold Train settlement and other Holocaust restitution claims made against the United States, see Michael J. Bazyler and Amber L. Fitzgerald, "Trading with the Enemy: Holocaust Restitution, the United States Government, and American Industry," 28 *Brooklyn J. Int'l L.* 683 (2003).
41. Complaint at 1, Abrams v. Société Nationale des Chemins de fer Français, 175 F. Supp. 2d 423 (E.D.N.Y. 2001) (No. CV00502), 2000 WL 34498150.
42. Litigation against European railroads for transporting Jews to concentration camps during the war continues. In January 2016, Holocaust survivors scored their first success when the Washington, D.C., Circuit Court of Appeals reversed the lower court's dismissal of one such suit. The unanimous panel of judges allowed Hungarian survivors to pursue a claim against the Republic of Hungary arising from the confiscation

of properties by the Hungarian national railway when Hungarian Jews were being transported to Auschwitz and other camps in 1944. Simon v. Republic of Hungary, No. 14-7082 (D.C. Cir. 2016) (Jan. 29, 2016).

43. The action was filed before the Administrative Tribunal for Toulouse against the French State and SNCF, and the tribunal in 2006 decided in favor of the plaintiffs. On appeal, however, the appellate tribunal in 2007 reversed by deciding that SNCF was acting under the command of the German authorities and therefore could not be held responsible. The Council of State, France's highest administrative tribunal affirmed the dismissal. The Lipietz case file is available at http://lipietz.net/spip.php?rubrique75.
44. Paul Vitello, "Leo Bretholz, 93, Dies; Escaped Train to Auschwitz," *N.Y. Times*, Mar. 29, 2014.
45. Ibid.
46. Katherine Shaver, "Seeking Accountability for the Sins of the Past," *Wash. Post*, Mar. 10, 2014, B1.
47. Emily Langer, "Made a Daring Escape from Nazis," *Wash. Post.*, Mar. 11, 2014, B5.
48. Ibid. During his testimony, Bretholz provided copies of an invoice showing that SNCF pursued payment for the transports even after Paris had been liberated. Ibid.
49. Keolis also operates the Virginia Railway Express commuter trains in the Washington, D.C., corridor.
50. Karen DeYoung, "France to Compensate American Survivors of Holocaust," *Wash. Post*, Dec. 5, 2014. SNCF also agreed to make a $4 million contribution over five years to Holocaust museums, memorials, and education programs.
51. Alfred C. Mierzejewski, "A Public Enterprise in the Service of Mass Murder: The Deutsche Reichsbahn and the Holocaust," 15 *Holocaust & Genocide Stud.* (2001), 35–36.
52. Raul Hilberg, "*German Railroads/Jewish Souls*" (Jan./Feb. 1998), 35 *Society* 162, *reprinted in The Nazi Holocaust: Historical Articles on the Destruction of the European Jews*, v.3 (Michael Marrus, ed.,1989), 520.
53. Raul Hilberg, *The Politics of Memory* (2003), 40.
54. For a perspective by an attorney defending many of these historical restitution claims in American courts, see Owen C. Pell, "Historical Reparations Claims: The Defense Perspective," *in Holocaust Restitution: Perspectives on the Litigation and Its Legacy* (Michael Bazyler and Roger P. Alford, eds., 2006), 331–344.
55. "Turkey Anger at Pope Francis Armenian 'Genocide' Claim," *BBC*, Apr. 12, 2015.
56. Ben Kiernan, *Blood and Soil: A World History of Genocide and Extermination from Sparta to Darfur* (2007), 386.
57. For discussion of the Herero genocide, see Jeremy Sarkin-Hughes, *Germany's Genocide of the Herero: Kaiser Wilhelm II, His General, His Settlers, His Soldiers* (2011); David Olusoga and Casper Erichsen, *The Kaiser's Holocaust: Germany's Forgotten Genocide and the Colonial Roots of Nazism* (2011); Dominik J. Shaller, *From Conquest to Genocide: Colonial Rule in German Southwest Africa and German East Africa* (2008).
58. See Allan Cooper, "Reparations of the Herero Genocide: Defining the Limits of International Litigation," 106 *Oxford Journal of African Affairs* 113 (2007).
59. Herero People's Reparations Corp. v. Deutsche Bank, A.G., 370 F.3d 1192 (D.C. Cir. 2004).

60. Hereros ex rel. Riruako v. Deutsche Afrika-Linien GmbH & Co., 232 F. App'x. 90 (3d Cir. 2007).
61. Linda Goetz Holmes, *Unjust Enrichment: How Japan's Companies Built Postwar Fortunes Using American POWs* (2001).
62. See Elizabeth Rosenthal, "Wartime Slaves Use U.S. Law to Sue Japanese," *N.Y. Times*, Oct. 10, 2000, A1.
63. Levenberg v. Nippon Sharyo Ltd., No. C-99-1554 (N.D. Cal. filed Mar. 16, 1999).
64. Cal. Civ. Proc. Code § 354.6.
65. In re World War II Era Japanese Forced Labor Litigation, 114 F. Supp. 2d 939 (N.D. Cal. 2000).
66. The court relied on Article 14(b) of the Peace Treaty, which states: "Except as otherwise provided in the present Treaty, the Allied Powers waive all reparations claims of the Allied Powers, other claims of the Allied Powers and their nationals arising out of any actions taken by Japan and its nationals in the course of the prosecution of the war, and claims of the Allied Powers for direct military costs of occupation." Treaty of Peace with Japan, Sept. 8, 1951, 3 U.S.T. 3169, 136 U.N.T.S. 45.
67. In re World War II Era Japanese Forced Labor Litigation, 164 F. Supp.2d 1160 (N.D. Cal. 2001).
68. Deutsch v. Turner Construction Corp., 324 F.3d 692 (9th Cir. 2003).
69. David Sanger, *Report on Holocaust Assets Tells of Items Found in the U.S., N.Y. Times*, Jan. 17, 2001.
70. David Wolpe, "Japanese Prime Minister's Non Apology for World War II Atrocities Is Damaging, *Time*, Aug. 14, 2015 (*quoting* Prime Minister Abe).
71. Ibid.
72. Abby Phillip, "Mitsubishi Apologizes for Using American POWs as Slaves During WWII," *Wash. Post*, July 20, 2015.
73. Justin McCurry, "Mitsubishi Offers Apology and $56m for Wartime Use of Chinese Labour," *The Guardian*, June 1, 2016.
74. Khulumani v. Barclays Nat'l Bank Ltd., No. 02 MDL No. 1499 (S.D.N.Y. Oct. 24, 2008); Ntsebeza v. Daimler AG, No. 02 MDL No. 1499 (S.D.N.Y. Oct. 27, 2008).
75. In re South African Apartheid Litigation, 238 F. Supp. 2d 1379 (J.P.M.L. 2002).
76. "Apartheid Lawsuit to Start Early August: Lawyer," *Agence France-Presse*, July 6, 2002.
77. See In re S. Afr. Apartheid Litig., 346 F. Supp. 2d 538, 549–55 (S.D.N.Y. 2004), *rev'd sub nom.*, Khulumani v. Barclay Nat'l Bank Ltd., 504 F.3d 254 (2d Cir. 2007) (per curiam); Khulumani v. Barclay Nat'l Bank Ltd., 504 F.3d 254 (2d Cir. 2007); In re S. Afr. Apartheid Litig., 617 F. Supp. 2d 228, 296 (S.D.N.Y. 2009); Balintulo v. Daimler AG, 727 F.3d 174, 194 (2d Cir. 2013). For summary, see Julian Ku, "The Case That Won't Die: U.S. Court Revives South Africa Apartheid Alien Tort Statute Lawsuit." *Opinion Juris*, Apr. 18, 2014.
78. See Edwin Black, *IBM and the Holocaust: The Strategic Alliance Between Nazi Germany and America's Most Powerful Corporation* (2001).
79. Balintulo v. Ford Motor Co., 796 F.3d 160 (2d Cir. 2015).
80. For a history of the African-American reparations movement, see Robert Wesley, *Many Billions Gone: Is It Time to Reconsider the Case for Black Reparations?*, 40 *B.C. L. Rev.* 429 (1998); Charles Ogletree Jr., "Repairing the Past: New Efforts in the Reparations Debate in America," 38 *Harv. C.R.-C.L. L. Rev.* 279 (2003).

81. Tamar Lewin, "Calls for Slavery Restitution Getting Louder," *N.Y. Times*, June 4, 2001.
82. Randall Robinson, *The Debt: What America Owes to Blacks* (1999).
83. Rick Montgomery, "Emotions High When the Issue Is Reparations; Push to Make Amends for Slavery Advances," *The Kansas City Star*, Mar. 11, 2001.
84. Cal. Ins. Code §§ 13811–13813.
85. "Calif. Law Forces Firms' Disclosures," *Reuters*, May 2, 2002.
86. Ogletree, 295.
87. Ibid., 298–307.
88. Ibid., 319.
89. For a discussion of the parallels between the two movements, see Eric K. Yamamoto, "Racial Reparations: Japanese American Redress and African American Claims," 19 *B.C. Third World L.J.* 477 (1998).
90. 50 U.S.C. § 1989(b)4 (1998).
91. Montgomery.
92. In re African-American Slave Descendants Litigation, 231 F. Supp. 2d 1357 (J.P.M.L. 2002).
93. Ogletree, 279.
94. Tamar Lewin, "Calls for Slavery Restitution Getting Louder," *N.Y. Times*, June 4, 2001.
95. No. 99-12073 (C.D. Cal. filed Jan. 17, 2000).
96. Cal. Civ. Proc. Code § 354.4.
97. Marootian v. New York Life Ins. Co., 2001 U.S. Dist. LEXIS 22274 (Nov. 20, 2001).
98. "Armenians Settle Genocide Insurance Case," *N.Y. Times*, Jan. 29, 2004.
99. Beverly Beyette, "He Stands Up in the Name of Armenians," *L.A. Times*, Apr. 27, 2001.
100. Ibid. For further discussion, see Michael J. Bazyler, "From 'Lamentation and Liturgy to Litigation': The Holocaust-Era Restitution Movement as a Model for Bringing Armenian Genocide-Era Restitution Suits in American Courts," 95 *Marquette L. Rev.* 247 (2011).
101. The author, as lead co-counsel, benefited from this precedent in a lawsuit representing a Jewish family against Argentina. The lawsuit, filed in Los Angeles federal court in 1982, arose out of torture and expropriation of properties that took place in Argentina during Argentina's so-called "dirty war" years, when a military junta held power between 1976 and 1983. Siderman De Blake v. Republic of Argentina, 965 F.2d 699 (9th Cir. 1992). The case settled in 1996. See Tim Golden, "Argentina Settles Lawsuit by a Victim of Torture," *N.Y. Times*, Sept. 14, 1996.
102. Filartiga v. Pena-Irala, 630. F.2d 876 (1980).
103. Michael J. Bazyler, *Holocaust Justice: The Battle for Restitution in America's Courts* (2003), 55.
104. *Filartiga*, 890.
105. 28 U.S.C. § 1350 (2006), originally enacted as part of the Judiciary Act of 1789, ch. 20, § 9, 1 Stat. 73, 77.
106. 28 U.S.C. § 1350 (2006).

107. The ATS also does not contain a limitation on the physical location of the torts at issue. From the plain language of the statute, the international law tort violation does not have to be committed in the United States for the alien to file suit in federal court under the ATS.
108. Michael Goldhaber, "Corporate Human Rights in Non-U.S. Courts: A Comparative Scorecard," 3 *U.C. Irvine L. Rev.* 127 (2013).
109. Jad Mouawad, "Shell to Pay $15.5 Million to Settle Nigerian Case," *N.Y. Times*, June 8, 2009.
110. Kiobel v. Royal Dutch Petroleum Co., 133 S. Ct 1659, 1663 (2013). For a recent analysis, Anna Grear and Burns H. Weston, "The Betrayal of Human Rights and the Urgency of Universal Corporate Accountability: Reflections on A Post-Kiobel Lawscape," 15 *Hum. Rts. L. Rev.* 21 (2015); Eugene Kontorovich. "Kiobel Surprise: Unexpected by Scholars but Consistent with International Trends," 89 *Notre Dame L. Rev.* 1671 (2014): Sarah H. Cleveland, "After Kiobel," 12 *J. Int'l Crim. J.* 551 (2014). Justice Breyer discusses *Kiobel* in his recent book, Stephen Breyer, *The Court and the World: American Law and the New Global Realities* (2015), 134–164.
111. *Kiobel*, 1669
112. Julian Ku, "Kiobel and the Surprising Death of Universal Jurisdiction under the Alien Tort Statute," *Agora: Reflections on Kiobel, asil.org* (2013).
113. 18 U.S.C. § 1091(e)(2)(d) ("There is jurisdiction over [prosecuting genocide] . . . regardless of where the offense was committed, [if] the alleged offender is . . . present in the United States.").
114. Michael Thad Allen, "The Limits of Lex Americana: The Holocaust Restitution Litigation as a Cul-de-Sac of International Human-Rights Law," 17 *Widener L. Rev.* 1, 67 (2011).

Chapter 6

1. Michael Shermer and Alex Grobman, *Denying History: Who Says the Holocaust Never Happened and Why Do They Say It?* (2000). For other studies, see, e.g., Robert A. Kahn, *Holocaust Denial and the Law: A Comparative Study* (2004); *Genocide Denials and the Law* (Ludovic Hennebel and Thomas Hochmann, eds., 2011); and *Extreme Speech and Democracy* (Ivan Hare and James Weinstein, eds., 2010).
2. Bradley R. Smith, *The Holocaust Controversy: The Case for Open Debate* (Committee for Open Debate on the Holocaust, 1992), *quoted in* Shermer and Grobman, xv. Denialist Bradley R. Smith should not be confused with Second World War historian Bradley F. Smith. See "Obituary, Bradley F. Smith: Military and Intelligence Historian," *Independent*, Sept. 12, 2012.
3. Shermer and Grobman, 40.
4. Simon Wiesenthal Center, "Hamas Leader Mashaal: Nazi Holocaust 'Exaggerated'—Wiesenthal Center Urges Repudiation by Arab Leaders," *SWC News*, July 17, 2007.
5. See "AHA Statement on Holocaust Denial," *Perspectives on History*, v. 29, no. 9, Dec. 1991, *available at* https://www.historians.org/publications-and-directories/perspectives-on-history/december-1991/aha-statement-on-holocaust-denial (website of the American Historical Association).

6. Deborah Lipstadt, *Denying the Holocaust: The Growing Assault on Truth and Memory* (1994).
7. *Quoted in* Steve Busfield, "Irving Loses Holocaust Libel Case," *The Guardian*, Apr. 11, 2000.
8. For discussion of the trial, see, e.g., Deborah E. Lipstadt, *History on Trial: My Day in Court with a Holocaust Denier* (2006); D. D. Guttenplan, *The Holocaust on Trial* (2001); Richard J. Evans, *Lying About Hitler: History, Holocaust and the David Irving Trial* (2001); Robert Jan van Pelt, *The Case for Auschwitz: Evidence from the Irving Trial* (2002). The last two authors are respected historians who served as expert witnesses for the defense. My own discussion can be found in *Jews on Trial* (Robert A. Garber, ed., 2005). The 2016 British-American film *Denial,* starring Rachel Weisz as Deborah Lipstadt and Timothy Spall as David Irving, dramatizes the trial.
9. Lipstadt, *Denying the Holocaust,* xiii.
10. Ibid., 28 (italics in original) Ironically, Lipstadt and her team of lawyers and historical experts were forced to do exactly that when sued by David Irving for labeling him a Holocaust denier.
11. Shermer and Globman, 14–15.
12. Ibid., 33.
13. The Italian law, enacted in June 2016, also criminalizes denial of other genocides and crimes against humanity, as defined by by International Court of Justice. The law prescribes prison sentences up to six years.
14. A good summary of the European Court of Human Rights cases on Holocaust and genocide denials can be found in "Factsheet—Hate Speech," European Court of Human Rights, Nov. 2015. *See also* Paolo Lobba, "Holocaust Denial Before the European Court of Human Rights: Evolution of an Exceptional Regime," 26 *Eur. J. Int'l. L.* 237 (2015).
15. Eugene Volokh, "No, There's No 'Hate Speech' Exception to the First Amendment," *Wash. Post,* May 7, 2015.
16. Ibid.
17. George Soroka, "The Spotless Mind: Behind Europe's Attempts to Legislate Memory," *Foreign Affairs,* July 14, 2015.
18. EU Presidency General Statement to the UN General Assembly: Resolution on Holocaust Denial, Statement of H.E. Mr. Thomas Matussek, Jan. 26, 2007. <http://www.eu-un.europa.eu>.
19. Kahn, 147.
20. The relevant portion of § 130 reads: "Whoever publicly or in a meeting approves of, denies or renders harmless an act committed under the rule of National Socialism of the type indicated in §220a subsection (1) [genocide], in a manner capable of disturbing the public peace shall be punished with imprisonment for not more than five years or a fine." The full English-language translation of this and related statutes can be found at <http://www.iuscomp.org> (German law archive containing statutes, literature, and bibliographies on German law in English language). For discussion of Penal Code § 220a, see Chapter 9, analyzing Germany's criminal prosecutions of genocidaires.
21. Eric Stein, "History Against Free Speech: The New German Law Against the 'Auschwitz'—and Other—'Lies,'" 85 *Mich. L. Rev.* 278, 282 (1986).

22. *Quoted in* Kahn, 66.
23. The swastika is an ancient symbol of peace appropriated by the Nazis. As such, Hindu and Jain temples are permitted to display swastikas, since religious symbols cannot be banned in Germany.
24. German Penal Code § 86 ("Dissemination of Means of Propaganda of Unconstitutional Organizations").
25. BVerfGe, 90 241–255. (1994). An English translation of the opinion is available at <https://law.utexas.edu/transnational/foreign-law-translations/german/case.php?id=621>.
26. Basic Law, Article 1, paragraph 1 reads: "Human dignity is inviolable. To respect and to protect it is the duty of all state authority."
27. Johannes Rau, "Foreword by the Federal President," *Basic Law for the Federal Republic of Germany* (2000 ed.), 5–6.
28. Kahn, 149. We examine Germany's militant democracy in Chapter 7.
29. See Sections 185–188 criminalizing "insult," "malicious gossip," "defamation," "malicious gossip and defamation against persons in political life," and "disparaging of memory of deceased persons."
30. Kahn, 6.
31. "Prize-winning Hitler Mask Breaks the Law," *Ottawa Citizen*, Feb. 21, 2002.
32. "German Company Fined for Selling Anti-Nazi Symbols," *Deutsche Welle*, Sept. 29, 2006.
33. Uwe Hessler, "Reversing Earlier Call, Court Allows Anti-Nazi Symbol Sale," *Deutsche Welle*, Mar. 15, 2007.
34. "German deported from the United States convicted of Holocaust denial," *Int'l Herald Trib.*, Mar. 15, 2007.
35. German Federal Criminal Code § 5 ("Acts Abroad Against Domestic Legal Interests") reads, in pertinent part: "German criminal law shall apply, regardless of the law of the place the act was committed, to the following acts committed abroad: . . . 3. endangering the democratic rule of law."
36. For detailed analyses of the Zündel criminal trials in Canada, see Kahn, 45–59, and Lawrence Douglas, *The Memory of Judgment: Making Law and History in the Trials of the Holocaust* (2001).
37. "German Neo-Nazi Lawyer Sentenced for Denying Holocaust," *Deutsche Welle*, Apr. 14, 2008.
38. Ibid.
39. Felicity Capon, "Former German Lawyer Imprisoned for Holocaust Denial for Second Time," *Newsweek*, Feb. 26, 2015.
40. Verbotsgesetz 1947 [National Socialism Prohibition Act 1947] Bundesgesetzblatt [BgBl] No. 148/1992, as amended, §3g-h (Austria).
41. "David Irving Jailed for Holocaust Denial," *The Guardian*, Feb. 20, 2006.
42. Ibid.
43. The Gayssot Law makes it a crime "to contest by any means the existence of one or more of the crimes against humanity as defined by Article 6 of the Statutes of the International Military Tribunal, attached to the London Agreement of August 8, 1945, committed either by the members of an organization declared criminal in application of Article 9 of the same Statutes, or by a person held guilty of such a crime by a French or international jurisdiction."

44. "France Upholds Law Singling Holocaust Denial as a Crime," *AP*, Jan. 8, 2016.
45. *Quoted in* Michael Curtis, "France Is Severe on Holocaust Denial," *American Thinker*, July 30, 2015.
46. Michel Arseneault, "Nazi Jailed in France for Denying Holocaust in Facebook Posts," *The Globe & Mail*, Feb. 12, 2015.
47. ECtHR Fact Sheet, "Hate Speech," Mar. 2016.
48. Council of the European Union Press Release 8364/07 (Press 77), Justice and Home Affairs, Framework Decision on Racism and Xenophobia (April 19, 2007).
49. Council Framework Decision on Racism and Xenophobia, 2008/913/JHA of Nov. 28, 2008, 2008 O.J. (L. 328) 55.
50. Ibid.
51. Ibid.
52. The EU Framework Decision's opt-out clause reads: [Member States] shall not have to take measures in contradiction to fundamental principles relating to freedom of association and freedom of expression, in particular freedom of the press and the freedom of expression." It affirms this point by noting: "[t]his Framework Decision shall not have the effect of modifying the obligation to respect fundamental rights and fundamental legal principles, including freedom of expression and association, as enshrined in Article 6 of the Treaty of the EU." As a final caveat, the Framework Decision states that "Member States may choose to punish only conduct which is either carried out in a manner likely to disturb public order or which is threatening, abusive or insulting." Ibid.
53. *Quoted in* Dan Bilefsky, "EU Adopts Measure Outlawing Holocaust Denial," *N.Y. Times*, Apr. 19, 2007.
54. Tony Blair and Moshe Kantor, "Intolerance Is Tearing the Fabric of Our Society," *The Times (London)*, June 4, 2015.
55. Daphne Antachopoulos, "Opinion: Hate Speech Has Nothing to Do with Freedom of Speech," *Deutsche Welle*, Feb. 16, 2007.
56. Douglas, 220.
57. Clare Murphy, "Irving Tests Europe's Free Speech," *BBC*, Feb. 20, 2006 (*quoting* Hajo Funke).
58. Douglas, 217.
59. *Quoted in* Mark Landler, "Austria Frees Holocaust Denier from Jail," *N.Y. Times*, Dec. 21, 2006.
60. Anti-genocide legal scholar Gregory Stanton, in his "Ten Stage of Genocide," believes the same: denial is the last stage of genocide. See Conclusion of this book.
61. Pierre Vidal-Naquet, *Assassins of Memory: Essays on the Denial of the Holocaust* (Jeffrey Mehlman, trans., 1993).
62. Geoffrey Hartman, "Introduction: Darkness Visible," *in Holocaust Remembrance: The Shapes of Memory* (Geoffrey Hartman, ed., 2004).
63. Rafael Medoff and Alex Grobman, "Holocaust Denial: A Global Survey—2006," The David S. Wyman Institute for Holocaust Studies, 2.
64. Ibid.
65. FRA European Union Agency for Fundamental Rights, "Antisemitism: Overview of Data Available in the European Union 2004-2014," Oct. 2015, 36.
66. JTA, "Anti-Semitic Attacks in France Climb 84% in 2015, Watchdog Says," *Haaretz*, July 13, 2015.

67. With the onset of the digital revolution, Europe's extreme right has stepped up efforts to spread its word through another medium attractive to the youth: pop music. The number of neo-Nazi and skinhead concerts in the country has doubled in the past seven years to 160, and the country is home to about one hundred right-wing rock bands. Despite being banned in Germany, music from neo-Nazi groups is distributed online through file-sharing networks.
68. Harold James, "There Are Good Reasons Why Europe's Jews Are So Worried," *Reuters*, Feb. 11, 2016.
69. Charles C. Haynes, *In Defense of the Indefensible*, First Amendment Center, Jan. 21, 2007.
70. Alec Brandon, "Censoring Holocaust Denial Is Hypocritical," *The Chicago Maroon*, Apr. 3, 2007.
71. Thomas Jefferson, in the same vein, said: "[There is nothing] to fear from the demoralizing reasons of some, if others are free to demonstrate their errors."
72. T. H. Teetens, *The New Germany and the Old Nazis* (1961).
73. *Quoted in* Erik Kirschbaum and Betham John, "At a Landmark Berlin Rally, Merkel Vows to Fight Anti-Semitism," *Reuters* , Sept. 14, 2014.
74. Keith B. Richburg and Alan Cooperman, "Swede's Sermon on Gays: Bigotry or Free Speech?," *Wash. Post*, Jan. 29, 2005.
75. "Anti-Gay Pastor Is Acquitted in Sweden," *Wash. Post*, Nov. 30, 2005.
76. Michael Shermer, "Free Speech, Even If It Hurts," *L.A. Times*, Feb. 22, 2006.
77. In 2007, Azerbaijan prosecuted a dissident journalist who disagreed with the official government narrative that during Azerbaijan's 1992 war with Armenia over Nagorny-Karabach, Armenian troops committed genocide in the town of Khojaly. In 2010, the European Court of Human Rights ruled that the conviction violated the European Convention on Human Rights and ordered the release of the journalist. See Fatullayev v. Azerbajian, Judgment, ECtHR, Apr. 22, 2010.
78. For discussion, see *Beyond Totalitarianism: Stalinism and Nazism Compared* (Michael Geyer and Sheila Fitzpatrick, eds., 2009).
79. Garin K. Hovannisian, "The Folly of Jailing Genocide Deniers," *Christian Science Monitor*, Nov. 6, 2006.
80. *Quoted in* Alexander Trowbridge, "French Arrests Draw Charges of Free Speech Hypocrisy," *CBS News*, Jan. 15, 2015.
81. Henry Weinstein, "Yahoo's Nazi Suit Tossed," *L.A. Times*, Jan. 13, 2006.
82. Jay Michaelson, "A Lawsuit Cannot Stop the Facebook Intifada. You Might.," *The Forward*, Nov. 4, 2015.
83. Kahn, vii.
84. Nigel Foster and Satish Sule, *German Legal System and Laws* (4th ed., 2010), 235–236.
85. Virginia v. Black, 538 U.S. 343 (2003).
86. Ibid., at 344.
87. California, Connecticut, the District of Columbia, New York, and Virginia, already have such laws on the books. The Connecticut statute, passed in 2008 in the wake of the 2007 Jena Six controversy, reads: "Any person who places a noose or a simulation thereof on any public property, or on any private property without the written consent of the owner, and with intent to intimidate or harass any other person

on account of religion, national origin, alienage, color, race, sex, sexual orientation, blindness or physical disability, shall be in violation [of the law]." For further discussion see Allison Barger, "Changing State Laws to Prohibit the Display of Hangman's Nooses: Tightening the Knot Around the First Amendment?," 17 *Wm. & Mary Bill Rts. J.* 263 (2008). *See also* Ellis Cose, "Ignore the Noose Makers," *Newsweek*, Oct. 27, 2007; Marisol Bello, "'Jena 6' Case in La. Spurs Copycats," *USA Today*, Oct. 10, 2007.

88. On the "Auschwitz Lie," "Letter from Professor Dr. Christian Meier," 87 *Mich. L. Rev.* 1026, 1030–1031 (1989).
89. "Slippery Slope," *The Economist*, Jan. 25, 2007.
90. Snyder v. Phelps, 562 U.S. 443 (2010).
91. According to Lipstadt, "I am not happy when censorship wins, and I don't believe in winning battles via censorship . . . The way of fighting Holocaust deniers is with history and with truth." *Quoted in* "Holocaust Denier Irving Is Jailed," *BBC*, Feb. 20, 2006.
92. AFP, "Holocaust-Denying 'Nazi Grandma' Gets 10 months in Jail," *Deutsche Welle*, Nov. 13, 2015.
93. Hugo Gye, "Holocaust-Denying Historian David Irving Organizes 'Disgusting' £2,000-a-head Holiday Tours of Former Concentration Camps and Hitler's HQ So People Can 'Make Up Their Own Mind About the Truth,'" *Daily Mail*, Aug. 31, 2015.
94. Perinçek v. Switzerland, App. No. 27510/08, ECHR, Judgment, Oct. 15, 2015. http://hudoc.echr.coe.int/eng?i=001-158235.
95. Ibid., para. 230.
96. Ibid., para. 209–212.
97. Ibid., para. 244.
98. Ibid., para. 242–243 (italics added).

Chapter 7

1. For some leading texts on post-Holocaust theology and philosophy, see, e.g., Richard L. Rubenstein, *After Auschwitz: Radical Theology and Contemporary Judaism* (1966); Emil L. Fackenheim, *To Mend the World: Foundations of Post-Holocaust Jewish Thought* (1994); John K. Roth, *Ethics During and After the Holocaust: In the Shadow of Birkenau* (2005); A. Roy Eckhart, *Post-Holocaust Theology and the Christian-Jewish Dialogue* (1987); Stephen R. Haynes, *Prospects for Post-Holocaust Theology* (1991).
2. John K. Roth, *The Failures of Ethics: Confronting the Holocaust, Genocide and Other Mass Atrocities* (2015), 49.
3. Arthur Kaufmann, "National Socialism and German Jurisprudence from 1933 to 1945," 9 *Cardozo L. Rev.* 1629, 1633, 1641 (1987).
4. Michael Stolleis, "Reluctance to Glance in the Mirror: The Changing Face of German Jurisprudence after 1933 and post-1945" (Fulton Lecture Series 2001), 14.
5. Vivian Grosswald Curran, "Fear of Formalism: Indications from the Fascist Period in France and Germany of Judicial Methodology's Impact on Substantive Law," 35 *Cornell Int'l L.J.* 101, 106 (2001) (italics added).
6. Yehuda Bauer, *Rethinking the Holocaust* (2001), 2.

7. Timothy Snyder, *Black Earth: The Holocaust as History and Warning* (2015), 326–327.
8. This is a given, and cannot be avoided. After 9/11, the US. government was blamed for failure to prevent the attack on America. It became its duty to prevent the next attack. Inevitably, laws were passed to increase police powers. The same was done by Britain after the July 7, 2005, attacks in London, by Spain after the train terror attacks in Madrid on March 11, 2004, and by France after the attacks in Paris in January and November 2015. See generally *Routledge Handbook of Law and Terrorism* (Genevieve Lennon and Clive Walker, eds., 2015).
9. Kaufmann, 1630.
10. Carl Schmitt, *The Concept of the Political* (expanded ed. 2008), 30.
11. Anna Schmidt, "The Problem of Carl Schmitt's Political Theology," *in Man and His Enemies: Essays on Carl Schmitt* (Svetozar Minkov and Piotr Nowak, eds., 2008), 107.
12. Paul Gottfried. "The Concept of Carl Schmitt," *in The American Conservative,* Oct. 15, 2015 (book review of *Carl Schmitt: A Biography by Reinhard Mehring* (2015).
13. Detlev Vagts, "Carl Schmitt's Ultimate Emergency: The Night of the Long Knives," 87 *Germanic Rev.* 203, 206 (2012).
14. Ibid.
15. *Quoted in* Raphael Gross, *Carl Schmitt and the Jews: The "Jewish Question," the Holocaust and German Legal Theory* (Joel Golb, transl., 2007), 66.
16. *Quoted in* Tom Sunic, "Carl Schmitt's 'Jews in Jurisprudence (Part I),'" *Occidental Observer* (Jan. 6, 2012).
17. Peter C. Caldwell, "Foreword," in Gross, xii.
18. *Quoted in* Manfred H. Wiegandt, *The Alleged Unaccountability of the Academic: A Biographical Sketch of Carl Schmitt,* 16 *Cardozo L. Rev.* 1569 (1995).
19. Gross, 4.
20. Gottfried.
21. "Law and the Human: The Challenge of Carl Schmitt," *available at* <http://isites.harvard.edu/course/colgsas-17587>.
22. Noah Feldman, "Baseball and Egypt," *N.Y. Post,* Aug. 11, 2013.
23. Gross, 226–228.
24. Ibid., 233.
25. Ibid., 234–235. Snyder likewise warns that there is "only the darkness that is consummate when gifted minds such as Schmitt's cloak evil with unreason." Snyder, 144.
26. Carl Schmitt, *Political Theology* (2005), 7.
27. Ibid, 15.
28. Tracy B, Strong, "The Sovereign and the Exception: Carl Schmitt, Politics, Theology and Leadership," Foreword to Carl Schmitt, *Political Theology* (2005), xvii.
29. And in line with Nazi thinking, universalism was invented by the Jews to subjugate non-Jews. See Gross, 13, discussing "Schmitt's critique of universalism and its ties to his assault on Judaism."
30. *Quoted in* Jan-Werner Müller, *A Dangerous Mind: Carl Schmitt in Post-war Legal Thought* (2003), Schmitt borrowed and modified the saying from the 19th century socialist philosopher Pierre-Joseph Proudhon's "Whoever invokes humanity, wants to cheat."

31. New books and articles on Schmitt and his philosophy continue abound, with the latest being *The Oxford Handbook of Carl Schmitt* (Jens Meierhenrich and Oliver Simons, eds., 2016).
32. See, e.g., Jason Ralph, *America's War on Terror: The State of the 9/11 Exception from Bush to Obama* (2015); *The International Political Thought of Carl Schmitt: Terror, Liberal War and the Crisis of Global Order* (Louiza Odyssseos and Fabio Petito, eds., 2007). See also Mark Danner, "After September 11: Our State of Exception," *N.Y. Review of Books*, Oct. 13, 2011.
33. Sandrine Baume, *Hans Kelsen and the Case for Democracy* (2012), 37.
34. This is to be contrasted with the American model of constitutionalism, where the guardian of the Constitution is the entire judiciary, with even a low-ranking judge being able to declare a law unconstitutional.
35. Goebbels is quoted in *Nationalsozialistische Diktatur, 1933–1945: Eine Bilanz* (K. D. Bracher et al., eds., 1983), 16.
36. For discussion of militant democracy, see, e.g., Svetlana Tyulkina, *Militant Democracy: Undemocratic Political Parties and Beyond* (2015); András Sajó, "From Militant Democracy to Preventive State," 27 *Cardozo L. Rev.* 2255 (2006); Gregory H. Fox and Georg Nolte, "Intolerant Democracies," 36 *Harv. Int'l L.J.* 1 (1995); Russell A. Miller, "Comparative Law and Germany's Militant Democracy," *in U.S. National Security, Intelligence and Democracy: From the Church Committee to the War on Terror* (Russell A. Miller, ed., 2008). Miller observes that it "[i]is unfortunate that the radically peaceful, thoroughly internationalist and uncompromisingly democratic Federal Republic must be associated with a constitutional construct that sounds so unflatteringly aggressive, so *Prussian*." (italics in original).
37. Karl Loewenstein, "Militant Democracy and Fundamental Rights," 31 *Am. Poli. Sci. Rev.* 417, 638 (1937). The journal published two separate articles, the second being the continuation of the first.
38. Ibid., 423–424.
39. Ibid., 424.
40. Ibid.
41. Ibid., 424.
42. The phrase was coined by French revolutionary Louis de Saint-Just during the Reign of Terror.
43. Grundgesetz für die Bundesrepublik Deutschland [Grundgesetz] [GG] [Basic Law], May 23, 1949, BGBl. I (Ger.) Art. XXI, § 2. In addition, Article 9 allows for certain social groups to be banned by the government when they are seen as hostile to the constitution. See ibid., Art. IX, § 2.
44. To date, these remain the only political parties to be banned by the Constitutional Court, though several unsuccessful attempts have been made in recent years to ban the far-right National Democratic Party.
45. Basic Law Art. XX, § 4.
46. Ibid., Art. I, §§ 1–2.
47. The Basic Law does not define the term. In 1952, the FCC defined it as "an order that establishes public powers that are bound by the rule of law and that exclude any violence or arbitrariness, and that are based on the self-determination of

the people according to the will of the majority as well as freedom and equality." Bundesverfassungsgerichtsentscheidungen (BVerfGE—Decisions of the Federal Constitutional Court) 2, 1 (12 ff.) (1952).

48. Miller, 240.
49. *Quoted in* Miller, 230.
50. Tuylkina, 16. For a post-9/11 collection of essays militant democracy, and whether it can be used to fight terror, see *Militant Democracy* (András Sajó, ed., 2004).
51. See Chapter 4.
52. The story of Radbruch as a postwar "lost positivist" was popularized by HLA Hart in his 1958 Harvard Law Review article. See note 63 *infra*. Whether the pre-war Radbruch was in fact a true positivist is still debated today. Likewise, debate still rages about whether Radbruch indeed abandoned his positivism after the war. For recent discussions, see the collection of essays found in "Discussion—A Symposium of Nazi Law," 3 *Jurisprudence* 341–463 (2012) and especially the essay by Raymond Critch, "Positivism in Post-War Jurisprudence," 3 *Jurisprudence* 347 (2012). As Critch explains: "Immediatelly following the Second World War, GLP [German Legal Positivism] came under fire as a potential answer to the question 'what went wrong in Germany and that could lead to Nazism and the Holocaust?' The best known of its accusers is Gustav Radbruch, who spent the war years in internal exile and before the war was regarded as a prominent GLPist academic and minister of justice in the Weimar Republic. However, there is considerable disagreement over the extent to which Radbruch was a GLPist before the Nazi period, and consequently on whether his renunciation of GLP after the war was a renunciation or simply a denunciation." Ibid, 349–350.
53. See Barney Bix, "Radbruch's Formula and Conceptual Analysis," 56 *Am. J. Juris.* 45 (2011).
54. Robert Alexy, "A Defense of Radbruch's Formula," *in Recrafting the Rule of Law: The Limits of Legal Order* (David Dizenhaus, ed., 1999), 17.
55. Ibid. The actual text of the Rabruch formula reads: "The positive law, secured by legislation and power, takes precedence even when its content is unjust and fails to benefit the people, *unless the conflict between statute and justice reaches such an intolerable degree that the statue, as 'flawed law', must yield to justice.*" Gustav Radbruch, *Statutory Lawlessness and Supra-Statutory Law* (1946) (italics added).
56. See Barney Reynolds, "Natural Law versus Positivism," 13 *Oxford J. L. Stud.* 441 (1993). American schoolchildren are first introduced to natural law in Thomas Jefferson's Declaration of Independence through the phrase "unalienable rights endowed by our Creator." "Unalienable" means absolute—not granted by any government and so cannot be taken away by any government. Because every human being is "endowed" with such rights, they are inseparable from our humanity. The American Constitution codifies these unalienable rights in the Bill of Rights. In the international law arena, the unalienable rights possessed by every human being are set out in the Universal Declaration of Human Rights, unanimously passed by the General Assembly on December 10, 1948 (and commemorated as International Human Rights Day).
57. William Blackstone, *Commentaries on the Laws of England, Book 2* (1793), 40.
58. To believe that any legal theory—whether natural law or positive law—can prevent humans from doing evil shows naïveté. As Richard Hemholz has pointed out in his

excellent study, natural law (the preferred legal doctrine in both common and civil law systems between the sixteenth and nineteenth centuries) "did not abolish slavery, . . . end judicial torture . . . [or] prevent the oppression of native peoples in the Americas." Richard Hemholz, *Natural Law in Court: A History of Legal Theory in Practice* (2015), 177–178.

59. Judgment of July 27,1949, Oberlandesgericht, Bamberg, 5 Siiddeutsche Juristen-Zeitung 207 (Germany 1950).
60. BGHSt 2, 234 [238] (1952), *quoted and translated in* Frank Haldemann, "Gustav Radbruch vs. Hans Kelsen: A Debate on Nazi Law," 18 *Ratio Juris* 162, 70 (2005).
61. *Quoted in* Lon L. Fuller, *American Legal Philosophy at Mid-Century* (1954), 485 (emphasis added).
62. It is beyond the scope of this study to present the Hart-Fuller debate in all its hues. The same goes for the philosophical views of professors Hart and Fuller. I invite the interested reader to turn to the vast amount of literature easily found through a Google search. My aim here is merely to introduce the reader to the subject. For the continuing vitality of the debate, see *The Hart-Fuller in the Twenty-First Century*, (Peter Cane, ed., 2010).
63. See H. L. A., "Hart, Positivism and the Separation of Laws and Morals," 71 *Harv. L. Rev.* 593 (1958); Lon L. Fuller, "Positivism and Fidelity to Law—A Reply to Professor Hart," 71 *Harv. L. Rev.* 630 (1958).
64. See H. L. A. *Hart, The Concept of Law* (1961); Lon L. Fuller, *The Morality of Law* (1964).
65. A good example is the Reich Citizenship Law of September 15,1935, limiting citizenship to those of "German or substantively related blood." It was passed unanimously by the Reichstat, the German parliament. It is thus law, says Hart. Likewise, Hitler's euthanasia letter decree, backdated to September 1, 1939, and personally signed by him, ordering the killing of physically and mentally handicapped, was also law.
66. See Fuller, "Reply to Professor Hart," 645.
67. Ibid, 660. In his later work, Fuller further elucidated this point: "It is truly astounding to what extent there runs through modern thinking in legal philosophy the assumption that law is like a piece of inert matter–it is there or not there. It is only such an assumption that could lead legal scholars to assume, for example that the "laws" enacted by the Nazis in their closing years, considered as laws in abstraction from their evil aims, were just as much laws as those of England and Switzerland." Fuller, *The Morality of Law* (1964), 123.
68. See Hart, "Positivism and Separation," 618–619.
69. Ibid.
70. Fuller, "Reply to Professor Hart," 655.
71. Alexy.
72. Ibid.
73. *Quoted in* Roger Cotterrell, *The Politics of Jurisprudence* (2nd ed., 1989), 14.
74. Kristen Rundle, "The Impossibility of an Exterminatory Legality: Law and the Holocaust," 59 *U. Toronto L.J.* 65 (2009). Rundle's article is a rejoinder in part to David Fraser's contention that the Holocaust was a legal event. See David Frasier, *Law After Auschwitz: Towards a Jurisprudence of the Holocaust* (2005). Fraser argues that the Holocaust was "perfectly lawful and legal" (at 5). Rundle's contrary

conclusion, relying on Fullerian notions of the meaning of *law*, is that "the extermination program . . . proceeded extra-legally" (at 65). In Chapter 1, I make the same point as Fraser, except that my focus is on the decrees and orders issued by the Nazis to carry out the Holocaust. I leave to others to argue whether these decrees and orders ultimately can be considered *law* or *notlaw*.

75. For Rundle's rich account of Fullerian philosophy and its importance to modern-day legal thinking see Kristen Rundle, *Forms Liberate: Reclaiming the Jurisprudence of Lon L. Fuller* (2012).
76. Rundle, The Impossibility of an Exterminatory Legality, 89.
77. See Herline Pauer-Studer and J. David Velleman, *Konrad Morgen: The Conscience of a Nazi Judge* (2015).
78. Rasul v. Bush, 542 U.S. 466 (2004).
79. Hamdi v. Rumsfeld, 542 U.S. 507 (2004).
80. Ibid., 536.
81. Ibid., 536–537.
82. Hamdan v. Rumsfeld, 548 U.S. 557 (2006).
83. Military Commissions Act of 2006, Pub. L. No. 109-366.
84. Boumediene v. Bush, 553 U.S. (2008).
85. *Citing and quoting* Murphy v. Ramsey, 114 U.S. 15, 44 (1885).
86. Boumediene, 727. *Citing and quoting* Marbury v. Madison, 1 Cranch 137, 177 (1803).
87. Scott Horton, "A Setback for the State of Exception," *Harper's*, June 13, 2008.
88. Ex parte Milligan, 71 U.S. (4 Wall.) 2 (1866).
89. At the same time, lower federal courts have not been keen to release Guantánamo suspects pursuant to the authority given to them under Boumediene. As of this writing, no federal court has granted a habeas corpus petition filed by a Guantánamo detainee.
90. The term "exceptional insecurity" was coined by Jason Ralph. See Ralph, passim.
91. In December 2015, the Second Circuit allowed those taken in preventive detention immediately after 9/11 to proceed with a civil suit against former Attorney-General John Ashcroft, former FBI Director Robert Mueller, and former Naturalization Service Commissioner James Zigler. Mark Hamblett, "Full Circuit Lets Stand Revival of 9/11 Detention Suit," *N.Y. L.J.*, Dec. 14, 2015.
92. The Anti-Torture Convention defines torture as "the intentional infliction of "severe physical or mental pain or suffering" under color of law. To ensure US compliance with the Convention's obligation to criminalize all acts of torture, the United States enacted Chapter 113C of the United States Criminal Code, which prohibits torture occurring outside the United States (torture occurring inside the United States was already generally prohibited under several federal and state statutes criminalizing acts such as assault, battery, and murder).
93. Article 2 of the Anti-Torture Convention states that "[n]o exceptional circumstance whatsoever, whether a state of war, internal political instability or any other public emergency, may be invoked as a justification for torture." In international law parlance, the freedom to be free from torture is a nonderogable right.
94. Opening Statement for the Prosecution, U.S. v. Brandt. Oxford legal historian William Holdsworth, writing in the early twentieth century, explains the detrimental

impact on law when torture is excused: "Once torture has become acclimatized in a legal system, it spreads like an infectious disease. It saves the labor of investigation. It hardens and brutalizes those who have become accustomed to it." Sir William Holdsworth, 5 *A History of English Law* (3rd ed., 1945), 194–195.

95. *Quoted in* Jack Goldsmith, *The Terror Presidency: Law and Judgment Inside the Bush Administration* (2007), 72.
96. See Evan Wallach, "Drop by Drop: Forgetting the History of Water Torture in U.S. Courts," 45 *Colum. J. Transnat'l. L.* 468 (2007); Glenn Kessler, "Cheney's Claim that the U.S. Did not Prosecute Japanese Soldiers for Waterboarding," *Wash. Post,* Dec. 16, 2014.
97. Ralph, 116–117. Literature about these two memos (one classified and one unclassified), written by Berkeley law professor John Yoo and signed by his superior Jay Bybee, now a federal judge on the Ninth Circuit Court of Appeals, is legion. Bybee was then head of the OLC. Yoo was his subordinate tasked with drafting an opinion on the legality of the proposed EITs. For overview, see "A Guide to the Memos on Torture," *N.Y. Times, available at* <http://www.nytimes.com/ref/international/24MEMO-GUIDE.html>. See also The Constitution Project's Task Force on Detainee Treatment, *available at* <http://detaineetaskforce.org/>.
98. "A little more than ten years ago, our government was employing interrogation methods that, as President Obama has said, any fair-minded person would believe were torture." Opening Statement, Tom Malinowski, Assistant Secretary for Democracy Human Rights and Labor, U.S. Department of State to UN Committee Against Torture, Nov. 12, 2014. See also Philippe Sands, *Torture Team, Uncovering War Crimes in the Land of the Free* (2009).
99. In addition to waterboarding, the interrogation program included beatings, week-long sleep deprivation, exposure to extreme cold, threats of death, threats of death to one's family members, sexual abuse, and medieval-type shackling.
100. Mark Mazzetti, "U.S. Says C.I.A. Destroyed 92 Tapes of Interrogations," *N.Y. Times,* Mar. 2, 2009.
101. "Prosecute Torturers and Their Bosses," *N.Y. Times,* Dec. 21, 2014.
102. Scott Horton, "When Lawyers Are War Criminals," *in The Nuremberg War Crimes Trial and Its Policy Consequences Today* (Beth A. Griech-Polelle, ed., 2009), 167. See also Jens David Ohlin, "The Torture Lawyers," 51 *Harv. Int'l L.J.* 193, 245–255 (2010).
103. Horton, 168.
104. Statement of Pat Philbin, Deputy Assistant Attorney General to Office of Professional Responsibility, in David Margolis, Memorandum of Decision Regarding the Objections to the Findings of Professional Misconduct in the Office of Professional Responsibility's Report of Investigation into the Office of Legal Counsel's Memoranda Concerning Issues Relating to the Central Intelligence Agency's Use of "Enhanced Interrogation Techniques" on Suspected Terrorists, Jan. 5, 2010, 20.
105. <http://www.breitbart.com/video/2014/12/15/ksm-interrogator-we-were-told-waterboarding-was-okayed-by-congress/>.
106. According to President Obama: "I don't believe that anybody is above the law. On the other hand, I also have a belief that we need to look forward as opposed

to looking backwards. And part of my job is to make sure that for example at the CIA, you've got extraordinarily talented people who are working very hard to keep Americans safe. I don't want them to suddenly feel like they've got to spend all their time looking over their shoulders and lawyering up." *Quoted in* Sam Stein, "Obama Leaves Door Open to Investigating Bush, But Wants to 'Look Forward,'" *Huffington Post,* Feb. 11, 2009. For a pro and con discussion about whether there should be prosecutions, see Ohlin, 255–256.

107. William H. Rehnquist, *All the Laws but One: Civil Liberties in Wartime* (1998). For a more recent analysis, penned by Justice Breyer in the post-9/11 era, see Stephen Breyer, *The Court and the World: American Law and the New Global Realities* (2015).
108. Ibid., 222–223.
109. Ibid., 224–225.
110. Kaufmann, 1643. American law professors Richard Weisberg and Vivian Grosswald Curran likewise have demonstrated how French jurists, schooled in the French Revolution norm of equality of all citizens, nevertheless easily adopted to the new wartime norm by simply excising Jews from the equality principle of the French Revolution. See Richard H. Weisberg, *Vichy Law and the Holocaust in France* (1998); Vivian Grosswald Curran, "Law's Past and Europe's Future," 6 *German L.J.* 483 (2005). In another article, Curran points out that "judicial positivism is not correlated strongly in a causal paradigm with the judicial propensity to countenance and implement unjust enacted laws"—nor does any other legal theory. Vivian Grosswald Curran, "Fear of Formalism: Indications from the Fascist Period in France and Germany of Judicial Methodology's Impact on Substantive Law," 35 *Cornell Int'l L.J.* 101, 105 (2002) For a study of judges enforcing tyrannical laws under various regimes, see Hans Petter Graver, *Judges Against Justice: On Judges When the Rule of Law Is Under Attack* (2015).
111. Kaufmann, 1649.
112. Ibid., 1643.

Chapter 8

1. See, e.g., Donald Bloxham and Devin O. Pendas, "Punishment as Prevention?," *in The Oxford Handbook of Genocide Studies* (Donald Bloxham and A. Dirk Moses, eds., 2010), 624 ("the collapse of Nuremberg in the 1950's").
2. In 1946 the UN General Assembly unanimously affirmed "the principles of international law recognized by the Charter of the Nuremberg Tribunal and the judgment of the Tribunal." The General Assembly then requested the newly established International Law Commission to formalize the Nuremberg Principles. The seven principles were enunciated in 1950, but then largely ignored, even in academic texts. See http://www.nurembergacademy.org/the-nuremberg-legacy/the-nuremberg-principles/.
3. See, e.g., Robert Cryer, *Prosecuting International Crimes: Selectivity and the International Criminal Regime* (2005), 50–51: "In the end, the lack of movement on an international criminal court was reflected in the excision of material relating to Nuremberg from standard [international law] textbooks. . . . A number of academics, including Cherif Bassiouni, Robert Woetzel and ex-Nuremberg prosecutor Benjamin Ferencz sought to keep the project for an international criminal court

going, but irrespective of the fortitude which they put forward their views, State officials heard their calls *pianissimo*, if at all."

4. István Deák, "Misjudgment at Nuremberg," *N.Y. Review of Books*, Oct. 1993. This negative view of Nuremberg began even as the trials were taking place. The most-quoted criticism of Nuremberg comes from US Supreme Court Chief Justice Harlan Fisk Stone, who wrote: "[Justice] Jackson is away conducting his high-grade lynching party in Nuremberg. I don't mind what he does to the Nazis, but I hate to see the pretense that he is running a court and proceeding according to common law. This is a little too sanctimonious a fraud to meet my old-fashioned ideas." *Quoted in* Gary Jonathan Bass, *Stay the Hand of Vengeance: The Politics of War Crimes Tribunals*, 25. In Congress, US Representative Lawrence H. Smith of Wisconsin declared: "The Nuremberg trials are so repugnant to the Anglo-Saxon principles of justice that we must forever be ashamed of that page in our history. . . . The Nuremberg farce represents a revenge policy at its worst." *Congressional Record*—Appendix, vol. 95, sec. 14, (June 15, 1949), A3741.
5. Because of extensive criticism of Nuremberg in the American and British legal communities, it became the task of many of the participants to make speeches and write articles explaining why Nuremberg should be seen as a triumph of law rather than an embarrassment. See, e.g., Robert H. Jackson, "Nuremberg in Retrospect: Legal Answer to International Lawlessness," 35 *A.B.A. Journal* 813 (1949); Henry Stimson, "The Nuremberg Trial: Landmark in Law," 25 *Foreign Affairs* 179 (1947); Sheldon Glueck, *The Nuremberg Trial and Aggressive War* (1946); Peter Calvocoressi, *Nuremberg: The Facts, the Law and the Consequences* (1947); Benjamin B. Ferencz, "Nurnberg Trial Procedure and the Rights of the Accused," 39 *J. Crim. Law & Criminology* 144 (1948). Calvocoressi's short monograph, written by one of the British prosecutors, is a forgotten classic.
6. The footage was filmed by reporters from the ITN television network, who came to the site of the camps on August 6, 1992. Their shock at what they encountered is comparable in some ways to the shock experienced by Allied troops that liberated Nazi concentration camps. The images can be accessed at https://iconicphotos.wordpress.com/2009/05/26/trnopolje-bosnia-1992/.
7. Madeleine Albright (with Bill Woodward), *Madam Secretary* (2003), 177. This was Resolution 808. Three months later, the Security Council passed Resolution 827 setting out the details of how the ICTY would be set up.
8. UN GA Res. 47/121, Dec. 18, 1992.
9. *Quoted in* David Scheffer, *All the Missing Souls: A Personal History of the War Crimes Tribunals* (2011), 22.
10. The plane was also carrying the president of Burundi and arriving from a regional summit in Tanzania. Who shot the plane down still remains disputed.
11. The formal names were the Special Court for Sierra Leone–SCSL, the Special Panels for the Dili District Court in East Timor, and the Extraordinary Chambers of the Courts of Cambodia–ECCC.
12. Guénaël Mettraux, *Perspectives on the Nuremberg Trial* (2008), xii.
13. Timothy Snyder, "Keeping Our Heads," *New Republic*, Aug. 23, 2012.
14. John Hagan, *Justice in the Balkans: Prosecuting War Crimes in The Hague Tribunal* (2003), 18 (*quoting* Louise Arbour).

15. Mark A. Drumbl, *Atrocity, Punishment and International Law* (2007), 48.
16. Bass, 203.
17. Ibid., 205. Bass also speaks of "the spectacular success of Nuremberg." Ibid., 147.
18. The war crimes trial in Tokyo by the International Military Tribunal for the Far East is rarely cited as precedent and little discussed. For a recent anthology, see *Beyond Victor's Justice? The Tokyo War Crimes Trial Revisited* (Yuki Tanaka, ed., 2011).
19. Humanitarian law deals with protection by a foreign government of civilians and combatants belonging to the adversary and applicable in time of armed conflict or war.
20. Today that prohibition is found Protocol I of 1977 to The Hague Convention, which define war crimes as including: (1) "making the civilian population or individual civilians the object of attack" and (2) "launching an indiscriminate attack affecting the civilian population or civilian objects in the knowledge that such attack will cause excessive loss of life, injury to civilians or damage to civilian objects."
21. Prosecutor v. Jovica Stanišić and Franko Simatović, Case No. IT-03-69-A, Judgment, Appeals Chamber, 9 Dec. 2015.
22. Article 21 of the ICTY Statute and Article 20 of the ICTR Statute set out the procedural guarantees granted to the accused.
23. The limits of that right were in fact tested in the trial of former Serb head of state Slobodan Milošević, who used it with much success to disrupt the proceedings before dying suddenly of a heart attack in 2006 in the middle of his trial.
24. "Judge Theodor Meron Reflects on His Quest for International Justice," *Euronews*, Nov. 19, 2015.
25. For further discussion, see Eric Stover, *The Witnesses: War Crimes and the Promise of Justice in The Hague* (2006).
26. Arbour is an academic. Del Ponte was a former Swiss prosecutor. Julian Borger credits the two women as "the two people who did more than any other individuals to ensure the [ICTY] suspects were all tracked down." Julian Borger, *The Butcher's Trail: How the Search for Balkan War Criminals Became the World's Most Successful Manhunt* (2016), 151. Del Ponte recounts her experiences as ICT prosecutor in Carla Del Ponte, *Madame Prosecutor: Confrontation with Humanity's Worst Criminals and the Culture of Impunity* (2009).
27. Scheffer, *All the Missing Souls*, 30 (*quoting* Madeleine Albright).
28. Theodor Meron, "The Case for War Crimes Trials in Yugoslavia," 72 *Foreign Affairs* 122 (1993).
29. Theodor Meron, *The Making of International Criminal Justice: A View from the Bench* (2011), 4.
30. Meron's counterpart at the International Court of Justice at The Hague, the judicial arm of the United Nations, was Thomas Buergenthal, another child Holocaust survivor who became a distinguished international law professor before being appointed as a judge to the World Court. See Thomas Buergenthal, *A Lucky Child: A Memoir of Surviving Auschwitz as a Young Boy* (updated ed., 2015).
31. Prosecutor v. Radislav Krstić, Case No. IT-98-33-A, Judgment, 19 April 2004, para. 37.
32. For list of acquittals cases at the ICTY of individuals prosecuted for genocide, see Wilson, 296, n.99.

33. For discussion, see Elies van Sliedregt, "Joint Criminal Enterprise as a Pathway to Convicting Individuals for Genocide," 7 *J. Int'l Crim. Just.* 184 (2007).
34. William Schabas, "Mens Rea in the Yugoslav International Tribunal," 37 *New Eng. L. Rev.* 1015, 1031 (2003) (italics added). For further discussion of JCE, see William Schabas, *Genocide in International Law: The Crime of Crimes* (2nd ed., 2008), 353–358.
35. Prosecutor v. Duško Tadić, Case No. IT-94-1-A, Judgment (AC), paras. 195–229 (July 15, 1999).
36. Schabas, "Mens Rea."
37. Klaus Bachmann and Aleksandar Fatić, *The UN International Criminal Tribunals: Transition Without Justice?* (2015), 219.
38. Article 3(c) of the Genocide Convention criminalizes incitement to genocide.
39. Richard Ashby Wilson, "Inciting Genocide with Words," 36 *Mich. J. Int'l L.* 277, 306 (2015).
40. Ibid., 278 (*quoting* Mathias Ruzindana).
41. Prosecutor v. Nahimana (ICTR Trial Chamber) (2003), para. 1001.
42. Prosecutor v. Nahimana (ICTR Appeals Chamber) (2007).
43. Prosecutor v. Bikindi, Judgment and Sentence (Dec. 2, 2008).
44. Meron's acquittals and reduction of sentences have been harshly criticized in some quarters. Critics argue that he has made it practically impossible to convict senior commanders or that the reversals provide a blueprint for how commanders can avoid criminal liability. See, e.g., David Rohde, "How International Justice Is Being Gutted," *The Atlantic*, July 14, 2012; David Scheffer, "Responses on Contemporary Responses to Atrocity Crimes," 10 *Genocide Stud. Int'l* 1 (2016). See also Borger, who contends that the "series of reversals represented a sharp about-face for the tribunal" and demonstrate "the ICTY's own role in undoing their legacy." Ibid., 325–326. For criticism of specific reversals on appeal, see Mark A. Summers, *The Surprising Acquittals in the* Gotovina *and* Perišić *Cases: Is the ICTY Appeals Chamber a Trial Chamber in Sheep's Clothing?*, 13 *Richmond J. Glob. L. & Bus.* 649 (2015).
45. *Krstić* Appeals Chamber Judgment, Apr. 19, 2004.
46. Tolimir was also convicted by the Trial Chamber of committing genocide in the Bosnian towns of Zepa and Trmovo, but these convictions were overturned on appeal.
47. In 2016, Tolimir, at age sixty-seven, died in his jail cell in the Netherlands, while serving his life sentence.
48. For excellent accounts of the capture of Karadžić and Mladić as well as others indicted by the ICTY, see Borger, 247–307.
49. See Chapter 9 for discussion of the *Tadić* prosecution.
50. *Quoted in* Borger, 332.
51. Alison Danner, "When Courts Make Law: How the International Criminal Tribunal Recast the Laws of War," 59 *Vand. L. Rev.* (2006) 1, 59.
52. Radina Gigova, "Rwanda Genocide Suspect Arrested after 21 Years," *CNN*, Dec. 11, 2015.
53. Heikelina Verrijn and Marlise Simons, *The Prosecutor and the Judge: Benjamin Ferencz and Antonio Cassese* (2010). Duško Tadić and Dragan Nikolić were the first

two defendants indicted by the ICTY prosecutor. Both were found guilty. Tadić's case is discussed in Chapter 8.

54. For Goldstone's reflections about his work on the tribunals, see Richard Goldstone, *For Humanity: Reflections of a War Crimes Investigator* (2010). According to Ambassador David Scheffer, "The success of the Yugoslav Tribunal can be credited, in no small measure, to Goldstone's leadership at the outset, when so much of the new court's operations remained problematic as the Balkan conflict raged on." Scheffer, *All the Missing Souls*, 33.
55. Patricia Wald, "Running the Trial of the Century: The Nuremberg Legacy," 27 *Cardozo L. Rev.* 1559, 1564 (2006) (United Nations votes for judges to the ICTs "on the basis of regional concerns and tradeoffs.") (author is a former US federal judge who served on the ICTY).
56. Michael G. Karnavas, "The ICTY Legacy: A Defense Counsel's Perspective," 3 *Goettingen J. Int'l L.* 1053, 1061 (2011).
57. Bachmann and Fatić, 232.
58. Prosecutor v. Prlić (Case No. IT-04-74). On April 5, 2004, six Croatian political and military leaders surrendered to the ICTY and charged with war crimes and crimes against humanity. The charges stemmed from the defendants' involvement in military operations between 1991 and1994 aiming to expel Muslims and other non-Croats from regions of Bosnia claimed by the Croatians. Trial commenced on April 26, 2006, and ended more than seven years later; on May 29, 2013, the Trial Chamber announced its verdict. All defendants were found guilty and received jail terms ranging from twenty-five to ten years. The Trial Chamber's judgment was 2,629 pages. See <http://www.icty.org/x/cases/prlic/tjug/en/130529_summary_en.pdf>. The case is presently on appeal.
59. Brandeis University, The Ad Hoc Tribunals Oral History Project, "An Interview with Karen Naimer" (2015), 38–39.
60. William Montgomery, "Carla Departs . . . Finally," *B92*, Jan. 6, 2008.
61. Lawrence Douglas, "Justice Denied at The Hague?," *L.A. Times*, Mar. 14, 2006.
62. Ibid.
63. Naimer Interview.
64. Hassan Jallow, a Gambian lawyer and jurist, who sat as the last chief prosecutor of the ICTR, is the chief prosecutor of the MICT.
65. One practical problem contributing to the cost is what to do with those brought to Arusha and then acquitted or those released after serving their time. Some of these Rwandans have remained in a safe house in Arusha for over a decade, with no country, including Rwanda, willing to take them.
66. Bosniak is the name being used by Bosnian Muslims since 1993.
67. Refik Hodzic, "Accepting a Difficult Truth: ICTY Is Not Our Court," *Balkan Transitional Justice*, Mar. 6, 2013.
68. Donald Bloxham and David O. Pendas "Punishment as Prevention?" *in The Oxford Handbook of Genocide Studies* (Donald Bloxham and A. Dirk Moses, eds., 2013), 628.
69. Scheffer, *All the Missing Souls*, 28–29.
70. Meron, 240. The ICTY and ICTR websites each devote a separate page to their respective achievements.
71. Borger, 324.

72. Ibid., 325.
73. Genocide Convention, Art. 6.
74. Telford Taylor, *Final Report to the Secretary of the Army on the Nuremberg War Crimes Trials Under Control Council Law No. 10* (1949), 112. The idea of an international criminal court dates back to the nineteenth century, with its first formal formulation taking place in 1937, when the Convention for the Creation of an International Criminal Court was opened for signature at the initiative of the League of Nations. Interestingly, the proposed court's jurisdiction was limited to terrorism, with the most immediate impetus being the assassination of King Michael of Yugoslavia in Paris in 1934. The Convention never took effect.
75. For report suggesting how the ICC and the Security Council could work more closely, see David Kaye, *The Council and the Court: Improving Security Council Support of the International Criminal Court* (2013).
76. These include: 2003: self-referral by Uganda, the first case referred to the ICC by a state party; 2003: self-referral by the Democratic Republic of Congo (DRC), the second case referred to the ICC by a state party (DRC); 2005: self-referral by the Central African Republic (CAR), the third case referred to the ICC by a state party; 2005: Sudan, referred for investigation by the Security Council in connection with the atrocities in Darfur; 2008: Kenya, with the ICC prosecutor initiating an investigation of violence that took place during the 2007 elections in Kenya, and investigation of the co-winners of the election, Kenyan President Uhuru Kenyatta Deputy President William Ruto; 2011: Libya, second referral by the Security Council, to investigate atrocities during the Khaddafi era; and 2014: self-referral by Uganda, for indictment of Joseph Kony, warlord heading the so-called Lord's Resistance Army in Uganda.
77. The pre-trial chamber confirmed the ICC prosecutor's arrest charges for Bashir for war crimes and crimes against humanity, but not for genocide. On appeal by Moreno Ocampo, an appellate panel reversed the pre-trial chamber, finding that enough evidence has been presented by the prosecution to allow it to pursue Bashir for genocide.
78. "ICC Secures First Arrest in Central African Republic Situation," Coalition for the International Criminal Court, May 25, 2008 (http://www.iccnow.org/documents/CICCAdvisoryCARBembaArrest_25May08_eng.pdf).
79. For video, see Dan Skinner, "Speech of Mr. Benjamin Ferencz at Closing of Lubanga Case," Filmed Aug. 2011. YouTube video 06:53. Posted Sept. 2011. https://youtu.be/TI3JhJOhBQo.
80. Alex Whiting, "From Paris to Africa," *justsecurity.org*, Nov. 24, 2015.
81. Ibid.
82. "ICC Authorises Russia–War Crimes Investigation," *BBC*, Jan. 27, 2016. Bensouda announced that a preliminary examination revealed that all three parties to the conflict—the Georgian armed forces, the Russian armed forces, and the South Ossettian forces—might have committed war crimes and crimes against humanity between July and October 2008.
83. ICC arrest warrants are also outstanding against: Abdel Muhammad Hussein, current Minister of Defense of the Republic of Sudan and former Minister of Interior Affairs; Ahmad Huran, Minister of State for the Interior Affairs and head of the "Darfur desk," and Ali Kushayb, a militia commander.

84. "Amid Growing Brutality in Darfur, International Criminal Court Prosecutor Urges Security Counsel to Rethink Tactics for Arresting War Crime Suspects," United Nations, Dec. 12, 2014. http://www.un.org/press/en/2014/sc11696.doc.htm.
85. For an anthology discussing options available to the ICC prosecutor, see *The First Global Prosecutor: Promise and Constraints* (Martha Minow, C. Cora True-Frost, and Alex Whiting, eds., 2015), 130.
86. Alex Whiting, "Investigations and Institutional Imperatives at the International Criminal Court," *in The First Global Prosecutor: Promises and Constraints* (Martha Minow et al., eds., 2015).
87. "A Handcuffed International Criminal Court," *L.A. Times*, June 18, 2015.
88. Ibid.
89. Duncan McCargo, "Transitional Justice and Its Discontents," 26 *J. Democracy* 5 (2015).
90. Alex Whiting, "Despite Ups and Downs, the ICC is Here to Stay," *Justice in Conflict*, Jan. 8, 2015 (posted by Mark Kersten).
91. Ibid.
92. Ibid.
93. Ibid., (*quoting* Judge Cassese).
94. Syria and Iraq can prosecute ISIS atrocities committed on their respective territories. Other states can prosecute any of their "Jihadi John" or "Jihadi Jane" nationals who join ISIS.

Chapter 9

1. Hitler, if captured, could not have been prosecuted for genocide since genocide did not become a "crime on the books" until the Genocide Convention came into force in 1951.
2. See ICTY Statute, Article 4 and ICTR Statute, Article 2.
3. Of the total 93 individuals indicted by the ICTR during its two-decade existence, 61 were found guilty. At the ICTY, 161 were indicted and 80 have been convicted as of January 2016. I am grateful to Research Law Librarian Sherry Leysen at Fowler School of Law, Chapman University, for compiling these statistics.
4. Akayesu was also found guilty of crimes against humanity, arising out of the extermination, murder, torture, rape, and "other inhumane acts" of the Tutsis in Taba.
5. Prosecutor v. Akayesu, ICTR-96-4-T, Trial Judgment, para. 706 (Sept. 2, 1998).
6. Prosecutor v. Akayesu, ICTR-96-4-A, Appeal Judgment, para. 423 (June 1, 2001).
7. Fourteen defendants were acquitted (two indictments were withdrawn), ten were referred to national prosecutions for trial, three died during trial, and three still remain as fugitives. See "The ICTR Remembers," *available at* <http://www.unmict.org>. See also Alastair Leihead, "Rwanda Genocide: International Criminal Tribunal Closes," *BBC*, Dec. 14, 2015.
8. Prosecutor v. Krstić, IT-98-33-T, Trial Judgment, para. 727 (Aug. 2, 2001).
9. Prosecutor v. Krstić, IT-98-33-A, Appeal Judgment, para. 134 (April 19, 2004).
10. Ibid., para. 137 (italics in original).
11. For an analysis, see *The Milosevic Trial: An Autopsy* (Timothy Waters, ed., 2014).
12. Marlise Simons, "Radovan Karadzic, a Bosnian Serb, Is Convicted of Genocide," *N.Y. Times*, Mar. 24, 2016.
13. See Gérard Prunier, *Darfur: A 21st Century Genocide* (3rd. ed., 2008); Nicholas Kristof, "Genocide in Slow Motion," *N.Y. Review of Books*, Feb. 9, 2006.

14. Both the victim and perpetrator groups in Darfur are Muslims.
15. Report of the International Commission of Inquiry on Darfur to the United Nations Secretary-General Pursuant to Security Council Resolution 1564 of September 18, 2004 (2005). In the words of the UN Report: "The Commission concluded that the Government of Sudan has not pursued a policy of genocide. . . . [T]he crucial element of genocidal intent is missing. . . . [T]he policy of attacking, killing, and forcibly displacing members of some tribes does evince a specific intent to annihilate, in whole or in part, a group of distinguished on racial, ethnic, national or religious grounds. Rather, it would seem that those who planned and organized attacks on villages pursued the intent to drive the victims from their homes, primarily for purposes of counter-insurgency warfare."
16. Andrew T. Cayley, "The Prosecutor's Strategy in Seeking the Arrest of Sudanese President Al Bashir on Charges of Genocide," 6 *J. Int'l Crim. L.* 829, 840 (2008).
17. Jorgić v. Germany (No. 74613/01), 2007-III Eur. Ct. H.R. 263.
18. The Nazi and Nazi Collaborators (Punishment) Law of 5710-1950. Taking both its inspiration from and also some lifting of its text directly from the Genocide Convention, the 1950 law in section (b) defines "crimes against the Jewish people" as: any of the following acts, committed with intent to destroy the Jewish people in whole or in part: (1) killing Jews; (2) causing serious bodily or mental harm to Jews; (3) placing Jews in living conditions calculated to bring about their physical destruction; (4) imposing measures intended to prevent births among Jews; (5) forcibly transferring Jewish children to another national or religious group; (6) destroying or desecrating Jewish religious or cultural assets or values; (7) inciting to hatred of Jews.
19. Attorney General v. Eichmann, Criminal Appeal 336/61, Judgment, para. 10 (Supreme Court of Israel May 29, 1962), 36 ILR 287.
20. The Crime of Genocide (Prevention and Punishment) Law of 5710-1950, SH No. 42 137 (Isr).
21. Jorgić, 281 at para. 46.
22. Gimzauskas immigrated as a refugee to the United States in 1956 and resided in Florida until the mid-1990s, when he lost his US citizenship for failing to disclose his wartime activity upon arrival forty years earlier. He was then deported back to Lithuania.
23. For summary of these convictions, see <http://www.preventgenocide.org/punish/domestic> (Latvia).
24. Bolivia has twice charged its former presidents with genocide. In 1993, the Supreme Court of Bolivia, acting as a trial court, convicted *in abstentia* former Bolivian military dictator Luis Garcia Meza Tejada of genocide for the killing of eight political opponents in 1981. In 2005, another former Bolivian president, Gonzalo Sanchez de Lozada, was charged with genocide for killings of demonstrators during his rule.
25. In 2002, § 220a became part of the new German Code on Crimes Against International Law, where it is now contained in Article 6. Article 1 provides for universal jurisdiction of genocide, war crimes, and crimes against humanity.
26. A good recitation of Jorgić's background and his crimes can be found in the European Court of Human Rights decision Jorgić v. Germany (No. 74613/01), 2007-III Eur. Ct. H.R. 263.
27. "Kriegsverbrechen: Der Tod in Der Drina," *Der Spiegel*, Sept. 1997.
28. *Jorgić*, 271 at para. 16.

29. Ibid.
30. Ibid.
31. "Kriegsverbrechen," *Der Spiegel.*
32. *Jorgić,* 271 at para. 15. The trial court later reopened the proceedings on the basis that a prosecution witness who testified that Jorgić was involved in the murder of twenty-two people in Grbaska might have committed perjury. It found, however, that the genocide conviction was still proper based on Jorgić's participation in the murder of eight other Bosnian Muslims. Ibid., 276 at para. 33. In all, six witnesses from Bosnia testified at trial for the prosecution. Ibid., 270 at para. 10.
33. Alan Cowell, "German Court Sentences Serb To Life for Genocide in Bosnia," *N.Y. Times,* Sept. 26, 1997, A5 (*quoting* Judge Krentz).
34. *Jorgić,* 272 at para. 19. See also Federal High Court of Germany Press Release No. 39, "Federal High Court Makes Basic Ruling on Genocide," Apr. 30, 1999. <http://www.preventgenocideinternational.org/punish/GermanFederalCourt.htm>.
35. *Jorgić,* 273 at para. 23.
36. The Prosecutor v. Nikola Jorgić, Bundesverfassungsgericht [BVerfG] [Federal Constitutional Court] 2 BvR 1290/99, Dec. 12, 2000.
37. *Jorgić,* 274 at para. 25.
38. *Quoted in Jorgić,* 279 at para. 42.
39. *Jorgić,* 282 at para. 53.
40. Ibid., 285 at para. 61. Or as put by the ECtHR another way: Article VI of the Genocide Convention, specifying the courts that have the power to prosecute genocide, is to be "understood as establishing a duty for the *courts named therein* to try persons suspected of genocide, while not prohibiting the prosecution of genocide by *other national courts.*" Ibid., 287 at para. 67.
41. Ibid., 295 at para. 99.
42. Ibid., 297 at para. 108.
43. Title 4, §57a of German Criminal Code.
44. Mark Caldwell, "Germany Gives Life Sentence to Rwandan for Genocide," *Deutsche Welle,* Dec. 29, 2015.
45. *Quoted in* Ludwig Berber, "German Court Finds Rwanda Mayor Guilty of Genocide," *Deutsche Welle,* Feb. 18, 2014.
46. *Quoted in* "Former Mayor Sentenced to Life over Role in Genocide," *AP,* Dec. 29, 2015.
47. *Quoted in* Stan Ziv, "German Court Sentences Former Rwandan Mayor to Life Imprisonment for His Role in 1994 Genocide," *Newsweek,* Dec. 29, 2015.
48. Maia de la Baume, "France Convicts Rwandan Ex-Officer of Genocide," *N.Y. Times,* Mar. 14, 2014.
49. Andrew Chung, "'Kill, Rape and Pillage': Rwandan Gets Life in Jail," *Toronto Star,* Oct. 30, 2009.
50. Ibid. Munyaneza could have asked for a jury trial, but agreed to a bench trial before Judge Denis.
51. *See* 18 U.S.C. Sec. 1091 (designating the federal crime of "Genocide"). For further discussion, see Chapter 2.
52. Their convictions were upheld in 2015. See Michelle McPhee, "Judge Upholds 10-Year Prison Sentence for 'Monster Next Door,'" *Boston Magazine,* Mar. 27, 2015

(sisters Beatrice Munyenyezi and Prudence Kantengwa convicted of visa fraud and stripped of US citizenship). One other prosecution, in upstate New York, is ongoing. See "Rwandan Native Indicted on Charges of Making False Statements and Lying to Government Agents," U.S. Attorney's Office, W. D. N.Y., Aug. 6, 2015 (indictment of Peter Kalimu).

Conclusion

1. Tom Segev, "The Holocaust and Israeli Identity." Interview by Barbara Plett. *BBC News*, Jan. 27, 2005, *available at* <http://news.bbc.co.uk/2/hi/europe/4211761.stm>.
2. The motto of Jewish World Watch, a California-based NGO focusing on genocide prevention, is "*Do Not Stand Idly By.*"
3. Gregory H. Stanton, "How Can We Prevent Genocide: Building an International Campaign to End Genocide," *available at* <http://www.genocidewatch.org/howpreventgenocide.html>.
4. David Kader, "Progress and Limitations in Basic Genocide Law," *in Genocide: A Critical Bibliographic Review, v. 2* (Israel W. Charny, ed., 1991), 141.
5. The Chapter VII invocation of the Genocide Convention by the United States led the Security Council to pass a resolution establishing "an international commission of inquiry in order immediately to investigate reports of violations of international humanitarian law and human rights law in Darfur by all parties, to determine also whether or not acts of genocide have occurred, and to identify the perpetrators of such violations with a view to ensuring that those responsible are held accountable." S.C. Res. 1564, P 12, U.N. Doc. S/RES/1564 (Sept. 18, 2004). As discussed in Chapter 2, the so-called Cassese Commission did not find genocide to be taking place in Darfur, a conclusion rejected by the prosecutor of the International Criminal Court.
6. For a list of organizations, centers and governmental bodies, see <http://genocideprevention.now>. A good description of the creation of the interdisciplinary field of genocide studies can be found in Adam Jones, *Genocide: A Comprehensive Introduction* (2010), 15–22.
7. Genocide Prevention Task Force, *Preventing Genocide: A Blueprint for U.S. Policymakers* (Madeleine K. Albright and William S. Cohen, co-chairs, 2008).
8. David Scheffer, "Chasing Leadership Impunity: The Rapid Evolution of International Criminal Law," 16 *Chapman L. Rev.* 395, 396 (2012).
9. Ibid., 400.
10. Directive on Creation of an Interagency Atrocities Prevention Board and Corresponding Interagency Review, 2011 Daily Comp. Pres. Doc. 549, 1 (Aug. 4, 2011), *available at* <http://www.gpo.gov/fdsys/pkg/DCPD-201100549/pdf/DCPD-201100549.pdf>.
11. Ibid., 1–2.
12. President Barack Obama (recorded by the Office of the Press Secretary), "Remarks by President Obama at the United States Holocaust Memorial Museum," *The White House*, Apr. 23, 2012, *available at* <https://www.whitehouse.gov/the-press-office/2012/04/23/remarks-president-united-states-holocaust-memorial-museum>.
13. Yishai Schwartz, "We Are Doing the Right Thing," *New Republic*, Aug. 11, 2014.

14. See, e.g., John G. Heidenrich, *How to Prevent Genocide: A Guide for Policymakers, Scholars, and the Concerned Citizen* (2001); Herbert Hirsch, *Anti-Genocide: Building an American Movement to Prevent Genocide* (2002); *The Prevention and Intervention of Genocide: A Critical Bibliographic Review* (Samuel Totten, ed., 2007); David A. Hamburg, *Preventing Genocide: Practical Steps Toward Early Detection and Effective Action* (2008); Daniel Jonah Goldhagen, *Worse Than War: Genocide, Eliminationism, and the Ongoing Assault on Humanity* (2009); Etienne Ruvebana, *Prevention of Genocide under International Law* (2014); James Waller, *Confronting Evil: Engaging Our Responsibility to Prevent Genocide* (2016).
15. Emanuel Stoakes, "We Need to Prevent Genocide of Rohingya Muslims—Before It's Too Late," *The World Post*, Nov. 6, 2015 (*quoting* Matthew Smith).
16. Israel W. Charny (in collaboration with Chanan Rapaport), "Toward a Genocide Early Warning System," *in How Can We Commit the Unthinkable?: Genocide, the Human Cancer* (Israel W. Charny, ed., 1982), 283–291. In 1983, the book was republished with a new title, *Genocide, the Human Cancer* (1983). A good summary of GEWS can be found in 1 *The Encyclopedia of Genocide* (Israel W. Charny, editor-in-chief, 1999), 253–261. Israel Charny of Jerusalem and Helen Fein of New York remain our still-living first generation of scholars in the field of genocide studies. See *Pioneers of Genocide Studies* (Samuel Totten and Steven L. Jacobs, eds., 2013).
17. Leo Kuper, *Genocide: Its Political Use in the Twentieth Century* (1981).
18. Leo Kuper, *The Prevention of Genocide* (1985).
19. Gregory H. Stanton, *The Eight Stages of Genocide*, Genocide Watch, *available at* <http://www.genocidewatch.org/genocide/8stagesofgenocide.html>.
20. Gregory H. Stanton, *The Ten Stages of Genocide*, Genocide Watch, *available at* <http://genocidewatch.net/genocide-2/8-stages-of-genocide/>.
21. US Holocaust Memorial Museum, *Early Warning Project, available at* http://www.ushmm.org/confront-genocide/how-to-prevent-genocide/early-warning-project.
22. Ibid. The Obama administration created the first-ever *National Intelligence Estimate on the Global Risks of Mass Atrocities* (NIE), to be compiled by the National Intelligence Council under the Director of National Intelligence. The NIE is classified and shared only with senior policymakers.
23. USHMM Early Warning Project, *Which Countries Are Most Likely to Suffer Onsets of State-Led Mass Killing in 2015? A Statistical Risk Assessment, available at* <http://www.earlywarningproject.com/2015/09/18/2015-statistical-risk-assessment>.
24. Ibid.
25. Nicholas Kristof, "Myanmar's Peace Prize Winner and Crimes Against Humanity," *N.Y. Times*, Jan. 9, 2016.
26. "Fulfilling the Humanitarian Imperative: Assisting Victims of ISIS Violence: Hearing Before the Subcomm. on Africa, Global Health, Global Human Rights, and Int'l. Org.," 114th Cong. 1 (Dec. 9, 2015) (statement of Gregory H. Stanton, President, Genocide Watch). In March 2016, the Obama administration, after months of pressure by human rights groups, declared that ISIS was indeed committing genocide. Secretary of State John Kerry, using the Arabic-language acronym for ISIS, announced at a press conference: "[I]n my judgment Daesh is responsible for genocide against groups in areas under its control. . . . Daesh is genocidal by

self-proclamation, by ideology, and by actions." John Kerry, "Remarks on Daesh and Genocide," US Department of State, March 17, 2016. Then came the hard part: what actions to take now that the G-word had been uttered? Former international war crimes prosecutor and law professor David Crane at a Congressional hearing on "what next?" suggested the establishment of a truth commission and a judicial tribunal of some sort (domestic, international or hybrid) to prosecute those responsible for ISIS atrocities: "These mechanisms can be headquartered in Iraq, Turkey or Jordan supported by members of the Arab League. The international community could assist and train commission or court personnel as requested and needed. The ideal is having Arab states, prosecuting Arabs, for crimes against Arab peoples, in violation of Arab laws." Testimony of David M. Crane, "Subcommittee Hearing: The ISIS Genocide Declaration: What Next?," *Hearing Before the Subcomm. on Africa, Global Health, Global Human Rights, and Int'l. Org.*, May 26, 2016. As to stopping the atrocities, Crane (like others) had no ready solutions other than defeating ISIS on the battlefield. Crane explained: "This is a multifaceted and decade's long struggle. It truly is kaleidoscopic. Our next steps should be to continue to try and contain ISIS. On the periphery create achievable regional and domestic programs. Consider that Marshall Plan! Let's take away the reason for ISIS to be . . . no hope in the future. We have and can offer a better alternative—freedom and jobs plan." Ibid.

27. Gregory H. Stanton, "Weak Words Are Not Enough," *Genocide Watch,* Dec. 9, 2015.
28. Gregory H. Stanton, "Choosing Social Justice over Hate: Two Stories of Community Success in the Pacific Northwest," *National Civic Review,* 2012. *available at* <http://www.genocidewatch.org/genocidepreventionctr.html>.
29. Ibid.
30. David Scheffer, "Genocide and Atrocity Crimes," 1 *Genocide Studies and Prevention* 229, 236–237, 248 (2006).
31. David Bosco, "Crime of Crimes: Does It Have to Be Genocide for the World to Act?," *Wash. Post,* Mar. 6, 2005.
32. Raphael Lemkin, "Letter to the Editor: Confusion With Discrimination Against Individuals Seen," *N.Y. Times,* June 12, 1953.
33. For an excellent NGO study explaining why the events in Darfur meet the legal definition of genocide, see Public International Law & Policy Group, *Genocide in Darfur: A Legal Analysis* (Sept. 2004), *available at* <http://www.publicinternationallaw.org>.
34. The United Nations' conclusion that no genocide was occurring in Darfur was based on the usual basis for such a finding: lack of *mens rea.* "[O]ne central element appears to be missing, at least as far as the [Sudan] central Government authorities are concerned: genocidal intent. Generally speaking, the policy of attacking, killing and forcibly displacing members of some tribes does not evince a specific intent to annihilate, in whole or in part, a group distinguished on racial, ethnic, national or religious grounds. Rather, it would seem that those who planned and organized attacks on villages pursued the intent to drive the victims from their homes, primarily for purposes of counter-insurgency warfare." International Commission of Inquiry on Darfur, *Report to the Secretary-General,* Jan. 25, 2005. In other words, the UN fact-finders could not find sufficient evidence that Bashir and his allies in their campaign of killings and displacement intended to destroy in whole or in part the local tribes

that make up the victims in the Darfur region. For a critique of the UN commission's conclusion, see Nsongurua J. Udombana, "An Escape from Reason; Genocide and the International Commission of Inquiry on Darfur," 40 *Int'l Lawyer* 41 (2006).

35. Bosco, "Crime of Crimes."
36. Schabas, "Genocide, Crimes Against Humanity, and Darfur," 1707.
37. Samantha Power, "Fulfilling a Responsibility to Protect: What Will It Take to End the 'Age of Genocide?' " Lecture delivered at US Holocaust Memorial Museum, May 4, 2004.
38. David Kader, "Progress and Limitations in Basic Genocide Law," *in* 2 *Genocide: A Critical Bibliographic Review* (Israel W. Charny, ed., 1991), 142.
39. Omer Bartov, "The Legacy of Raphael Lemkin," (Interview with Jerry Fowler), Voices on Genocide Prevention, US Holocaust Memorial Museum Podcast, Mar. 8, 2007, *available at* http://web.archive.org/web/20070525165226/http://www.ushmm.org/conscience/analysis/details.php?content=2007-03-08.
40. Ibid.
41. Remarks by the President at the US Holocaust Memorial Museum, 2012 Daily Comp. Pres. Doc. 296, 2 (Apr. 23, 2012).
42. Samantha Power, *A Problem from Hell: America and the Age of Genocide* (2004).
43. Power, "Fulfilling a Responsibility to Protect."
44. Power, *A Problem from Hell*, 514.
45. Colum Lynch, "Samantha Power's Problem from Hell: Can a Humanitarian Firebrand Help Forge a Deal with Syria's Dictator," *Foreign Policy*, Sept. 23, 2013 (discussing the Syrian crisis).
46. "Remarks by President Obama and President Benigno Aquino III of the Philippines in Joint Press Conference, April 28, 2014, *available at* <http://whitehouse.gov>.
47. Evan Osnos, "In the Land of the Possible: Samantha Power Has the President's Ear. To What End?" *The New Yorker*, Dec. 22, 2014 (profile of Samantha Power).
48. Ibid.
49. Colm Quinn, "The CIA Torture Report and Ambassador Samantha Power at CSIS." Audio blog post. *The CSIS (Center for Strategic and International Studies) Podcast.* Center for Strategic and International Studies, Released Dec. 14 2014 (interview with Samantha Power), *available at* <https://itunes.apple.com/us/podcast/the-csis-podcast/id214886950?mt=2>.
50. Ibid.
51. Sarah Sewall, "Preventing Mass Atrocities: Progress in Addressing an Enduring Challenge," Council on Foreign Relations, Mar. 30, 2015, *available at* <http://www.state.gov/j/remarks/239968.htm>.
52. Israel Charny, who is a decade younger than Ferencz, after a half-century of studying genocide and its causes also makes the same point. See Israel W. Charny, "Requiem for the Prevention of Genocide in Our Time: Working Toward an Improbable Possibility But Not Giving Up," 7 *Genocide Stud. & Prevention* 108 (2012).

Index

Please note: "*n*" refers to footnotes. Page numbers in *italics* refer to photographs/illustrations.